Global Monetary Governance

Benjamin J. Cohen has long been recognized as one of the world's leading authorities on the political economy of international money and finance. This book provides an overview of his contribution to the field, grouped around the central theme of global monetary governance.

Divided into three sections, the first four essays address the changing nature of challenges to international monetary management, with particular emphasis on the impact of financial liberalization on efforts to promote monetary reform or cooperation. These papers stress the extent to which the role of states in systemic governance has been transformed by the accelerating growth of private capital mobility. A second set of essays turns to efforts to deal effectively with financial crises, exploring the reciprocal influences between governments and banks in the management of international debt problems. Case studies include the Asian financial crisis and several other key instances of instability in world markets. The final set of essays addresses implications of the remarkable growth in recent years of cross-border currency competition – the "new geography of money," where governing authority appears to be exercised now more by market forces than by sovereign states.

Cohen concludes by evaluating the merits and prospects of alternative policy options available to governments and explores some of the geopolitical ramifications involved. The papers are placed in historical and intellectual context by an introduction outlining the development of Cohen's thought. *Global Monetary Governance* will be useful to all students of international political economy or international money/finance.

Benjamin J. Cohen is Louis G. Lancaster Professor of International Political Economy, University of California, Santa Barbara, USA.

Global Monetary Governance

Benjamin J. Cohen

LONDON AND NEW YORK

First published 2008
by Routledge
2 Park Square, Milton Park, Abingdon, Oxon OX14 4RN

Simultaneously published in the USA and Canada
by Routledge
270 Madison Ave, New York, NY 10016

*Routledge is an imprint of the Taylor & Francis Group,
an informa business*

© 2008 Benjamin J. Cohen

Typeset in Times New Roman by
Newgen Imaging Systems (P) Ltd, Chennai, India
Printed and bound in Great Britain by
TJ International Ltd, Padstow

British Library Cataloguing in Publication Data
A catalogue record for this book is available
from the British Library

Library of Congress Cataloging in Publication Data
A catalog record for this book has been requested

ISBN10: 0–415–77313–X (hbk)
ISBN10: 0–415–77314–8 (pbk)
ISBN10: 0–203–96258–3 (ebk)

ISBN13: 978–0–415–77313–3 (hbk)
ISBN13: 978–0–415–77314–0 (pbk)
ISBN13: 978–0–203–96258–9 (ebk)

For Peter, Edna, Fritz, Susan, and Martin
With everlasting gratitude

Contents

Preface

Over the course of a career spanning more than four and a half decades, one naturally accumulates quite a few debts of gratitude. This book is dedicated to five individuals who were particularly important influences on my life when my interest in global monetary governance was first being formed. Each occupies a very special place in my heart.

First was Peter Kenen, a world-class international economist and, I am proud to say, my mentor. Peter was the first to introduce me to the mysteries of international trade and finance, both in the classroom and as the supervisor of my doctoral dissertation. Through the force of his formidable intellect as well as through the depth of the passion he brought to the scholarly enterprise, he inspired me to pursue my fascination with global monetary issues – in effect, to follow in his footsteps. It was as a result of a phone call from Peter that I was offered my first job after graduate school, as a research economist at the Federal Reserve Bank of New York.

Next was Edna Ehrlich, a kind and gentle woman who was my Division chief at the New York Fed. Responsible for our work assignments, Edna graciously relieved me of most routine duties so I could concentrate on more fundamental research. In return, I did my best to justify her faith in me, though I was never able to proofread my own work as carefully as she would have liked. One paper that I wrote at her behest was directly responsible for the invitation I received to accept my first teaching appointment, at Princeton University in 1964.

At Princeton I came under the wing of Fritz Machlup, one of the leading international economists of his day. A transplanted Viennese Austrian, Fritz had a formal manner that may have seemed distant and disinterested; it was only after seven years of addressing one another as Professor, for example, that he suggested we might now shift to a first-name basis. But he was in fact a caring and thoughtful gentleman who took pains to further the career of a younger colleague. In 1968, unbeknownst to me, he nominated me for an International Affairs Fellowship at the Council on Foreign Relations, thus enabling me to travel to London for a year to write a book on the pound sterling. (This was in the fellowship program's first year, when I had the honor of receiving an award in the company of a handful of future stars of the academic firmament, including Robert Keohane and Graham Allison.) And shortly thereafter it was Fritz who proposed me for an available faculty position at the Fletcher School of Law and Diplomacy at Tufts University, where I was to teach from 1971 until 1991.

A fourth influence was Susan Strange, whose role in defining the course of my career is described in the Introduction to this volume. Susan was the first serious scholar I met who really made me think about the political dimension of international economic relations. She was like an Old Testament prophet, persistently challenging me and others to abandon our wastrel ways. The mutual neglect that had long prevailed between international economics and international relations, she urged us, must be overcome. No one who knew her would deny that she was an excellent motivator.

Finally, there was Martin Kessler, editor at the New York publishing house Basic Books, who in 1970 invited me to commission and edit a series of original treatises on international political economy – the first such project ever conceived. Ultimately, five books were published in the Political Economy of International Relations Series, including Robert Gilpin's classic *U.S. Power and the Multinational Corporation* as well as two volumes of my own, *The Question of Imperialism* and *Organizing the World's Money*. The rest, as they say, is history.

In addition, I wish to thank Craig Fowlie of Routledge, who first proposed the idea of putting together this collection of papers. I am grateful to him for the confidence he expressed in me and my work. Apart from the Introduction, which was written expressly for this volume, all of the chapters appear here as they did when they were originally published.

I also wish to thank my good friends Dave Andrews, Eric Helleiner, Randy Henning and Lou Pauly for helpful comments on my Introduction, and Heather Arnold for her efficient research assistance.

Acknowledgements

The publisher would like to thank the following for permission to reprint material in this book:

"The Political Economy of Monetary Reform Today" (1976), *Journal of International Affairs* **30:1** (Spring/Summer), 37–50, reprinted with permission of Wiley-Blackwell.

"Balance-of-Payments Financing: Evolution of a Regime" (1982), *International Organization* **36:2** (Spring), 457–478, reprinted with permission of The MIT Press.

"The Triad and the Unholy Trinity: Lessons for the Pacific Region" (1993), in *Pacific Economic Relations in the 1990s: Cooperation or Conflict?* edited by Richard Higgott, Richard Leaver, and John Ravenhill. Copyright © 1993 by the Australian Fulbright Commission. Used by permission of Lynne Rienner Publishers, Inc.

"Phoenix Risen: The Resurrection of Global Finance" (1996), *World Politics* **48:2** (January), 268–296, reprinted with permission of The Johns Hopkins University Press.

"International Debt and Linkage Strategies: Some Foreign-Policy Implications for the United States" (1985), *International Organization* **39:4** (Autumn), 699–727, reprinted with permission of The MIT Press.

"Developing-Country Debt: A Middle Way" (1989), *Princeton Essays in International Finance* No. 173, Princeton, NJ: International Finance Section, reprinted with permission of Princeton University Press.

"Taming the Phoenix: Monetary Governance after the Crisis" (2000), in *The Asian Financial Crisis and the Architecture of Global Finance*, edited by Greg Noble and John Ravenhill, Cambridge University Press, 192–212, reprinted with permission of Cambridge University Press.

"Capital Controls: The Neglected Option" (2003), in *International Financial Governance Under Stress: Global Structures versus National Imperatives*, edited by Geoffrey R.D. Underhill and Xiaoke Zhang, Cambridge University Press, 60–76, reprinted with permission of Cambridge University Press.

"The New Geography of Money" (1999), in *Nation-States and Money: The Past, Present and Future of National Currencies*, edited by Emily Gilbert and Eric Helleiner, Routledge, 121–138, reprinted with permission of Taylor & Francis Books UK.

"Monetary Governance in a World of Regional Currencies" (2003), in *Governance in a Global Economy*, edited by Miles Kahler and David A. Lake, Princeton University Press, 136–167, reprinted with permission of Princeton University Press.

"The Geopolitics of Currencies and the Future of the International System" (2003), Real Instituto Elcano, Madrid, working paper available online at http://realinstitutoelcano.org/documentos/69.asp. Reprinted with permission of Real Instituto Elcano.

"Dollarization: Pros and Cons" (2000), Center for Applied Policy Research, Munich, working paper available online at http://www.cap.uni-muenchen.de/ transatlantic/papers/americas.html. Reproduced with permission of Center for Applied Policy Research (C.A.P.), Munich.

"Are Monetary Unions Inevitable?" (2003), *International Studies Perspectives* **8:3** (August), 275–292, reprinted with permission of Wiley-Blackwell.

1 Introduction

Back in my student days, nearly half a century ago, the issue of global monetary governance attracted little attention from scholars of international affairs. The celebrated conference at Bretton Woods, New Hampshire, in 1944, which had resulted in the creation of the International Monetary Fund (IMF), was supposed to permanently relegate management of monetary relations to the realm of "low politics." The aim of the Bretton Woods "system" was to "depoliticize" the challenge of governance – to ensure that problems of money and finance would be left largely to the technicians to resolve. Insofar as possible, debates over exchange rates or the balance of payments would be severed from the "high politics" of national security and interstate rivalries. What was there in the intricacies of finance that could possibly be of interest to specialists in international relations?

At the time, the wall between low politics and high politics in international affairs seemed natural, reflecting the academic world's larger divide between the established disciplines of economics and political science. Ever since the late nineteenth century, international economics and international relations (IR) had been treated as distinctly separate specialties, each with its own language, concerns, and standards. Communication between the two was rare. For the most part, scholars working on either side of the wall simply did not speak to each other.

My own experience as a university student was typical. In my one IR course, taken while still an undergraduate, the emphasis was all on the high politics of conflict and national survival in a dangerous, anarchic world. The policy agenda was preoccupied, not to say obsessed, with the Cold War and the threat of nuclear weapons. The low politics of economic relations were not really deserving of serious attention. Conversely, in the several courses on international economics that I sat through, first as an undergraduate and later in pursuit of a PhD, the spotlight was on issues of efficiency and stabilization, with public policy evaluated solely in terms of its implications for consumer welfare. No account was taken of the influence of differing institutional contexts or the political underpinnings of economic relations. The only dimension of power acknowledged was market power, stripped of any connection to interstate politics or issues of war and peace. When I wrote my doctoral dissertation, in the early 1960s, it hardly occurred to me to link analysis of monetary relations to broader issues of world politics.

Today, of course, we know better. Monetary relations are nothing if not political. Global monetary governance is, by definition, high politics. But awareness grew slowly, spurred by the birth of the new field of International Political Economy (IPE) in the late 1960s and early 1970s. Gradually a pioneer generation of scholars began to explore diverse political dimensions of the international monetary system. In 1968, economist Richard Cooper published *The Economics of Interdependence* (Cooper 1968), highlighting the political challenges posed by an accelerating interdependence of national economies. Adjustment to widening payments imbalances imposed difficult choices on governments, risking tension and conflict among states. The same theme was also developed by Charles Kindleberger in a short treatise entitled *Power and Money*, published in 1970 (Kindleberger 1970), soon to be followed by his justly celebrated *The World in Depression* (Kindleberger 1973). And in 1971 came Susan Strange's monumental *Sterling and British Policy*, stressing the politics of international currency use.

Until exposed to pioneering efforts like these, my own career path remained firmly on the economics side of the wall between the disciplines. With my PhD in hand, I worked for two years as a research economist at the Federal Reserve Bank of New York, and even after beginning my teaching career at Princeton University in 1964, I continued to stick to the standards of orthodox economic analysis. A turning point came in 1968, when I arrived in London to spend a year writing a book on the pound sterling (Cohen 1971). If I was going to research the pound, I was told, I should meet Susan Strange, who was working on *Sterling and British Policy* at the time. So I sought her out. When we got together, I dutifully told her about my plan to do a strictly economic cost-benefit calculus of sterling's role as an international currency. "Oh, Jerry," she replied, squinting at me through hooded eyes, "you can't possibly write about the pound without talking about the politics, too" – a remonstration that she would subsequently repeat on every possible occasion. At the time I resisted, with a stubbornness born of my conventional economics training. The loss was mine: her book turned out to be far more interesting.

Ultimately, however, Strange's message did get through. By the time I got back to the United States, I was determined – thanks, in good part, to her – to dip my toe into this new current of International Political Economy. In time this led me to produce a successor to my sterling book, *Organizing the World's Money* (Cohen 1977), which may legitimately be described as the first comprehensive integration of the economic and political dimensions of global monetary relations. *Organizing the World's Money* marked the completion of my conversion to the emerging field of IPE – "one of the rare cases of an economist," one observer wrote of me, "who came in from the cold of the dismal science" (Underhill 2000: 811). For a third of a century, I have continued to explore the political economy of a diverse range of monetary and financial issues, often prefiguring new analytical perspectives.

After all this time I may claim, perhaps immodestly, to have attained something of the aura of senior-scholar status. In a recent *festschrift* produced in my honor (Andrews *et al.* 2002), the editors described me as "a political economist of the first rank.... among the first to explore systematically the interaction between the 'high politics' of foreign affairs and the 'low politics' of economic management."

In a review essay, a younger colleague generously linked me with Strange (now regrettably deceased) as one of the two leading influences on the study of monetary governance today. Strange and I, the essay asserts, "establish landmarks around which competing schools of thought will organize.... Each author provides a new roadmap for navigating the international political space transformed by the ascendance of money" (Kirshner 2000: 408). More pithily, in private correspondence, another young colleague has called me "godfather of the monetary mafia." I like to think he meant it as a compliment.

From the beginning, monetary governance has been a recurrent theme in my work. The challenge of governance is understood to involve all the main features of monetary relations among states – the processes and institutions of financial intermediation (mobilization of savings and allocation of credit) as well as the creation and management of money itself. Who makes the rules and who exercises authority in monetary matters? The thirteen papers collected in this volume are representative of the long-term evolution of my thinking on these questions in response to changing events and my own continuing education. Chapters are arranged under three headings: Part 1: challenges to systemic governance; Part 2: dealing with financial crisis; and Part 3: the new geography of money. Each set of chapters may be located within the wider historical setting that over time has set the agenda for my research.

The historical setting

The key feature that distinguishes the international monetary system from purely domestic analysis is the existence of separate national currencies. Legally, the concept of state sovereignty has long been understood to include an exclusive right to create and manage money. Within national frontiers no currency but the local currency is expected, normally, to serve the traditional functions of money: medium of exchange, unit of account, and store of value. Formally, there is no money for the world as a whole, though selected national currencies have informally played important international roles. Hence when we speak of the global monetary system (or, synonymously, the global financial structure), we are talking of a universe of diverse national monetary spaces, not one homogenous entity – a universe where the territorial state, still the world's basic unit of formal governance, remains the core (though far from exclusive) actor.

The existence of separate national currencies has both economic and political implications. Economically, monetary sovereignty means that currencies that are legal tender in one place are unlikely, with few exceptions, to be fully useable elsewhere. From that tradition stems the need for mechanism and arrangements, such as the foreign-exchange market and other financial institutions, to facilitate transactions and interchanges between national moneys and credit systems. Politically, monetary sovereignty means that governments must necessarily be concerned about the balance of payments – the overall relationship between foreign revenues and expenditures. More precisely, they must somehow reconcile the twin – and often conflictual – macroeconomic policy goals of "internal balance" (full employment with low inflation) and "external balance" (equilibrium in the balance of payments). Since, normally, domestic money is not generally accepted outside the state's territorial frontiers, payments deficits cannot ordinarily be managed simply by printing more of one's own currency. Either adequate financing ("international liquidity") must be found or appropriate policy adjustments must be undertaken via changes of domestic spending, the exchange rate, or trade and capital controls. From that tradition stems the need for mechanisms and arrangements, concerning such matters as currency values and access to credit, to minimize frictions and, if possible, to facilitate cooperation in financial management.

It is in the interaction of these twin economic and political imperatives – the ever-shifting relations among states and between states and markets – that we find the challenge of global monetary governance.

From Bretton Woods to "non-system"

The Bretton Woods system is commonly understood to refer to the monetary regime that prevailed from the end of World War II until the early 1970s. The result of protracted wartime discussions, the Bretton Woods system was history's first example of a fully negotiated order intended to govern monetary relations among sovereign states. Based on a formally articulated set of principles and rules, the regime was designed to combine binding legal obligations with multi-lateral decisionmaking conducted through an international organization, the IMF, endowed with limited supranational authority.

Central to the Bretton Woods system was an exchange-rate regime of "adjustable pegs." Countries were obligated to declare a par value (a parity or "peg") for their national money and to intervene in currency markets to limit exchange-rate fluctuations within certain margins (a "band"), though they also retained the right, in accordance with agreed procedures, to alter their parity when needed to correct a "fundamental disequilibrium" in their external payments. The IMF was created to assure governments of an adequate supply of financing, if and when required, as well as to provide a permanent institutionalized forum for inter-state cooperation on monetary matters. International liquidity was to consist of national reserves of gold or currencies convertible, directly or indirectly, into gold – the so-called "gold-exchange standard" – later supplemented by Special Drawing Rights (SDRs), a negotiated form of "paper gold." The main component of liquidity was the U.S. dollar – America's fabled greenback – the only currency at the time that was directly convertible into gold.

The history of the Bretton Woods system is generally divided into two periods: the era of dollar "shortage," lasting roughly until the late 1950s, when world liquidity needs were fed primarily by deficits in the U.S. balance of payments; and a subsequent period of dollar "glut," when America's persistent deficits culmi-nated in termination of the greenback's gold convertibility in 1971 and collapse of the par-value system in 1973. With the closing of Washington's gold window, the gold-exchange standard passed into history, to be succeeded by a polyglot collection of national currencies, gold, and SDRs in the reserves of central banks. Likewise, with the end of par values, the exchange-rate regime was transformed into a mixed bag of choices, some governments continuing to peg more or less firmly to a single "anchor" currency like the dollar or to some form of "basket" of anchor currencies while others opted for more flexible arrangements, up to and including free floating.

Some elements of the old system survived, of course – not least, the IMF itself, which has continued to perform vital roles as a source of finance and as a forum for interstate cooperation. Moreover, new albeit less formal mechanisms of monetary management gradually emerged to cope with subsequent threats to stability such as the oil shocks of the 1970s, the Latin American debt crisis of the 1980s, and the financial-market crises of the 1990s. Exchange-rate policies, in principle, remain subject to "multilateral surveillance" by the Fund. Access to liquidity can still be secured, though without the degree of assurance promised at Bretton Woods. And new procedures for consultation and policy coordination have been developed and regularized, not only through the IMF but also in such now well-established bodies as the Group of Seven (G-7) and the Bank for International Settlements (BIS). Still there is no question that, on balance, the system has become more decentralized and diffuse. As compared with the elaborate rule-based design laboriously negotiated at Bretton Woods, what has evolved since the early 1970s seems both less restrictive and more rudderless. In the eyes of some, it is little more than a "non-system" bordering on anarchy if not chaos.

From hegemony to "privatization"

Dominating the evolution of monetary relations over the last half-century have been two major trends in the locus of influence over outcomes. The first is a redistribution of power *among states*, principally involving a relative decline in the overwhelming preeminence once enjoyed by the United States. The second is a redistribution of power *from states to markets*, involving a relative increase in the role of non-state actors in deciding such fundamental matters as currency values or access to credit. Simultaneously, the system has become less hegemonic and more market-determined – less centralized and more "privatized," to recall a term I introduced in this context as early as 1981 (Cohen 1981). Together, these two trends have largely defined the research agenda for students of global monetary governance.

That America's dominance of the monetary system has declined, especially in relation to Europe and East Asia, is widely accepted. Washington cannot act with quite the same degree of authority as during the era of dollar shortage, when the United States was universally acknowledged as monetary leader. Other states have also gained an influential voice on matters of money and finance. The main question is empirical: *How much* has U.S. dominance declined? At one extreme is the view, especially common in the 1970s and 1980s, that the day of American hegemony is irretrievably over. We are faced with the challenge of living in a world "after hegemony," wrote Robert Keohane in 1984 (Keohane 1984). The

United States, echoed Robert Gilpin, "had forfeited its role of monetary leadership" (Gilpin 1987: 142). At the other extreme are scholars like Strange, who even in her last books continued to maintain that the supposed loss of American hegemony was little more than a "myth" (Strange 1996, 1998). Most observers today would acknowledge that reality, as is so often the case, undoubtedly lies somewhere between these polar views.

Likewise, that the role of non-state actors in the monetary system has increased is also widely accepted. In fact, the transformation has been dramatic. A half century ago, after the ravages of the Great Depression and World War II, currency and credit markets everywhere (with the notable exception of the United States) were generally weak, insular, and strictly controlled, reduced from their previously central role in the world economy to offer little more than a negligible amount of trade financing. Starting in the late 1950s, however, private lending and invest-ment once again began to gather momentum, generating a phenomenal growth of cross-border capital mobility. First came the development of offshore currency markets – otherwise known as the Euro-currency market – and then a gradual liberalization of restrictions at the national level, all leading to a degree of financial integration not seen since the end of the nineteenth century. While it is as yet premature to speak of a single world financial market, it is by no means an exaggeration to speak of "financial globalization" – a genuine resurrection of global finance, embodying the pro-market principles of "neoliberal" economics. The monetary system was becoming increasingly privatized.

By the end of the twentieth century, the growth of capital mobility had proceeded to the point where the authority of governments seemed directly threat-ened. Again the main question is: *How much?* At a minimum states have been thrown on the defensive, no longer able to enforce their will without constraint. At a maximum states appear on the verge of total emasculation, with monetary sovereignty soon to be transferred in its entirety from national governments to "stateless" markets. Here too it seems most likely that reality lies somewhere in between.

Challenges to systemic governance

These twin changes in the monetary system are well reflected in the evolution of my thinking about the broad problem of systemic governance. My earliest work on the topic, best represented by *Organizing the World's Money* (Cohen 1977), was firmly state-centric in tone and focused mainly on issues of policy and statecraft, with particular emphasis on the role of the United States. Governments were the main units of interest, conceived as rational utility-maximizing agents. The essential elements of *Organizing the World's Money* are captured in Chapter 2 of this volume, the first chapter of Part 1.

A state-centric approach seemed natural to me at the time, given my background in economics. In my chosen specialty of international economics, standard theory always tended to treat governments as the equivalent of atomistic actors with well-defined utility functions. Over time, however, as financial globalization began to take hold, I learned to appreciate the growing role of markets and non-state actors as well, seen as a direct challenge to the authority and capacity of governments. Increasingly, I found it impossible to speak of monetary governance without taking account of the growth and ever more pervasive influence of capital mobility over outcomes in monetary affairs. The trend is evident in the remaining three chapters of Part 1, which originally appeared at intervals over the next two decades.

After hegemony?

By the time the old Bretton Woods system collapsed in the early 1970s, economists had been debating monetary reform for more than a decade. The trigger for discussion had been the sudden transition from dollar shortage to dollar glut, coinciding with publication of Robert Triffin's classic *Gold and the Dollar Crisis* (Triffin 1960). The days of monetary stability resting on U.S. hegemony, Triffin declared, were over. With swollen U.S. deficits now flooding the world with greenbacks, the international community faced a dilemma. The gold-exchange standard was built on the illusion of the convertibility of the dollar into gold. The Bretton Woods system, meanwhile, still relied on America's deficits to supply liquidity to a growing world economy. To secure confidence in the dollar, the deficits would have to cease. But that would confront governments with a liquidity problem. To forestall the liquidity problem, the deficits would have to continue. But that would confront governments with a confidence problem. Governments could not have their cake and eat it, too.

Over the course of the 1960s myriad reforms were proposed, envisioning everything from a return to the classical gold standard of the nineteenth century to a regime of fully floating exchange rates. Academics and policymakers alike struggled mightily to find some way out of the Triffin dilemma. For its part, the U.S. Government undertook a number of initiatives to reduce America's deficits or build defenses around the greenback. Collectively, leading governments sought to find some way to successfully rewrite the rules and regulations underlying the system. One significant reform was agreed – a first amendment of the Articles of Agreement of the IMF in 1968, bringing the SDR into existence. But the SDR proved to be too little and too late. In the end, none of these efforts were able to forestall breakdown of either the gold-exchange standard or the par-value system. The international community was simply unable to arrive at anything like a new constitution for the monetary regime.

In *Organizing the World's Money* (Cohen 1977), I asked the question: Why was monetary reform so difficult to achieve? Certainly there was no shortage of technically attractive alternatives. Economists were nothing if not inventive in addressing the governance issue. But safely ensconced on their side of the wall between international economics and IR, they failed to take account of the fundamental *politics* involved. States, I noted, must be understood as endogenous and purposive actors. The goal, therefore, was not just to attain some minimum level of economic efficiency – what I called the *efficiency objective*. Monetary reform must also ensure some minimum degree of consistency among the political objectives of separate national governments – a *consistency objective*. None of the many proposals on the table proved workable because in seeking to address the Triffin dilemma, economists ignored the deeper political dilemma: how to reconcile and balance the efficiency and consistency objectives. The point may seem obvious today, but at the time it was little understood.

Could some means be found to satisfy both objectives? Well before widespread acceptance of the notion of regimes in the IPE literature, I was already wrestling with the question of how legal or conventional frameworks might be developed to provide a measure of governance in monetary matters. *Organizing the World's Money* outlined four alternative principles by which the global system might be constituted to realize consistency as well as efficiency. These were: (1) automaticity – a self-disciplining regime of norms and rules binding for all governments; (2) supranationality – a regime founded on collective adherence to the decisions of some autonomous international institution; (3) hegemony – a regime organized around a single state with acknowledged responsibilities and privileges as leader; or (4) negotiation – a regime of shared responsibility and decisionmaking. Effective governance, I argued, had to be based on one or some combination of these four organizing principles. As I wrote in Chapter 2, "That is the real issue of world monetary reform."

After privatization

My first inkling of the growing impact of financial globalization came early, during my two years at the New York Fed. The bulk of my time at the Fed was spent dealing with the increasing outflow of capital from the United States. In 1963 I even played a small role in one of Washington's initiatives to reverse America's growing payments deficits – a tax on foreign bond issues known as the Interest Equalization Tax, which some have credited (in a fine example of the law of unintended consequences) with providing the stimulus for the phenomenal growth of the Euro-currency market in subsequent years. And two years later, now a full-time academic, I found myself engaged in a colloquy in the pages of the *American Economic Review* over the merits of capital controls, which some economists were promoting at the time. My own position then was mostly skeptical, stressing incentives for circumvention that tend to erode the effectiveness of restraints. Controls, I argued, ultimately have to be reinforced if their impact is to be preserved. In my dogmatic youth, I was even willing to raise that observation to the status of an economic law – what I boldly labeled the Iron Law of Economic Controls. To wit, "to be effective, controls must reproduce at a rate faster than that at which means are found for avoiding them" (Cohen 1965: 174). Today, of course, I am less inclined to be quite so categorical.

It was not until 1976–77, however, when I spent a year in Paris as a consultant on international monetary questions at the Organization for Economic Cooperation and Development (OECD), that I began to address the issue of financial globalization more systematically. Member governments at the time were struggling desperately to cope with the financing problems caused by the first oil shock of 1973. The enormous surpluses enjoyed by oil exporters, following a four-fold increase in the price of petroleum, were matched by the deficits of oil importers. Where would the requisite liquidity come from? For many, the answer turned out to be: international banks. For reasons of their own, oil exporters found it convenient to deposit the bulk of their surplus earnings in the offshore currency markets of London, New York, and other financial centers. Banks, in turn, had to look for customers for their excess funds – and found them among the oil importers, who were in desperate need of loans. And so the process of "petrodollar recycling" was born, funneling the surpluses of oil exporters through the banks to oil importers and, ultimately, back again – a process that was only reinforced when the second oil shock hit in 1978–79, following the Islamic revolution in Iran. A new source of international liquidity creation had come into existence, complementing and at times overshadowing the financing role of the IMF.

Building on my experience at the OECD, I first wrote about the privatization of liquidity creation in *Banks and the Balance of Payments* (Cohen 1981), the earliest comprehensive study of the political implications of the transformation of the financing process. As a result of the two oil shocks, I noted, the largest part of world liquidity growth now stemmed from the financial intermediation of private banking institutions. The development was bound to have an impact on global monetary governance. Microeconomic commercial interests had become irrevocably intertwined with national and international macroeconomic issues. Key decisions regarding access to liquidity were now in the hands of the private sector. Could banks be usurping the powers and authority of governments and the IMF?

At issue, it seemed, was a fundamental change in the regime that had been set up at Bretton Woods to govern access to balance-of-payments financing. But was this a change of degree or a transformation of kind? My answer, spelled out in Chapter 3, was that the phenomenon, for all its profound implications for monetary governance, was best understood as no more than a change of degree – an example of "norm-governed" evolution in monetary arrangements. The chapter was written for the landmark volume on *International Regimes* organized and edited by Stephen Krasner (1983), which first appeared as a special issue of the journal *International Organization* in 1982. The notion of "norm-governed change" was borrowed from John Ruggie's contribution to the same collection (Ruggie 1983). The large-scale privatization of liquidity creation represented a significant change at the level of formal rules and decisionmaking procedures, I argued, but not at the level of underlying principles and norms. At Bretton Woods it was generally agreed that deficit countries should not enjoy unlimited access to external financing. That stricture had not been fatally compromised, nor had commonly agreed standards of behavior been significantly altered. In terms of the regime's deeper tenets, there was a strong element of continuity.

One response to the growth of capital mobility in the 1960s and 1970s was a revival of interest in the 1980s in collective approaches to monetary management (re-emphasizing, in effect, the organizing principle of negotiation). The turning point came in 1985 with the so-called Plaza Agreement negotiated by the Group of Seven, formally pledging governments to a coordinated realignment of exchange rates. In principle, the G-7 countries were now to collaborate regularly to manage currency relations and macroeconomic conditions across Europe, North America, and Japan – the area referred to by many, simply, as the Triad. In practice, however, cooperation in ensuing years turned out to be episodic at best, with commitments tending to ebb and flow like the tides. The mutual commitment to monetary cooperation was honored more often in word than in deed. In Chapter 4, first published in 1993, I attempted to explain why.

The reason, I suggested, is systematic and had to do with the intrinsic incompatibility of three key desiderata of governments: exchange-rate stability, capital mobility, and monetary-policy autonomy. That dilemma is a core proposition of the so-called Mundell–Fleming model of open-economy macroeconomics long familiar to economists, which suggests that in an environment of fixed exchange rates and fully integrated financial markets, a government loses all control over domestic money supply and interest rates. My label for the dilemma was the Unholy Trinity, a term that now seems to have passed into the lexicon of IPE. The effect of the Unholy Trinity is to erode collective commitments to monetary collaboration. At times of speculative pressure on exchange rates, when the benefits of stabilization become paramount, governments may be willing to enter into policy compromises in an effort to restore market confidence. But once the sense of crisis subsides, the desire to exercise monetary autonomy tends to reassert itself, encouraging defection and free riding. The result is a cyclical pattern that provides little assurance of effective governance over time. Monetary cooperation, as I wrote in Chapter 4, may be a good thing but "like passionate love [is] difficult to sustain."

By the 1990s, capital mobility had become *the* central issue for international monetary management. Globalized financial markets, it seemed, had become something akin to a structural feature of world politics: an exogenous attribute systematically constraining state action, rewarding some behavior and punishing others. The ever-present threat of capital flight had created irresistible pressures for a convergence of national policies. David Andrews, building on the logic of the Unholy Trinity, called this the Capital Mobility Hypothesis (CMH): "The central claim associated with the capital mobility hypothesis is that financial integration has increased the costs of pursuing divergent monetary objectives, resulting in structural incentives for monetary adjustment" (Andrews 1994: 203). Not all analysts agreed with the CMH. Indeed, Andrews himself urged caution, directing attention to qualifications and limits of the proposition. But others were even more adamant. Debate raged over both the causes and consequences of financial globalization.

At mid-decade, I attempted to take stock of the debate in a review essay (Chapter 5). The CMH, I argued, had to be understood as something of an oversimplification. The practical impacts of financial globalization were really more nuanced and contingent than appeared at first glance. There could be no doubt that capital mobility had increased the costs of going it alone. But it also seemed reasonable to assume that some room for independent policy choice might yet remain, depending on the priorities of policymakers. The logic of the Unholy Trinity could be escaped – or at least evaded to a degree – if governments were willing to make trade-offs. Officials might sacrifice fixity of the exchange rate or financial openness. Alternatively, they might renew efforts to promote monetary cooperation. The problem was that no available option was without cost. The question was: Would governments be prepared to pay the necessary price? That question remains salient even to the present day.

Dealing with financial crisis

About one consequence of financial globalization there could be no doubt. That was the increasing vulnerability of the system to the eruption of financial crisis. The growth of capital mobility meant that governments, more and more, were hostage to abrupt shifts of market sentiment. Today access to liquidity might seem assured; tomorrow, denied. Money that flowed in one day might flow out the next. From the 1980s onward, crisis prevention and management became central to the challenge of global monetary governance. Increasingly, like many other specialists, I found myself drawn to address some of the issues involved.

Sovereign debt

During the 1980s, the critical issue was sovereign debt. The petrodollar recycling process had resulted in a rapid accumulation of debt by many governments around the world, most notably in Latin America. So long as export revenues kept growing and interest rates stayed low, borrowers had encountered few problems. But then came the second oil shock, contributing to both a recession in global markets and a sharp spike in the cost of debt service. Calamity soon struck. Unable to manage their liabilities, governments were forced to postpone debt service and institute severe austerity measures. Threatened with default on their massive claims, banks teetered on the verge of bankruptcy. Most of the decade of the 1980s was taken up with the crisis of sovereign debt in Latin America and elsewhere.

My first response to the crisis was Chapter 6, originally published in 1985. The article broke new ground in explicitly addressing implications of the crisis for the foreign policy of the United States. American banks had been among the heaviest lenders to sovereign borrowers. Now they were among the most threatened by the possibility of default. How, I asked, had these developments influenced the power of the U.S. Government in international affairs? To what extent did the crisis alter Washington's ability to realize its foreign-policy preferences?

Banks, it was clear, had become influential actors in their own right. If the privatization of payments financing meant anything, it was that banking institutions were now full participants in the realm of foreign relations. Through their ongoing commercial decisions vis-à-vis sovereign debtors, they could substantially alter issues of salience for policy or the nature or scope of options available to government officials. Yet given their status as private enterprises, answerable ultimately only to their own shareholders, there was no assurance at all that their interests would necessarily coincide with those of the public sector. From Washington's point of view, I argued, the main impact of these developments was to be found in the number and substance of potential linkages that might be exploited to promote foreign-policy objectives.

U.S. power, it was evident, was not always enhanced by the overseas activities of banks. Indeed, at times when bank priorities turned out to be substantially at variance with the goals of Washington officials, the effectiveness of existing policy instruments was to some extent compromised. But foreign-policy capabilities could clearly also be enhanced when preferences were more convergent, as in Latin America, where banks and the government alike shared an interest in avoiding default. My argument was later spelled out in greater detail in a book commissioned by the Council on Foreign Relations, published under the title *In Whose Interest?* (Cohen 1986).

Subsequently, as debt problems persisted, my attention turned to the broader issue of crisis resolution. In Chapter 7, a short monograph that appeared in 1989, I asked how we might overcome the obstacles to effective solution of the difficulties of hard-pressed debtors. Borrowing governments seemed caught in a "low-growth, high-debt-service trap." The stubbornness of the problem, I contended, could most accurately be attributed to underlying configurations of power in the political arena, both within individual debtor countries and in their broader strategic inter-action with creditors. Major changes in the political equation conditioning creditor-debtor relations seemed called for: a "middle way" that would recognize the need for mandatory collective action while at the same time stressing voluntary and market-oriented solutions. The solution could best be achieved, I suggested, through imaginative institutional innovation modeled on Chapter 11 of the U.S. Bankruptcy Code or analogous regulations elsewhere. Much of the monograph was taken up with a detailed elaboration of what such a "Global Chapter 11" might look like – something that had not previously been attempted by any other commentator. Though the idea has never yet been formally imple-mented – despite a brief flurry of interest after 2001 prompted by a similar proposal from the deputy managing director of the IMF – my pioneering role on the issue has frequently been acknowledged (e.g., Rogoff and Zettelmeyer 2002; Rieffel 2003).

Capital controls?

In time, of course, the crisis of the 1980s subsided, thanks in good part to the so-called Brady Plan, named after Nicholas Brady, Treasury Secretary during the term of the first President Bush. First proposed in early 1989, the Brady Plan called on banks to agree to debt forgiveness or debt-service reductions, or both, for selected borrowers in return for various forms of financial support from the IMF and World Bank or creditor governments. The reality of the low-growth, high-debt-service trap was finally acknowledged; banks, after years of building up their financial defenses, were now in a position to accept some losses as part of a general solution. Very soon, beginning with Mexico, settlements were negotiated that effectively permitted the reopening of global capital markets for a widening circle of countries. International lending again took off, this time mainly in "securitized" form – purchases of bonds and stocks – rather than as direct bank loans.

But that was by no means the end of the problem. Soon new crises erupted – *inter alia*, in Mexico in 1994–95, East Asia in 1997–98, Russia in 1998, Brazil in 1999, and Argentina in 2001–2002. Most dramatic was the storm that hit the emerging market countries of East Asia after a run on the Thai baht in mid-1997. Within months, some of the seemingly most successful economies of the developing world were thrown into turmoil by a flight of mobile capital. Exchange rates went into a tailspin, with depreciations ranging in magnitude from some 10–20 percent in Taiwan and Singapore to as much as (at one time) 80 percent in Indonesia. Growth came to halt and poverty soared. The price to be paid for reliance on privatized financing seemed exceptionally high.

Was there a way out? Controversially, in a conference paper published in 2000 (Chapter 8), I raised the questions of whether in the aftermath of the Asian crisis, the time had come to reconsider the case for capital controls. In Chapter 5, I described the resurrection of global capital as a kind of phoenix risen from the ashes of the Great Depression and World War II. Few analysts dispute the benefits of open financial markets. But as the logic of the Capital Mobility Hypothesis makes clear, there are costs as well, particularly in moments of crisis. The crisis in East Asia appeared to pose an opportunity to think again about the priority attached to financial liberalization. Why should governments be forced to make all kinds of sacrifices to appease market forces? Perhaps it would be better to cage the wilder impulses of the phoenix – to tame it, if not slay it, by restoring limitations of some kind on the cross-border mobility of capital.

My own position was clear. The Asian crisis, it seemed to me, had brought new respectability to the old case for capital controls. Once scorned as a relic of the past, limitations on capital mobility suddenly looked as if they might become the wave of the future. One country in the Asian region, Malaysia, had imposed comprehensive restraints for a year, with striking success, and lived to tell the tale. And China, of course, had never relaxed the panoply of controls that have long restricted the inflow or outflow of capital. So why not others? The question, I suggested, was no longer whether limitations on capital mobility might be restored but rather when, how, and under what rules governments might reconsider their commitment to financial liberalization. The time was ripe for reviving controls as a legitimate tool of public policy.

But my prediction was wrong. As matters turned out, Malaysia remained a lonely exception. Governments of other emerging market economies, once committed to liberalization, still hesitated to raise or restore impediments to the free flow of capital. Despite the demanding discipline of the Unholy Trinity, controls remained the neglected option. In another conference paper (Chapter 9), I asked why. The answer, I proposed, lay in a combination of external and internal influences on decisionmaking in debtor countries. From the outside came pressures from the U.S. Government and the IMF, both firmly opposed to any significant revival of controls. From the inside came pressures from key societal interests that, having gained from liberalization in the past, made clear their preference for keeping financial markets open in the future. In effect, a powerful transnational coalition appeared to be at work to prevent any turning back of the clock. Capital controls remained – and largely remain – very much off the table.

The new geography of money

But what, then, could states do to defend their currencies? By the 1990s, it was becoming evident that something radically new was afoot. Capital mobility had already become a central issue for monetary management. Increasingly, though, one could see that this was just the tip of the iceberg – the beginning of the story, not the end. Financial globalization meant more than just a constraint on government behavior. Beyond that, it meant erosion of the last effective barriers between national monetary systems, encouraging intense competition between currencies. More and more, the domains within which individual currencies traditionally served the standard functions of money were diverging from the legal jurisdictions of governments. Where currencies had once been essentially "territorial," money was now becoming "deterritorialized." A fundamental transformation was occurring in what I began to call the *geography* of money – the spatial organization of currency relations.

Over the last decade, the changing geography of money has been the principal focus of my scholarship. At issue is nothing less than a challenge to the long-standing convention of national monetary sovereignty. In *The Geography of Money* (1998), I was the first to spell out the dimensions and main consequences of today's accelerating deterritorialization of currencies. In *The Future of Money* (2004), I extended this line of analysis by systematically exploring alternative policy strategies available to governments to cope with the rising tide of currency competition. Core arguments drawn from these two books are highlighted in the five chapters of Part 3 of this volume.

Challenging monetary sovereignty

The political significance of the new geography of money is spelled out in Chapter 10. Money's deterritorialization, I emphasize, radically transforms the structure of monetary governance. Where national governments once, in principle, reigned supreme – each claiming the right to an absolute monopoly within its own borders – the users of money now increasingly have choice. The balance between states and markets, therefore, is being dramatically altered. Practical authority is becoming more and more diffuse, incorporating key private-sector actors as well as agents of the state.

The development has both positive and negative elements. A primary advantage, I argue, is the check that is provided on the arbitrary exercise of governmental power. The greater the range of choice that becomes available to the users of money, the less can policymakers abuse their monopoly privileges to extract seigniorage from the general population. The main disadvantage lies in the fact that market actors are less accountable than politicians to the wider electorate, raising serious questions about legitimacy and representation in this critical realm of decisionmaking. Are we really better off loosening the link between government and governance in monetary matters?

Deterritorialization does not mean that governments have been totally deprived of their capacity to act on behalf of their citizens. The pendulum has not swung that far. But the new geography of money does oblige states now to *share* authority with market agents, each side playing a key endogenous role in an ongoing dialectical process. Governance no longer is exercised solely by political actors. Authority now emerges in more complex fashion from the "invisible hand" of competition, states *interacting with* private societal forces in the functional spaces created by currency competition. The challenge to monetary sovereignty may not be absolute, but it is real.

Responding to the challenge

How might governments respond to the challenge? The main policy choices available to states are described and analyzed in Chapter 11. Broadly, four options may be identified. One, available only to governments with the most competitive currencies, is *market leadership*: an aggressive unilateralist policy intended to maximize use of the national money both home and abroad. The other three options, available to the vast majority of states with less competitive currencies, are (1) *market preservation*: a status-quo policy intended to defend the national currency against encroachment; (2) *market followership*: an acquiescent policy of subordinating monetary sovereignty to a stronger foreign currency via a currency board or "dollarization" (substituting a foreign currency like the dollar for local money); or (3) *market alliance*: a policy of sharing monetary sovereignty in a monetary union of some kind. The choices that states make among these diverse options, I contend, constitute the central issue of monetary governance today.

The aim of Chapter 11 is to provide the essential building blocs for a positive theory of currency choice. Five key factors can be expected to dominate the calculations of rational policymakers in thinking about the available options. These include (1) transactions costs; (2) macroeconomic stabilization; (3) the distribution of seigniorage; (4) social symbolism; and (5) diplomatic influence. Taking all these factors into account, I contend, it is clear that for many states traditional monetary sovereignty will remain the preferred strategy. A look at the empirical record suggests that outcomes will depend most on country size, economic linkages, political linkages, and domestic politics. The world's monetary map, I expect, will look more like a messy, highly variegated mosaic than the historical model of distinct territorial currencies.

The remaining chapters look at the separate options in greater detail. In Chapter 12, I address the relationship among the three most competitive currencies in the world, the dollar, euro, and yen, all of which have the capacity to promote a policy of market leadership. At present, we know, America's greenback is the only truly global currency, used for all the familiar functions of money in every corner of the globe. Can the euro or yen challenge the dollar's dominance? If we look to the logic of market competition alone, I argue, a successful challenge seems improbable. The greenback will continue to prevail. However, once we factor in government preferences as well, the outlook becomes cloudier. That the Europeans and Japanese will do all they can to sustain the market appeal of their currencies may be taken for granted. But whether they will go further, to seek formation of organized monetary blocs with foreign governments, is less certain. Japan may well seek to challenge the dollar's present dominance in East Asia; likewise, Europe could be tempted to make a battleground of the Middle East. My prediction, however, is that neither is likely to carry currency confrontation with the United States to the point where it might jeopardize more vital political and security interests.

In Chapter 13, I take up the option of dollarization, focusing on pros and cons both for potential dollarizers and for the United States. For potential dollarizers, advantages would include lower administrative costs, a firm basis for a sounder financial sector, and lower interest rates. Disadvantages would include the loss of monetary autonomy, seigniorage, and a vital national symbol as well as greater vulnerability to foreign influence. For the United States, conversely, advantages would include gains of seigniorage, prestige, and political authority. Disadvantages would include possible constraints on U.S. monetary policy and pressures to accommodate the special needs of dollarizing economies. Early in the new millennium two Latin American states, Ecuador and El Salvador, did in fact dollarize. Will many others follow? Much will depend on whether the sovereign rights of both sides can be adequately protected – not an easy task.

Finally, in Chapter 14, I consider monetary union – the option of market alliance. With the rapid growth of competition among currencies, many analysts have predicted that new monetary unions are virtually inevitable in many parts of the world. In fact, I argue, predictions of such alliances are misleading and almost certainly wrong. Monetary unions necessarily imply a measure of *collective* action in the issue and management of money. An alliance requires allies – other states with similar preferences and a disposition to act cooperatively. A survey of proposed monetary unions shows that willing partners among sovereign states are just not all that plentiful. Conceivably some governments could be attracted to less demanding forms of monetary alliance, depending on bargaining context. But prospects for many full new monetary unions are dim at best.

Conclusion

So what have we learned after all these years? For me, the main lesson is simple. Global monetary governance is a moving target. At many times over the course of my career, I heard the claim that we were in a period of transition. In fact, change has been the only constant. The best definition I know of a transition period is that interval of time between two transition periods. The historical setting is always in transition.

A third of a century ago, the critical issues in monetary governance involved a collapsing par-value system and gold-exchange standard. The main actors were states. The principal challenge was to find some new organizing principle to return stability to the overall system. Later, financial globalization added new actors to the mix – banks, international investors, and the like – increasingly privatizing the processes by which exchange rates and access to liquidity were determined. Growing capital mobility gave markets and market agents new authority to set standards and determine outcomes. It also raised the risk of financial crisis, putting a new premium on crisis prevention and management. And most recently we have seen a rise of cross-border currency competition, radically transforming the geography of money. States are being forced to respond to a fundamental challenge to their monetary sovereignty.

The question is: Where do we go from here? The world today seems as far as ever from effective monetary governance. In the late 1990s, following East Asia's devastating crisis, there was much talk of reform of the "international financial architecture." In practice, however, little was accomplished at the global level other than a modest increase of IMF lending capacity and a couple of new committees. The exchange-rate regime continues to be a mixed bag of choices, as it has since the end of the old Bretton Woods system. Access to liquidity remains hostage to abrupt shifts of market sentiment, as it has since the resurrection of global finance. Worst, states have been left essentially on their own to cope with the deterritorialization of money. Governments now compete not only with each other but also with markets and societal actors. Yet decisionmaking remains entirely decentralized. Without some effective coordinating mechanism to institutionalize cooperation, there is no guarantee that the policies adopted by individual governments – no matter how rational in terms of each country's own circumstances – will turn out to be compatible on a global scale. The "non-system" has never seemed more rudderless.

Ultimately, the issue remains the same as I first articulated it in *Organizing the World's Money*. Monetary reform must successfully reconcile the twin objectives of efficiency and consistency. But given the ever-widening circle of actors and interests involved today, that task would appear to be far easier said than done. Chapter 4 argues that chances for cooperation are best in times of crisis, when the benefits of collaboration trump other considerations. Short of a major crisis, I fear, prospects for effective governance remain regrettably dim.

References

Andrews, David M. (1994) "Capital Mobility and State Autonomy: toward a structural theory of international monetary relations," *International Studies Quarterly* 38: 2 (June): 193–218.

Andrews, David M., Henning, C. Randall, and Pauly, Louis W. (eds) (2002) *Governing the World's Money*, Ithaca, NY: Cornell University Press.

Cohen, Benjamin J. (1965) "Capital Controls and the U.S. Balance of Payments: comment," *American Economic Review* 55:1 (March): 172–176.

—— (1971) *The Future of Sterling as an International Currency*, London: Macmillan.

Cohen, Benjamin J. (1977) *Organizing the World's Money: the political economy of international monetary relations*, New York: Basic Books.

—— (1981) *Banks and the Balance of Payments: private lending in the international adjustment process*, Montclair, NJ: Allenheld Osmun.

—— (1986) *In Whose Interest? International banking and American foreign policy*, New Haven, CN: Yale University Press.

—— (1998) *The Geography of Money*, Ithaca, NY: Cornell University Press.

—— (2004) *The Future of Money*, Princeton, NJ: Princeton University Press.

Cooper, Richard N. (1968) *The Economics of Interdependence: economic policy in the atlantic community*, New York: McGraw-Hill.

Gilpin, Robert (1987) *The Political Economy of International Relations*, Princeton, NJ: Princeton University Press.

Keohane, Robert O. (1984) *After Hegemony: cooperation and discord in the world political economy*, Princeton, NJ: Princeton University Press.

Kindleberger, Charles P. (1970) *Power and Money: the politics of international economics and the economics of international politics*, New York: Basic Books.

—— (1973) *The World in Depression 1929–1939*, Berkeley and Los Angeles: University of California Press.

Kirshner, Jonathan (2000) "The Study of Money," *World Politics* 52:3 (April): 407–436.

Krasner, Stephen D. (ed.) (1983) *International Regimes*, Ithaca, NY: Cornell University Press.

Rieffel, Lex (2003) *Restructuring Sovereign Debt: the case for ad hoc machinery*, Washington, DC: Brookings Institution.

Rogoff, Kenneth and Zettelmeyer, Jeromin (2002) "Bankruptcy Procedures for Sovereigns: a history of ideas, 1976–2001," *IMF Staff Papers* 49:3: 470–507.

Ruggie, John Gerard (1983) "International Regimes, Transactions, and Change: embedded liberalism in the postwar economic order," in Krasner, Stephen D. (ed.) *International Regimes*, Ithaca, NY: Cornell University Press: 195–231.

Strange, Susan (1971) *Sterling and British Policy: a political study of an international currency in decline*, London: Oxford University Press.

—— (1996) *The Retreat of the State: the diffusion of power in the world economy*, London: Cambridge University Press.

—— (1998) *Mad Money*, Manchester: Manchester University Press.

Triffin, Robert (1960) *Gold and the Dollar Crisis*, New Haven, CN: Yale University Press.

Underhill, Geoffrey R.D. (2000) "State, Market, and Global Political Economy: genealogy of an (inter?) discipline," *International Affairs* 76:4 (October): 805–824.

Part 1

Challenges to systemic governance

2 The political economy of monetary reform today

Source: *Journal of International Affairs*, 30, 1, Spring/Summer 1976.

In recent years the world monetary order has been in a state of rapid flux. The rules and conventions that went by the name of the "Bretton Woods system" are honored now more in the breach than in the observance. Repeated efforts to reform the structural framework of international monetary relations so far have ended in near total failure. The few superficial changes in global monetary arrangements that have recently been introduced have been almost purely cosmetic. Why has monetary reform proved so difficult to achieve? What must be done in order to restore stability to international monetary relations? The objective of this article is to examine the principal issues of monetary reform today. The major stress of the article will be on the political economy of the problem. I shall argue that underlying and conditioning all of the purely economic aspects of monetary reform is the fundamental political dilemma of how to ensure a minimum degree of consistency among the political objectives of separate national governments. That is the real issue of world monetary reform.

The failure of reform

Monetary reform has not failed for want of trying. Intensive discussions of the needs, prospects, and possibilities for reform began more than a decade and a half ago.[1] In the intervening years, few subjects in international economic relations have attracted so much attention. During the 1960s, the debate on reform tended to focus mainly on the triad of broad, interrelated problems known as adjustment, liquidity, and confidence.[2] By "adjustment" was meant the problem of assuring an efficient mechanism for the maintenance and restoration of equilibrium in international payments. "Liquidity" referred to the problem of assuring an adequate supply and rate of growth of official monetary reserves. "Confidence" stood for the problem arising from the coexistence of different kinds of reserve assets and the danger of disturbing shifts among them.

At the level of governmental and intergovernmental agencies, most discussions stressed the latter two problems. To cope with the confidence problem, a variety of partial reforms were introduced into the monetary order. Among them were the General Arrangements to Borrow (GAB) in the International Monetary Fund (IMF); a network of reciprocal swap facilities among central banks; a gold pool;

and a two-tier gold price system. All were intended to help governments handle destabilizing shifts among various international monetary assets. To cope with the liquidity problem, deliberations in the so-called Group of Ten culminated in 1968 in the creation of an entirely new international reserve asset, inelegantly labelled the Special Drawing Right (SDR).[3] Most observers at the time hoped that these reforms would be enough to keep the monetary order operating smoothly at least into the medium-term future. Events, however, were to prove them wrong. On August 15, 1971, international monetary arrangements suffered a severe jolt resulting from former President Nixon's declaration of the New Economic Policy of the United States.[4] Within a year and a half, despite the "greatest monetary agreement in the history of the world" at the Smithsonian Institute in December 1971, the world monetary order collapsed completely.

That is not to say that the world monetary system itself collapsed. Analytically, a clear distinction must be drawn between the international monetary system and the international monetary order.[5] A system is "an aggregation of diverse entities united by regular interaction according to some form of control."[6] In the context of international monetary relations, this describes the aggregation of individuals, commercial and financial enterprises, and governmental agencies that are involved, either directly or indirectly, in the transfer of purchasing power between countries. The international monetary system exists because, like the levying of taxes and the raising of armies, the creation of money has always been considered one of the fundamental attributes of political sovereignty. Within national frontiers only the local currency is accepted to serve the three traditional functions of money: medium of exchange, unit of account, and store of value. Consequently, across national frontiers some integrative mechanism must exist to facilitate interchanges between local money systems. That mechanism is the international monetary system.

The international monetary order, by contrast, is the legal and conventional framework within which this mechanism of interchange operates. Control is exerted through policies implemented at the national level and interacting at the international level. By specifying which instruments of national policy may be used and which targets of policy may be regarded as legitimate, the monetary order establishes both the setting for the monetary system and the understanding of the environment by all of the participants in it. As Robert Mundell says: "A monetary order is to a monetary system somewhat like a constitution is to a political or electoral system. We can think of the monetary system as the modus operandi of the monetary order."[7]

What collapsed after 1971 was the monetary order. The monetary system continued to function. Indeed, world trade and payments continued growing at record rates. Now, however, the system was no longer subject to any stabilizing form of control. This was the real change in global monetary relations. In 1972, the so-called Committee of 20 (formally, the Committee on Reform of the International Monetary System and Related Issues) was organized under the auspices of the IMF in hopes that agreement on a new framework of rules and conventions could be reached before the end of 1973. Unfortunately, such agreement proved elusive, and, in June 1974, the Committee wound up its affairs without final accord on a comprehensive plan for reform.[8] Instead, the Committee declared that henceforth the process of putting a reformed monetary order into practice would have to be treated as evolutionary, rather than as a task to be concluded in the short one-to-two year period originally envisioned. In the words of the chairman of the deputies of the Committee of 20, "some aspects of reform should be pushed forward and implemented early, while other aspects could be developed over time."[9] In effect, a British-style approach to constitution writing would have to be substituted for an American-style approach. No estimate was given of how long the evolutionary process of reform might actually take.

These aspects of reform, pushed forward by the Committee of 20, were all relatively superficial – mainly, a new system of valuation of and high interest rate on the SDR, and the establishment of an Interim Committee of the Fund's Board of Governors to continue the former Committee's work. The same description of superficiality applies as well to the subsequent decisions of the Interim Committee at its meeting last January in Jamaica, which apart from acknowledging the reality of floating exchange rates, principally concerned enlargement of national quotas in the IMF and disposition of the Fund's own gold holdings.[10] On the specific technical issues which, over the years, have truly agitated governments – issues such as the rules for exchange intervention by central banks, the convertibility of the dollar, and the consolidation of the dollar "overhang" – no significant progress has been made. Reform, to date, has been almost purely cosmetic.

There are several reasons for this. For one thing, deliberations in the Committee of 20, and subsequently the Interim Committee have been stymied by inertia. The basic issues of reform have been under discussion for so long that most governmental positions have become inflexible. A second cause has been the emergence of unanticipated and unprecedented international economic developments, including rampant global inflation and enormous increases of oil prices since late 1973. International negotiators were taken unawares by these developments. As is so often true of generals, they were caught preparing for the last war instead of for the next.

The principal cause, however, is simply that negotiators have been caught looking in the wrong direction. Negotiators have kept their eyes on the same triad of problems that dominated the debate through the 1960s. Adjustment, liquidity, and confidence, however, are not really the main threat to the monetary system, even if they remain technical issues in urgent need of resolution. The genuine danger goes much deeper – to the absence of some agreed mechanism to ensure compatibility among the external policy objectives of separate national governments. This is the problem of "consistency." Essentially political in nature, it underlies and conditions all of the traditional economic issues of reform. No economic problem can be solved until the political consistency problem is satisfactorily dealt with. Yet negotiators in the Committee of 20 and Interim Committee have never explicitly confronted this problem. Little wonder, then, that monetary reform has remained an elusive goal.

The options for reform

Basically, there are only five possible ways to respond to the consistency problem. Each represents an alternative organizing principle for the international monetary order. These are: (1) anarchy, what Richard Cooper calls a "free-for-all" regime;[11] (2) automaticity, a self-disciplining regime of rules and conventions binding for all nations; (3) supranationality, a regime founded on collective adherence to the decisions of some autonomous international organization; (4) hegemony, a regime organized around a single country with acknowledged responsibilities and privileges as leader; and (5) negotiation, a regime of shared responsibility. An international monetary order must be based on one of these five abstract principles, or on some combination of them. The five together effectively exhaust all possible options for monetary reform.

Which option should governments be aiming for in the evolutionary process of reform that has now begun? In my opinion, the choice clearly lies between hegemony and negotiation. Automaticity and supranationality both have their attractions, but they are politically naive. Sovereign governments will not voluntarily surrender their decision-making powers either to automatic rules or to a supranational agency. A free-for-all regime is even less appealing to governments, even though it might conceivably achieve a fairly high degree of technical efficiency through exclusive reliance on private market decisions. Anarchy does not cope with the political consistency problem – it cops out. As Cooper says:

> A free-for-all regime does not commend itself. It would allow large nations to exploit their power at the expense of smaller nations. It would give rise to attempts by individual nations to pursue objectives that were not consistent with one another (e.g., inconsistent aims with regard to a single exchange rate between two currencies), with resulting disorganization of markets. Even if things finally settled down, the pattern would very likely be far from optimal from the viewpoint of all the participants.[12]

Is hegemony possible? There is no question that the Bretton Woods system was hegemonic. The charter drafted at Bretton Woods in 1944 clearly reflected the dominant position and vital interests of the United States at the time. As David Calleo has written: "Circumstances dictated dollar hegemony."[13] The postwar world needed an elastic supply of new international reserves; the United States desired freedom from any balance-of-payments constraints in order to pursue whatever policies it considered appropriate and to spend as freely as it thought necessary to promote objectives believed to be in the national interest. The result, unplanned but effective, was a gold-exchange standard based on the dollar as the principal reserve asset, with the flow of new monetary reserves being determined mainly by the magnitude of America's annual payments deficit. America's deficits were the universal solvent that kept the machinery of Bretton Woods running. Other countries set independent balance-of-payments targets; the external financial policy of the United States was essentially one of "benign neglect." In effect, America surrendered any payments target of its own in favor of taking responsibility for the operation of the monetary order itself. Consistency was assured by America's willingness to play a passive role in the adjustment process: "Other countries from time to time changed the par value of their currencies against the dollar and gold, but the value of the dollar itself remained fixed in relation to gold and therefore to other currencies collectively."[14]

Naturally, this responsibility was advantageous to the United States – it preserved America's privilege to act abroad unilaterally in promoting its perceived national interest. So too was it advantageous to other countries, which were thereby given assurance of a more stable international monetary environment. America's hegemony was not exploitative. Quite the contrary, it reflected a positive-sum game in which all of the principal players would benefit. At the heart of this order was an implicit bargain, struck early in the postwar period between the United States and the countries of Western Europe, the only countries at the time conceivably capable of challenging America's hegemony. As I have written elsewhere:

> Implicitly, a bargain was struck. The Europeans acquiesced in a system which accorded the United States special privileges to act abroad unilaterally to promote U.S. interests. The United States, in turn, condoned Europe's use of the system to promote its own regional economic prosperity, even if this happened to come largely at the expense of the United States.[15]

Ultimately, however, the fabric of the bargain frayed as discontent over its terms grew on both sides of the Atlantic. European governments (especially the French) became increasingly resentful of what Charles de Gaulle called "the exorbitant privilege" given the United States by the dollar's preeminence, to pursue policies many considered abhorrent, such as the U.S. involvement in Vietnam. In the meantime, the U.S. government was becoming increasingly uncomfortable about the economic costs of European regionalism, and, by extension, the economic costs of its benign neglect policies toward third regions such as Japan. America's trade balance was deteriorating badly. By 1970, protectionist forces were running rampant in the U.S. Congress. Furthermore, in 1971, the United States faced a serious threat of a run on its remaining gold stockpile in Fort Knox. The New Economic Policy of August 1971 was a direct response to these and related developments. The postwar bargain was scuttled because the Nixon Administration decided that the United States could no longer afford to play a passive role in the payments adjustment process. Consequently, the Bretton Woods system lost its assurance of consistency.

Today, it is difficult to imagine being able to reconstruct anything like America's postwar hegemony in international monetary arrangements. Circumstances have changed too much. Western Europe and Japan both have long since emerged from under the American shadow, and, more recently, the energy crisis has promoted the countries of OPEC to a new position of prominence as well. No longer are these nations content to play the world money game strictly by American rules. In the Committee of 20 and the Interim Committee, for instance, negotiators were preoccupied with ensuring a greater degree of "symmetry" in the international monetary order. For European governments at least, this was simply a semantic disguise to cloak the more fundamental ambition of ending dollar hegemony.

At the same time, however, none of these nations has grown strong enough to write its own rules for the monetary order. The European Community still has not made significant progress toward making the political concessions necessary for monetary unification. Without a common currency the Community can hardly hope to reduce or eliminate the asymmetries in the global economy that derive directly or indirectly from the dollar's leading role as international "vehicle" currency. The governments of Europe still have not demonstrated that they are prepared to make the fundamental political concessions that a common currency would require. As Fred Hirsch has argued,

> In this sense one can conclude that European monetary integration is not a serious issue. It belongs to the category of commitments that are endorsed by national authorities at the highest level, but are in fact ranked low in their priorities when it comes to the test.[16]

Likewise, Japan, for all its industrial might, can hardly hope to replace the United States as the dominant power. At the same time, the oil states, lacking any financial markets of their own, have actually reinforced America's position by favoring New York and the dollar for the investment of their surplus earnings. The United States may no longer be as clearly dominant as it was in 1944. But it is still the world's leading national economy.

The United States, therefore, must continue to bear the responsibility of leadership, even if it can no longer enjoy all its privileges. "Leadership without hegemony," Marina Whitman calls it: "the replacement of leadership based on hegemony, with leadership based on persuasion and compromise."[17] Like Samson, we may still be strong enough to bring the temple crashing down around us if we wish; our power of veto remains. If our role is to be constructive rather than destructive, however, we must, as I have argued elsewhere,

> acknowledge that the United States is no longer the dominant economic power in the 'world. Deeds must speak as loud as words: the United States must demonstrate that it is in fact prepared to adjust to the new reality in reorganizing economic space – not assertively or in excessively self-interested terms, but on the basis of a genuine reciprocity of interests and purposes.[18]

We must be prepared to give up our "exorbitant privilege" and to accord a greater voice in monetary councils to Western Europe, Japan, and OPEC. The new international monetary order that is evolving must be negotiated rather than imposed, pluralistic rather than hegemonic. The only alternative is inconsistency and the consequent danger of splintering into a congeries of competing monetary blocs: a free-for-all regime.

Such self-sacrificing leadership is not easy to achieve. Calleo notes: "It is a hard lesson for an imperial power to learn that it cannot be omnipotent."[19]

Can the United States be happy with such an arrangement? Harry Johnson stresses, "This is a problem in political economy, not in technical economic analysis."[20] Technical economic analysis can illustrate what monetary reforms might be desirable; it can also demonstrate America's shared interest in an order that promotes stability for all. In the end, however, it will not be economics that matters, but politics.

The adjustment problem

To give some substance to this general argument, consider again the three technical problems of adjustment, liquidity, and confidence. All are issues still in urgent need of a solution. I have said that in the 1960s the stress of most discussions was on liquidity and confidence. In the 1970s, emphasis must be changed somewhat in the light of recent developments. The collapse of the Bretton Woods system was in essence a breakdown of the rules for central bank intervention in the foreign-exchange market. This means, on the one hand, that attention must now be focused much more on the adjustment problem. On the other hand, the rise of OPEC means that the liquidity and confidence problems have been significantly transformed. At a time when all oil consumers are scrambling to pay for their higher priced oil imports, much less importance need be attached to such traditional concerns as dollar convertibility and consolidation of the dollar overhang. The key aspect of the liquidity-confidence problem today is the issue labelled "petrodollars." I shall discuss these problems of adjustment and petrodollars in turn.

With regard to the adjustment problem, there used to be a great prejudice, at the level of governmental and intergovernmental agencies, against any form of exchange-rate mechanism that would allow currency values to float freely. The Bretton Woods system was a par value (or "pegged-rate") regime: each government was expected to declare a par value for its currency and to defend its parity within narrow limits by intervening in the exchange market as buyer or seller of last resort. Par values (pegs) were supposed to be shifted only infrequently in response to something called "fundamental disequilibrium." The comparative rigidity of the postwar regime reflected the chaotic experience of the interwar period which, the negotiators at Bretton Woods were convinced, had amply demonstrated the disadvantages of floating rates. With the collapse of the Bretton Woods system, and the subsequent move to generalized floating in 1973, many feared the advent of a new era of wildly fluctuating currency values and competitive exchange depreciations. As events have turned out, however, such fears were excessive. In fact, floating rates have worked remarkably well, considering the unprecedented economic developments of recent years, and governments have been educated about their advantages. With exchange-market pressures now being absorbed mainly by changing currency values – rather than, as in the past, by reserve movements, controls, or adjustments of the level of domestic activity – countries find themselves enjoying an extra degree of freedom in the pursuit of national economic and social objectives. Official opinion is now amenable to greater exchange-rate flexibility than had previously been considered either possible or desirable.

In the Committee of 20, this opinion was expressed by the acceptance (in principle) of a formula of "stable but adjustable par value," indicating the possible willingness of governments but only provided they have the right to make frequent small adjustments of their parities when and if the need arises. The formula itself was ambiguous. What was clear, though, was that any difference between a "stable but adjustable" regime and a regime of "managed" floating under multilateral surveillance would likely be more apparent than real. A reasonable conclusion, therefore, was that reform ought to do away entirely with the fiction of par values, and concentrate instead on establishing rules and procedures to guide a regime of continuously floating exchange rates. The reality of floating exchange rates was formally acknowledged by the Interim Committee, at its January meeting in Jamaica, in the form of a new draft amendment of the IMF Charter legalizing abolition of par values.[21]

The principal advantage of floating rates is that they provide a mechanism for continuing adjustment in the face of all the myriad influences that impinge daily on a country's balance of payments. The principle disadvantage of floating rates is that they are prone to destabilizing activity by private speculators or government officials. Private speculators may increase the frequency and amplitude of fluctuations of exchange rates around their long-term trend; government officials may be tempted to intervene to influence in mutually inconsistent ways the long-term trends themselves ("dirty floating"). Both types of activity create uncertainties and exchange risks that could discourage a certain amount of legitimate foreign trade and investment. Economic theory teaches that normally private speculation tends to be stabilizing except when the economic environment is clouded by unpredictable governmental policies. This suggests that the first need of a floating-rate regime is agreement on guidelines for official intervention in the foreign-exchange market. Intervention must be encouraged to reduce the frequency and amplitude of fluctuations of rates around trend, but not to influence the trends themselves ("clean floating"). A tentative set of such guidelines was recommended by the Committee of 20 when it wound up its affairs in 1974, but these were too general to be of much practical use to governments[22] Unfortunately, the new draft amendment adopted by the Interim Committee at Jamaica did nothing to make the guidelines more specific. Further refinement of intervention rules and prodedures is still necessary.

The second need of a floating-rate regime is agreement on the respective adjustment obligations of countries in balance of payments surplus or deficit. This is a subject discussed at considerable length in the Committee of 20 and the Interim Committee. During the 1960s, a serious political conflict developed between the United States, which was demanding currency revaluations by

Western Europe and Japan, and the countries of continental Europe, led by France, which were insisting upon devaluation by the United States. This was the origin of the "symmetry" issue. It reflected the weakening of the postwar bargain between the United States and Europe. The Europeans felt that they were being discriminated against by America's exorbitant privilege to finance deficits by issuing what amounted to IOUs. America felt discriminated against because it had no effective control over its own rate of exchange. Since other governments used the dollar not only as their main reserve asset but also as their principal intervention medium to support par values, the U.S. could not change its exchange rates unilaterally unless all other countries agreed to intervene appropriately in the exchange market. This was an asymmetry in the monetary order that favored the Europeans rather than the U.S., which could not easily devalue to be rid of its deficit.[23]

In the negotiations in the Committee of 20 and the Interim Committee, both the United States and Europe have agreed that a more symmetrical adjustment process is needed. Since they are talking about different kinds of symmetry, however, they find it difficult to agree on an approach to the problem. Each side is prisoner of its own perception of the past. As Peter Kenen wrote in 1973:

> As usual, the parties are arguing from history as each reads it. Americans believe that the U.S. deficits of the 1950s and 1960s were prolonged and led finally to the collapse of the par value system because surplus countries – the Europeans and Japan – could not be compelled to alter their policies, and the United States could not easily initiate a change in exchange rates. Europeans read this same post-war history to argue that the blame and obligation to change policies rested with the United States, yet it was not compelled to act because it was not losing reserves.[24]

What criteria might be used for refining intervention procedures and the respective adjustment obligations of countries in payment surplus or deficit? Clearly, this is one of those areas where politics must take precedence over economics. No monetary order can remain stable for long if some governments feel seriously discriminated against. As Anthony Lanyi has pointed out:

> If the cost of cooperation is too great for a country at a particular time, it will prefer to take measures which, if often only in a minor or partial way, "break down" or diverge from the purposes and methods of the agreed-upon system.... Therefore, the more equally the costs of cooperation are distributed, the better is the chance that the system will be maintained unimpaired.[25]

In short, procedures and obligations must be shared more or less equally. This does not mean that governments must submit to automatic rules enjoining specific policies in the event of particular types of disturbances; nor does it mean that they must always follow the dictates of some autonomous international organization. I have already argued that sovereign states will not voluntarily surrender their decision-making powers either to automatic rules or to a supranational agency. Governments demand a certain leeway in their effective range of policy options. What it does mean is that all governments must be expected to take an active role in the management of the exchange-rate regime – countries in payments surplus as well as those in deficit, reserve centers as well as those who do not enjoy an exorbitant privilege. All must share in the collective costs of cooperation. That indeed is the essence of a negotiated order.

Special responsibility falls on the largest countries which, because of their power to disrupt, have no choice but to take a constructive attitude toward the problem of adjustment. This includes the United States, of course; it also includes, in particular, Germany and Japan, the next two largest economies of the non-communist world, which share with America an interest in a stable exchange-rate regime. Among currencies today, the currencies of these three countries are clearly dominant – the Deutsche Mark in Europe (as linchpin of the European "snake," which is as close to monetary unification as Europeans have yet been able to come), the yen in the Far East, and the dollar in Latin America and elsewhere. Successful stabilization of relations among these three currencies is a prerequisite for stabilization of the exchange-rate mechanism as a whole. In 1936, the monetary chaos of the interwar period was finally brought to a close by a Tripartite Agreement among the three most influential currencies of that day – the dollar, the pound, and the French franc. In the 1970s, a similar sort of tripartite agreement is needed among the dollar, the mark, and the yen in order to end present uncertainties about exchange intervention procedures and payments adjustment obligations.

Such a stabilization agreement could be more or less formal.[26] Preferably, it should be carried out under the auspices of the IMF, in order to confer a certain "legitimacy" on the rules and procedures agreed to by the major financial powers. The Fund is an ideal forum for this because it can provide an institutional mechanism for the management of the exchange-rate regime without imposing on governments any special elements of supranationality. Fund recommendations tend to reflect a consensus of views of all the principal members. Consequently, governments can accede more easily to its recommendations than to the decisions of one or a few large countries acting unilaterally. Still, any agreement at all is better than none. There is a need for some form of managed floating under multilateral surveillance. If negotiation within the Fund proves too slow or cumbersome, a tripartite agreement among the major powers would be far preferable to the only conceivable alternative, an unpalatable free-for-all regime.

The petrodollar problem

With regard to the petrodollar problem, the key question is what to do about the huge surplus earnings of OPEC. The oil-price increases since 1973 have resulted in enormous current-account surpluses for oil producers as a group – $60 billion in 1974, $92 billion in 1975, with additional large surpluses projected for 1976 and thereafter.[27] The world has never been confronted with such an immense transfer of wealth. As Winston Churchill said in another context, never before have so many owed so much to so few. Projections of future OPEC surplus accumulations vary considerably, depending on the source.[28] According to even the most sanguine projections, petrodollar surpluses are expected to reach a minimum of $180–190 billion (in current dollars) by 1980. Even that is a substantial sum and the situation has profound implications for global economic and political relations. Two issues in particular stand out as far as the international monetary order is concerned: how governments can ensure that petrodollars will be effectively "recycled" to the oil consumers that are most in need of them, and how they can ensure that OPEC surplus accumulations will not become a new source of instability in world monetary arrangements.

The recycling issue highlights the fact that oil price increases affect different oil consuming countries differently. Some consumers are more dependent on oil imports than others; some are less able to offset the higher cost of oil imports either by increasing exports of goods and services to OPEC members, or by attracting loans and investments from them. Consequently, some consumers have found themselves in serious payments difficulty since the energy crisis, while others have been enjoying relatively healthier external accounts. In the long run, consumer countries must evolve toward a structure of trade relations compatible with the emerging pattern of OPEC capital flows to consumers as a group. In the short run, however, the key need is to channel oil revenues from consumers presently receiving the benefit of OPEC capital flows to those who are most in need of them. Private international financial markets cannot be relied upon to perform this financial intermediation function entirely on their own. There is no assurance that an allocation of loans based on traditional banking considerations (creditworthiness, relative interest rates, etc.) will coincide with the requirements of global balance of payments equilibrium. In the words of the managing director of the IMF Johannes Witteveen: "[T]he Euro-currency markets alone cannot cope with the new situation because they cannot channel funds on reasonable terms to countries whose economic position is precarious. The need of these countries is perhaps the most urgent, but precisely for this reason their ability to attract private funds is weakest."[29] For this reason, the private markets must be supplemented by bilateral and multilateral credit facilities among governments, such as the IMF "oil facility" and the OECD Financial Support Fund.

Until now, such governmental recycling facilities have not been used frequently. This has led some observers to suggest that the private markets, indeed can be relied upon to handle the problem by themselves. This is, however, an overly sanguine conclusion based on an unrepresentative sample of experiences. In 1974, the first year of the energy crisis, there was still much scope in international financial markets for absorbing the higher cost of oil imports. The most seriously affected industrial countries, such as Britain and Italy, as well as many less developed countries, were able to borrow extensively to cover their oil deficits. Now, however, many of these same countries seem to be reaching the limit of their foreign borrowing capacity. Fully 80 per cent of the combined current-account deficit of oil consumers in 1974 was borne by primary-producing countries, including primary producers in the periphery of Europe and in Australia. The deficits of Third World primary producers alone totaled $28 billion in 1974 and $35 billion in 1975.[30] These poor countries have already attracted about as much private money as they are capable of doing; for most of them, monetary reserves are simply too low to take up much of the remaining burden of financing. Without access to governmental recycling facilities, they will be forced to endure cutbacks in imports and development programs, and perhaps even starvation. LDCs are not participants in the OECD Financial Support Fund, and the amounts of funds that were committed to the IMF oil facility before it was allowed to lapse this year were derisively small. For these poorest countries, an expansion of intergovernmental recycling facilities is still a fundamental imperative.

All this imposes a special responsibility on the United States. Because of our favorable endowments of oil and alternative energy resources, our balance of payments has been less adversely affected by higher oil prices than have the external accounts of most other consumer nations. At the same time, a disproportionate share of OPEC surpluses have been placed either in the United States or in Euro-dollars. (Either way, the American balance of payments benefits, since the dollars paid to oil producers are returned to the United States – in the former instance directly, in the latter, indirectly – rather than converted into foreign currencies.) New York is an especially attractive investment center as it is probably the only financial market in the world large enough to absorb without serious strain sustained capital movements of the magnitudes involved. The dollar is an especially attractive investment medium because it continues to be the world's leading vehicle currency for private transactions. The United States, therefore, must take the lead in facilitating the recycling of OPEC funds. In the interest of promoting prosperity at home as well as abroad, the U.S. must see that other governments are not forced into mutually harmful payments policies by oil induced deficits.

The second issue is the disposition of OPEC surplus accumulations. OPEC countries have begun to diversify a portion of their investments. Yet for a long time to come, a large proportion will undoubtedly continue to be concentrated in short maturity assets (bank deposits, etc.). By the end of 1975, the official monetary reserves of Saudi Arabia had soared to over $24 billion, second only to Germany's; reserves of the oil producers as a group had risen to $55 billion, one-quarter of the world total. In the next few years, OPEC countries could accumulate reserves in excess of $100 billion, most of which will be concentrated in the hands of five Persian Gulf nations and Libya. A monetary order cannot remain stable when such a large proportion of international liquidity is unilaterally controlled by such a small number of countries – particularly countries with such a poor record of economic and political volatility. In the interest of assuring monetary stability, multilateral controls should be instituted to ensure that these funds are not shifted about frequently in a chaotic or irresponsible fashion. The objective should be to induce OPEC nations to treat their surpluses as long-term savings rather than as short-term investments.

This would require new investment facilities to absorb OPEC's surplus funds. There has been no lack of proposals along these lines.[31] The problem is to ensure that such facilities are sufficiently attractive to induce OPEC participation. OPEC nations might have to be offered concessions to protect the purchasing power of their investments against losses from exchange-rate depreciation or price inflation. They might have to be offered a role in the administration of such facilities as well as some degree of control over the terms by which their funds are re-lent to final borrowers. Without such concessions, the oil producers might not consider cooperation worthwhile.

The three largest economies of the non-communist world have a clear common interest in the problem of adjustment. With regard to the petrodollar problem, however, the interests of the United States, Germany, and Japan are more divergent. Because the latter two countries are more dependent on OPEC oil than the United States, they are less reluctant to offer concessions to OPEC in order to attract a reflow of their surplus earnings. The U.S., in constrast, is in a position to make fewer concessions to oil producers because of its more favorable energy endowment. Nowhere has this divergence of interests been more apparent than in the debate, in 1974, over the relative merits of the IMF oil facility versus the OECD Financial Support Fund. The Germans and Japanese favored a considerable expansion of the IMF oil facility, which would have offered OPEC countries not only a relatively riskless haven for funds but also a substantial voice in administration. For these reasons, however, Secretary of State Kissinger preferred to by-pass the IMF with his alternative proposal for a "safety net" to be established solely within the OECD. Ultimately, the American position prevailed. Therefore, the petrodollar threat to the stability of the monetary order remains acute.

Successful solution of the petrodollar problem also requires agreement among the largest national economies; the divergent interests of the United States, Germany, and Japan must be reconciled. Again, it would be preferable to implement such agreement through the IMF, in order to confer a certain degree of legitimacy on decisions, and as with the adjustment problem, any agreement at all would be better than none. The key need is to avoid a situation in which inconsistency of national policies, a failure to compromise, leads to great instability. The United States is no longer in a position to dictate from a position of hegemony. Others are not yet ready to pick up the mantle of leadership. Consistency can be assured today only in the context of a negotiated system – more a matter of politics than economics. One can only hope that the politicians are up to the job.

Notes

1 Credit for initiating the modern debate on world monetary reform must go to Robert Tiffin. See his landmark *Gold and the Dollar Crisis* (New Haven: Yale University Press, 1960).
2 This trichotomy goes back to the deliberations of a celebrated international study group of 32 economists in 1964. See Fritz Machlup and Burton G. Malkeil, eds., *International Monetary Arrangements: The Problem of Choice* (Princeton: International Finance Section, 1964).
3 For more on the reforms of the 1960s, see Fritz Machlup, *Remaking the International Monetary System* (Baltimore: Johns Hopkins Press, 1968).

4 See Benjamin J. Cohen, "The Revolution in Atlantic Economic Relations: A Bargain Comes Unstuck," in Wolfram Hanrieder, ed., *The United States and Western Europe: Political, Economic and Strategic Perspectives* (Cambridge, Mass.: Winthrop Publishers, 1974), pp. 106–133.

5 See Robert A. Mundell, "The Future of the International Financial System," in A. L. K. Acheson, J. F. Chant, and M. F. J. Prachowny, eds., *Bretton Woods Revisited* (Toronto: University of Toronto Press, 1972), p.92; and Richard N. Cooper, "Prolegomena to the Choice of an International Monetary System," *International Organization*, Vol. 29, No. 1 (Winter 1975), p.64. The terminology of "order" and "system" employed in the text is Mundell's. Cooper prefers the term "regime" to "order."

6 Mundell, *op. cit.*

7 *Ibid.*

8 The results of the Committee's deliberations were published in the form of an Outline of Reform, detailing areas of both agreement and disagreement among the negotiators. See *International Monetary Reform: Documents of the Committee of Twenty* (Washington: International Monetary Fund, 1974).

9 Jeremy Morse, as quoted in *IMF Survery*, 8 April 1974, p.97.

10 See *IMF Survey*, 19 January 1976.

11 Cooper, *op. cit.*, p.64.

12 *Ibid.*, p.65.

13 David P. Calleo, "American Foreign Policy and American European Studies: An Imperial Bias?", in Hanrieder, *op. cit.*, p.62.

14 Marina V. N. Whitman, "The Current and Future Role of the Dollar: How Much Symmetry?", *Brookings Papers on Economic Activity*, No. 3 (1974), p.542.

15 Cohen, *op. cit.*, p.118.

16 Fred Hirsch, "The Politics of World Money," *The Economist*, 5 August 1972, p.57.

17 Marina V. N. Whitman, "Leadership Without Hegemony," *Foreign Policy*, No. 20 (Fall 1975), p.160.

18 Cohen, *op. cit.*, p.133.

19 Calleo, *op. cit.*, p.70.

20 Harry G. Johnson, "Political Economy Aspects of International Monetary Reform," *Journal of International Economics*, Vol. 2, No. 4 (September 1972), p.405.

21 *IMF Survey*, 19 January, 1976.

22 See *International Monetary Reform: Documents of the Committee of Twenty*, Annex 4.

23 A second asymmetry unfavorable to the United States, also deriving from the dollar's exclusive intervention role, was the fact that market exchange rates involving the dollar could move by only half as much as the exchange rate between any other pair of currencies. This is an asymmetry that persists even today, and will continue to persist as long as governments intervene in the exchange markets principally in dollars.

24 Peter B. Kenen, "After Nairobi – Beware of the Rhinopotamus," *Euromoney*, November 1973, p.19.

25 Anthony Lanyi, *The Case for Floating Exchange Rates Reconsidered*, Princeton Essays in International Finance No. 72 (Princeton: International Finance Section, 1969), pp.23–24.

26 For a formal proposal along these lines, see Ronald I. McKinnon, *A New Tripartite Monetary Agreement or a Limping Dollar Standard?* Princeton Essays in International Finance, No.106 (Princeton: International Finance Section, 1974). For a similar proposal involving just the dollar and the mark, see C. Fred Bergsten, *"The United States and Germany: The Imperative of Economic Bigemony,"* in C. Fred Bergsten, *Toward a New International Economic Order: Selected Papers of C. Fred Bergsten, 1972–1974* (Lexington, Mass.: D. C. Heath, 1975), ch. 23.

27 International Monetary Fund, *Annual Report 1975*, pp. 12–16.

28 See, e.g., Morgan Guaranty Trust Company, *World Financial Markets*, 21 January 1975; First National City Bank, *Monthly Economic Letter*, June 1975; Thomas

D. Willett, "The Oil Transfer Problem," *Department of the Treasury News*, 30 January 1975; Hollis B. Chenery, "Restructuring the World Economy," *Foreign Affairs*, Vol. 53, No. 2 (January 1975), pp.242–263; and W. J. Levy Consultants, *Future OPEC Accumulation of Oil Money: A New Look at a Critical Problem* (New York: June 1975).

29 Quoted in *IMF Survey*, 6 May 1974.

30 International Monetary Fund, *Annual Report 1975, loc. cit.* The deficits of the primary producers reflect the severe deterioration of their terms of trade in 1974 and 1975 – partly caused by the high rate of inflation in the industrial world, which sharply reduced the prices of their exports.

31 See, e.g., Khodada Farmanfarmaian, Armin Gutowski, Saburo Okita, Robert V. Roosa, and Carroll L. Wilson, "How Can the World Afford OPEC Oil?," *Foreign Affairs*, Vol. 53, No. 2 (January 1975), pp.201–222.

3 Balance-of-payments financing

Evolution of a regime

Source: *International Organization* 36, 2, Spring 1982.

In few areas of international economic relations has there been as much change in recent years as in the area of monetary relations. At the start of the 1970s, the international monetary system was still essentially that established at Bretton Woods, New Hampshire, a quarter of a century earlier. Exchange rates were still "pegged" within relatively narrow limits around declared par values. Currency reserves were still convertible, directly or indirectly, into gold at the central-bank level. And the main source of external financing for balance-of-payments deficits was still the International Monetary Fund (IMF).

A decade later, all that has changed. Exchange rates of major currencies are no longer pegged; they float. Currency reserves are no longer convertible into gold; they are inconvertible. And the main source of balance-of-payments financing is no longer the IMF but private banking institutions. The role of the private banks in international monetary relations has been greatly enhanced as a result of repeated increases in oil prices since 1973, which have generated enormous financing problems for many oil-importing countries (the petrodollar recycling problem). The recycling of the surplus earnings of OPEC countries, via bank credits and bond issues, to nations in balance-of-payments deficit has, in lieu of commensurate increases in financing from official sources, fallen primarily to private credit markets. As a result, the markets have come to play a role once reserved (in principle) exclusively for official institutions such as the Fund. As one former central banker has put it, "the private banking system took over the functions proper to an official institution possessed of the power to finance balance-of-payments disequilibria through credit-granting and to create international liquidity.... The function of creating international liquidity has been transferred from official institutions to private ones."[1]

Not that the practice of private lending for balance-of-payments purposes is entirely new. Even in the late 1960s, as much as one-third of all payments financing was intermediated by banking institutions between surplus countries (in those days, mainly countries of the Group of Ten) and deficit countries. But up to 1973, the private markets' role tended to be relatively modest. It was only with the emergence of the petrodollar recycling problem that the markets came into their own as an alternative source of payments financing. A special report to the OECD in 1977 (the McCracken Group Report) perhaps best described the development in historical perspective:

> The shift to increased reliance on private lenders for official financing purposes marked the culmination of a secular transformation of the process of liquidity creation. This transformation had already been going on for some time. Its roots lay in the development of the international financial markets – in particular, the growth of the Euro-dollar market – which gradually made it easier for governments to rely on private international financial intermediation rather than on the deficits of reserve centres to obtain new monetary reserves. The international markets act as worldwide financial intermediaries between the lenders and borrowers of loanable funds (including official as well as private lenders and borrowers). Private capital and the accumulated reserves of surplus countries flow into the market and then ultimately are lent on to countries in balance-of-payments difficulties. Increases of demand for credit in borrowing countries are financed by the markets, within the usual institutional and legal constraints, by borrowing or attracting deposits from the banking systems of surplus countries with available loanable funds. The events of 1974–76 simply confirmed and accelerated a trend in the process of liquidity creation that had been evident well before the oil price increases of 1973.[2]

This may be only a change of degree – but it is a change of degree so profound that it appears to border on a transformation of kind. This seeming transformation of the regime governing access to balance-of-payments financing is the subject of this article.

I shall first summarize the role of balance-of-payments financing in international monetary relations, and then describe the key elements of the financing regime that was established at Bretton Woods. Next, the evolution of the regime will be analyzed, and I shall argue that no matter how profound the regime's recent change may appear, it does not in fact add up to a transformation of kind. Rather, to borrow John Ruggie's phrase, it represents an example of "norm-governed change." At the level of principles and norms, the regime remains very much as it was. In the final two sections of the article, I shall briefly consider what inferences may be drawn from the analysis regarding, first, the relationship between the financing regime and behavior; and second, the jurisdictional boundaries between this and other international economic regimes.

The role of financing

The regime for payments financing encompasses the set of implicit or explicit principles, norms, rules, and decision-making procedures governing access to external credit for balance-of-payments purposes. This is clearly a very disaggregated notion of a substantive issue-area. In fact, payments financing as an issue is firmly embedded in the broader question of balance-of-payments adjustment (which in turn is embedded in the still broader question of the structure and management of international monetary relations in general). My choice of issue-area for analysis is based on convenience for a relatively narrow case study; it implies no claim regarding what may or may not be the most appropriate level of aggregation for the study of regimes in other international issue-areas.

Payments financing arises as an issue essentially because of the insistence of national governments on their sovereign right to create money. The existence of separate national moneys requires some integrative mechanism to facilitate economic transactions between states. In practical terms, this function is performed by the foreign-exchange market, which is the medium through which different national moneys are bought and sold. The basic role of the foreign-exchange market is to transfer purchasing power between countries – that is, to expedite exchanges between a local currency and foreign currencies ("foreign exchange"). This role will be performed effectively so long as the demand for foreign exchange in any country (representing the sum of the demands of domestic importers, investors, and the like, all of whom must normally acquire foreign currencies in order to consummate their intended transactions abroad) and the supply of foreign exchange (representing the sum of demands by foreigners for domestic goods, services, and assets, which must be paid for with local currency) remain roughly in balance at the prevailing price of foreign exchange – that is, so long as the exchange market is in *equilibrium*. Difficulties arise when demand and supply do not tend toward balance at the prevailing price – that is, when the market is in *disequilibrium*. Then, either the price of foreign exchange (the exchange rate) must be brought to a new equilibrium level or other actions must be taken or tolerated in order to remove or suppress the disequilibrium. This is the problem of balance-of-payments adjustment.

When confronted by a payments disequilibrium, national governments have two basic policy options. Either they may *finance* the disequilibrium, or they may *adjust* to it. Adjustment implies that the authorities are prepared to accept an immediate reallocation of productive resources (and hence of exchanges of real goods, services, and investments) through changes of relative prices, incomes, exchange rates, or some combination thereof. In effect, they are prepared to accept a reduction of domestic spending on goods, services, and investments (in technical terms, real domestic absorption) relative to national output (real national income). Financing, by contrast, implies that the authorities prefer to avoid an immediate reallocation of resources or a reduction of the ratio of real absorption to production by running down their international monetary reserves or borrowing from external credit sources or both. Politics aside, decisions by individual governments regarding the preferred mix of these two options tend to reflect the comparative economic costs of each.

The economic costs of adjustment have both macroeconomic and microeconomic dimensions. At the macroeconomic level, there may be a decline in the overall level of employment of resources, an increase in the rate of price inflation, or both. At the microeconomic level, there may be a decline in the overall productivity of resources because of distortions introduced into the pattern of resource allocation, as well as frictional costs of the sort that occur whenever resources are reallocated. The magnitude of the costs of adjustment will depend not only on the macroeconomic and microeconomic conditions of the economy but also on the particular strategy of payments adjustment that is chosen – whether that strategy relies most heavily on income changes via variations of monetary policy and fiscal policy (expenditure-reducing policies), or on relative price changes via a modification of the exchange rate, or on direct restrictions on trade or capital movements (expenditure-switching policies). The distinguishing characteristic of adjustment costs is that they must be borne currently, whatever happens to the balance of payments in the future (even if subsequently the causes of the deficit should prove to have been transitory).

The costs of financing, by contrast, are borne not in the present but in the future, when monetary reserves must be replenished and foreign debts repaid. The country will then have to generate a greater net volume of exports to gain the requisite increment of foreign exchange. But until that time, no reduction of current absorption relative to production is required.

The choice between adjustment and financing thus reduces to a choice between reducing the absorption-production ratio today and reducing it tomorrow. Put differently, it reduces to a (necessarily subjective) evaluation of the present values of two different kinds of cost, one (the cost of adjustment) to be borne in the present and one (the cost of financing) in the future – a classic discounting problem.

For political and other reasons, governments often prefer to attach a rather high discount rate to future costs as compared with present costs; that is, they prefer to postpone nasty decisions for as long as possible. Consequently, the greater the level of their reserves or access to external credit or both, the greater is the risk that they may be tempted to alter their policy mix away from adjustment and toward financing – even in situations where an immediate reallocation of resources might be the more appropriate response. Thus it has long been felt that, on principle, governments ought not to enjoy unlimited access to balance-of-payments financing. That principle was formally incorporated into the design of the international monetary system established by a conference of forty-four allied nations at Bretton Woods in 1944.

The Bretton Woods system

The Bretton Woods conference represented the culmination of more than two years of planning, particularly in the Treasuries of Great Britain and the United States, for reconstruction of the monetary system after World War II. In agreeing on a charter for an entirely new international economic organization, the International Monetary Fund, the conferees in effect wrote a constitution for the postwar monetary regime – what later became known as the Bretton Woods system.[3]

Provision of supplementary financing

One of the cardinal principles established at Bretton Woods was that nations should be assured of an adequate supply of international liquidity. Since it was widely believed at the time that the interwar period had demonstrated (to use the words of one authoritative source) "the proved disadvantages of freely fluctuating exchanges,"[4] the conferees decided that countries should be obligated to declare a par value (a "peg") for their currencies and to intervene in the exchange market to limit fluctuations within relatively narrow margins. But since, at the same time, it was also widely recognized that exchange-market intervention "presupposes a large volume of…reserves for each single country as well as in the aggregate," the conferees agreed that there should be some "procedure under which international liquidity would be supplied in the form of prearranged borrowing facilities."[5] It was in order to ensure the availability of such supplementary financing that the IMF was created.

Access to the IMF's resources, however, was not to be unlimited. On the contrary, access was to be strictly governed by a neatly balanced system of subscriptions and quotas. In essence, the Fund was created as a pool of national currencies and gold subscribed by each member country. Members would be assigned quotas, according to a rather complicated formula intended roughly to reflect each country's relative importance in the world economy, and would be obligated to pay into the Fund a subscription of equal amount. The subscription was to be paid 25 percent in gold or currency convertible into gold (effectively the U.S. dollar, which was the only currency still convertible directly into gold) and 75 percent in the member's own currency. In return, each member would be entitled, when short of reserves, to "purchase" (i.e., borrow) amounts of foreign exchange from the Fund in return for equivalent amounts of its own currency. Maximum purchases were set equal to the member's 25 percent gold subscription (its "gold tranche") plus four additional amounts each equal to 25 percent of its quota (its "credit tranches"), up to the point where the Fund's holdings of the member's currency would equal 200 percent of its quota.[6] (If any of the Fund's holdings of the member's initial 75% subscription in its own currency were to be borrowed by other countries, the member's borrowing capacity would be correspondingly increased: this was its "super-gold tranche.") The member's "net reserve position" in the Fund would equal its gold tranche (plus super-gold tranche, if any) less any borrowings by the country from the Fund. Net reserve positions were to provide the supplementary financing that the Bretton Woods conferees agreed was essential.[7]

Formally, within these quota limits, governments were little constrained in their access to Fund resources. The IMF charter simply provided that "the member desiring to purchase the currency [of another member] represents that it is presently needed for making in that currency payments which are consistent with the provisions of the Agreement"[8] – for example, that it "avoid competitive exchange depreciation" and that it "correct maladjustments in [its] balance of payments without resorting to measures destructive to national or international prosperity."[9] In short, the member would play by the agreed rules of the game. It was only with the passage of time that access to financing from the Fund came to be governed explicitly by what has become known as policy "conditionality."[10]

As such, the word "conditionality" does not appear anywhere in the IMF Articles of Agreement. Indeed, in the Fund's early years, there was some question whether the organization even had a legal authority to make borrowing subject to conditions; and for a time debate raged over the issue. Very soon, however, as a result of accumulating experience and precedent, a recognized interpretation of the Fund's prerogatives did in fact emerge to govern members' access to credit. Two landmark decisions of the Fund's governing Board of Executive Directors[11] stand out in this connection. In the first, in 1948, the Board agreed that the IMF could challenge a member's request for finance on the grounds that *inter alia* it would not be "consistent with the provisions of the Agreement," and indeed that the Fund could "postpone or reject the request, or accept it subject to *conditions.*"[12] In the second, in 1952, "conditions" were defined to encompass "policies the member will pursue ... to overcome the [balance-of-payments] problem"[13] – in other words, policies that promise a genuine process of adjustment to external deficit. Since 1952, this has been the accepted meaning of the term "conditionality."

The 1952 decision was also important for establishing a practical distinction between a member's gold tranche and its four credit tranches, by ruling that borrowing in the gold tranche (plus the super-gold tranche, if any) would receive "the overwhelming benefit of any doubt."[14] Subsequent practice also created a distinction between a member's first credit tranche and its remaining ("upper") credit tranches, as summarized in the Fund's 1959 *Annual Report*:

> The Fund's attitude to requests for transactions within the first credit tranche ... is a liberal one, provided that the member itself is also making reasonable efforts to solve its problems. Requests for transactions beyond these limits require substantial justification.[15]

Integral to the evolution of these distinctions were two further developments in IMF practice – stabilization programs and stand-by arrangements.

Over the course of the 1950s, the Fund evolved a practical expression of policy conditionality in the form of stabilization programs, which members were obliged to submit when applying for financing in their credit tranches. Such a program may be quite comprehensive, covering monetary, fiscal, credit, and exchange-rate policies as well as trade and payments practices. In the case of a request in the first credit tranche, members may express their policy intentions at a relatively high level of generality. But for upper credit tranches, programs have to be correspondingly more precise and rigorous in design. Common to most stabilization agreements are, first, a "letter of intent" from the member-government to the Fund spelling out its program to correct its external deficit; and, second, the use of "performance criteria" to express, in quantitative terms, the policy objectives of its program.

Also over the course of the 1950s, the Fund evolved what has become one of the primary instruments used in applying policy conditionality – the stand-by arrangement. Under a stand-by, a member is assured of access to a specified amount of Fund resources for a fixed period of time under agreed conditions, without further consideration of the member's position beyond that provided for in the initial agreement. A key characteristic of most stand-bys is "phasing," which provides that specified amounts of finance will be made available at specified intervals during the stand-by period. At each interval the member's access to finance is made dependent on compliance with the performance criteria spelled out in its stabilization program. These criteria usually operate automatically to suspend (in Fund terminology, "interrupt") the member's access to finance if the policy objectives of its program are not being observed.[16]

Stand-bys normally originate from negotiations between a mission composed of officials of the Fund Secretariat, operating under the instructions of the Fund's Managing Director, and representatives of the member-government. From these negotiations, which may be quite protracted, a letter of intent emerges, usually signed by the member's Finance Minister or central-bank Governor (or both). The Fund Secretariat then, through a decision process involving both "area" departments (responsible for individual countries and regions) and "functional" departments (responsible for individual policy issues such as exchange and trade restrictions, fiscal or monetary policy, etc.), formulates the stand-by arrangement by reference to the letter of intent. That arrangement in turn is submitted by the Managing Director to the Executive Board for final approval. The Board then makes its decision, usually without benefit of a formal vote. If a formal vote is required, Executive Directors vote on behalf of all the members, with the vote of each member weighted in proportion to its individual quota.[17]

The financing regime summarized

The regime for payments financing embedded in the postwar Bretton Woods system can be readily summarized in terms of the four elements of the conventional definition of an international regime.

Principles. The basic principle underlying the regime was that nations should be assured of an adequate but not unlimited supply of supplementary financing for balance-of-payments purposes. The principle was formally articulated in the IMF Articles of Agreement and backed by explicit organizational arrangements in the Fund.

Norms. Standards of behavior were defined in terms of formally articulated treaty rights and obligations accepted by each nation pursuant to its membership in the Fund. Rights consisted of access to IMF resources within quota limits. Obligations consisted of the general pledge to avoid policies inconsistent with the provisions of the IMF charter (i.e., to play by the agreed rules of the game).

Rules. Specific prescriptions or proscriptions for action derived from the Fund's prerogative of policy conditionality. Members' access to financing, particularly in the upper credit tranches, was subject to explicit conditions embodied in Fund stabilization programs and stand-by arrangements.

Decision-making procedures. Arrangements for determining the amount of financing to be made available and the policy conditions, if any, to be imposed in individual instances combined bargaining (in negotiations between the deficit country and the Fund), administrative decision making (within the Fund Secretariat) and, if necessary, voting (in the Executive Board).

Evolution of the regime

The regime remained relatively intact until barely more than a decade ago. What accounted for its creation and subsequent maintenance for more than a quarter of a century? And what then explains its dissipation and subsequent changes in the 1970s?

Creation

To a certain extent, creation of the postwar financing regime may be attributed to enlightened self-interest on the part of the forty-four nations represented at Bretton Woods. All understood the need for adequate liquidity in any exchange-rate regime other than a pure float. All remembered the so-called "gold shortage" of the 1920s – a by-product of extreme price inflation in almost all countries during and immediately after World War I, which had sharply reduced the purchasing power of monetary gold stocks (then still valued at their prewar parities). And all remembered the financial chaos of the 1930s that had ensued when Britain was forced to depart from the gold standard in 1931. None wanted to risk repeating any of that dismal history.

But all understood as well the need to set some upper limit on the availability of supplementary financing for balance-of-payments purposes. The question was, what form should that limit take?

Planning for the postwar monetary system was dominated by the two great reserve centers of the day, Great Britain and the United States. Prior to Bretton Woods the British government, in the person of John Meynard Keynes, had pushed hard for the establishment of an international clearing union endowed with some characteristics of a central bank and in particular, with authority to create a new international currency ("bancor") for lending to countries in deficit. Access to financing, within very broad and flexible limits, would have been automatic and repayment would have followed only after the external imbalance had been reversed. But the Keynes plan was opposed by the American government – in particular, by the chief American negotiator, Harry Dexter White – as being excessively biased in favor of financing rather than adjustment. A much firmer limit on borrowing was needed, White felt: financing should be conditional rather than automatic, and repayment should be at a set time rather than indefinite.

The respective positions of the two governments reflected, in good measure, their national concerns. Britain, facing an enormous task of reconstruction, did not want to be hampered by an inability to finance prospective payments deficits. The United States, by contrast, potentially the largest creditor in the system, did not want in effect to write a blank check. For America, the problem was to avoid financing a massive "giveaway" of U.S. exports. For the U.K., the problem was to avoid constraints on the process of postwar recovery.

In the end, the American position prevailed – reflecting, of course, the predominant position of the United States among the allied nations during World

War II. What was agreed at Bretton Woods was a compromise between the Keynes and White plans. But as one author has put it, "the compromise contained less of the Keynes and more of the White plans."[18] A contractarian route was used, in effect, to legitimate America's view of what constituted rectitude in monetary affairs. Supplementary financing would be made available to deficit countries, but only subject to strict quantitative limits and contingent upon appropriate policy behavior. Hence the Fund's neatly balanced system of subscriptions and quotas.

Only in one respect did the American position on borrowing not prevail at Bretton Woods, and that was on the issue of repayment. In a compromise with the British, the United States initially agreed to an "automatic" provision requiring members to repay credits only when their reserves were rising (with repayments normally to equal one-half the net increase of reserves in each year).[19] But not long thereafter (in 1952), under U.S. pressure, the Fund's Executive Board agreed to a more precise and rigorous temporal limit, requiring repayment within three to five years at the outside.[20] Thus here, too, America's view ultimately won out.

Maintenance

Two factors were principally responsible for the maintenance of the postwar financing regime in the 1950s and 1960s. On the demand side, the need for supplementary financing generally did not exceed what the IMF could provide. On the supply side, there were few alternative sources of financing to compete with the Fund or compromise its authority to exercise policy conditionality.

The demand side. Implicit in the original charter of the IMF was a remarkable optimism regarding prospects for monetary stability in the postwar era. Underlying the choice of a pegged-rate exchange regime seemed to be a clear expectation that beyond the postwar transition period (itself expected to be brief) payments imbalances would not be excessive. The pegged-rate regime was manifestly biased against frequent changes of exchange rates, reflecting the bitter memory of the 1930s, yet nations were left with few instruments under the charter other than capital controls to deal with external disturbances. Few of the conferees at Bretton Woods appeared to doubt that the new Fund's resources would be sufficient to cope with most financing problems.

As matters turned out, this optimism was not entirely justified, at least not in the near term. In fact, in the immediate postwar period monetary relations were anything but stable, and the Fund's resources were anything but sufficient. Most nations were too devastated by war – their export capacities damaged, their import needs enormous, their monetary reserves exhausted – to pay their own way; and their financing needs far exceeded what the IMF could offer. Consequently, the initial burden fell instead to the United States, which in the years 1946 to 1949 disbursed $26 billion through the Marshall Plan and other related aid programs for deficit countries. Fund lending, meanwhile, after a short burst of activity during its first two years, mainly to the benefit of European nations, shrank to an extremely low level. In 1950, the Fund made no new loans at all.[21]

By the mid 1950s, however, the situation had altered substantially. Economies had recovered from wartime destruction and reserve levels were increased by the U.S. balance-of-payments deficit (which averaged approximately $1.5 billion annually between 1950 and 1956). Thereafter, until the emergence of the petrodollar recycling problem in the 1970s, payments imbalances of most countries tended to be more manageable than formerly, and financing needs tended not to strain Fund resources unduly – particularly after 1962, when the Fund's potential lending authority was substantially augmented by negotiation of an arrangement with ten of its main industrial members (the "General Arrangements to Borrow") to borrow additional amounts of their currencies when necessary.[22] During these years, monetary relations corresponded much more closely than previously to the expectations of the conferees at Bretton Woods. And this in turn reinforced the regime that had been designed there.

The supply side. The regime was also reinforced by the absence of important alternative sources of balance-of-payments financing. Some alternative sources did exist, but none seriously threatened to undermine the central role of the Fund.

For example, from 1950 to 1958 the countries of Western Europe enjoyed access to a limited amount of payments financing through the European Payments Union.[23] Similarly, in the 1960s the larger industrial countries could avail themselves of short-term credit through the network of central-bank swap lines initiated by the American Federal Reserve System as well as through other special arrangements at the Bank for International Settlements (BIS) at Basle (e.g., the special stand-bys arranged for Great Britain between 1964 and 1968).[24] And of course a number of countries also had the standing to obtain a certain amount of financing in private credit markets via bank credits or bond issues. But none of these sources was ever posed as a competitor to conditional lending by the Fund. Indeed, most were designed to complement rather than to substitute for IMF credit.

The existence of these alternatives did, of course, bias the system somewhat in favor of the relatively small group of rich industrial countries able to take advantage of them. In effect, only the poorer countries of Europe and Third World nations were fully subject to the ostensible rules of the game. The richer countries had room for a certain amount of "cheating," by borrowing either from one another or (to a limited extent) from the private markets. But it should also be noted that the room for such cheating was not unlimited; witness the fact that Britain required $3.6 billion of IMF loans during the 1964–68 period, despite its access to other lines of credit through the Federal Reserve and the BIS. In any event, the most important of these alternative sources of financing were still official rather than private, thus tending to ensure, in practice, no great inconsistency with Fund conditionality.

In fact, there was only one country at the time that truly had the capacity to avoid Fund conditionality through access to an alternative source of financing. That, ironically enough, was the principal author of the postwar regime, the United States, through the central role of the dollar in international monetary affairs. Because other countries, eager to build up their currency reserves, were largely prepared to accumulate America's surplus dollars (in effect, America's IOUs), the United States was for the most part freed from any balance-of-payments constraint to spend as freely as it thought necessary to promote objectives believed to be in its national interest. In brief, the United States could simply "liability-finance" its deficits. Not that this meant that America's "exorbitant privilege" (as Charles De Gaulle called it) necessarily exploited or disadvantaged others. In fact, as I have argued elsewhere, the element of mutual self-interest in this arrangement was very strong.[25] But it did mean that the regime was potentially vulnerable to abuse by the reserve center, and eventually, as we know, America's deficits did indeed become too great for the postwar system to bear.

Dissipation

With the emergence of the petrodollar recycling problem in the 1970s, changes occurred on both the demand side and the supply side to alter substantially the appearance of the postwar regime. On the demand side the need for supplementary financing expanded enormously, overwhelming what the IMF alone could provide, while on the supply side the private credit markets emerged as an increasingly important rival to the Fund as a source of such financing.

The demand side. Once oil prices began to rise in late 1973, it was clear that oil-importing countries as a group would for some time face extremely large current-account deficits in their relations with oil producers. Some of the largest members of OPEC simply could not increase their imports of goods and services as quickly as their revenues: their "absorptive capacity," at least in the short term, was too low. Accordingly, the balance of their earnings – their "investable surplus" – perforce would have to be invested in foreign assets or otherwise lent back to oil-importing nations as a group.[26] But since reflows of funds from OPEC could not be counted upon to match up precisely with the distribution of deficits among oil importers, some of the latter (industrialized as well as developing countries) were bound to find themselves in serious payments difficulties. The aggregate need of such countries for supplementary financing far exceeded what the IMF alone could provide.

The IMF tried, of course. What was needed, plainly, was not just an increase of quotas (which in fact occurred twice during the 1970s), but, even more importantly, an increase of members' access to Fund resources beyond the strict limit set by their quotas. Precedent for this already existed in two special facilities that had been created during the 1960s to help members cope with particular types of payments problems. The Compensatory Financing Facility was established in 1963 to assist countries, particularly producers and exporters of primary products, experiencing temporary shortfalls of export revenues for reasons largely beyond their own control. The Buffer Stock Financing Facility was established in 1969 to assist countries participating in international buffer-stock arrangements designed to stabilize the price of a specific primary product. Each of these two facilities initially permitted a member to borrow an amount equal to 50 percent of its quota over and above its regular credit tranches.[27]

Building on these precedents, the Fund in the 1970s erected several more special facilities in an effort to cope with its members' increased need for financing. These included a temporary one-year Oil Facility (1974), to help countries meet the initial balance-of-payments impact of higher oil prices; a second one-year Oil Facility (1975); an Extended Fund Facility (1974), to provide financing for longer periods (up to ten years) and in larger amounts (up to 140% of quota) for members experiencing "structural" balance-of-payments problems; a Trust Fund (1976), to provide special assistance to the Fund's poorest members (for up to ten years) out of the proceeds of sales of a portion of the Fund's gold holdings; and a Supplementary Financing Facility (1979), also known as the Witteveen facility, to provide extra credit to members experiencing very large deficits in relation to their quotas. By 1979, as a result of these initiatives, a country could in principle borrow as much as 467.5 percent of its quota, as compared with the 125 percent authorized under the original Articles of Agreement.[28]

But even this was not enough. Although the Fund found itself lending more money to more countries than ever before, the magnitude of deficits after 1973 was simply too great,[29] and much of what the Fund did was really a case of too little and too late. Deficit countries had to look elsewhere. What they found were the private credit markets.

The supply side. The increased role of the private markets as an alternative source of payments financing was a natural consequence of OPEC's comparatively low absorptive capacity. Insofar as the imports of the largest oil exporters failed to keep pace with their revenues, their investable surplus had to be placed somewhere; and the most attractive options were to be found in Western financial markets. Coincident with the weakening of domestic investment demand in industrialized countries, this in turn spurred Western banking institutions to search for new outlets for their greatly enhanced liquidity. Seemingly among the most attractive of such outlets were countries in need of supplementary financing for balance-of-payments purposes.

After 1973, accordingly, private lending to deficit countries increased enormously, primarily by way of bank credits or bonds issued in national or international (offshore) markets. Private banking institutions came to represent, in quantitative terms, the single most important source of payments financing in the world.[30] Not all countries were able to avail themselves of such financing, of course. Poorer less developed countries, lacking any standing at all in the markets, still had to rely on official bilateral or multilateral sources for most of their foreign borrowing. But for developing countries that were regarded by private lenders as sufficiently "creditworthy," as well as for most industrial countries, the bulk of external assistance now came from private sources. Much as in the manner of the United States after World War II, the markets took over from the IMF the main burden of providing supplementary financing for payments purposes.

The result appeared fundamentally to challenge the IMF's presumed role as final arbiter of access to such financing. Private banking institutions had neither the legal authority nor (usually) the inclination to make loans to sovereign governments subject to policy conditions. As a consequence, countries that were regarded by the markets as creditworthy were formally unconstrained in their access to financing, so long as they were willing and able to pay the going rate of interest. This created a danger that some countries might be tempted by the availability of such relatively "easy" (i.e., unconditional) financing to postpone painful – even if necessary – adjustment measures. Put differently, it suggested that the cardinal principle underlying the postwar financing regime – that governments ought not to enjoy unlimited access to balance-of-payments financing – might have been fatally compromised.

Transformation?

The danger was widely acknowledged. Said Wilfried Guth, a prominent German banker, in 1977: "The banks as today's main international creditors are unable to bring about by themselves a better balance between external adjustment and financing."[31] His sentiment was echoed by Arthur Burns, chairman of the Federal Reserve Board of Governors, who admitted that "Countries thus find it more attractive to borrow than to adjust their monetary and fiscal policies."[32] The problem was best summarized by the IMF:

> Access to private sources of balance-of-payments finance may . . . in some cases permit countries to postpone the adoption of adequate domestic stabilization measures. This can exacerbate the problem of correcting payments imbalances, and can lead to adjustments that are politically and socially disruptive when the introduction of stabilization measures becomes unavoidable.[33]

Nor was the danger merely hypothetical. In fact, the IMF was describing what actually came to pass in a number of individual instances. In Peru, for example, in 1976, at a time when the country's balance of payments was under severe pressure owing to plummeting prices for copper (a major Peruvian export) as well as to a mysterious disappearance of anchovy stocks from offshore waters (essential for fishmeal, another major Peruvian export), the government used a new $385 million syndicated bank credit to avoid painful adjustment measures, such as credit restraints or cutbacks of fiscal expenditures. The government even announced, less than a month after the credit was negotiated, plans to purchase $250 million worth of fighter-bombers from the Soviet Union. The result was further deterioration of Peru's external balance, domestic social and political unrest, and eventually stringent austerity measures when the government was finally obliged to adopt an effective stabilization program in 1978.[34]

Similar cases could be cited elsewhere, for example, in both Turkey and Zaïre after 1975. In these countries, access to market financing apparently encouraged the authorities to postpone needed adjustment measures, with consequences ultimately very much like those in Peru.

But not all countries yielded to the temptation to postpone needed adjustment measures. In fact, for any example such as Peru, one could cite a variety of counterexamples of countries that at one time or another used their access to market financing to underwrite immediate and effective actions to restore balance-of-payments equilibrium. Particularly impressive was the case of South Korea following the rise of oil prices in 1973 and the onset of recession in its principal export markets in the United States and Japan in 1974. While relying on borrowing in international credit markets to bridge a widening balance-of-payments gap, the Korean authorities instituted an intensive program of export promotion supplemented by a modest relaxation of monetary and fiscal policy to cushion the domestic impact of recession in foreign markets. In effect, market financing was used to give the economy a breathing space to reallocate resources to the export sector in a context of continuing real growth. Similar cases could be cited, such as Argentina in 1976 and Spain in 1977.

Still, little comfort could be drawn from such "success stories." As the Peruvian case demonstrated, the danger inherent in the availability of relatively "easy" financing from the markets was real – and no one was more aware of it than private banking institutions themselves. Certainly the banks recognized that it was not in their interest to make loans to any country that would do little to ensure its future capacity to service such debt. They had no wish to throw good money after bad, but the problem from their point of view was one of leverage. What, in practice, could they do to ensure that sovereign borrowers would indeed undertake policies that promised a genuine process of adjustment to external deficit?

Variations of terms on offer in the marketplace (e.g., a rise of interest rates or a shortening of maturities) seemed to have little influence on the policies of borrowing governments. As one central banker conceded, it was difficult to "regard this as more than a very marginal contribution to adjustment."[35] Potentially more effective might have been variations of *access* to the market (whatever the terms on offer) – that is, shifts in market sentiment regarding a sovereign borrower's creditworthiness. But the difficulty with that approach was that it might cut off a country's access to financing just when it was most needed. It was certainly not in the banks' interest to force a nation into outright default on its foreign debt.

An alternative approach might have been to exert discipline directly on a borrower through imposition of comprehensive policy conditions. In fact, this was attempted only once – in the syndicated credit to Peru in 1976, which was split into two installments, the first to be drawn immediately and the second in early 1977. Peru's creditors thought that they could ensure adherence to an effective stabilization program by establishing a system for continuous monitoring of the Peruvian economy and by making the second installment of their loan formally contingent upon satisfactory performance. The effort was unique. It was also a failure. In the end, when the loan's second installment came due, no delay was ever seriously mooted despite Peru's evident failure to meet its policy commitments. The banks, as private institutions, simply did not have the legal or political leverage to dictate policy directly to a sovereign government. Since that episode, they have not even tried.

Instead, private lenders have turned increasingly to the IMF, the one lender that, as a multilateral institution backed by formal treaty commitments, *does* have such legal and political leverage. In a growing number of instances, where doubts have developed regarding a country's prospective policy stance, borrowers have been told to go to the IMF first: formally or informally, new financing from the markets has been made contingent upon negotiation of a satisfactory stabilization program with the Fund. As a result, the Fund has come to play a role as a de facto certifier of creditworthiness in the markets – the official issuer of an unofficial "Good Housekeeping Seal of Approval."[36] As one banker has said: "Conditional credit from the Fund is increasingly viewed as an 'international certificate of approval' which enhances the ability of a country to borrow in the private market place."[37] The procedure is favored by lenders because of the Fund's high professional standards, access to confidential information, and – above all – recognized right to exercise policy conditionality. The procedure is acceptable to the Fund because, in effect, it "gears up" the IMF's own lending while ensuring that new financing in such cases will indeed be used to support a well conceived process of adjustment.

To this extent, therefore, the Fund's role as arbiter of access to financing has been preserved: for countries whose creditworthiness comes into doubt, it is still the Fund that formally imposes specific prescriptions or proscriptions for action. This suggests that the change in the regime is really less than it first appears.

That profound change has occurred is clear. At the level of decisionmaking procedures, the amounts or conditions of lending are in most instances no longer a matter for negotiation solely between the authorities of a country and the IMF. Now a third set of actors is often prominently involved – private banking institutions. And in the many instances where a borrower's policy stance has not come into doubt, the IMF may not be involved at all. To that extent the Fund's monitoring role has indeed been eroded.[38] Nonetheless, I would argue that this falls short of a transformation of kind.

In the first place, just as the practice of private lending for balance-of-payments purposes is itself not entirely new, neither is the role of the Fund as informal certifier of creditworthiness in the markets. Even as far back as the 1950s, cases could be cited where an IMF stabilization program proved the key to unlocking supplementary financing from private sources.[39] Admittedly, use of that procedure prior to 1973 was relatively infrequent. Still, the very fact that it existed at all suggests that there has been more of an element of continuity in the financing regime than might have been thought.

Even more importantly, there has been a strong element of continuity in the basic principles and norms underlying the regime. The idea that deficit countries ought not to enjoy unlimited access to balance-of-payments financing has not been fatally compromised; nor have commonly agreed standards of behavior been significantly altered. Rather, what has happened is that all the key players – governments, banking institutions, the IMF – have made operational adaptations to the changed circumstances on both the demand and the supply sides of the system. True, as a result norms and rules have tended to become somewhat less formally articulated than before; decision-making procedures have become more ambiguous; and the room for cheating (for countries with unquestioned creditworthiness) now is greater than it used to be. But these are changes of degree only – "norm-governed changes," once again to borrow Ruggie's phrase.

The important point is that all players, even while making their operational adaptations, still acknowledge the fundamental need to play by the rules of the game. In its maintenance of a balance of recognized rights and obligations for deficit countries, the financing regime remains very much the same as before. In its deeper tenets, it has not in fact changed.

The relationship between regime and behavior

What conclusions may we draw, from this stylized sketch of the evolution of the postwar financing regime, regarding the relationship between the regime and behavior?

At the time of its creation, it is clear, the regime was the product not of actual behavior but rather of other, endogenous factors – in particular, the experiences of the interwar period and World War II. The interwar experience had generated a broad consensus in favor of establishing some kind of mechanism to provide limited amounts of supplementary payments financing. World War II had confirmed the economic and political predominance of the United States. The fact that a regime emerged from Bretton Woods at all reflected the allies' collective perception of self-interest in monetary affairs. The specific shape of that regime reflected largely the individual concerns and influence of the United States.

Moreover, over the next quarter of a century, it was mostly the regime that influenced behavior rather than the reverse. Deficit countries, with the important exception of the United States, did in fact generally respect IMF policy conditionality when availing themselves of supplementary payments financing – although, to be sure, this reflected conditions on both the demand and the supply sides of the system as much as it did the influence of the regime as such. Governments played by the formal rules agreed at Bretton Woods not only because they were legally committed to do so by an international agreement but also because their need for supplementary financing did not in general exceed what the IMF could provide and because there were few alternative sources of financing to compete with the Fund. Maintenance of the regime in the 1950s and 1960s was attributable as much to the general absence of either need or means to circumvent the regime as it was to the enlightened self-interest of nations.

Conversely, when conditions changed dramatically in the 1970s, so did behavior. The vast increase in the need for financing led countries to search for new sources of external credit; the vast increase of liquidity in financial markets led banking institutions to search for new customers. The result was a profound change in the appearance of the regime as the markets emerged as a major alternative source of financing for deficit countries. No longer did the IMF stand alone as arbiter of access to payments support.

But this cannot be regarded as a transformation of kind. Owing to the informal working relationship that has gradually developed between the IMF and the markets whereby private lenders, in cases of serious payments difficulties, treat negotiation of a Fund stand-by (with attendant policy conditionality) as a prerequisite for lending, the basic principle underlying the regime as well as commonly agreed standards of behavior for deficit nations have, for the most part, been preserved. While rules and decision-making procedures admittedly have become somewhat vaguer than they were, and for some countries the room for cheating has been increased, these changes have been for the most part "norm-governed" in character. In its essential purpose, the financing regime continues to have a real effect on behavior.

Jurisdictional boundaries of the regime

Finally, it is of interest to consider the impact of recent events on the jurisdictional boundaries of the financing regime.

Originally, a very clear division of labor was intended to distinguish the work of the IMF from that of its sister organization created at Bretton Woods, the World Bank (formally, the International Bank for Reconstruction and Development). The mandate of the Fund was to lend for relatively short periods of time to help maintain international payments equilibrium. The mandate of the Bank was to lend for much longer periods to help support postwar economic recovery and, subsequently, economic development in poorer countries. The regime to govern access to IMF financing was firmly embedded in the broader question of balance-of-payments adjustment. The regime to govern access to Bank financing was firmly embedded in the broader question of development assistance.

More recently, however, as a result of repeated increases in world oil prices since 1973, the line dividing the Fund's mandate from the Bank's has grown rather more ambiguous. In fact, the Fund has come under a great deal of pressure to extend increased amounts of credit to deficit countries – particularly in the Third World – for longer periods and with more flexible policy conditions.[40] In an era of persistent OPEC surpluses, it is argued, deficits in nonoil developing countries cannot be treated simply as a short-term phenomenon caused by faulty domestic policies and amenable to traditional policy prescriptions (e.g., devaluation or monetary and fiscal restraint). Oil-induced deficits perforce must be expected to continue for much longer periods, until such time as the nations involved can make the necessary "structural" adjustments to the altered relative cost of energy. In the meantime, the Fund should make a greater effort to supplement private lending by reforms of its own lending policies, such as making more money available for longer-term, structural measures to narrow net dependence on oil imports and to broaden the foreign-exchange earning capacity of deficit countries.

To some extent, the Fund has tried to respond to these pressures. In 1979, the Executive Board issued a new set of guidelines on policy conditionality explicitly acknowledging that adjustment in many cases might require a longer period of time than traditionally assumed in Fund stabilization programs, and pledging to "pay due regard to ... the circumstances of members, including the causes of their balance of payments problems."[41] And in 1980 and 1981 a new policy of "enlarged access" to the Fund's resources was brought formally into effect, along with a 50 percent increase of all members' quotas. Under the new policy, the maximum amount that a country may in principle cumulatively borrow from the

Fund has been raised from 467.5 percent of its quota to 600 percent.[42] In addition, an increasing proportion of Fund lending is now being directed through the Extended Fund Facility, thus making available more financing for longer periods of time than had generally been available in the past.

However, as these changes have been carried out, the Fund has found itself moving closer to the traditional province of the World Bank – just as, simultaneously, the Bank has been moving the other way. Also under pressure to do more for countries hit hard by the increased relative cost of energy, the Bank in 1979 began to shift from its usual emphasis on long-term project lending to more, relatively short-term, program lending for "structural adjustment" purposes. The object of such lending, in the words of a senior Bank official, is "to provide support for member countries already in serious BOP [balance-of-payments] difficulties, or faced in the years ahead with the prospect of unmanageable deficits arising from external factors which are not likely to be easily or quickly reversed."[43] This sounds remarkably similar to the IMF's explanations of its own lending policies.

In fact, we are witnessing a partial convergence of the roles of the Fund and the Bank – that is, a partial overlapping of the regimes governing access to payments financing and development assistance. Here, in the blurring of the jurisdictional boundary between these two regimes, is perhaps the most significant impact of the events of the 1970s. In the 1980s it will be increasingly difficult to maintain a clear distinction between these two forms of lending.

Notes

1 Guido Carli, *Why Banks Are Unpopular*, The 1976 Per Jacobsson Lecture (Washington: IMF, 1976), pp. 6, 8.
2 *Towards Full Employment and Price Stability*, A Report to the OECD by a Group of Independent Experts, chaired by Paul McCracken (Paris: OECD, 1977), para. 159. In a still longer historical perspective, Charles Kindleberger has pointed out that – on an intermittent basis – private bankers at least since the Medici have made a practice of last-resort lending to governments at times of financial crisis; see his *Manias, Panics, and Crashes: A History of Financial Crises* (New York: Basic Books, 1978), chap. 10. Only with the growth of the Eurocurrency market, however, has balance-of-payments lending from private sources tended to become a *regular* practice.
3 Comprehensive histories of the wartime discussions and Bretton Woods conference can be found in J. Keith Horsefield, ed., *The International Monetary Fund, 1945–1965*, vol. 1: *Chronicle* (Washington: IMF, 1969), Part I; and Richard N. Gardner, *Sterling-Dollar Diplomacy* (Oxford: Clarendon Press, 1956), chaps. 5, 7.
4 League of Nations, *International Currency Experience* (1944), p. 211.
5 Ibid., pp. 214, 218.
6 Although the original Fund charter contained a provision prohibiting members in most circumstances from borrowing more than 25% of quota in any twelve-month period, in practice, as IMF operations evolved, this provision was frequently waived and was finally eliminated entirely in the Second Amendment of the Articles of Agreement of the IMF in 1976.
7 As a result of the Second Amendment in 1976, gold was eliminated from the Fund system of subscriptions and quotas. In lieu of gold, members now subscribe Special Drawing Rights or national currencies; and in lieu of a gold tranche, members now have a reserve tranche.

8 *Articles of Agreement of the International Monetary Fund*, Art. V., Section 3 (a) (i). The original Articles are reprinted in Horsefield, *The IMF*, vol. 3: *Documents*, pp. 185–214.

9 *Articles of Agreement*, Art. I (iii) and (v).

10 For the evolution of the concept of policy conditionality, see Horsefield, *The IMF*, vol. 2: *Analysis*, chaps. 18, 20, 21, 23; Joseph Gold, *Conditionality*, IMF Pamphlet Series, no. 31 (Washington: IMF, 1979); Manuel Guitian, "Fund Conditionality and the International Adjustment Process: The Early Period, 1950–70," *Finance and Development* 17, 4 (December 1980), pp. 23–27; and Frank A. Southard Jr., *The Evolution of the International Monetary Fund*, Essays in International Finance, no. 135 (Princeton: Princeton University, International Finance Section, 1979), pp. 15–21.

11 Formally, the Fund is governed by its Board of Governors, consisting of one Governor (usually the Finance Minister or central-bank Governor) from each member-country. However, since the Board of Governors only meets once a year, in practice most of its powers have been delegated to the Executive Board, which functions in continuous session. Executive Directors now (1981) number twenty-two, seven representing the five largest members of the Fund together with Saudi Arabia (one of the Fund's two largest creditors) and China, and fifteen representing various constituencies comprising collectively the remaining membership.

12 Decision No. 284-4, 10 March 1948, reprinted in Horsefield, *The IMF*, 3:227. Italics supplied.

13 Decision No. 102-(52/11), 13 February 1952, reprinted in Horsefield, *The IMF*, 3:228.

14 Ibid., p. 230.

15 IMF, *Annual Report*, 1959, p. 22.

16 For a model stand-by arrangement, see Joseph Gold, *Financial Assistance by the International Monetary Fund: Law and Practice*, IMF Pamphlet Series, no. 27 (Washington: IMF, 1979), Appendix B.

17 For more on the Fund's decision-making procedures, see Horsefield, *The IMF*, 2, chap. 1; and Southard, *Evolution of IMF*, pp. 2–15.

18 Sidney E. Rolfe, *Gold and World Power* (New York: Harper & Row, 1966), p. 78.

19 *Articles of Agreement*, Art. V, Section 7.

20 See, e.g., Southard, *Evolution of IMF*, pp. 16–17.

21 Inadequacy of resources was not the only reason for the Fund's meager contribution during these years. In addition, there was the running debate over conditionality, which was not finally resolved until the Executive Board's landmark 1952 decision. See Southard, *Evolution of IMF*, p. 17.

22 The text of the arrangement is reprinted in Horsefield, *The IMF*, 3:246–56.

23 For more detail on EPU, see Robert Triffin, *Europe and the Money Muddle* (New Haven: Yale University Press, 1957), chaps. 5–6.

24 For more detail on the various support operations arranged for Britain during this period, see Benjamin J. Cohen, *The Future of Sterling as an International Currency* (London: Macmillan, 1971), pp. 97–98.

25 Benjamin J. Cohen, *Organizing the World's Money* (New York: Basic Books, 1977), pp. 95–97.

26 In fact, OPEC's absorptive capacity after the first round of oil price increases in 1973–74 surpassed expectations, and by 1978 its investable surplus (which averaged some $45 billion annually, 1974–76) had fallen to below $10 billion. But with the second round of price increases starting in late 1978, the surplus soared to $68 billion in 1979 and $112 billion in 1980. Most observers expect this OPEC surplus to persist for much longer. See, e.g., Morgan Guaranty Trust Company, *World Financial Markets*, September 1980, pp. 1–13, and May 1981, pp. 3–5; *Citibank Monthly Economic Letter*, April 1981, pp. 5–6; IMF, *World Economic Outlook* (Washington, D.C., June 1981).

27 More recently, the Compensatory Financing Facility has been liberalized to permit borrowings up to 100% of quota.

28 For more detail on the Fund's various special facilities, see Gold, *Financial Assistance*; and *IMF Survey*, May 1981, "Supplement on the Fund," pp. 6–10. It should be noted that of these facilities, only three – the Compensatory Financing Facility, the Buffer Stock Financing Facility, and the Extended Fund Facility – represent *permanent* additions to the IMF's lending authority.

29 For more detail, see Benjamin J. Cohen, *Banks and the Balance of Payments*, in collaboration with Fabio Basagni (Montclair, N.J.: Allenheld, Osmun, 1981), chap. 1.

30 Ibid.

31 Wilfried Guth, in Guth and Sir Arthur Lewis, *The International Monetary System in Operation*, The 1977 Per Jacobsson Lecture (Washington: IMF, 1977), p. 25.

32 Arthur F. Burns, "The Need for Order in International Finance," in *International Banking Operations*, Hearings before the Subcommittee on Financial Institutions Supervision, Regulation, and Insurance of U.S. Congress, House Committee on Banking, Finance and Urban Affairs (Washington, D.C., March-April 1977), p. 860.

33 IMF, *Annual Report*, 1977, p. 41.

34 For more detail on the Peruvian and other examples cited in this section, see Cohen, *Banks and the Balance of Payments*, chap. 4 and Appendix.

35 J. A. Kirbyshire, "Should Developments in the Euro-Markets be a Source of Concern to Regulatory Authorities?", *Bank of England Quarterly Bulletin* 17, 1 (March 1977), p. 44.

36 See, e.g., Giovanni Magnifico, "The Real Role of the IMF," *Euromoney*, October 1977, pp. 141–44; Charles Lipson, "The IMF, Commercial Banks, and Third World Debts," in Jonathan David Aronson, ed., *Debt and the Less Developed Countries* (Boulder, Col.: Westview Press, 1979); and Carl R. Neu, "The International Monetary Fund and LDC Debt," in Lawrence G. Franko and Marilyn J. Seiber, eds., *Developing Country Debt* (New York: Pergamon Press, 1979).

37 Richard D. Hill, in *International Debt*, Hearings before the Subcommittee on International Finance of U.S. Congress, House Committee on Banking, Housing and Urban Affairs (Washington, D.C., 1977), p. 127.

38 There seems little to be done to reverse this erosion, at least by way of formal reforms, without losing the acknowledged benefits of private lending for balance-of-payments purposes. See Cohen, *Banks and the Balance of Payments*, pp. 171–76.

39 See, e.g., Peter B. Kenen, *Giant Among Nations* (New York: Harcourt, Brace, 1960), pp. 93–94.

40 See, e.g., Group of 24, *Outline for a Program of Action on International Monetary Reform*, reprinted in *IMF Survey*, 15 October 1979, pp. 319–23; *North-South: A Programme for Survival*, Report of the Independent Commission on International Development Issues, chaired by Willy Brandt (Cambridge: MIT Press, 1980), chap. 13; and Sidney Dell and Roger Lawrence, *The Balance of Payments Adjustment Process in Developing Countries* (New York: Pergamon Press, 1980). I have associated myself with this point of view in Benjamin J. Cohen, "Balancing the System in the 1980s: Private Banks and the IMF," in Gary Clyde Hufbauer, ed., *The International Framework for Money and Banking in the 1980s* (Washington: International Law Institute, 1981).

41 See *IMF Survey*, 19 March 1979, pp. 82–83; and Gold, *Conditionality*, pp. 14–37.

42 In practice the limit is even higher, since the 600% figure does not take into account loans from either the Compensatory Financing Facility or the Buffer Stock Financing Facility. See *IMF Survey*, May 1981, "Supplement on the Fund," p. 10. The first country to borrow up to this new maximum was Turkey, in June 1980. See *IMF Survey*, 25 June 1980, p. 177. The IMF had never previously lent more than 400% of a member's quota.

43 E. Peter Wright, "World Bank Lending for Structural Adjustment," *Finance and Development*, September 1980, p. 21.

4   The Triad and the Unholy Trinity
Lessons for the Pacific Region

Source: From R. Higgott, R. Leaver and J. Ravenhill (eds), *Pacific Economic Relations in the 1990s: Cooperation or Conflict?*, 1993.

Economic cooperation is now on the agenda of the Pacific Region. As the chapters in this collection testify, governments throughout the area are becoming increasingly aware of the many interests they share in common; even more importantly, there is now growing appreciation of the value of collective approaches to help promote regional objectives or to resolve tensions where mutual interests differ. Until now, understandably, most attention has focused on the high-profile issues of trade and investment. But as the countries of the Pacific move into the 1990s, the challenge of cooperative management of monetary relations is taking on increasing salience as well. The question addressed in this chapter is: what are the prospects for successful monetary cooperation in the Pacific Region in the 1990s? Since to date there has been little experience within the region itself to draw on, the analysis of this chapter will focus primarily on implications that can be drawn from the most prominent example of monetary cooperation elsewhere – specifically, the regularised process of 'multilateral surveillance' that has recently been developed and refined by the governments of the Group of Seven (G-7).

Among the G-7 countries (the United States, Britain, Canada, France, Germany, Italy and Japan), procedures for monetary cooperation have been gradually intensified since the celebrated Plaza Agreement of September 1985, which formally pledged participants to a coordinated realignment of exchange rates. Ostensibly the aim of these evolving procedures is to jointly manage currency relations and macroeconomic conditions across Europe, North America and Japan – the area referred to by many simply as the Triad. Finance ministers from the G-7 countries now meet regularly to discuss the current and prospective performance of their economies; policy objectives and instruments are evaluated for possible linkages and repercussions; the principle of mutual adjustment in the common interest is repeatedly reaffirmed in official communiqués (for details see Dobson 1991, chs 3–5). Yet for all their promises to curb unilateralist impulses, the governments involved frequently honour the process more in word than deed. In fact, if there has been one constant in the collaborative efforts of the Triad, it has been their lack of constancy. Commitments in practice have tended to ebb and flow cyclically like the tides. In its essence, G-7 monetary cooperation has had a distinctly episodic quality to it.

The main premise of this chapter is that international monetary cooperation, like passionate love, is a good thing but difficult to sustain. The reason, I argue, is systematic and has to do with the intrinsic incompatibility of three key desiderata of governments: exchange-rate stability, capital mobility, and national policy autonomy. Together these three values form a kind of 'Unholy Trinity' that operates regularly to erode collective commitments to monetary collaboration. The impact of the Unholy Trinity has been evident in the experience of the G-7. The principal implication for the countries of the Pacific Region is that the conditions necessary for a serious and sustained commitment to monetary cooperation are not easy to satisfy and, without major effort, appear unlikely to be attained any time soon. The irony is that even without such a commitment most regional governments will find their policy autonomy increasingly eroded in the coming decade – in a manner, moreover, that may seem even less appealing to them than formal cooperation.

The organisation of this chapter is as follows. Following a brief evaluation in Part 1 of the basic case for monetary cooperation, Part 2 reviews the experience of the G-7 countries since 1985 noting, in particular, a distinctly cyclical pattern in the Triad's collective commitment to policy coordination. Reasons for the episodic quality of monetary cooperation with emphasis on the central role of the Unholy Trinity are explored in Part 3, and the question of what might be done about the resulting inconstancy of policy commitments is addressed in Part 4. The chapter concludes in Part 5 with possible lessons for the Pacific Region.

The case for policy cooperation

Conceptually, international cooperation may take many forms, ranging from simple consultation among governments, or occasional crisis management, to partial or even full collaboration in the formulation and implementation of policy. In this chapter, following the lead of standard scholarship on international political economy (e.g., Keohane 1984, pp. 51–4), cooperation will be identified with a mutual adjustment of national policy behaviour in a particular issue-area, achieved through an implicit or explicit process of inter-state bargaining. Related terms such as 'coordination' and 'joint' or 'collective' decision-making will, for our purposes, be treated as essentially synonymous in meaning.

In the issue-area of international monetary relations, the theoretical case for policy cooperation is quite straightforward (see e.g., Cooper 1985; Artis & Ostry 1986, ch. 1). It begins with the undeniable fact of intensified interdependence across much of the world economy. In recent decades, states have become increasingly linked through the integration of markets for goods, services and capital. Structurally, the greater openness of economies tends to erode each country's insulation from commercial or financial developments elsewhere. In policy terms it means that any one government's actions will generate a variety of 'spillover' effects – foreign repercussions and feedbacks – that can significantly influence its own ability, as well as the ability of others, to achieve preferred macroeconomic or exchange-rate objectives. (Technically the size, and possibly even the sign, of policy multipliers is altered both at home and abroad.) Such 'externalities' imply that policies chosen unilaterally, even if seemingly optimal from an individual country's point of view, will almost certainly turn out to be sub-optimal in a global context. The basic rationale for monetary cooperation is that it can *internalise* these externalities by giving each government partial control over the actions of others, thus relieving the shortage of instruments that prevents each one separately from reaching its chosen targets on its own.

At least two sets of goals may be pursued through policy coordination. At one level, cooperation may be treated simply as a vehicle by which countries together move closer to their individual policy targets. (In the formal language of game theory favoured by many analysts, utility or welfare-seeking governments bargain their way from the sub-optimality of a so-called Nash equilibrium to something closer to a Pareto optimum.) Peter Kenen (1988, pp. 75–7) calls this the *policy-optimising* approach to cooperation. At a second level, mutual adjustments can also be made in pursuit of broader collective goals, such as defence of existing international arrangements or institutions against the threat of economic or political shocks. Kenen calls this the *regime-preserving* or *public-goods* approach to cooperation. Both approaches derive from the same facts of structural and policy interdependence. Few scholars question the basic logic of either one.

What is accepted in theory, of course, need not be favoured in practice – however persuasive the logic. As Martin Feldstein (1988, p. 3), a sceptic on the value of policy cooperation, has written:

> Although [theory] might suggest that international coordination is unambiguously better than the uncoordinated pursuit of national interest, it is important to distinguish between the theoretical possibilities of idealized coordination and the realistic potential gains of practical coordination. In practice, despite its aspirations, international coordination may produce results that are not as satisfactory as those that result from each country's uncoordinated pursuit of national sell-interest.

Few scholars question the logic of Feldstein's scepticism either. Quite the contrary, in fact. Samuel Brittan (1991, p. 37) may be correct when he asserts that 'being in favor of coordination is like being in favor of virtue or motherhood'. But even virtue and motherhood can be said to have their drawbacks. In recent years there has been a virtual avalanche of formal literature citing various qualifications to the basic case for monetary cooperation and casting doubt on its practical benefits. The irony is evident: even as policy coordination since the mid-1980s has ostensibly become fashionable again among governments, it seems to have gone out of style with many analysts. At least five major issues have been raised for discussion by economists working in this area.

First is the question of the *magnitude of the gains* to be expected. Although in theory the move from a Nash equilibrium to Pareto optimality may seem dramatic, in practice much depends on the size of the spillovers involved. If externalities are small, so too will be the potential benefits of cooperation.

Many analysts cite a pioneering study by Oudiz and Sachs (1984) designed to measure the effects of monetary and fiscal policy coordination by Germany,

Japan and the United States, using data from the mid-1970s. Estimated gains were disappointingly meagre, amounting to no more than half of one per cent of GNP in each country as compared with the best noncooperative outcomes. Although some subsequent studies have detected moderately greater income increases from coordination, most tend to confirm the impression that on balance very large gains should not be expected (Kenen 1989, pp. 23–9; Currie et al. 1989, p. 25–7).

Second is the other side of the ledger: the question of the *magnitude of the costs* to be expected. Theoretical models typically abstract from the costs of coordination. In reality, however, considerable time and effort are needed to evaluate performance, negotiate agreements, and monitor compliance among sovereign governments. Moreover, the greater the number of countries or issues involved, the more complex are the policy adjustments that are likely to be required of each (Artis & Ostry 1986, pp. 17–18). All this demands expenditure of resources that may loom large when compared with the possibly meagre scale of anticipated benefits. For some analysts, this suggests that the game may simply not be worth the candle. For others, it implies the need for a more explicit framework for cooperation – some formally agreed set of rules – that could substitute for repeated negotiations over individual issues, such as the Williamson–Miller (1987) extended target-zone proposal or Jeffrey Frankel's (1988) plan for nominal-income targeting. The advantage of an articulated rule-based regime is that it would presumably be more cost-effective than endless *ad hoc* bargaining. The disadvantage is that it would require a greater surrender of policy autonomy than many governments now seem prepared to tolerate (a point to which I shall return below).

Third is the so-called *time–inconsistency* problem: the risk that agreements, once negotiated, will later be violated by maverick governments tempted to renege on policy commitments that turn out to be inconvenient (e.g., Canzoneri & Gray 1985). The risk, in principle, is a real one. In relations between sovereign states, where enforcement mechanisms are weak or nonexistent, there is always a threat that bargains may be at some point broken. But whether the possibility of unilateral defection constitutes much of a threat in practice is hotly debated among specialists, many of whom stress the role of reputation and credibility as deterrents to cheating by individual governments (e.g., Kenen 1989, pp. 29–33). In the language of game theory, much depends on the details of how the strategic interactions are structured, for example, the number of players in the game, whether and how often the game is iterated, and how many other related games are being played simultaneously. Much depends as well on the historical and institutional context, and how the preferences of decision-makers are formed – matters about which it is inherently difficult to generalise. In the absence of more general specifications, few definitive judgements seem possible *a priori*.

Fourth is the possible *distortion of incentives* that might be generated by efforts at policy coordination. In an early and influential article, Kenneth Rogoff (1985) argued that international cooperation could actually prove to be counterproductive – welfare-decreasing rather than Pareto-improving – if the coordination process were to encourage governments collectively to choose policies that are more politically convenient than economically sound. Formal coordination of monetary policies, for example, could simply lead to higher global inflation if governments were all to agree to expand their money supplies together, thus evading the balance-of-payments constraint that would discipline any country attempting to inflate on its own. More generally, there is always the chance that ruling élites might exploit the process to promote particularist or even personal interests at the expense of broader collective goals. This risk too is widely regarded as realistic in principle and is hotly debated for its possible importance in practice. And here too few definitive judgements seem possible *a priori* in the absence of more general specifications.

Finally, there is the issue of *model uncertainty*: the risks that policymakers simply are badly informed and do not really understand how their economies operate and interact. Frankel and Rockett (1988) in a widely cited study demonstrated that when governments do differ in their analytical views of policy impacts, coordination could well cause welfare losses rather than gains for at least some of the countries involved. For some analysts, this is more than enough reason to prefer a return to uncoordinated pursuit of national self-interest. For others, however, it suggests instead the value of consultation and exchanges of information to avoid misunderstandings about transmission mechanisms and the size and sign of relevant policy multipliers. As Holtham and Hughes Hallet (1987) and Ghosh and Masson (1988) have each shown, the success rate of policy cooperation can be expected to be much higher if governments design their policies cautiously to take explicit account of the possibility of model uncertainty.

Where, then, does all this discussion come out? None of the five issues that have been so thoroughly aired in the literature is unimportant; sceptics have been right to raise and emphasise them. But neither do any of these qualifications appear to deal a decisive blow to the underlying case for cooperation, which retains its essential appeal. For this reason most analysts, myself among them, still remain disposed to view policy cooperation for all its imperfections in much the same light as virtue or motherhood – an inherently good thing. Net gains may be small; motivations may get distorted; outcomes may not always fulfil expectations. Nonetheless, despite all the risks the effort does seem justified. Robert Solomon (1991, p. 51) said it best when he wrote:

> Serious obstacles stand in the way of effective macroeconomic coordination... Nonetheless, there have been occasions when the world economy would clearly have benefited from coordination, and such occasions will undoubtedly arise again. On balance, therefore, coordination of macroeconomic policies is worth pursuing.

The ebb and flow of policy commitments

A problem remains, however. To be effective, the collective commitment to cooperation must appear credible; and to be credible, that commitment must above all be *sustained*. Individual governments may play the maverick on occasion (the time–inconsistency problem); a little cheating at the margins is after all hardly unexpected, or even unusual, in international relations. But the commitment of the collectivity must be seen to be enduring: there can be no room for doubt about the continuing relevance, the *seriousness*, of the process as such. Otherwise incentives will indeed be distorted for state and non-state actors alike, and outcomes could well turn out to be every bit as counterproductive as many analysts fear. As Peter Kenen (1991, p. 31) has warned, 'Sporadic management may be worse than no management at all'. Yet, as noted at the outset, that is precisely the pattern that policy coordination has tended to display in practice. The history of international monetary cooperation is one long lesson in the fickleness of policy fashion.

During the early inter-war period, for example, the central banks of the major industrial nations publicly committed themselves to a cooperative attempt to restore something like the pre-World War I gold standard, only to end up in the 1930s energetically battling one another through futile rounds of competitive devaluations and escalating capital controls. And similarly during the Bretton Woods era, early efforts at cooperative institution-building and joint consultations ultimately terminated in mutual recriminations and the demise of the par-value system. In the middle 1970s, endeavours to revive some kind of rule-based exchange-rate regime were overwhelmed by policy disagreements between the Carter administration in the United States and its counterparts in Europe and Japan, leading to a record depreciation of the US dollar. At the turn of the decade renewed attempts at joint stabilisation were cut short by the go-it-alone policies of the new Reagan administration, leading to the record appreciation of the dollar which, in turn, set the stage for the Plaza Agreement of 1985. The broad picture of monetary relations in the twentieth century is clearly one of considerable ebbs and flows in the collective commitment to policy cooperation.

Moreover, the big picture – much in the manner of Mandelbrot fractals – tends broadly to be replicated in the small. (A fractal is an object or phenomenon that is self-similar across different scales.) Often superimposed on longer waves of enthusiasm or disillusionment with policy cooperation have been briefer 'stop–go' cycles of commitment and retreat, such as the short-lived attempts of the London Monetary Conference and later Tripartite Agreement to restore some measure of monetary stability in the 1930s. In the 1960s and early 1970s, even as the Bretton Woods system was heading for breakdown, the major financial powers cooperated at one point to create a new international reserve asset, the Special Drawing Right (SDR), and then at another to temporarily realign and stabilise exchange rates in the Smithsonian Agreement of December 1971. And even before the Plaza Agreement in 1985 there were already regular meetings of finance ministers and central bankers to discuss mutual policy linkages, as well as of lower-level officials in such settings as the Organisation for Economic Cooperation and Development (OECD) and the Bank for International Settlements (BIS). The now-fashionable process of multilateral surveillance was, in fact, first mandated by the leaders of the G-7 countries at the Versailles summit in 1982.

Most significantly, the same cyclical pattern has been evident even during the brief period since the announcement of the Plaza Agreement. The appetite for mutual accommodation in the Triad continues to wax and wane episodically; inconstancy remains the rule. Formally the G-7 governments are now fully committed to the multilateral-surveillance process. In actual practice, despite regular meetings and repeated reaffirmations of principle, policy behaviour continues to betray a certain degree of recurrent recidivism. At least four distinct rounds of stop–go motion can be identified in the trend of events since 1985.

Round I: September 1985–February 1987

This round, lasting from the Plaza Agreement up to the so-called Louvre Accord, was typical in starting promisingly but ending raggedly. The Plaza Agreement itself was, of course, responsible for making policy coordination formally fashionable again after several years of disrepute. But it did not take long for the process in practice to begin losing momentum as policy divergences reasserted themselves. As has so often occurred in monetary history, the governments involved found it difficult to sustain their collective commitment to cooperate in the common interest.

The key to the Plaza Agreement was the willingness of the Reagan administration, at the start of its second term under the leadership of incoming Treasury Secretary James Baker, to abandon its earlier unilateralist impulses, owing above all to the accelerating deterioration of the US balance of trade. The story is well known and has been well described elsewhere (e.g., Funabashi 1988, ch. 3; Destler & Henning 1989, ch. 3). Suffice it to note here that Secretary Baker was determined to head off protectionist pressures in the Congress, first and foremost by engineering a sharp depreciation of the dollar from the astronomical heights it had reached by early 1985. Quite understandably, he also wanted to ensure that his policy strategy would not be compromised by offsetting actions elsewhere. Emphasis was placed, therefore, on negotiating the concurrence of the other major financial powers, using the forum conveniently provided by the informal meetings of the finance ministers of the so-called Group of Five (the United States, Britain, France, Germany and Japan) that had already been going on for nearly a decade. It was the G-5 ministers that had been directed by the Versailles Summit to develop a process of multilateral surveillance of one another's policies and performance. It seemed only natural to build on that emerging process to implement a critically needed realignment of exchange rates.

Fortunately, the other governments involved were in accord and joined enthusiastically in setting out to burst the exchange market's speculative bubble. Although in retrospect it appears that the dollar may already have peaked by mid-1985, fears were widespread throughout the northern summer that a new rebound might be imminent. Thus, after meeting at the Plaza Hotel in New York in September, the G-5 ministers declared in a widely publicised communiqué that an 'orderly appreciation of the main non-dollar currencies is desirable', and pledging to 'stand ready to cooperate more closely to encourage this' outlined a series of explicit policy initiatives to be undertaken by each country. By the standards of diplomatic discourse, these commitments amounted to an unusually unambiguous signal of policy intention. The Plaza Agreement was also unusually successful, helping to consolidate and accelerate a shift of market sentiment that in less than two years wholly reversed the dollar's previous appreciation.

Initially the goal of the Agreement could be considered essentially regime-preserving – in Kenen's words (1988, p. 77), 'to defend the trade regime rather than alter the exchange-rate regime'. But soon the goal of policy optimisation came to be included too as US officials, flush with their achievements in exchange-rate management, pressed the other governments to strengthen their still-embryonic multilateral-surveillance procedures. In May 1986 the G-7 summit in Tokyo formally directed finance ministers to articulate a new framework for cooperation, including the use of so-called objective indicators of economic performance (for example, growth, interest and exchange rates, current-account balances and fiscal deficits) to review and evaluate the 'mutual compatibility' of national policies. Summit leaders also added Italy and Canada to the coordination process, effectively making the G-7 ministerial group rather than the G-5 the central forum for decision-making (although, in practice, outcomes not surprisingly tend to be determined largely by the views of the Big Three – the United States, Germany and Japan).

At the time, this new-found zeal for policy cooperation seemed quite remarkable. In retrospect it is clear that the turnabout largely resulted from a rather fortuitous coincidence of national preferences. No government in the Triad wanted to see a damaging resurgence of protectionism in the United States.

A depreciation of the dollar, achieved in part by a reduction of US interest rates, also promised to serve broad macroeconomic needs at a time of comparatively low inflation and weak growth, by providing room for greater monetary ease in both Europe and Japan to stimulate internal demand. In effect, no major conflict existed for the moment between the aims of domestic policy and the goal of realigning exchange rates – in the words of Yoshio Suzuki (1990, p. 566), a former executive director of the Bank of Japan, 'a rare case of a happy harmony between autonomy and coordination'. As Robert Keohane (1984, pp. 51–5) has reminded us, however, there is an enormous difference between harmony (understood as a situation in which actors' policies pursued in their own self-interest happen automatically to facilitate attainment of others' goals as well) and cooperation (understood as an active process of mutual accommodation). Declaring a collective commitment to policy cooperation seemed innocuous enough when no real compromises of national interests were required.

Unfortunately, such a happy harmony was bound to prove fleeting. By the end of 1986, it was already evident that the interests of the major players were beginning to diverge again as the dollar's depreciation carried beyond what many regarded as desirable. In September, the first formal meeting of the finance ministers of the full Group of Seven agreed that there was no need for 'further significant exchange rate adjustment', in effect declaring that the realignment had now gone far enough. Yet over the following months the dollar continued to weaken, exacerbating concerns in Europe and Japan about the harm being done to the competitiveness of their export industries. Tensions were further aggravated by calls from Washington for more expansionary policies in the major surplus countries, in particular Germany and Japan, despite fears in these countries of renewed inflationary pressures. The idea was to give further impetus to an improvement of America's current balance. For the Europeans and Japanese, however, the cause of the US trade deficit lay in America's low savings rate – due especially to the Reagan administration's massive fiscal deficits – rather than in the performance of others. Conflicts between domestic objectives and exchange-rate policies were clearly on the rise.

Round II: February 1987–October 1987

The response of the Triad countries was the Louvre Accord announced in February 1987 after another ministerial meeting, this time at the old headquarters of the French Treasury in Paris (Funabashi 1988, ch. 8; Destler & Henning 1989, ch. 4). Once again the goal was essentially regime-preserving (Dobson 1991, p. 61) – to demonstrate anew the Triad's collective commitment to the principle of policy cooperation as such. Indeed, for many observers the Accord represented a new high-water mark in the multilateral-surveillance process. Yet again, however, national divergences quickly re-emerged to undermine faith in the process, and ultimately to contribute to the 'Black Monday' stockmarket crash in October.

Although the Louvre Accord, unlike the Plaza Agreement, aimed to stabilise exchange rates rather than realign them, the two pacts were similar in outlining a series of explicit policy initiatives to be undertaken by each country. Asserting that currency values were now 'broadly consistent with underlying economic fundamentals', the G-7 governments 'agreed to cooperate closely to foster stability of exchange rates around current levels'. Central to this were the formal policy commitments of the Big Three – Germany and Japan on the one hand promising new fiscal stimulus; the United States on the other pledging again to cut its budget deficit. As at the Plaza, ministers were determined to send an unambiguous signal of policy intentions.

In terms of its exchange-rate objective, the Louvre Accord was reasonably successful. Despite some renewed dollar weakness in the months March to May and again in September, a fair degree of currency stability was in fact attained. Most of this achievement, however, could be attributed to massive exchange-market interventions rather than to internal fiscal or monetary adjustments. In terms of its domestic objectives, the Louvre Accord only managed to highlight policy tensions in the Triad. By the end of the northern summer, Washington was again calling on Germany and Japan for more expansionary measures including, in particular, lower interest rates to prevent a further depreciation of the dollar; and once again the Germans and Japanese were resisting for fear of rekindling inflationary pressures. In September, the president of the German central bank openly repudiated the US approach by insisting 'that prevention of inflation should be priority over the achievement of exchange rate stability'. In early October, Secretary Baker equally openly rebuked Germany's Finance Minister for his country's high interest rates. What had begun at the Louvre as a proud reaffirmation of common purpose ended little more than a half year later in public bickering and recrimination.

The denouement, of course, came with the stockmarket crash in the middle of October. The Louvre Accord contributed directly to the arrival of Black Monday by setting a goal of exchange-rate stabilisation without firmly ensuring the requisite mutual adjustments of domestic policies. German and Japanese resistance to lower interest rates, at a time of continuing pressure on the dollar, inevitably meant the prospect of higher rates in the United States; and this, in turn, widened the differential between bond and stock yields to the point where some adjustment of equity prices had to be expected. Overt policy conflict among the G-7 governments, by adding to the atmosphere of uncertainty in financial markets, only made matters worse. In the words of *The Economist* (24 October 1987), Secretary Baker's public criticism of German interest-rate policy 'put the market in the mood to crash'. Destler and Henning (1989, p. 63) call his remarks 'the greatest mistake that Baker made as Treasury Secretary... Open verbal warfare among the G-7 apparently undermined the markets' confidence... when the markets were already anxious... fearful... and shaken'. In the event, it did not take much more to trigger the steepest meltdown of global stock values since 1929.

Round III: October 1987–September 1990

Once more, the response of the G-7 was to demonstrate anew their collective commitment to policy cooperation – first by concerted intervention to support the dollar, which quickly came under accelerated selling pressure following the crash; and then, after some hesitation, by a new exchange of domestic policy commitments outlined in late December in yet another ministerial communiqué (the so-called 'Telephone Accord'). And once more policy divergences eventually emerged to strain faith in the process.

Currency intervention began almost immediately and remained substantial until the dollar, after hitting new lows, finally bottomed out in January 1988. The goal, as at the Plaza and the Louvre, was again clearly regime-preserving, as minds were concentrated by the spectre of a possible worldwide financial collapse. And when it became evident that more than just intervention alone would be needed to fully restore stability of exchange rates, additional domestic measures were announced in the Telephone Accord in December, reaffirming 'the basic objectives and economic policy directions agreed in the Louvre Accord'. As in the earlier agreements, policy pledges included more fiscal stimulus by Germany and Japan, and implementation of a new deficit-reduction plan in the United States. Endorsements of these mutual commitments have been ritually repeated at virtually every G-7 meeting since the Telephone Accord.

Six months later, currency intervention picked up again and continued until after November leading to the first strengthening of the dollar after nearly three years of decline. Whether this renewed activity was in any way directly related to the US presidential election in 1988 is unclear (although it does seem evident that a healthier dollar did nothing to hurt the prospects of candidate George Bush, then the incumbent Vice President). What is clear is that the stronger dollar gradually enabled the other G-7 nations to shift their concerns from the exchange market to the increasingly critical problem of resurgent inflation. Interest rates, which had been cut sharply in anticipation of possible liquidity problems following the stockmarket crash, were now starting to rise again in the Triad countries, particularly after the middle of the year. A stronger dollar meant that governments in Europe and Japan no longer felt so compelled to hold down asset yields to deflect purchases of their currencies. By the time of the first G-7 ministerial meeting of 1989 in February, it was clear that policy-makers now wished to concentrate more on domestic price stabilisation. As in 1985, for the moment at least no real compromises of national interests seemed required. Once again so long as the dollar remained buoyant, a happy harmony could exist between the aims of domestic policy and the demands of exchange-rate management. But as before such a fortuitous conjuncture of preferences was bound to prove fleeting. As time moved on, differences over interest-rate policy gradually intensified into more and more open conflict.

In April 1989, for example, tensions were provoked when Germany suddenly raised its interest rates without giving any warning to others in the Triad. 'There was some degree of surprise', admitted one US official (*New York Times*, 12 May 1989). And a month later feelings were further soured when the Germans then declined to join Japan and the United States in an additional coordinated adjustment of rates to help stem an escalating appreciation of the dollar. 'There appears to have been a breakdown in collaboration on interest rates', commented the *New York Times* (12 May 1989) drily. Said one private commentator: 'They have a common preoccupation with inflation, and they can dress that up as a common international concern and say they're fighting inflation together. But they're not. They're fighting it separately' (*New York Times*, 12 May 1989).

A year later at a ministerial meeting in Paris in April, even greater strains were generated when Germany and the United States rejected a Japanese request for a concerted rate cut to help bail out the yen, which was then under attack. Both the German and US governments were evidently too preoccupied with their own inflation problems at the time to worry about the Japanese, who in turn were so infuriated that they refused to send any representative to the next ministerial meeting in Washington in May. The collective commitment to multilateral-surveillance was visibly weakening. Indeed, by the northern summer of 1990, many observers were openly questioning the relevance of the whole process. Commented one analyst: 'Active macroeconomic policy coordination currently appears to be in abeyance' (Webb 1991, p. 334). It was certainly becoming difficult to take the G-7's ritual reaffirmations of principle very seriously.

Round IV: September 1990–present

And then came Saddam Hussein's invasion of Kuwait in August, triggering a sharp spike of oil prices and fears of a new global economic crisis. Once again, in the interest of regime-preservation, ministers sought to project an impression of determined and coordinated action; and once again policy divergences among the G-7 governments soon reasserted themselves.

The main challenge facing the G-7 was a renewed run on the dollar after two years of relative strength. The group's main response, as in the aftermath of the 1987 stockmarket crash, was to reaffirm the members' mutual commitment to exchange-rate stability. At their next meeting in September, ministers declared that 'exchange rates were now broadly in line with continued adjustment of external balances'. They also insisted that they would 'continue to cooperate closely on exchange markets in the context of the economic policy coordination process'. Over the following months, however, few actions were taken to back up their determined words. In the delicate phrasing of the International Monetary Fund (IMF), the statements of the G-7 'indicated a preference for exchange rate stability. On the other hand, the extent to which this preference affected policy actions may at times have seemed unclear; the decline in the dollar... encountered virtually no resistance from official operations in foreign exchange markets... and the objective of exchange rate stability may have appeared not to have had a major influence on monetary policy actions' (IMF 1991, pp. 91, 95). In short, credibility was quickly strained. By January, *The Economist* (26 January 1991) was openly questioning whether policy cooperation could still be considered *à la mode*.

During 1991, conflicts over interest rates dominated relations in the Triad. In February, German rates were raised, despite US objections and the continued weakness of the dollar. And then in April, after the dollar began to rebound, a new battle erupted when Germany and Japan rejected a proposal by Nicholas Brady, who had succeeded James Baker as Treasury Secretary in 1988, for a coordinated easing of monetary policies. In June, efforts to achieve a new consensus at the G-7 meeting in London ended inconclusively, with ministers in effect agreeing to do little more than disagree. By the time of their next meeting in October, members found it more convenient to talk about the disintegrating Soviet Union than haggle over interest rates, but they once again 'reaffirmed their continued support for economic policy coordination'. By the end of the year in December, the Deutsche Bundesbank felt free to tighten policy again without even consulting Germany's G-7 and EC partners, in a move that had the *New York Times* talking of 'economic warfare, 1991 style' (22 December 1991, Section 3, p. IF). What October's words now meant in terms of practical commitments was no longer very clear.

Summary

It is obvious that the G-7 governments do, indeed, find it difficult to sustain the collective commitment to cooperation. Recidivism does recur. This is not to suggest that the multilateral-surveillance process has been utterly without redeeming social value. On the contrary, one can reasonably argue that for all its episodic quality the effort has on balance been beneficial, both in terms of what has in fact been accomplished and in terms of what has been avoided (Dobson 1991, pp. 126–30). Anecdotal evidence seems to suggest that policy-makers have had their consciousness genuinely raised regarding the foreign externalities of their domestic actions; in any event, the regularity of the schedule of ministerial meetings now clearly compels officials to integrate the international dimension much more fully than ever before into their own national decision processes. At the same time potentially severe challenges to regime stability have been successfully averted, including in particular the rising wave of US protectionism in 1985 and the stockmarket crash of 1987.

Collective initiatives have been designed cautiously to avoid the pitfalls of model uncertainty and have not typically been chosen simply for their political convenience. Overall, gains do appear to have outweighed costs.

The gains might have been larger, however. One can also reasonably argue that the positive impact of the process might have been considerably greater than it was had there been less inconstancy of behaviour. That is perhaps the chief lesson to be learned from this brief recitation of recent monetary history. Governmental credibility has undoubtedly been strained by the cyclical ebb and flow of commitments since 1985. With each retreat to unilateralism market scepticism grows, requiring ever more dramatic *démarches* when, once again, joint initiatives seem warranted. *Net* benefits, as a result, tend to be diminished over time. Multilateral surveillance may have redeeming social value, but its stop–go pattern makes it more costly than it might otherwise be. In a real sense we all pay for the fickleness of policy fashion.

The influence of the Unholy Trinity

Why is international monetary cooperation so episodic? To answer that question it is necessary to go back to first principles. Blame cannot be fobbed off on 'karma', accidental exogenous 'shocks', or even that vague epithet 'politics'. Consideration of the underlying political economy of the issue suggests that the dilemma is, in fact, systematic – endogenous to the policy process – and not easily avoided in relations between sovereign national governments.

The central analytical issue, which has been well understood at least since the pioneering theoretical work of economist Robert Mundell (1968, chs 16–18), is the intrinsic incompatibility of three key desiderata of governments: exchange-rate stability, private-capital mobility, and monetary-policy autonomy. As I wrote in the introduction to this chapter my own label for this is the 'Unholy Trinity'. The problem of the Unholy Trinity, simply stated, is that in an environment of formally or informally pegged rates and effective integration of financial markets, any attempt to pursue independent monetary objectives is almost certain, sooner or later, to result in significant balance-of-payments disequilibrium, and hence provoke potentially destabilising flows of speculative capital. To preserve exchange-rate stability, governments will then be compelled to limit either the movement of capital (via restrictions or taxes) or their own policy autonomy (via some form of multilateral surveillance or joint decision-making). If they are unwilling or unable to sacrifice either one, then the objective of exchange-rate stability itself may eventually have to be compromised. Over time, except by chance, the three goals cannot be attained simultaneously.

In the real world, of course, governments might be quite willing to limit the movement of capital in such circumstances – if they could. Policy-makers may say they value the efficiency gains of free and integrated financial markets. If polled 'off the record' for their private preferences, however, most would probably admit to prizing exchange-rate stability and policy autonomy even more. The problem, from their point of view, is that capital mobility is notoriously difficult to control. Restrictions merely invite more and more sophisticated forms of evasion, as governments from Europe to South Asia to Latin America have learned to their regret. More than a quarter of a century ago, quite early in my professional career, I asserted an Iron Law of Economic Controls: once implemented, I contended, limits on capital mobility must be multiplied at a rate at least equal to that at which means are found to circumvent them (Cohen 1965). Although the labelling may have been pretentious, the thought is arguably even more valid today in an era when financial markets have become more ingeniously innovative than ever. As an alternative James Tobin (1982, ch. 20) has proposed a tax on financial transactions, to limit capital mobility by 'putting some sand in the wheels' of the markets. But this idea too poses problems for practical implementation, as Rudiger Dornbusch (1988, pp. 220–2) and others have pointed out. Not only would such a tax be costly to administer, to be effective it would also have to be applied jointly by financial centres everywhere – a very demanding condition. More realistically most governments, in the area of the Triad at least, have tended to resign themselves to the inevitable if not always welcome presence of a high degree of capital mobility.

In practice, therefore, this means that in most instances the Unholy Trinity reduces to a direct trade-off between exchange-rate stability and policy autonomy. Conceptually, choices can be visualised along a continuum representing varying degrees of monetary-policy cooperation. At one extreme lies the polar alternative of a common currency or its equivalent – full monetary integration – where individual governments sacrifice policy autonomy completely for the presumed benefits of a permanent stabilisation of exchange rates. Most importantly, these benefits include the possible improvement in the usefulness of money in each of its principal functions: as a medium of exchange (owing to a reduction of transaction costs as the number of required currency conversions is decreased), store of value (owing to a reduced element of exchange risk as the number of currencies is decreased), and unit of account (owing to an information saving as the number of required price quotations is decreased). Additional gains may also accrue from the possibility of economies of scale in monetary and exchange-rate management as well as a potential saving of international reserves due to an internalisation through credit of what would otherwise be external trade and payments (Mundell 1973; Robson 1980, ch. 6). Any saving of reserves through pooling in effect amounts to a form of seigniorage for each participating country.

At the other extreme lies the polar alternative of absolute monetary independence, where individual governments sacrifice any hope of long-term exchange-rate stability for the presumed benefits of policy autonomy. Most importantly, as Mundell demonstrated as early as 1961 (Mundell 1968, ch. 17), these benefits include the possible improvement in the effectiveness of monetary policy as an instrument to attain national macroeconomic objectives. Today, of course, it is understood that much depends on whether any trade-off can be assumed to exist between inflation and unemployment over a time horizon relevant to policy-makers – technically, whether there is any slope to the Phillips curve in the short-term (Robson 1980, ch. 6). In a strict monetarist model of the sort popular in the 1970s, incorporating the classical neutrality assumption ('purely monetary changes have no real effects'), such a trade-off was excluded by definition. The Phillips curve was said to be vertical at the so-called 'natural' (or 'non-inflation-accelerating') unemployment rate, determined exclusively by microeconomic phenomena on the supply side of the economy. More recently, however, most theorists have tended to take a more pragmatic approach, allowing that for valid institutional and psychological reasons Phillips-curve trade-offs may well persist for significant periods of time – certainly for periods long enough to make the preservation of monetary independence appear worthwhile to policy-makers. From this perspective, any movement along the continuum in the direction of a common currency will be perceived as a real cost by individual governments.

The key question is how this cost compares with the overall benefit of exchange-rate stabilisation. Here we begin to approach the nub of the issue at hand. My hypothesis is that for each participating country both cost and benefit vary systematically with the degree of policy cooperation, and that it is through the interaction of these costs and benefits that we get the episodic quality of the cooperation process we observe in practice.

Assume absolute monetary independence to start with. Most gains from exchange-rate stabilisation, I would argue, can be expected to accrue 'up front' and then decline at the margin for successively higher degrees of policy cooperation. That is because the greatest disadvantage of exchange-rate instability is the damage done to the usefulness of money in its various functions. Any move at all by governments to reduce uncertainty about currency values is bound to have a disproportionate impact on market expectations and, hence, transaction costs in foreign exchange; further steps in the same direction may add to the credibility of the collective commitment but will yield only smaller and smaller savings to participants. Most of the cost of stabilisation, on the other hand, can be expected to be 'back-loaded' in the perceptions of the relevant policy-makers. That is because governments have an understandable tendency to discount the disadvantages of foreign agreements until they find themselves really constrained in seeking to attain their domestic objectives – at which point disproportionate importance comes to be attached to the compromises of interests involved. Where initial moves towards coordinated decision-making may be treated as virtually costless, further steps in the same direction tend to be seen as increasingly threatening. Thus, the marginal cost of policy cooperation for each country tends to rise systematically even as the marginal benefit may be assumed to fall.

The relationship is illustrated in Figure 4.1. Points along the horizontal axis represent successively greater degrees of policy cooperation, from absolute monetary independence at the left to full currency union at the right. Points along

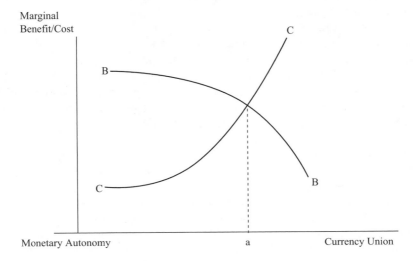

Figure 4.1 Benefits and costs of policy cooperation: static equilibrium.

the vertical axis represent successively higher levels of marginal cost or benefit (measured for convenience on the same scale). Curve BB measures the marginal benefit of exchange-rate stabilisation for a single country, assumed to decline as policy cooperation is increased. Curve CC measures the marginal cost for the country, assumed to rise as cooperation is increased. Static equilibrium is represented by point E, where the two curves intersect. If the country finds itself to the left of point E, it will have an incentive to commit itself to an intensified process of policy cooperation. If it finds itself to the right it will be tempted to retreat from its commitment, moving towards greater unilateralism in national behaviour instead. In political-economy terms point E may be understood as the degree of cooperation that maximises the utility of governments in the political marketplace, analogous to the level of production that maximises profit for competing firms in the economic marketplace.

Dynamics enter if we consider the stability of the positioning of the two curves. Curve CC may be considered to be stationary since it directly reflects governments' domestic policy preferences, which are determined exogenously. Curve BB, on the other hand, is more likely to shift about significantly since it largely reflects market expectations, which can be assumed to vary considerably over time. Anything that independently enhances confidence in the stability of exchange rates, and thus reduces the need for deliberate currency management, will shift curve BB to the left; anything that shakes market confidence, conversely will shift it to the right. Correspondingly, for each shift of BB along curve CC there will be a new static equilibrium, altering incentives for governments to agree to policy compromises. My argument is that it is precisely because of such shifts that we observe so marked a pattern of stop–go cycles in international monetary cooperation.

Consider, for example, the original impetus for the Plaza Agreement of 1985 – the rising tide of protectionist pressures in the United States. The threat to the trading system was plainly adding to nervousness in currency markets, in effect shifting curve BB to the right where a renewed commitment to policy coordination seemed attractive to all the governments concerned. In turn, market confidence was independently reinforced by the growth-promoting easing of monetary conditions that followed, reflecting the fortuitous 'happy harmony' of policy interests at the moment. BB as a result drifted back to the left again completing the cycle, and by reducing the felt need for currency management, helping to account for the increasingly acrimonious policy divergences that began reasserting themselves before the end of 1986. And these policy conflicts, in turn, triggered Round II by renewing market concerns and tensions, shifting BB once more to the right and setting the stage ultimately for the Louvre Accord in early 1987. Similar rightwards shifts of the BB curve caused by the stockmarket crash later in 1987 and the Gulf crisis in 1990, each followed by a period of drift to the left, would appear to explain the subsequent Rounds III and IV as well. In all four instances the collective commitment to cooperation was initially stimulated by an exogenous or policy-induced, confidence-shaking shock. And in each instance the commitment was eventually undermined, once confidence was restored, by a growing discrepancy between the perceived costs and benefits of that commitment.

These four cycles were clearly no accident. Quite the contrary, they must be regarded as an endogenous feature of the ongoing policy process. The typical pattern is stylised in Figure 4.2. Starting at an initial equilibrium E, the cycle

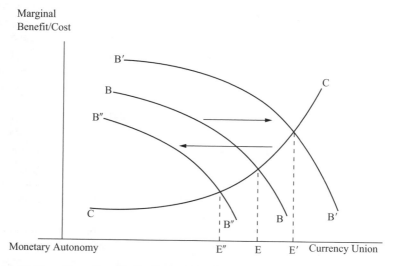

Figure 4.2 Benefits and costs of policy cooperation: dynamic equilibrium.

begins with some confidence-shaking shock that sends the BB curve to the right (B'B'), creating a new enthusiasm among governments for some form of policy cooperation (E'). It continues with a subsequent drift of curve BB back to the left again (B"B"), reflecting the confidence-building impact of the cooperation effort, and ends ultimately with a corresponding retreat by policy-makers from their collective commitment (E"). Point E", of course, may be either to the left or right of the original point E. The only exogenous element of the process is the shock that first triggers each cycle, which is by definition unpredictable. But this one random note in no way makes the overall pattern less systematic. In the real world, like it or not, shocks do have a nasty habit of repeatedly happening, even if we can know neither their nature nor their timing in advance. And once they do happen, they clearly seem to generate a distinct ebb and flow in the appetite for mutual accommodation. Recidivism not only recurs; it is explicable.

Can cooperation be 'locked in'?

The dilemma posed by the Unholy Trinity thus helps us to understand why international monetary cooperation is so episodic. The question remains: what, if anything, can be done about it?

One answer can be ruled out from the start: the proposition that the observed inconstancy of policy behaviour could be overcome if only governments could be educated to comprehend their own best interests. If my hypothesis is correct, governments are already acting in their own best interests and behaving in a manner consistent with a rational calculus of their own costs and benefits. The issue is not myopia: policy-makers surely are not unaware of the impacts of their behaviour on market expectations (as reflected in the cyclical movements of the BB curve), and would stick to their commitments if that seemed desirable. Rather, it is a question of how policy incentives change over time as a result of the shifting tide of events. Fundamentally, my reasoning may be understood as a variant of the logic of collective action first elucidated by Mancur Olson more than a quarter of a century ago (Olson 1965). A common interest is evident to all, yet individually rational behaviour can, at least part of the time, lead to distinctly sub-optimal outcomes. This is true whether the common interest is understood in terms of policy optimisation or regime preservation.

Moreover, my hypothesis has the advantage of being consistent with a wide range of alternative paradigms that have been employed in the standard international political-economy literature. It is certainly compatible with traditional realist or structuralist approaches in which the sovereign state, for reasons of analytical parsimony, is automatically assumed to behave like a rational unitary actor with its own set of well-defined national interests. It is also consistent with more pluralist models of policy-making, in which conceptions of interest are distilled from the interplay of differing combinations of domestic political and institutional forces; and even with models drawn from public-choice theory, in which policy behaviour is assumed to reflect first and foremost the personal interests of policy-makers (the principal-agent problem). For the purposes of my hypothesis, it really does not matter where the policy preferences of governments come from. It only matters that they act systematically on them.

Assuming education is not the answer, the crux of the issue becomes whether any collective commitment to cooperation once made can be 'locked in' in some way. If the problem is that governments find it difficult to sustain their enthusiasm for the process, can a solution be found that will effectively prevent them from retreating?

One obvious possibility is the extreme of a common currency, where individual autonomy is – in principle – permanently surrendered by each participating country. In practice, of course, not even full currency unions have proved indissoluble, as we saw in the case of the East African shilling in the 1970s or as evidently we are about to see in the case of the (former) Soviet Union today. But cases like these usually stem from associations that were something less than voluntary to begin with. When undertaken by consenting sovereign states, full monetary unification generally tends to be irreversible – which is precisely the reason why it is seen so seldomly in the real world. During the *laissez-faire* nineteenth century, when monetary autonomy meant less to governments than it does now, two fairly prominent currency unions were successfully established among formally independent nations – the Latin Monetary Union dating from 1865, and the Scandinavian Monetary Union created in 1873 – each built on a single, standardised monetary unit (respectively the franc and the krone). Both groupings, however, were effectively terminated with the outbreak of World War I. In the twentieth century, the only comparable arrangement has been the Belgium–Luxembourg Economic Union, established in 1921. (Other contemporary currency unions, such as the CFA franc zone and the East Caribbean dollar area, had their origins in colonial relationships.) The recent difficulties experienced by the European Community (EC) in negotiating the details of a formal Economic and Monetary Union (EMU) illustrate just how tough it is to persuade governments even as closely allied as these to make the irrevocable commitment required by a common currency.

Short of the extreme of a common currency, an effective solution would require participating governments to voluntarily pre-commit to some form of external authority over their individual policy behaviour. The authority might be supplied by an international agency armed with collectively agreed decision-making powers – corresponding to what I have elsewhere (Cohen 1977) called the organising principle of supranationality. It might also be supplied by one single dominant country with acknowledged leadership responsibilities (the principle of hegemony), Or it might be supplied by a self-disciplining regime of norms and rules accepted as binding on all participants (the principle of automaticity). Unfortunately, neither experience nor the underlying logic of political sovereignty offers a great deal of hope in the practical potential of any of these alternatives. Supranationality and automaticity, for example, have always tended to be heavily qualified in international monetary relations. In the G-7 multilateral-surveillance process, the International Monetary Fund (in the person of its managing director) has been given a role, but limited only to the provision of essential data and objective analytical support, and public articulation of any sort of binding rules (regarding, for example, exchange-rate targets) has been strenuously resisted by most governments (Dobson 1991). Hegemony, in the meantime, may be tolerated where it is unavoidable, as in the sterling area during the 1930s or the Bretton Woods system immediately after World War II. But as both these historical episodes illustrate, dominance also tends to breed considerable resentment and a determined eagerness by most countries to assert individual autonomy as soon as circumstances permit.

The principal exception in recent years has been the joint currency float (the 'snake') of the European Community, first implemented in the 1970s by a cluster of smaller countries effectively aligned with West Germany's Deutschmark, and later extended and formalised under the European Monetary System (EMS) starting in 1979. Under the rules of the EC's joint float, national monetary discretion for most members has been distinctly constrained, despite relatively frequent realignments of mutual exchange rates and, until the end of the 1980s, the persistence of significant capital controls in some countries. German policy, on the other hand, has not only remained largely autonomous but has effectively dominated monetary relations within the group. In effect, therefore, the snake has successfully locked in a collective commitment to cooperation through a combination of automaticity and hegemony. Yet not only has the arrangement proved tolerable to its members, over time it has gradually attracted new participants; and now, despite the difficulties of gaining irrevocable commitments to a common currency, may be about to be extended again in the form of EMU.

The reasons for this success quite obviously are unique and have to do most with the distinctive character of the institutional ties that have developed among EC members. Over time, as Robert Keohane and Stanley Hoffmann (1991) have recently noted, the EC has gradually built up a highly complex process of policy-making in which formal and informal arrangements are intricately linked across a wide range of issues. Decisions in one sector are closely affected by what is happening elsewhere and often lead to the sort of inter-sectoral 'spillover' effects that were first emphasised in early neo-functional theory (Tranholm-Mikkelsen 1991). (Note that these effects are quite different from those featured in the theoretical case for policy cooperation, which stresses spillovers in a single sector or issue-area.) More generally, member governments have come to fully accept a style of political behaviour in which individual interests are jointly realised through an incremental, albeit fragmented, pooling of national sovereignty – what Keohane and Hoffmann (1991, p. 13) call a 'network' form of organisation, 'in which individual units are defined not by themselves but in relation to other units'. And this, in turn, has been made possible only because of the existence of a real sense of commitment and attachment – of *community* – among all the countries involved. In this sense, the EC truly is the exception that proves the rule. Among states less intimately connected, resistance to any form of external authority over individual policy behaviour is bound to be correspondingly more stubborn and determined.

Does this mean then that nothing can be done about the episodic quality of monetary cooperation? Not at all. In principle, any number of technical innovations can be imagined to moderate underlying tendencies towards recidivism by cooperating governments. As in the G-7 process, for example, meetings could be put on a regular schedule and based on an agreed analytical framework to help ensure greater continuity of policy behaviour. Much the same impact might also be attained by giving more precision as well as greater publicity to policy guidelines and commitments. And there might also be some benefit to be had from establishing a permanent, independent secretariat to provide an institutional memory and ongoing objective analysis of priorities and issues. The issue, however, is not administrative creativity but political acceptability. Each such innovation makes it just that much more difficult for policy-makers to change their minds when circumstances might seem to warrant it. Is the underlying relationship among the states involved sufficiently close to make them willing to take such a risk? This is not a question that can be answered *a priori;* as the exceptional case of the EC demonstrates, it is certainly not a question of monetary relations alone. Ultimately prospects for sustaining any cooperative effort in this crucial area of public policy will depend on how much basic affinity governments feel in other areas as well – in effect, on the extent to which they feel they share a common destiny across the full spectrum of economic and political issues.

Lessons for the Pacific Region

What lessons can be drawn from this discussion for the question of managing monetary relations in the Pacific Region in the 1990s? The principal implication is that a serious and sustained commitment to monetary cooperation requires a real sense of *community* among the countries involved, meaning, in particular, a real willingness to pool elements of state sovereignty across a range of issues, as in the EC's 'network' form of organisation. Unfortunately, the conditions necessary to establish such a style of political behaviour are not easy to satisfy and without major effort appear unlikely to be attained in the Pacific region any time soon. The irony, as indicated at the outset, is that even without such a commitment most regional governments will find their policy autonomy increasingly eroded in the coming decade – and in a manner that may seem even less appealing to them than formal cooperation.

We know that there is not much of a tradition of shared destiny in the Pacific Region. Indeed, it is not even clear how the region is to be defined. Is it to include all countries in or bordering on the Pacific – an enormously diverse group which, apart from geography, has almost nothing in common either economically or politically? Or are we talking about some less differentiated subgroup, including only a limited selection of states and excluding others? Are the United States and Canada part of the region? Latin America? China? (Which China?) The Russian Federation? The problems of defining the Pacific Region are well known and have long plagued efforts to promote economic cooperation in the area (Higgott et al. 1990; Harris 1991). Proposals in the past have ranged from a Pacific Free Trade Area (PAFTA) limited to just the five relatively developed economies of Japan, the United States, Canada, Australia, and New Zealand (Kojima 1971) to an idea for a far more comprehensive Organization for Pacific Trade, Aid and Development (OPTAD) modelled on the OECD (Drysdale & Patrick 1979). None of these schemes has ever come to fruition.

The challenge in fact is daunting. How can cooperation be promoted on any scale among countries more noted for their sustained antagonisms, ethnic and cultural conflicts, and border disputes? Many, having only recently emerged from colonial status, are understandably resistant to any surrender of their newly won political sovereignty. Most are more intent on individual nation-building than on regional interdependence. Few have yet demonstrated much inclination (borrowing from the language of Keohane and Hoffmann) to define themselves in relation to one another rather than in their own terms. Most still behave as if state interests can best be pursued unilaterally.

At present, the only institutionalised version of economic cooperation in the region is the so-called Asia Pacific Economic Co-operation (APEC) group, first proposed by Australian Prime Minister Bob Hawke in 1989. Participants include the six nations of the Association of Southeast Asian Nations, otherwise known as ASEAN (Brunei, Indonesia, Malaysia, the Philippines, Singapore, and Thailand), plus Australia, Canada, Japan, Korea, New Zealand and the United States. To date APEC has met three times: in Canberra in November 1989, Singapore in July 1990, and Seoul in November 1991. So far, however, little has been accomplished in terms of practical policy collaboration. If any serious affinity is beginning to develop among these states on commercial or financial issues, it has yet to be convincingly demonstrated.

Nor, focusing just on the issue of monetary relations alone, does there appear to be much *practical* basis for enhanced cooperation in the region. Financial links of Pacific countries have always tended to centre bilaterally on the United States, with the dollar still serving as the main currency of choice for both trade and investment purposes; direct connections among national capital markets in East Asia and Oceania remain rudimentary at best. Likewise, nearly all Pacific governments including Japan continue to use the dollar as their principal vehicle for exchange-market intervention; apart from the yen, no significant amounts of local currency are retained in reserves to help promote multilateral management of exchange rates. And, of course, any effort at coordination of domestic credit or fiscal policies would be severely hampered by the vast differences of economic, political, and institutional development that are evident in the region. These are all potent barriers to effective monetary collaboration.

This is not to suggest that such barriers cannot be overcome. With the appropriate will, initiatives could be designed to broaden financial links and permit more cross-trading of regional currencies. In lieu of existing exchange controls, for instance, a system of joint restrictions could be instituted on the model of the old sterling area to promote freedom of capital movement among Pacific countries. Likewise, in lieu of continued reliance on the dollar for intervention purposes, a network of reciprocal credit lines on the model of the European Monetary System's short-term lending facilities could be agreed to help efforts to stabilise mutual exchange rates. And in lieu of today's decentralised decision-making, a regularised procedure on the model of the G-7's ministerial meetings (preferably improved to include more publicity and a permanent secretariat) could be organised to ensure greater consistency of national macro-economic policies. But does the will exist? As in the G-7, political acceptability remains the ticklish issue. To date, governments in the Pacific Region have seemed more impressed by the benefits of formal monetary sovereignty than by potential costs. Although in other issue areas regional policy-makers may be showing increasing awareness of the limits of unilateralism, none have yet shown any appetite for the major effort that would be required to reverse existing attitudes on monetary matters.

Unfortunately, such attitudes are short-sighted. Regional governments behave as if the choice in the monetary area is between autonomy and cooperation – and they still prefer autonomy. In fact, that behaviour overlooks two essential considerations, one analytical and one empirical. Analytically it overlooks the crucial message of the Unholy Trinity. If the recent experience of the Triad teaches us anything, it is that monetary independence in a world of growing capital mobility is increasingly illusory or else can be purchased only at the cost of greater and greater exchange-rate instability. Empirically it overlooks the spreading financial influence of Japan in the Pacific Region. More and more, the economies of East Asia and Oceania are finding themselves drawn into Japan's gravitational orbit by ties of trade, aid, and investment; and this in turn, as a recent award-winning study by Jeffrey Frankel (1991) clearly demonstrates, is making them increasingly sensitive to Japanese monetary conditions and policies. While as recently as 1988 local interest rates were still affected most by yields on dollar assets, Frankel shows that by 1991 yen rates had come to dominate in many local capital markets. Regional use of Japan's currency, albeit still second to the dollar, is also growing, and Tokyo is rapidly becoming the area's acknowledged financial centre. Over the course of the 1980s, the proportion of central-bank reserves held in yen rose from 13.9 per cent to 17.5 per cent, while the fraction of external debt denominated in yen nearly doubled to about 40 per cent. *De facto*, if not *de jure*, a kind of 'yen bloc' quite clearly is gradually coalescing in the region, in a manner not unlike the clustering of some of Europe's smaller currencies around the Deutschmark in the 1970s.

Together these considerations suggest that the choice for regional governments is not between autonomy and cooperation as such but rather between *different forms* of monetary cooperation or integration. In the 1990s countries can actively promote formal and mutually acceptable procedures for collective decision-making, perhaps building on the model of the G-7 multilateral-surveillance process. Or else they can procrastinate, which, in effect, would mean passively accepting the gradual emergence of a yen bloc instead. One way or another, they are bound to find their individual policy behaviour increasingly constrained. The question is where that external authority will come from – as a result of voluntary mutual accommodation (possibly incorporating elements of automaticity or supra-nationality) or from the unilateral decisions of an increasingly hegemonic Japan. Many in the region still remember Japan's role in World War II and remain suspicious of Japanese values and motivations; if history is any guide, many more would undoubtedly be resentful of a growing Japanese dominance in monetary affairs. It would be ironic, indeed, if they nonetheless soon find themselves part of a new version of a Greater East Asia Co-Prosperity Sphere by virtue of nothing more than their own indecisiveness and inaction.

References

Artis, M. and Ostry, S. 1986, *International Economic Policy Coordination*, Chatham House Papers No. 30, Royal Institute of International Affairs, London

Brittan, S. 1991, 'Defects in the Policy Model', *Partners in Prosperity*, Report of the Twentieth Century Fund Task Force on the International Coordination of National Economic Policies, Priority Press, New York

Canzoneri, M. and Gray, J. 1985, 'Monetary Policy Games and the Consequences of Non-Cooperative Behavior', *International Economic Review*, vol. 26, no. 3, pp. 547–64

Cohen, B.J. 1965, 'Capital Controls and the US Balance of Payments: Comment', *American Economic Review*, vol. 55, no.1, pp. 172–6

—— 1977, *Organizing the World's Money: The Political Economy of International Monetary Relations*, Basic Books, New York

Cooper, R.N. 1985, 'Economic Interdependence and Coordination of Economic Policies', *Handbook of International Economics*, eds R.W. Jones & P.B. Kenen, North-Holland, Amsterdam and New York

Currie, D.A., Holtham, G. and Hughes Hallett, A. 1989, 'The Theory and Practice of International Policy Coordination: Does Coordination Pay?', *Macroeconomic Policies in an Interdependent World*, eds R.C. Bryant, et al., International Monetary Fund, Washington, DC

Destler, I.M. and Henning, C.R. 1989, *Dollar Politics: Exchange Rate Policymaking in the United States*, Institute for International Economics, Washington, DC

Dobson, W. 1991, *Economic Policy Coordination: Requiem or Prologue?*, Policy Analyses in International Economics No. 30, Institute for International Economics, Washington, DC

Dornbusch, R. 1988, 'The Adjustment Mechanism: Theory and Problems', *International Payments Imbalances in the 1980s*, ed. N.S. Fieleke, Federal Reserve Bank of Boston, Boston

Drysdale P. and Patrick, H. 1979, *An Asian-Pacific Regional Economic Organization: An Exploratory Concept Paper*, Washington Library of Congress, Congressional Research Service, Washington, DC

Feldstein, M. 1988, International Economic Coorperation: Introduction', *International Economic Coorperation*, ed. M. Feldstein, University of Chicago Press, Chicago

Frankel, J.A. 1988, 'International Norminal Trageting: A Proposal for Policy Coordination', *International Payments Imbalances in the 1980s*, ed. N.S. Fieleke, Federal Reserve Bank of Boston, Boston

Frankel, J.A. 1991, 'Is a Yen Bloc Forming in Pacific Asia?', *AmEx Bank Review*, November

Frankel, J.A. and Rockett, K.E. 1988, 'International Macroeconomic Policy Coordination When Policymakers Do Not Agree on the True Model', *American Economic Review*, vol. 78, no. 3, pp. 318–40

Funabashi, Y. 1988, *Managing the Dollar: From the Plaza to the Louvre,* Institute for International Economics, Washington, DC

Ghosh, A.R. and Masson, P.R. 1988, 'International Policy Coordination in a World with Model Uncertainty', *IMF Staff Papers*, vol. 35, no. 2, pp. 230–58

Harris, S. 1991, Varieties of Pacific Economic Cooperation', *The Pacific Review*, vol. 4, no. 4, pp. 301–11

Higgott, R., Cooper, A.F. and Bonnor, J. 1990, 'Asia–Pacific Economic Cooperation: An Evolving Case-Study in Leadership and Co-operation Building', *International Journal*, vol. 45, no. 4, pp. 823–66

Holtham, G. and Hughes Hallett, A. 1987, 'International Policy Cooperation and Model Uncertainty', *Global Macroeconomics: Policy Conflict and Cooperation*, eds R. Bryant & R. Portes, Macmillan, London

International Monetary Fund 1991, *World Economic Outlook, May 1991*, International Monetary Fund, Washington, DC

Kenen, P.B. 1988, *Managing Exchange Rates*, Council on Foreign Relations, New York

—— 1989, *Exchange Rates and Policy Coordination*, University of Michigan Press, Ann Arbor

—— 1991, 'Comment', *Partners in Prosperity*, Report of the Twentieth Century Fund Task Force on the International Coordination of National Economic Policies, Priority Press, New York

Keohane, R. *After Hegemony: Cooperation and Discord in the World Political Economy*, Princeton University Press, Princeton, NJ

Keohane, R.O. and Hoffmann, S. 1991, 'Institutional Change in Europe in the 1980s', *The New European Community: Decisionmaking and Institutional Changes*, eds R.O Keohane & S. Hoffmann, Westview Press, Boulder, CO

Kojima, K. 1971, *Japan and Pacific Free Trade Area*, Macmillan, London

Mundell, R.A. 1968, *International Economics*, Macmillan, New York

—— 1973, 'Uncommon Arguments for Common Currencies', *The Economics of Common Currencies*, eds H.G. Johnson & A.K. Swoboda, George Allen and Unwin, London

Olson, M. 1965, *The Logic of Collective Action*, Harvard University Press, Cambridge, MA

Oudiz, G. and Sachs, J. 1984, 'Macroeconomic Policy Coordination Among the Industrial Economies', *Brookings Papers on Economic Activity*, vol. 1, pp. 1–75

Robson, P. 1980, *The Economics of International Integration*, George Allen and Unwin, London

Rogoff, K. 1985, 'Can International Monetary Policy Coordination Be Counter-productive?', *Journal of International Economics*, vol. 18, no. 3/4, pp. 199–217

Solomon, R. 1991, 'Background Paper' , *Partners in Prosperity*, Report of the Twentieth Century Fund Task Force on the International Coordination of National Economic Policies, Priority Press, New York

Suzuki, Y. 1990, 'Autonomy and Coordination of Monetary Policy in a Global Economic Order', *Cato Journal*, vol. 10, no. 2, pp. 565–71

Tobin, J. 1982, *Essays in Economics: Theory and Policy*, The MIT Press. Cambridge, MA

Tranholm-Mikkelsen, J. 1991, 'Neo-Functionalism: Obstinate or Obsolete? A Reappraisal in the Light of the New Dynamism of the EC', *Millennium: Journal of International Studies*, vol. 20, no. 1, pp. 1–22

Webb, M.C. 1991, 'International Economic Structures, Government Interests, and International Coordination of Macroeconomic Adjustment Policies', *International Organization*, vol. 45, no. 3, pp. 309–42

Williamson. J. and Miller, M.H. 1987, *Targets and Indicators: A Blueprint for the International Coordination of Economic Policy*, Policy Analyses in International Economics No. 22, Institute for International Economics, Washington, DC

5 Phoenix risen*

The resurrection of global finance

Source: *World Politics* 48, 2, January 1996.

John B. Goodman. *Monetary Sovereignty: The Politics of Central Banking in Western Europe.* Ithaca, N.Y.: Cornell University Press, 1992, 238 pp.

Eric Helleiner. *States and the Reemergence of Global Finance: From Bretton Woods to the 1990s.* Ithaca, N.Y.: Cornell University Press, 1994, 244 pp.

Ethan B. Kapstein. *Governing the Global Economy: International Finance and the State.* Cambridge: Harvard University Press, 1994, 224 pp.

Paulette Kurzer. *Business and Banking: Political Change and Economic Integration in Western Europe.* Ithaca, N.Y.: Cornell University Press, 1993, 261 pp.

Andrew C. Sobel. *Domestic Choices, International Markets: Dismantling National Barriers and Liberalizing Securities Markets.* Ann Arbor: University of Michigan Press, 1994, 211 pp.

Of all the many changes of the world economy in recent decades, few have been nearly so dramatic as the resurrection of global finance. A half century ago, after the ravages of the Great Depression and World War II, financial markets everywhere – with the notable exception of the United States – were generally weak, insular, and strictly controlled, reduced from their previously central role in international economic relations to offer little more than a negligible amount of trade financing. Starting in the late 1950s, however, private lending and investment once again began to gather momentum, generating a phenomenal growth of cross-border capital flows and an increasingly close integration of domestic financial markets. Like a phoenix risen from the ashes, global finance took flight and soared to new heights of power and influence in the affairs of nations.

How can we explain the remarkable globalization of financial markets of recent years, and what are its economic and political implications? Such questions have lately spawned a veritable cottage industry of popular commentary, some of it frankly sensationalist if not down-right alarmist in tone.[1] Even otherwise level-headed scholars have at times allowed themselves to be carried away by gnawing fears of instability and chaos.[2] A new generation of political economists, however, is beginning to focus its attention on the phenomenon, casting the cool eye of objective analysis on both the causes and consequences of financial globalization. A survey of this emerging literature, including the five books under review here,[3] suggests just how much can be learned about such a topical issue from more serious and substantive scholarship.

* I am indebted to David Andrews, Joe Grieco, Miles Kahler, Helen Milner, and Louis Pauly for helpful comments and suggestions. The able assistance of Kathleen Collihan is also gratefully acknowledged.

The aim of this article is both to summarize present understanding of the political economy of global finance and to identify key elements of an agenda for future research. For our purposes, global finance is assumed to encompass all types of cross-border portfolio-type transactions – borrowing and lending, trading of currencies or other financial claims, and the provision of commerical banking or other financial services. It also includes capital flows associated with foreign direct investment – transactions involving significant control of producing enterprises. Financial globalization (or internationalization) refers to the broad integration of national markets associated with both innovation and deregulation in the postwar era and is manifested by increasing movements of capital across national frontiers. The more alternative assets are closely regarded as substitutes for one another, the higher the degree of capital mobility.

The scope of financial globalization should not be exaggerated. As much as capital flows have grown, it is still premature to speak of a single, world financial market. In the words of Jeffry Frieden, "International investment is by no means yet a seamless web."[4] Careful econometric studies demonstrate that even for the most liquid of monetary assets, capital mobility remains imperfect because of inherent country and currency risks.[5] Market segmentation persists, both within states (among different sectors) and between them. Debt instruments are less transferable than cash, long-term claims are less substitutable than short-term, and equity markets are less integrated still. The scope of globalization, however, also should not be underestimated. Though frictions between markets remain, they are far fewer and weaker today than they used to be; both domestically and internationally, functional and institutional linkages have greatly increased. The trend in finance has been toward ever higher levels of global interdependence.

This survey will begin with a brief synopsis of the five books under review, highlighting the core concerns and conclusions of each. Though individually quite diverse, the five as a group constitute a reasonably representative sample of work currently under way in this specialized subfield of international political economy. The following sections will then take up three of the most critical questions posed by the globalization of financial markets: How did it happen? What does it mean for economic performance or policy? What can governments do about it? Answers vary considerably, suggesting much room for further research, particularly on implications for the central political-economy dialectic between politics and markets. At a minimum, financial globalization has put governments distinctly on the defensive, eroding much of the authority of the contemporary sovereign state. At a maximum, it may have irreversibly altered the meaning of geography in the world economy today. The phoenix has risen. Does it also rule the roost?

The globalization of finance

Recent scholarship, as indicated, has addressed both the causes and the consequences of financial globalization. The question of causes is taken up by Eric Helleiner and Andrew Sobel in two admirably detailed historical studies. Both agree on the key role played by states, particularly the major industrial powers, in deregulating domestic markets and liberalizing external controls. They disagree sharply, however, on how to explain the policies they observe.

For Helleiner, the story lies in a combination of structural and ideational factors. At the systemic level, "competitive deregulation" by governments maneuvering unilaterally to attract the business of mobile financial traders was reinforced as early as the 1960s by policy initiatives from the two leading financial powers of the day, the United States and Britain, both with a strong interest in promoting a more open international order. At the cognitive level, an ideological shift from postwar Keynesianism to a neoclassical or neoliberal policy framework gained strength from the preexistence of a sophisticated epistemic community of central bankers based around the Bank for International Settlements (BIS). The bulk of Helleiner's discussion is an account of the role played by each of these factors in the resurrection of global finance over the postwar period.

For Sobel, by contrast, the process is best explained by purely domestic considerations – competition between organized interests within national political economies that has spilled over to affect the international environment. Focusing specifically on recent developments in the securities markets of Britain, Japan, and the United States, Sobel rejects structural or ideational interpretations of globalization, which he labels "outside-in" explanations. "In these explanations, the primary stimulus motivating change arises outside the domestic political economy, but compels changes that impact the domestic political economy" (p. 15). Sobel prefers instead an alternative "inside-out" explanation, which he defends with extensive evidence of persistent national distinctions and "home bias" in bond and equity markets. "Paradoxical inconsistencies in behavior across the three markets pose dilemmas for outside-in explanations" (p. 15).[6] Incomplete convergence, he argues, suggests that "the international outcome is solidly rooted in domestic policy dilemmas and distributional debates" (p. 19).[7]

Consequences rather than causes are the principal concerns of the remaining three authors, again with strikingly divergent results. All three concur that financial globalization has indeed put government on the defensive, but they part company on what policymakers can do about it.

A fairly pessimistic view is represented by Paulette Kurzer, who sees rather little scope for effective state responses to global finance. Kurzer's densely textured comparative study examines the fate in the 1980s of tripartite distributive arrangements between business, labor, and government in four small European democracies: Austria, Belgium, the Netherlands, and Sweden. In all four countries, traditional policies of "social concertation" have recently been abandoned. The timing of these changes varied across the countries, which may be explained by differences in such factors as business preferences, administrative rulings, and the historical stance of foreign economic policies. But the overall outcome ultimately was the same in each and may be attributed, Kurzer insists, to a single cause – financial globalization: "As business and finance became more mobile, their power resources increased, and those of labor decreased.... [T]he greater mobility of capital and deepening financial integration corroded social concertation" (p. viii). As a result, Kurzer concludes grimly, "governments have lost the ability to carve out national economic strategies and to sustain social accords" (p. viii).

An alternative, rather more sanguine view is proposed by Ethan Kapstein in an informed and insightful survey of regulatory responses to the internationalization of commercial banking over the postwar period. Focusing in particular on prudential and supervisory agreements that have been negotiated by major central banks through the BIS, Kapstein identifies a formula, "international cooperation based on home country control," which, in his view, has enabled governments to mount an effective response to the challenges of financial globalization. Though imperfections remain, he argues, a workable framework for governing global financial markets has been created and may even suggest a "generic policy solution" to the conflicting demands of systemic and societal forces in other issue-areas as well: "International cooperation based on home country control provides a way for states to enjoy the benefits of interdependence while maintaining national responsibility for the sector in question" (p. 180).

Finally, a third view is offered by John Goodman in a highly instructive comparative analysis of central banking practices in three big West European economies: France, Germany, and Italy. Goodman's primary concern is with the role played by institutional differences, particularly differences in the degree of central-bank independence that "govern the extent to which domestic political pressures influence national monetary policy" (p. 221). His discussion, however, is distinguished from most institutional studies in its assumption not of a closed economy but rather a context of deepening financial interdependence. The globalization of finance, he argues, drives states voluntarily to limit their own monetary autonomy by means of cooperation – in Europe, his specific area of focus, up to and including the possible creation of a full monetary union. Authority may be lost at the national level but might be regained through a convergence of policies at a higher level. In effect, therefore, Goodman strikes a middle ground between Kurzer's pessimism and Kapstein's optimism. Governments have not necessarily lost the ability to carve out effective economic strategies, but cooperation based on home country control is unlikely to prove sufficient. If they are to be successful, states must do the job collectively.

How did it happen?

As the contrasting views of Helleiner and Sobel suggest, little consensus exists concerning the causes of financial globalization. Not that this is particularly surprising. Historical interpretation is never easy, even in a field as well documented as international finance. The discord, however, is significant insofar as the past may be assumed to have some impact on the course of events in the future. One does not have to hold a particularly rigid view of path dependency to recognize the extent to which tomorrow's choices may be delimited by yesterday's actions. An understanding of antecedents does matter.

Competing hypotheses may be categorized in any number of ways. Helleiner contrasts two classes of causal interpretation – those explanations that see globalization as a direct product of "unstoppable technological and market forces [that] discount the role played by states" (p. 1); and those, like his own, that stress instead the central role of government policies. Sobel, on the other hand, distinguishes three types of interpretation. Two are his so-called outside-in explanations, one positing change "as a response to systemic conditions that affect all states" (p. 14), including technological developments and ideological shifts; the second viewing liberalization and internationalization as "a foreign policy outcome" (p. 15) reflecting the direct exercise of state influence. The third is his preferred inside-out interpretation. Yet another classification is proposed by Philip Cerny, a frequent contributor to the globalization literature, who also distinguishes three types of explanation: (1) market-based explanations; (2) institutional-technological explanations; and (3) political explanations, which in turn are subdivided into interpretations that, like Sobel's, stress internal political processes, or, like Helleiner's, stress the autonomous state.[8] The organization of inquiry seems to be treated very much as a matter of personal taste.

If historical interpetation is to be of much value to social scientists, however, it should, ideally, be framed to facilitate the closest possible comparison with prevailing theoretical perspectives and approaches – in effect, to offer a form of empirical test of alternative analytical models. In the IPE field today three broad paradigms dominate most discussion, the familiar three levels of analysis: the systemic (or structural) level of analysis, the domestic (or unit) level, and the cognitive.[9] Specific theories tend to represent a variation on one or more of these general themes. It would seem preferable, therefore, as a general principle, to organize inquiry into the sources of financial globalization along the same lines.

This suggests a taxonomy of four main hypotheses for investigation. At the systemic level, two variants can be identified, replicating Helleiner's distinction between the contrasting roles of market forces and government policies. One variant, with roots in standard neoclassical economics, stresses the powerful impacts of competition and innovation in the financial marketplace. It also emphasizes advances in communications and information technologies, which have literally swept away institutional and legal barriers to market integration and the free flow of capital. This variant might be labeled the "liberal model." The second, more consistent with an older tradition in international relations theory, emphasizes the determining role of policy rivalry among governments in an insecure world, each calculating how best to use its influence and capabilities to promote state interest. Call this the "realist model." A third approach, pitched at the unit level of analysis characteristic of most comparative political economy, corresponds to Sobel's inside-out explanation, highlighting the role of domestic politics and institutions in driving international developments. This may be labeled the "pluralist model." A fourth approach, embodying Helleiner's ideational factors, underscores the role of belief systems and epistemic communities as catalysts for change. Call this the "cognitive model."

The question is: What does the historical evidence suggest about the relative utility of each of these four models? Which comes closest to actually explaining the resurrection of global finance? And what are the linkages among them?

Each model has its champions. The liberal model, not surprisingly, is the personal favorite of most economists. Typical is Ralph Bryant, a well-known international monetary specialist, who confidently asserts that "technological nonpolicy factors were so powerful...that they would have caused a progressive internationalization of financial activity even without changes in government separation fences."[10] On the political science side, the case has been put equally firmly by David Andrews, who emphasizes both the degree to which capital mobility appears to have increased independently of changes in national regulatory frameworks and the degree to which liberalization at the national level has seemingly occurred in response to market pressures at the systemic level.[11] Appearances, however, can be deceiving. An approach that causally links an outcome (globalization) to its own defining characteristics (competition and innovation) borders on the tautological. It also leaves no room for politics in an arena, the interstate system, that is inherently politicized.

A possible antidote is offered by the realist model, which is nothing if not political. Reversing the arrow of causation, the approach is best represented by Helleiner. "The contemporary open global financial order," he argues, "could never have emerged without the support and blessing of states" (p. vii). Capital mobility may have been facilitated by innovations in financial instruments and advances in communications and information technologies. Without explicit policy decisions by governments, however, national markets would have remained as insulated from one another as ever. Political authorities promoted the resurrection of global finance by granting more freedom to market operators, refraining from imposing more effective controls on capital movements, and acting to prevent or manage international financial crises.

Three issues, however, are raised by the realist model. First, if states were so pivotal in the globalization process, could they also turn back the clock if they wish? Reversibility would appear to be a logical corollary of the realist model. Certainly this is the conclusion drawn by Helleiner, who in more recent commentary has argued quite forcefully that since "financial globalization [was] heavily dependent on state support and encouragement...a reversal of the liberalization trend is more likely than is often assumed."[12] Others, however, attack the implication, insisting instead on a kind of hysteresis in financial market development. Globalization has progressed so far, it is said, that capital mobility must now be regarded as tantamount to an exogenous feature of the international system. In the words of David Andrews, "The constraints imposed on states by capital mobility are structural in nature, or at a minimum can usefully be construed as structural by analysts."[13]

In fact, both sides of this debate seem too categorical. Central to the issue is an implicit calculation of the costs, economic or political, that would be associated with any attempt to restrict capital mobility. Reversibility would not appear to be ruled out in principle. In practice, however, limits seem likely only insofar as governments are prepared to pay the requisite price. As Louis Pauly has contended,

> Capital mobility constrains states, but not in an absolute sense.... Analysts should therefore be cautious when interpreting the current dimensions of

international capital flows as constituting an exogenous structure that irrevocably binds societies or their states.... A collective movement away from capital decontrol may be undesirable, but it remains entirely possible.[14]

We will return to this crucial point below.

A second issue has to do with matters of power and hegemony in the globalization process. Helleiner and Sobel alike stress the role that American and British leadership played in opening up financial markets. To borrow from the language of Scott James and David Lake,[15] however, we may ask which "face" of hegemony was at work here: the first face of direct government-to-government influence, exercised through positive and negative sanctions; the second face of market power, altering incentive structures; or the third face of ideas and ideology, shaping the climate of opinion. Except in the special case of Japan, neither Helleiner nor Sobel suggests much evidence of overt inducements or threats by Washington or London to compel liberalization by other governments.[16] Indeed, as indicated, Sobel explicitly rejects any explanation positing direct exercise of state influence. They differ sharply, however, about which of the other two faces mattered more in this context.

For Helleiner, it was the second face – initially, the pressures created by U.S. and U.K. policy decisions facilitating creation of a foreign-currency deposit market, the Euromarket, in London. "When these two states supported growth of the Euromarket...foreign financial centers...were forced to follow the lead of Britain and the United States by liberalizing and deregulating their own financial systems" (p. 12). For Sobel, by contrast, it was the third face, exhibited in particular by the United States – the privileging of American-style rules, institutions, and trading technologies in foreign securities markets:

> Through innovation and invention of financial and regulatory technologies, U.S. actors established the agenda and boundaries of changes in other markets.... This embedded influence produces an outcome generally consistent with U.S. actors' preferences, as others choose options already enacted in the U.S. market, reducing transaction costs for American firms and professionals overseas, and at far less cost than direct pressure. (pp. 151–52)

In fact, there is nothing inherently contradictory about these two views; they are complementary rather than mutually exclusive. They do suggest, however, different inferences about the comparative importance of government policies versus market forces, and thus ultimately about the explanatory power of the realist versus the liberal model. More detailed empirical studies to help disentangle the two forms of influence would clearly be useful.

A third issue, finally, has to do with the motivations for state behavior suggested by the realist model. Were states operating as classic rational unitary actors, single-mindedly competing within systemic constraints to maximize some objective measure of national interest? Or were other, more subtle forces at work to shape government preferences and perceptions? This, of course, is the issue posed by the pluralist and cognitive models, both of which effectively open up the black box of public policy.

Sobel's inside-out explanation offers a prime example of a pluralist model. His view that "internationalization [was] motivated domestically" (p. 155) is echoed by such scholars as Ron Martin, who asserts that globalization was in fact "politically engineered ... a reassertion by the state of an underlying disposition towards financial interests."[17] Similarly, Helleiner's references to ideological shifts and epistemic communities exemplify well the main elements of the cognitive model, also echoed by others. The former element, the role of ideas, is highlighted as well by Cerny, who stresses "an ideological backlash against state economic interventionism" as a key part of the dynamic driving market deregulation.[18] The latter element is highlighted as well by Stephen Gill and David Law, who in quasi-Marxist language stress

> international patterns of elite interaction ... [which] are explicitly concerned to foster ... a shared outlook among the international establishments of the major capitalist countries ... [and] to produce a transnational capitalist class or class fraction with its own particular form of "strategic" class consciousness.[19]

Plainly, the array of potential influences behind state policy is both diverse and complex.

So how did globalization happen? Amidst the cacophony of voices championing one or another version of events, the relative utility of the four models and the interrelationships among them remain unclear. Most sources, wary of mono-causal interpretations of history, appear to concur with Cerny's assertion that "it is impossible to rely on any one form of explanation."[20] Many seem tempted to fudge the issue simply by citing multiple factors more or less indiscriminately. With their carefully executed historical studies, Helleiner and Sobel stand as worthy exceptions to more general practice. Yet even their treatments fall rather short of the demands of complete and formal comparative analysis. Helleiner, while stressing the role of government policies, may certainly be faulted for failing to go behind observed decisions to explore fully alternative motivations for state behavior. Sobel, meanwhile, intent on proving his inside-out hypothesis, appears to understate greatly the role that external forces undoubtedly played in eroding internal resistance to change. Sobel also appears to contradict himself by insisting on the significance of residual distinctions between national markets even while simultaneously alleging homogenization of financial technologies through the embedded influence of U.S. actor preferences. Given such gaps and inconsistencies, it is evident that we are still far from resolving the central question of causation.

A fuller explanation would focus on dynamic linkages among factors highlighted by the four models, particularly as they influenced state calculations of interests over time. A hint of what this might look like is suggested by John

Goodman and Louis Pauly, who note a powerful dialectic at work in the relationship between market forces and public policy – government actions in one period leading to increases of capital mobility that in turn have generated pressures for widening liberalization in subsequent periods.[21] A prime example was the Interest Equalization Tax imposed by the United States in 1963 in an effort to stem foreign-bond sales in New York. One consequence was the stimulus this provided to growth of the Eurocurrency market in London, which in turn eroded the effectiveness and raised the cost of existing restrictions on financial flows and eventually led governments to grant even more freedom for private operations. "In this sense," Goodman and Pauly write, "the diminishing utility of capital controls can be considered the unintended consequence of other and earlier policy decisions."[22] What we need now is more rigorously detailed study along such lines, not just to compare alternative hypotheses but, more importantly, to explore the complex underlying connections among them.

What does it mean?

Even less consensus exists concerning the consequences of financial globalization. As the divergent results of the remaining books make clear, views range from the hopeful to the hopeless. Some economists, with their faith in neoclassical theory, might argue optimistically that the resurrection of global finance represents, in effect, the best of all possible worlds. Other observers, more pessimistically, might simply nod their heads sadly in agreement. At issue is the role of markets versus governments in the management of international capital. Are we better off if the phoenix rules the roost? Or do we simply have no choice?

Analytically, the consequences of globalization may be addressed at two very different levels – at the macro level, with implications for aggregate economic performance and the effectiveness of national stabilization policies; and at the micro level, with implications for domestic distribution and the role of public policy in structuring private activity. Sensationalist sources tend cavalierly to compound the two. "Governments at all levels...have lost the vestiges of unchecked economic sovereignty," says one;[23] "politicians these days have no doubt where the power lies," asserts another.[24] The distinction between the two levels, however, is critical to a full understanding of practical consequences.

The macro level

The core issue at the macro level, long familiar to economists, is best summarized in terms of what I have elsewhere labeled the "unholy trinity" – the intrinsic incompatibility of exchange-rate stability, capital mobility, and national policy autonomy:[25]

> The problem...simply stated, is that in an environment of formally or informally pegged rates and effective integration of financial markets, any

attempt to pursue independent monetary objectives is almost certain, sooner or later, to result in significant balance-of-payments disequilibrium, and hence provoke potentially destabilizing flows of speculative capital. To preserve exchange-rate stability, governments will then be compelled to limit either the movement of capital (via restrictions or taxes) or their own policy autonomy (via some form of multilateral surveillance or joint decisionmaking). If they are unwilling or unable to sacrifice either one, then the objective of exchange-rate stability itself may eventually have to be compromised. Over time, except by chance, the three goals cannot be attained simultaneously.[26]

As capital mobility has increased, so too has concern about its implications for the effectiveness of independent monetary and fiscal policies.[27] Goodman's study, though focused on central banking alone, is typical. With accelerating financial globalization, he suggests, a government's room for maneuver is necessarily reduced. In effect, the stringent logic of the unholy trinity imposes an increasingly stark trade-off on policymakers. Autonomy of national policy can be preserved only by giving up some degree of currency stability; an independent exchange-rate target can be maintained only at the cost of reduced control over domestic macro-economic performance. Over time, states begin to pay a higher price for divergent behavior owing to the risk of capital flight. Ultimately, the cost of defending policy independence may simply become too high to bear. In Goodman's view, these developments have therefore "increased the overall pressure for monetary convergence [and] created new incentives for monetary policy cooperation" (p. 217). Andrews, concurring, calls this the "capital mobility hypothesis":[28] "The central claim associated with the capital mobility hypothesis is that integration has increased the costs of pursuing divergent monetary objectives, resulting in structural incentives for monetary adjustment."[29]

How serious is the challenge of the capital mobility hypothesis? Certainly examples abound that would seem to testify to the strength of the constraint imposed on governments. Goodman cites the case of France in 1983, where at a time of sluggish growth in Europe a new socialist administration was compelled to abandon its agenda of unilateral expansion by a speculative run on the franc (pp. 126–39). More recently, beginning in late 1994, much the same happened to Mexico when foreign as well as domestic investors lost confidence in the country's economic management, forcing incoming President Ernesto Zedillo to introduce an austerity program of unprecedented severity. Once Mexico's bond rating was marked down by agencies like Moody's Investors Services, the handwriting was on the wall. Policymakers had to do whatever they could to restore their own credibility. As one commentator observed:

That makes Moody's one powerful agency. In fact, you could almost say that we live again in a two-superpower world. There is the U.S. and there is Moody's. The U.S. can destroy a country by leveling it with bombs; Moody's can destroy a country by downgrading its bonds.[30]

In reality, however, the discipline of the financial marketplace may be less than it appears for at least three reasons. In the first place, there are limits to just how much can be accomplished by independent monetary and fiscal policies even in the absence of a high degree of capital mobility. The challenge to policy autonomy matters only to the extent that available policy instruments (the money supply or government budget) can be assumed to have a genuine influence on "real" economic variables like output and employment. In effect, there must be some sustained trade-off between unemployment and inflation – technically, a negative slope to the Phillips curve. Today, however, the conventional view among economists, inspired by so-called rational-expectations theory, is that there is no such trade-off, at least not for long – no permanent slope to the Phillips curve. Over relatively extended time horizons, policy is more apt to be neutral with respect to real output, influencing only prices or interest rates. Monetary or fiscal initiatives may have a significant impact on aggregate performance, but their effects are not likely to be lasting. Insofar as policy autonomy continues to matter, therefore, it is mostly for the short term.

Second, it is also important to recall the still limited scope of financial globalization in the contemporary world. The power of Moody's to destroy a country is effectively contained to the extent that capital mobility remains short of absolutely perfect. As Sylvia Maxfield has pointed out, moreover, not all international investors are equally sensitive to monetary or fiscal changes in host countries.[31] Governments thus still retain some room for maneuver to pursue independent policy objectives.

Finally, it is important to recall that, within limits, a trade-off continues to exist between policy autonomy and currency stability. Even if a capital flight does develop, officials have some choice – to sacrifice either domestic targets or the exchange rate. Investors anxious to switch out of local assets must, collectively, find buyers for their claims. Unless the central bank steps in as residual buyer of its own currency, however, the impact of a loss of confidence will be seen in asset prices and the exchange rate rather than in the government's own programs. In other words, economic policies at home need not be fatally compromised as long as the authorities are willing and able to tolerate a degree of currency volatility abroad.

In practice, to be sure, this is a luxury that not all economies are able to afford. The insulation provided by a floating exchange rate is partial at best: most countries find it difficult to protect themselves completely from all the negative consequences of currency instability. For economist Barry Eichengreen, this means that the logic of the unholy trinity has now in effect eliminated the policy-autonomy trade-off altogether. Governments, he argues, can no longer hope to contain market pressures by means of contingent exchange-rate rules. In the future, "countries that have traditionally pegged their currencies will be forced to choose between floating exchange rates on the one hand and monetary unification on the other.... The middle ground of pegged but adjustable rates and narrow target zones is being hollowed out."[32] But this conclusion rests on an unspoken, and highly debatable, judgment about the political calculations involved. Eichengreen asserts that "the capital mobility characteristic of the late twentieth century" makes pursuit of independent policy objectives "extremely costly and potentially unsustainable politically."[33] Note, however, that it does not make national autonomy impossible. The option continues to exist, albeit at a price. How can we be sure what price will turn out to be unsustainable politically?

Thus while the challenge of the capital mobility hypothesis is obviously serious, and no doubt growing, governments do not appear in fact to have been wholly deprived of macroeconomic authority – at least, not yet. The interesting question, therefore, is not whether financial globalization imposes a constraint on sovereign states; it most clearly does. Rather, we should now be asking how the discipline works and under what conditions. What accounts for the remaining room for maneuver, and why do some countries still enjoy more policy autonomy than others? These issues point the way for future research in this area. It is time to move beyond broad generalizations about the logic of the unholy trinity to more disaggregated analysis of the complex linkages between global finance and domestic performance.

On these linkages, only a few intriguing hints can be found in the literature to date. Goodman, for example, stresses the role of central-bank independence in enhancing the credibility of a state's macroeconomic policies. A monetary authority that is legally distinct from the elected government can give greater assurance that decisions will be insulated from domestic political pressures. The argument appears to have something of a catch-22 quality about it, since it suggests that the only way to avoid speculative capital flows is to do what the market wants; in effect, to save policy autonomy, it must be surrendered. There may nonetheless be an important insight here, if reputation today provides some room for maneuver, if needed, tomorrow. The degree of central-bank independence, along with structural differences in relations between private banks and industry, is also stressed by Randall Henning as a crucial determinant of national-policy choices involving the exchange rate.[34] Along somewhat different lines, Goodman and Pauly emphasize "generic types of external pressure,"[35] which are identified with persistent current-account surpluses or deficits in the balance of payments. Since in standard monetary theory such imbalances are understood to reflect an economy's underlying saving and investment propensities, this amounts to suggesting a systematic difference between capital importers and capital exporters in their respective vulnerabilities to market forces. Andrews, meanwhile, mentions size and openness as factors that may help account for variations in state willingness to tolerate trade-offs of currency volatility for policy autonomy.[36]

Plainly, more could be done to explore linkages of these kinds. Particular use might be made of the contemporary theory of optimum currency areas (OCAs), well developed by economists, which highlights the advantages or disadvantages, as seen from a single country's point of view, of abandoning monetary sovereignty to participate in a currency union or an equivalent regime of irrevocably fixed exchange rates.[37] OCA theory identifies a number of key characteristics that may be regarded as instrumental in a government's decision to surrender authority over its exchange rate. In addition to a country's size and openness, these include such economic variables as wage and price flexibility, factor mobility, geographic trade patterns, the degree of commodity diversification, inflation trends, and the source and timing of payments disturbances. These particular characteristics are singled out because they may be assumed to influence, to a greater or lesser extent, the degree of insulation afforded by a floating currency. To this list one might also add political variables such as state capacity, electoral politics, and foreign alliance or treaty commitments. The number of conditions that might influence the preferred trade-off between policy autonomy and exchange-rate stability is quite large. What is needed is more careful applied investigation of how each works in today's financially integrated world.

The micro level

The core issue at the micro level is the familiar one of whose ox is gored: who wins and who loses? As Frieden has reminded us, increased capital mobility may be "expected to have a significant impact on the interests of various domestic economic interest groups."[38] It is also likely to influence government's ability to structure economic activity by remaking political coalitions and changing the pattern of lobbying over national policies.[39] Here too increasing concern is expressed about possible barriers to the attainment of politically determined social goals. In Paulette Kurzer's words:

> The growth of financial activities and the availability of many different kinds of financial instruments are major stumbling blocks for governments that desire to induce an increase in production or investments or a change of prices.... High capital mobility and deepening financial integration prompt governments to remove or alter institutions and practices objectionable to business and finance. (pp. 7, 245)

The key, of course, is the financial sector's increased ability simply to take its money elsewhere. Recalling the language of Albert Hirschman, the bargaining strength of different groups in an economy may be thought to depend on the relative availability of the options of exit, voice, and loyalty.[40] The greater a group's capacity to evade the preferences of public officials (exit), the more likely it is to give voice within the political system to promote its own desires and objectives. The government's ability to command loyalty will be correspondingly weakened. Financial globalization clearly enhances the leverage of investor interests by reducing barriers to exit. Owners of mobile capital thus gain influence at the expense of less fortunate sectors, including so-called national capital as well as labor. As Gill and Law put it, "The impact of increased capital mobility...has worked to the advantage of large-scale transnational capital, relative to national capital...and to labor, especially in the core capitalist states.... These changes can be interpreted as signs of the emergence of a new regime of accumulation."[41]

The result, many scholars fear, is likely to be both a dramatically more regressive income distribution and an effective veto over public policy. Wages will tend to fall relative to returns on capital, eroding the living standards of many citizens.[42] Even worse, governments will increasingly find themselves hostages to financial-market sentiment, compelled to take account of investor concerns at every turn. More than a decade ago Robert Bates and Da-Hsiang Lien explained how, historically, increases in the mobility of taxable property have always obliged political authorities "to bargain with those who possessed property rights over the moveable tax base and to share with them formal control over the conduct of public affairs."[43] Today, with the resurrection of global finance, that imperative seems stronger than ever. Redistributive strategies are out; tax relief for financial interests is in.

Certainly Kurzer's study would seem to confirm the validity of such fears. In each of the four countries she examines, the abandonment of policies traditionally associated with social democracy – including numerous entitlement programs; redistributive incomes policies; and consensual tripartite exchanges among business, labor, and government – clearly appears linked to the postwar internationalization of finance. "This mobility allows business and finance to move with ease across borders into different money-making ventures and away from arrangements considered inflexible and outdated" (pp. 4–5). Ultimately, in all four countries, officials concluded that the cost of policy independence had become more or less unacceptable. None wished to provoke a major capital flight. Jonathan Moses offers a similar interpretation of the parallel experiences of Sweden and Norway:

> Despite the fact that Sweden and Norway can be said to have relied on different strategies for meeting social democratic objectives, both strategies have proved ineffective in the new international economic environment.... A new international economic regime, characterized by increased levels of capital mobility, has made traditional tools for government steering ineffective.... [A]ll participants are subject to an iron law of policy.[44]

Broad evidence suggesting such an iron law can also be found in the recent evolution of national tax regimes, not only in Europe but in many other countries as well, including the United States. During the 1980s, which has been described as the "decade of tax reform," governments on every continent initiated major revisions in their tax codes designed inter alia to reduce marginal tax rates on capital and to restrict the use of tax policy as an instrument of economic management. Most specialists agree that a principal cause of these moves has been the fear of investor exodus made easier by the growing integration of financial markets. In the words of Sven Steinmo, "The battle for progressive (if not redistributive) taxation has been a difficult one.... But as the power resources available to capital increase with its growing internationalism, it may be that the difficult battle will become a futile one."[45]

In practice, however, here too the discipline of the marketplace may be less than it appears. The indictment of global finance seems extreme. First, factors other than capital mobility may also have contributed to the outcomes described by Kurzer and others. To single out financial internationalization alone may be to mistake correlation for causation.[46] Even with greater options for exit, moreover, capital's veto is not absolute. The globalization of finance obviously has increased pressures for general policy convergence toward an agenda set by investors. But a closer look suggests that room may still exist for implementation or preservation of distinctive national strategies and structures. Geoffrey Garrett and Peter Lange, for example, stress the role of more selective supply-side programs, such as policies targeted to shape investment incentives or labor-market practices, which have enabled "governments of the left" to maintain traditional redistributive and welfare goals while simultaneously adjusting to the demands of investor interests.[47] Financial-market integration has not made separate social goals impossible, they argue. Rather, it "has altered the policy instruments through which governments can pursue their partisan objectives."[48] Likewise, Pauly has emphasized the extent to which diversity in national financial structures persists despite increasing international mobility of capital.[49] The iron law would appear to be less of a handicap than commonly thought.

Hence once again the interesting question is not whether financial globalization imposes a constraint, but how and under what conditions. Here too it is time to move beyond broad generalizations to a more disaggregated analysis of the diverse relationships at work. One key might lie in the distinction between national and transnational capital, which could help to explain observed differences in pressures for convergence at the sectoral level. As Frieden has noted, "Inasmuch as capital is specific to location, increased financial integration has only limited effects on policies targeted at particular industries."[50] Other keys might be located in domestic institutional variations of the sort examined by Kurzer or in differential interest-group pressures as emphasized by Helen Milner.[51] These could be thought to affect the ability or willingness of political authorities to bear the costs of policy independence. At the micro level no less than at the macro level, more careful applied investigation is needed to see how any of these linkages might actually work.

What can governments do about it?

The practical consequences of financial globalization thus seem rather more nuanced and contingent than they appear at first glance. Increases of capital mobility have clearly diminished the effective autonomy of states. On the other hand, public officials still retain some room to pursue independent policy agendas. Across countries as well as over time, outcomes may vary considerably depending on an identifiable range of economic and political factors. From a political-economy perspective, therefore, it would seem important to ask what governments can do, if anything, to promote outcomes more to their liking. Even if it does not rule the roost, the phoenix can make life difficult for policymakers. Can it be tamed?

This brings us back to the issue of reversibility. To relax the constraint on policy, capital mobility would have to be reduced significantly, or at least managed more successfully. This would no doubt be both difficult and costly. Are governments prepared to pay the price? Two broad strategies seem possible, one unilateral and one collective. Neither is without problems.

The first approach would be the more direct. States would simply seek to limit capital mobility on an individual basis. In principle, any government has the means available to reverse the process of financial integration for its own economy. All it requires is the will to impose new taxes or controls of sufficient severity to effectively eliminate opportunities for substitution between domestic and foreign claims. As Pauly suggests, "states can still defy markets" if they so desire.[52] The costs involved, both economic and administrative, are apt to be quite high, however, unless all governments are prepared to act in concert. In practice, therefore, comprehensive unilateral initiatives would seem unlikely except in the most dire of circumstances, such as a foreign-exchange or national-security crisis.

The alternative, collective approach would seek to promote policies of active collaboration to ease or eliminate the constraints imposed by financial integration. This is the path advocated by both Goodman and Kapstein. While disagreeing on specifics, both scholars concur on a general need for political governance to catch up with global finance. In Kapstein's words, "The idea of globalization challenges public officials, who are responsible to their societies for ensuring economic welfare and national security. In an international system which lacks any higher authority, citizens must look to the state for the protection of their well-being" (p. 1). Governments thus must be prepared to merge selected elements of their sovereignty to preserve their capacity to fulfill established responsibilities.

Is cooperation feasible? Skepticism would appear justified by recent history. During the 1980s, the so-called Group of Seven industrial states (the United States, Britain, Canada, France, Germany, Italy, and Japan) repeatedly declared their commitment to principles of mutual surveillance of their macroeconomic policies and a coordinated management of exchange rates. Yet for all their promises to curb unilateralist impulses, the governments involved more often than not ended up going their separate ways as policymakers wearied of the frequent concessions required. Collaboration in practice tended to ebb and flow like the tides. Apparently, as I have written before, international monetary cooperation, like passionate love, is a good thing but difficult to sustain.[53] The episodic quality of such efforts has also been demonstrated by more recent events in Europe. The march toward a European monetary union, which Goodman approvingly discusses in considerable detail, has seemingly been stalled by currency crises occurring since the completion of his study. Goodman's barely qualified positive tone plainly reflects the enthusiasm and sense of momentum generated by passage of the Maastricht treaty in 1991, when he was writing. Today, it seems fair to say, prospects for a single European currency and central bank appear rather dim.

Reasons for the problematic quality of cooperation are not difficult to find. At the domestic level, as indicated, financial globalization remakes political coalitions and creates vested interests in the new status quo. In the words of Goodman and Pauly, "Global financial structures affect the dynamics of national policy-making by changing and privileging the interests and actions of certain types of firms. Once those interests have been embedded in policy, movement back is not necessarily precluded but is certainly rendered much more difficult."[54] At the systemic level, states are always tempted to vie for advantage at the expense of rivals. To the extent that governments act as "defensive positionalists,"[55] compromise will be inhibited by fears of noncompliance abroad as well as of relative loss at home. Factors at both levels enhance the attractiveness of policies of unilateralism and even aggressive neomercantilism in financial matters. For some observers, they virtually guarantee a world dominated by the "competition state."[56]

Yet again, some caution is warranted in the face of such bold generalizations. If the extensive literature on international regimes teaches us anything, it is that even the most self-interested of states will on occasion find it advantageous to voluntarily limit their own autonomy.[57] This will especially be so when governments are confronted with what Arthur Stein calls "dilemmas of common aversions" rather than "dilemmas of common interests."[58] Dilemmas of common aversions, or coordination games, exist when all actors share a concern to avoid a particular outcome. The only question is how to establish a norm, or focal point, around which behavior may coalesce. Beyond agreeing to play by some standard set of rules (for example, driving on the righthand side of the road), no compromise of underlying preferences is called for. This is in contrast to dilemmas of common interests, or conflictual games, where reciprocal concessions are indeed required to avoid suboptimal (Pareto-deficient) outcomes. Collective action in such situations will obviously be more difficult to achieve or sustain. The difference between the two classes of dilemma is reflected in the distinction economist Peter Kenen draws between two types of cooperation – the "policy-optimizing" approach, where governments seek to bargain their way from suboptimality to something closer to a Pareto optimum; and the regime-preserving, or public-goods approach, where mutual adjustments are made for the sake of defending existing arrangements or institutions against the threat of economic or political shocks.[59] The more difficult of the two is clearly the policy-optimizing approach. Happily, though, not all of the challenges posed by global finance are quite so demanding.

In fact, many of the issues involved clearly are more in the nature of coordination games, where "regime preservation" rather than "policy optimization" is at stake. One example is the problem studied by Kapstein, international banking regulation. Prudential supervision, Kapstein suggests, presented a "challenging case" because it

> is an issue-area in which state power appears to be relatively weak and ineffective.... If, despite these unpromising background conditions, states

have somehow managed to build a reasonably sound structure for the
regulation and supervision of [banks], maybe this tells us something of more
general importance. (p. 178)

In reality, the case may have been less challenging than alleged.[60] All states, after
all, share an interest in ensuring prudent behavior in the banking sector, owing to
the industry's central role in the operation of the payments system. None was
eager to become enmeshed in a competition in laxity. As Kapstein's own analysis
demonstrates, few truly serious compromises were actually required to reach
agreement on common standards for capital adequacy, accounting rules, and the
like. Nonetheless, the case does tell us something of more general importance –
that cooperative action is indeed feasible, at least in circumstances where states
find themselves confronted with common aversions rather than fundamentally
divergent interests.

Such circumstances can be found at both the micro and macro levels. In Sobel's
analysis of securities markets, the evidence clearly points to opportunities for
regulatory agreements parallel to those highlighted by Kapstein in the banking
sector. "The greater the frequency of international trading, the greater the
demands for national regulators to coordinate internationally. The more such regulators coordinate, the more regulatory styles will converge" (p. 159).[61] Likewise,
even in the G-7's disappointing record of performance in the exchange-rate area,
experience testifies to the willingness of governments to act together effectively
when broader collective goals have appeared at risk (for example, the Plaza
Agreement of 1985, the joint response to the stock-market crash of 1987). While
genuine policy-optimizing cooperation in the monetary area remains rare,
regime-preserving collaboration has not proved impossible.[62]

Hence, here too the interesting question is not whether but how and under what
conditions. The difficulties of coordinating state action, whether at the micro or
macro level, should certainly not be underestimated. Neither, however, should the
problematic quality of cooperative strategies be exaggerated. Some issues by their
nature require little more than agreement on mutual recognition of standards.
Even in areas where conflicts of interest are more directly involved, it may be
possible to preserve or promote a collective approach by switching the focus of
attention from one class of policy instruments to another.[63] Short of a genuine
systemic crisis, governments may never be willing to pay the undoubtedly steep
price that would be required to tame the phoenix completely. But it does appear
feasible to arrange life so that states and markets may cohabit a bit more
comfortably.

The end of geography?

There is no question that the globalization of finance is one of the most striking
political-economy developments of the post–World War II era. Governments have
clearly been thrown on the defensive. For many analysts, the rise of the phoenix
means a possibly irreversible erosion of state authority. For some, it signifies

much more: a fundamental change in the meaning of the state itself in relation to transcendent market forces – in effect, a transformation of geography as we know it. No longer is economic activity bounded by the political jurisdiction of the traditional territorial state. Increasingly, the globe itself is the only domain that matters. As economist Richard O'Brien puts it, "The closer we get to a global, integral whole, the closer we get to the end of geography."[64]

Is this the end of geography? At least three intepretations can be attached to O'Brien's proposition. In one sense it could be construed in material terms, to mean a decline in the importance of place – physical location – as markets are increasingly integrated by the forces of competition and technical innovation. New communications and information technologies already permit market actors to operate with impunity across national frontiers. A future could be imagined where financial services are provided and transactions conducted solely in cyberspace, regardless of specific location. This is evidently the meaning that O'Brien mainly has in mind: "As markets...become integrated...the need to base decisions on geography will alter and often diminish."[65] In effect, business will be done anywhere.

Such a scenario, however, tends to strain credulity. In reality, the importance of place is unlikely to be erased completely as long as economies of agglomeration can still be gained from concentrating operations in close proximity. Benefits include the more efficient use of information where contact between market actors is facilitated, the spreading of costs of needed public services, and the ready availability of specialist skills and supporting cognate functions. Even O'Brien admits that "certain activities will still be transacted within a relatively limited physical area, in which a collection of expertise is valuable.... Where deals require the personal touch...location of the players will still matter."[66] It is no accident that financial markets historically have always tended to gather together in a few select locales; nor that financial centers, once established, generally resist encroachment from newer rivals for long periods of time. As Paul Krugman has reminded us, "increasing returns and cumulative process are pervasive" in influencing the placement of economic activity.[67] Rational actors will continue to be attracted to certain locations as long as gains exceed the costs of congestion.

In a second sense the end of geography could be understood in political terms, as referring to the decline of state authority brought on by financial globalization – the transfer of effective sovereignty from national governments to "stateless" markets. The more public policy is hemmed in by private activities, the less relevant are the legal boundaries that have traditionally been drawn between political jurisdictions. Ultimately, all power might be drained off in favor of transnational capital. The nation-state, as Charles Kindleberger once predicted, would be "just about through as an economic unit."[68] But this interpretation too tends to strain credulity. As the preceding discussion has sought to make clear, the more plausible scenario is rather more mundane – a world of incomplete discipline and constant tension on both sides of the state-market divide. While national sovereignty is undoubtedly being challenged, it is not yet ready to be tossed quietly into the dustbin of history.

Finally, in a third sense, the end of geography might be interpreted in cognitive terms, as a shorthand expression for a required long-term shift of intellectual paradigm. Traditionally, in political economy studies of global finance, the central *problematique* has been the uneasy dialectic between states and markets. As in the books reviewed here, scholars typically focus on the challenge posed by mobile capital to the autonomy of national governments. The existence of an international system, based on state sovereignty as the central organizing principle of world politics, is taken more or less for granted, with markets assumed to operate within a framework defined in terms of the familiar territorial state. As financial activities become increasingly integrated, however, arguably a new organizing principle could be needed, a competing transnational model,[69] based not on political space but on economic space, which is becoming truly global in character. For a widening circle of scholars today, the key to understanding contemporary finance is indeed globalization. As Cerny has contended: "It is not merely the erosion of state financial power, but also the way that separate national currencies themselves are increasingly inextricably locked into wider financial trends and structures, which has become the central issue."[70] Geography has ended in the sense that the very meaning of borders has allegedly dissolved.

In essence, this final interpretation is just another way of arguing for the exogeneity of global finance – the notion that capital mobility must now be regarded as a truly structural constraint on state behavior. The limitations of that perspective have already been addressed. Insofar as the integration of financial markets remains contingent on government calculations of costs and benefits, the traditional state-centric paradigm continues to be relevant. Nonetheless, for students of IPE the competing transnational model is not easy to ignore. It represents, in fact, but one tributary of a much broader stream of criticism of standard international relations scholarship that has been gathering force in recent years.[71] The focus of debate is the "territorial trap,"[72] the deceptively simple notion that world politics can be best understood in terms of "neatly divided spatial packages."[73] In reality, as Stephen Rosow argues, "the entire territorial imagery of current IPE has been rendered ambiguous. . . . Modern conceptualization fails to illuminate the networks and flows of power, and the paths people attempt to carve out within them, which operate in global economic life."[74] To stay useful, contemporary IR scholarship must take more serious account of alternative and potentially complementary conceptualizations of rule and dominion in the modern world – nonterritorial "spaces-of-flows," in the language of John Ruggie, as well as the more traditional territorial "spaces-of-places."[75] The resurrection of global finance can be fully comprehended only in this much broader context.

Notes

1 See, e.g., Howard M. Wachtel, *The Money Mandarins: The Making of a New Supranational Economic Order* (Armonk, N.Y.: M. E. Sharpe, 1990); Richard

B. McKenzie and Dwight R. Lee, *Quick-silver Capital: How the Rapid Movement of Wealth Has Changed the World* (New York: Free Press, 1991); Joel Kurtzman, *The Death of Money: How the Electronic Economy Has Destabilized the World's Markets and Created Financial Chaos* (New York: Simon and Schuster, 1993); Gregory J. Millman, *The Vandals' Crown: How Rebel Currency Traders Overthrew the World's Central Banks* (New York: Free Press, 1995); and Steven Solomon, *The Confidence Game: How Unelected Central Bankers Are Governing the Changed Global Economy* (New York: Simon and Schuster, 1995).

2 Susan Strange, *Casino Capitalism* (New York: Basil Blackwell, 1986).

3 Other recent contributions of note include Stephen R. Gill and David Law, "Global Hegemony and the Structural Power of Capital," *International Studies Quarterly* 33 (December 1989); Geoffrey R. D. Underhill, "Markets beyond Politics? The State and the Internationalisation of Financial Markets," *European Journal of Political Research* 19 (March–April 1991); Tariq Banuri and Juliet B. Schor, eds., *Financial Openness and National Autonomy: Opportunities and Constraints* (Oxford: Clarendon Press, 1992); John B. Goodman and Louis W. Pauly, "The Obsolescence of Capital Controls? Economic Management in an Age of Global Markets," *World Politics* 46 (October 1993); Philip G. Cerny, ed., *Finance and World Politics* (Aldershot, England: Edward Elgar, 1993); David M. Andrews, "Capital Mobility and State Autonomy: Toward a Structural Theory of International Monetary Relations," *International Studies Quarterly* 38 (June 1994); Stuart Corbridge, Nigel Thrift, and Ron Martin, eds., *Money, Power and Space* (Cambridge: Basil Blackwell, 1994); and Eric Helleiner, ed., "The World of Money: The Political Economy of International Capital Mobility," *Policy Sciences* 27, no. 4 (1994).

4 Jeffry A. Frieden, "Invested Interests: The Politics of National Economic Policies in a World of Global Finance," *International Organization* 45 (Autumn 1991), 429.

5 See, e.g., Jeffrey A. Frankel, *On Exchange Rates* (Cambridge: MIT Press, 1993), chap. 2; Barry P. Bosworth, *Saving and Investment in a Global Economy* (Washington, D.C.: Brookings Institution, 1993), chap. 1; William F. Shepherd, *International Financial Integration: History, Theory and Applications in OECD Countries* (Brookfield, Vt.: Ashgate Publishing, 1994), chap. 4; Richard J. Herring and Robert E. Litan, *Financial Regulation in the Global Economy* (Washington, D.C.: Brookings Institution, 1995), chap. 2; and Atish R. Ghosh, "International Capital Mobility amongst the Major Industrialised Countries: Too Little or Too Much?" *Economic Journal* 105 (January 1995). Country (or political) risk refers to the possibility that assets may be treated differently by different sovereign governments; currency (or foreign-exchange) risk, to the possibility of exchange-rate movements that may alter the rate of return on investments. For some useful discussion, see Richard J. Herring, ed., *Managing International Risk* (Cambridge: Cambridge University Press, 1983).

6 Though unacknowledged by Sobel, use of the terms "outside-in" and "inside-out" to describe alternative approaches to the study of international relations was pioneered by Kenneth Waltz. See Waltz, *Theory of World Politics* (Reading, Mass.: Addison-Wesley, 1979), 63.

7 For parallel arguments concerning the critical role of domestic politics in shaping distinctive national patterns of financial liberalization, see Louis W. Pauly, *Opening Financial Markets: Banking Politics on the Pacific Rim* (Ithaca, N.Y.: Cornell University Press, 1988); Frances McCall Rosenbluth, *Financial Politics in Contemporary Japan* (Ithaca, N.Y.: Cornell University Press, 1989); and Sylvia Maxfield, *Governing Capital: International Finance and Mexican Politics* (Ithaca, N.Y.: Cornell University Press, 1990).

8 Philip G. Cerny, "The Deregulation and Re-regulation of Financial Markets in a More Open World," in Cerny (fn. 3), chap. 3.

9 Each of these levels of analysis has its analogue in one of Kenneth Waltz's three "images" of international relations – respectively, the third, second, and first image. See Waltz, *Man, the State and War* (New York: Columbia University Press, 1959).

10 Ralph C. Bryant, *International Financial Intermediation* (Washington, D.C.: Brookings Institution, 1987), 69.

11 Andrews (fn. 3). See also Philip G. Cerny, "The Dynamics of Financial Globalization: Technology, Market Structure, and Policy Response," *Policy Sciences* 27, no. 4 (1994).

12 Eric Helleiner, "Post-Globalization: Is the Financial Liberalization Trend Irreversible?" in Daniel Drache and R. Boyer, eds., *The Future of Nations and the Limits of Markets* (forthcoming).

13 Andrews (fn. 3), 197. See also idem, "Capital Mobility and Monetary Adjustment in Western Europe, 1973–1991," *Policy Sciences* 27, no. 4 (1994); Philip G. Cerny, "The Political Economy of International Finance," in Cerny (fn. 3), chap. 1; and idem (fn. 11).

14 Louis W. Pauly, "Capital Mobility, State Autonomy and Political Legitimacy," *Journal of International Affairs* 48 (Winter 1995), 373, 385. Andrews himself (fn. 3) admits that "this is not to say that the current degree of capital mobility cannot be reduced, but instead that reduction is likely to be both difficult and costly" (p. 198).

15 Scott C. James and David A. Lake, "The Second Face of Hegemony: Britain's Repeal of the Corn Laws and the American Walker Tariff of 1846," *International Organization* 43 (Winter 1989).

16 Uniquely, Japan was the object of considerable and quite direct pressure from the United States to liberalize its financial markets, particularly during the 1980s. For detail, see Rosenbluth (fn. 7), chap. 3. Overt exercise of influence by the U.S. as well as Britain has been much more evident in the negotiation of regulatory responses to financial globalization, as Kapstein emphasizes (chap. 5).

17 Ron Martin, "Stateless Monies, Global Financial Integration and National Economic Autonomy: The End of Geography?" in Corbridge, Thrift, and Martin (fn. 3), 271.

18 Cerny (fn. 8), 51. Andrews (fn. 3), similarly speaks of the critical role of "widely shared ideological commitments" and "mindsets" (pp. 200–201).

19 Gill and Law (fn. 3), 483–84.

20 Cerny (fn. 8), 79.

21 Goodman and Pauly (fn. 3), 79. Andrews (fn. 3) criticizes Goodman and Pauly for this suggestion, charging that, by stressing both market forces and preexisting levels of financial integration, they in effect "treat capital mobility as both an independent and dependent variable" (p. 197). In fact, this is a bit unfair, since Goodman and Pauly clearly have in mind a kind of dynamic sequencing model or step-function in which today's dependent variable is tomorrow's independent variable (and vice versa).

22 Goodman and Pauly (fn. 3), 79.

23 McKenzie and Lee (fn. 1), xi.

24 Millman (fn. 1), 24.

25 Benjamin J. Cohen, "The Triad and the Unholy Trinity: Lessons for the Pacific Region," in Richard Higgott, Richard Leaver, and John Ravenhill, eds., *Pacific Economic Relations in the 1990s: Co-operation or Conflict?* (Boulder, Colo.: Lynne Reinner, 1993). Adding free trade to the equation produces what Tommaso Padoa-Schioppa calls the "inconsistent quartet." See Padoa-Schioppa, "The European Monetary System: A Long-term View," in Francesco Giavazzi, Stefano Micossi, and Marcus Miller, eds., *The European Monetary System* (Cambridge: Cambridge University Press, 1988).

26 Cohen (fn. 25), 147.

27 See esp. Michael C. Webb, "International Economic Structures, Government Interests, and International Coordination of Macroeconomic Adjustment Policies," *International*

Organization 45 (Summer 1991); Goodman and Pauly (fn. 3); Cohen (fn. 25); Andrews (fn. 3).

28 Andrews (fn. 3).

29 Ibid., 203.

30 Thomas A. Friedman, "Don't Mess with Moody's," *New York Times*, February 22, 1995, p. A15. For a more general analysis of the role that credit-rating agencies may play in constraining public policy, see Timothy J. Sinclair, "Between State and Market: Hegemony and Institutions of Collective Action under Conditions of International Capital Mobility," *Policy Sciences 27*, no. 4 (1994). For more specific detail on the Mexican experience, see Moises Naim, "Mexico's Larger Story," *Foreign Policy 99* (Summer 1995).

31 Sylvia Maxfield, "International Portfolio Flows to Developing/Transitional Economies: Impact on Government Policy Choice" (Manuscript, Yale University, 1995).

32 Barry Eichengreen, *International Monetary Arrangements for the 21st Century* (Washington, D.C.: Brookings Institution, 1994), 5–6.

33 Ibid., 60.

34 C. Randall Henning, *Currencies and Politics in the United States, Germany, and Japan* (Washington, D.C.: Institute for International Economics, 1994).

35 Goodman and Pauly (fn. 3), 51.

36 Andrews (fn. 3), 206–7.

37 For recent surveys of OCA theory, see Paul R. Masson and Mark P. Taylor, "Currency Unions: A Survey of the Issues," in Masson and Taylor, eds., *Policy Issues in the Operation of Currency Unions* (New York: Cambridge University Press, 1993); and George S. Tavlas, "The 'New' Theory of Optimum Currency Areas," *World Economy* 16 (November 1993).

38 Frieden (fn. 4), 433.

39 Ibid.

40 Albert O. Hirschman, *Exit, Voice and Loyalty: Responses to Decline in Firms, Organizations, and States* (Cambridge: Harvard University Press, 1970).

41 Gill and Law (fn. 3), 486–88.

42 See, e.g., Thomas I. Palley, "Capital Mobility and the Threat to American Prosperity," *Challenge* (November–December 1994).

43 Robert H. Bates and Da-Hsiang Donald Lien, "A Note on Taxation, Development, and Representative Government," *Politics and Society* 14 (March 1985), 57. Bates and Lien note that their argument leads them to precisely the opposite conclusion from Hirschman, who reasoned that it was owners of immobile resources who would be more likely to take the political initiative. Hirschman's error, they suggest, was to focus on the motivations of private groups alone without regard to their strategic interaction with government. Political authorities anxious to preserve their tax base will always pay more attention to the owners of mobile resources. Ibid., 61.

44 Jonathan W. Moses, "Abdication from National Policy Autonomy: What's Left to Leave?" *Politics and Society* 22 (June 1994), 140–42.

45 Sven Steinmo, "The End of Redistribution? International Pressures and Domestic Tax Policy Choices," *Challenge* (November–December 1994), 17.

46 Thus Ton Notermans criticizes Jonathan Moses for his preoccupation with capital mobility in explaining the Swedish and Norwegian experiences, to the exclusion of what Notermans regards as even more important domestic factors. Notermans, "Social Democracy in Open Economies: A Reply to Jonathan Moses," *Politics and Society* 22 (June 1994).

47 Geoffrey Garrett and Peter Lange, "Political Responses to Interdependence: What's 'Left' for the Left?" *International Organization* 45 (Autumn 1991).

48 Ibid., 541.

49 Louis W. Pauly, "National Financial Structures, Capital Mobility, and International Economic Rules: The Normative Consequences of East Asian, European, and American Distinctiveness," *Policy Sciences* 27, no. 4 (1994).

50 Frieden (fn. 4), 430.

51 Helen V. Milner, "Bargaining and Cooperation: Domestic Games and International Relations" (Manuscript, Columbia University, 1995).

52 Pauly (fn. 14), 373.

53 Cohen (fn. 25), 134.

54 Goodman and Pauly (fn. 3), 52.

55 Joseph M. Grieco, "Anarchy and the Limits of Cooperation: A Realist Critique of the Newest Liberal Institutionalism," *International Organization* 42 (August 1988).

56 Cerny (fn. 8); and idem, "The Infrastructure of the Infrastructure? Toward 'Embedded Financial Orthodoxy' in the International Political Economy," in Ronen P. Palen and Barry Gills, eds., *Transcending the State-Global Divide: A Neostructuralist Agenda in International Relations* (Boulder, Colo.: Lynne Rienner, 1994).

57 For a useful recent survey, see Volker Rittberger, ed., *Regime Theory and International Relations* (New York: Oxford University Press, 1993).

58 Arthur A. Stein, *Why Nations Cooperate: Circumstance and Choice in International Relations* (Ithaca, N.Y.: Cornell University Press, 1990), chap. 2.

59 Peter B. Kenen, *Managing Exchange Rates* (New York: Council on Foreign Relations, 1988), 75–77.

60 Herring and Litan (fn. 5), chap. 5.

61 For evidence of developing cooperation in the regulation of securities markets, see Tony Porter, *States, Markets and Regimes in Global Finance* (New York: St. Martin's Press, 1993); and William D. Coleman and Tony Porter, "Regulating International Banking and Securities: Emerging Co-operation among National Authorities," in Richard Stubbs and Geoffrey R. D. Underhill, eds., *Political Economy and the Changing Global Order* (New York: St. Martin's Press, 1994). For some observers, regulatory convergence amounts to a "re-regulation" of financial markets. See Underhill (fn. 3), Cerny (fn. 8).

62 Cohen (fn. 25); Kenen (fn. 59).

63 Webb (fn. 27).

64 Richard O'Brien, *Global Financial Integration: The End of Geography* (New York: Council on Foreign Relations, 1992), 5. See also Kenichi Ohmae, *The Borderless World: Power and Strategy in an Interdependent Economy* (New York: Harper Business, 1990); Martin (fn. 17).

65 O'Brien (fn. 64), 2.

66 Ibid., 76.

67 Paul Krugman, *Geography and Trade* (Cambridge: MIT Press, 1991), 25.

68 Charles P. Kindleberger, *American Business Abroad* (New Haven: Yale University Press, 1969), 207.

69 Marcello De Cecco, "Financial Relations: Between Internationalism and Transnationalism," in Roger Morgan et al., eds., *New Diplomacy in the Post–Cold War World: Essays for Susan Strange* (New York St. Martin's, 1993).

70 Philip G. Cerny, "Money and Finance in the International Political Economy: Structural Change and Paradigmatic Muddle," *Review of International Political Economy* 1 (Autumn 1994), 591.

71 John Gerard Ruggie, "Territoriality and Beyond: Problematizing Modernity in International Relations," *International Organization* 47 (Winter 1993); Stephen D. Krasner, "Westphalia and All That," in Judith D. Goldstein and Robert O. Keohane, eds., *Ideas and Foreign Policy: Beliefs, Institutions, and Political Change* (Ithaca, N.Y.: Cornell University Press, 1993); and Janice E. Thomson, "State Sovereignty in

International Relations: Bridging the Gap between Theory and Empirical Research,"
International Studies Quarterly 39 (June 1995).

72 John A. Agnew, "The Territorial Trap: The Geographical Assumptions of International
Relations Theory," *Review of International Political Economy* 1 (Spring 1994).

73 John A. Agnew, "Timeless Space and State-Centrism: The Geographical Assumptions
of International Relations Theory," in Stephen J. Rosow, Naeem Inayatullah, and Mark
Rupert, eds., *The Global Economy as Political Space* (Boulder, Colo.: Lynne Reinner,
1994), 89.

74 Stephen J. Rosow, "On the Political Theory of Political Economy: Conceptual
Ambiguity and the Global Economy," *Review of International Political Economy*
1 (Autumn 1994), 473–75.

75 Ruggie (fn. 71), 172.

Part 2
Dealing with financial crisis

6 International debt and linkage strategies

Some foreign-policy implications for the United States*

Source: *International Organization* 39, 4, Autumn 1985.

Recent debt crises in Eastern Europe and the Third World have vividly highlighted the close connections between high finance and high politics. "Money brings honor, friends, conquest, and realms," said John Milton; or, as the old French proverb puts it. "l'argent fait le jeu"–money talks. The connections, however, are anything but simple. Money may talk but it does so, as it were, out of both sides of its mouth. The game that money makes is a highly complex one in which it is not at all clear who conquers, who is conquered, or even what conquest means.

My purpose in this article is to explore some of the foreign-policy implications of international debt from the point of view of a major creditor country. Specifically, my focus is on the United States, whose banks have been among the heaviest lenders to sovereign borrowers in recent years. Foreign policy, in this analysis, is understood to encompass the full range of strategies and actions developed by the U.S. government's decision makers in America's relations with other nations. Foreign policy aims to achieve specific goals defined in terms of national interests as decision makers themselves perceive them. National interests may included economic objectives no less than political or security concerns. The central issue for analysis is the extent to which, if at all, the global debt problem has influenced the power of the U.S. government in foreign affairs, power being understood to imply leverage or control not only over resources and actors but also over the outcome of events. Has the global debt problem altered the ability of public officials in Washington to realize their foreign-policy preferences?

What makes this question analytically interesting is the fact that most international debt is owed to private creditors rather than to governments or multilateral agencies. Following the first oil shock in 1973 the private financial markets, and in particular the major commercial banks, became the principal source of external finance for much of Eastern Europe and the Third World, and banks have been intimately involved in all of the major debt crises of recent years. In short, banks have become full participants in the realm of foreign policy: they are now

* An earlier version was presented at the Lehrman Institute, New York City, in the spring of 1984 as part of its seminar series on Politics and International Debt, which was supported in part by a grant from the Ford Foundation and directed by Miles Kahler of Yale University.

important independent actors on the world stage. Yet there is no assurance at all that the banks' interpretation of their private interests in the marketplace will necessarily converge with the public interest as interpreted by policy makers in Washington. As one astute observer has commented, "U.S. foreign policy actions and the overseas activities of the private banks have come increasingly to overlap. The interests of the two sides do not always coincide and indeed may at times be contradictory."[1] Or to quote Ronald Reagan's first under secretary of state for economic affairs,

> There are areas of shared interests ... as well as areas of potential friction. ... The bankers must be guided by the interests of their stockholders. ... Governments, on the other hand, are guided by a mix of political, humanitarian, strategic and economic objectives. ... Banks may differ with government in their assessment of political factors. ...[2]

In formal terms the situation described here corresponds to Robert Keohane and Joseph Nye's "complex interdependence," in which direct interstate relations are affected by the presence of important transnational actors, including banks. As Keohane and Nye write, "These actors arc important not only because of their activities in pursuit of their own interests, but also because they act as transmission belts, making government policies in various countries more sensitive to one another."[3] Certainly the lending practices of banks, insofar as they have contributed to the origin or exacerbation of the debt problem, have increased the mutual sensitivities of the United States and major sovereign debtors and complicated considerably the U.S. government's pursuit of policy objectives in relation to those countries. Complex interdependence, Keohane and Nye remind us, means that power in foreign policy must be exercised through a political bargaining process. The participation of banks in the process, with their own interests to pursue, can significantly affect outcomes. Through their ongoing commercial decisions vis-à-vis sovereign debtors, the banks affect the general foreign-policy environment – and their effects may substantially alter the issues of salience for policy or the nature and scope of policy options available to government officials.

In short, high finance intersects with high politics. Strategic interactions between governments – the traditional focus of foreign-policy analysis–are increasingly linked with strategic interactions between public and private institutions in both debtor and creditor countries. The roster of players in the "money game" is rich and varied.

From the point of view of a major creditor country, such as the United States, the principal impact of these interactions is on the number and substance of potential "linkages" in foreign policy (that is, the joining for bargaining purposes of otherwise unrelated policy instruments or issues). Policy makers may be forced to make connections between different policy instruments or issues that might not otherwise have been felt necessary; opportunities for connections may be created that might not otherwise have been thought possible. In a world of complex interdependence power in foreign affairs is very much a function of a government's "linkage strategies" – that is, how well the government can make use of instruments or issues where its bargaining position is relatively strong in order to promote or defend interests where it is weaker.[4] These considerations shape the analysis to follow. My discussion will center on the implications that the global debt problem holds for the linkage strategies of the United States as a major creditor country.

I start by introducing some general considerations that bear on the relationship between international debt and the foreign-policy capabilities of the United States. The discussion is deliberately abstract, in effect creating a set of empty analytic "boxes." In the following three sections I attempt to put some empirical content into those boxes by looking at a limited selection of recent experiences – the Polish debt crisis of 1981–82, the Latin American debt crisis (or crises) of 1982–83, and the International Monetary Fund quota increase of 1983. In all three cases the cutoff point for discussion is mid-1984. The treatment in the three sections is necessarily cursory but nonetheless suggestive. I conclude the article with a brief summary of conclusions and implications for the politics of stabilization of the international financial system.

Debt and foreign policy

The intersection of high finance and high politics in the context of the global debt problem highlights the potential for reciprocal influences between governments and banks.[5] Changes that banks induce in a government's decisionmaking environment may alter foreign-policy capabilities; in turn, a government may be able to supplement its power resources by relating bank decisions, directly or indirectly, to foreign-policy considerations. Either form of influence could affect the power of a government in foreign affairs, but neither can be predicted a priori with any confidence.

Some observers do not doubt that the banks' lending practices in Eastern Europe and the Third World have weakened the ability of the U.S. government to realize its foreign-policy preferences. By their decisions affecting sovereign borrowers – to lend or reschedule debt? to which countries'? how much? when? at what cost? under what conditions (if any)? – banks establish priorities among capital-importing nations that amount, in effect, to decisions about foreign aid. And since these decisions may depart quite substantially from the goals and priorities of official policy, they can significantly hamper the effectiveness of existing policy instruments. The government may find it more difficult to support or reward its friends or to thwart or punish its enemies. Generous debt assistance to countries with poor records on human rights, for instance, or to regimes that support international terrorism may easily undermine efforts by Washington to exercise influence through the withholding of public moneys: states deemed vital to U.S. security interests may be seriously destabilized if they are suddenly "red-lined" by the financial community. Contends Congressman Jim Leach of Iowa, "The large money center banks are the true foreign aid policy makers of the United States."[6]

Clearly, there is some truth in this charge. As the *Banker* has commented, "bankers assume a political role...through the mere act of lending on any large scale. The provision of finance to sovereign borrowers...immediately involves financial intermediaries in passively helping to determine priorities."[7] But equally clearly, it is an exaggeration to argue, as Jack Zwick and Richard Goeltz do, that therefore "private banks are effectively making United States foreign economic policy."[8] Public officials still make policy. What has changed is the nature of the constraints and opportunities that now confront those public officials in the international arena. It is not at all clear that these changes are, on balance, necessarily disadvantageous for foreign policy.

In the first place is an empirical question: How serious is the problem? The fact that banks *may* establish priorities at variance with the goals of official policy does not mean that they inevitably *will* do so. Banks naturally pay attention to foreign relations in the ordinary course of business and, to some extent at least, tailor their commercial decisions accordingly. It is obvious that insofar as movements of finance correlate positively with movements of the diplomatic barometer, bank decisions may actually enhance rather than diminish the effectiveness of existing foreign-policy instruments. The drying up of private credits in Chile, for example, undoubtedly strengthened the Nixon administration's campaign against Salvador Allende after his election in 1971. Current U.S. government support of such strategic allies as South Korea and the Philippines is undoubtedly reinforced by a continued high level of bank lending there. Sometimes private and public interests converge and sometimes, as we shall see in the discussions of Poland and Latin America, they do not.

Furthermore, even where bank operations appear to diverge from official priorities, the resulting impacts on policy effectiveness could turn out to be little more than trivial. To say that policy *could* be affected is not to say that any such influences are necessarily *significant*. That remains to be seen.

Finally, and most importantly, any impacts on foreign-policy capabilities will depend a great deal on the policy linkages that bank decisions generate. Debt-service difficulties are a natural breeding ground for policy linkages. When key sovereign borrowers get into trouble, Washington may feel forced to respond, however reluctantly, with some sort of support – in effect, to underwrite the debts in some way. Some borrowers are considered crucial for U.S. interests and cannot be ignored. As the Senate Foreign Relations Committee staff has written, America "has important security interests in other debtor countries.... It can hardly afford to stand by and watch the economies of these countries collapse, or to have their governments undermined politically by financial difficulties."[9] In other cases borrowers may stimulate concerns about possible repercussions on the health and stability of American banks or the wider financial or economic system. Either way, debtors gain a new kind of political leverage to extract from the U.S. government concessions that might not otherwise be obtainable. These concessions may be financial, trade, or even political.

Financial concessions are the most familiar variety. Back in 1979, for example, at a time of near-bankruptcy, Turkey was able to exploit its strategic position within NATO to persuade the United States and other Western allies to come to its rescue with pledges of special assistance totaling nearly one billion dollars. Subsequent aid packages for similar amounts were pledged for 1980 and 1981 as well.[10] Likewise, more recently, financial assistance has been arranged for several Latin American debtors when they had trouble meeting their obligations to foreign creditors.

There may also be trade concessions, which have been increasingly mooted lately despite strongly protectionist domestic pressures. U.S. policy makers have been forced to acknowledge the obvious linkage between trade and finance – that import liberalization by industrialized countries may be the only way to enable major borrowers to earn their way out of their debt morass. In the words of Meyer Rashish,

> We must face the interdependence of the financial and trading systems. External debt only makes sense if the borrower has a reasonable prospect for servicing the debt by exporting goods and services to the lenders .... Ultimately, we, the lenders, will be confronted with a decision – either to open our markets in order to provide outlets to the borrowers for their exports, thus generating revenues in the borrowing countries for debt repayment, or to yield to protectionist pressures and be forced to deal with resultant financial failures .... [11]

Finally, even political concessions may be felt necessary. In 1977 the Senate Foreign Relations Committee staff worried that "there appears to be a direct correlation between economic hardship and political repression in many countries. The Carter Administration may therefore have to choose between pressing its international human rights effort, and supporting creditor demands for drastic austerity programs that can only be achieved at the expense of civil liberties in the countries that undertake them."[12] In the first half of the 1980s this dilemma confronted the Reagan administration as well, in Latin America and elsewhere. In the case of the Philippines, for example, Asia's second-largest debtor to the banks, the United States clearly chose to maintain support for the martial-law "New Society" of Ferdinand Marcos on broad foreign-policy grounds. U.S. policy makers justified strict Filipino controls, including the continued stifling of political opposition, by the need to preserve the financial viability of an important strategically.

Can we generalize about the implications of these policy linkages for the foreign-policy capabilities of the United States? I shall stress three considerations that bear on this question. First is the nature of the concessions themselves. Concessions are not necessarily disadvantageous. In fact, the constraints and opportunities created for the U.S. government's linkage strategies in individual instances may actually enhance rather than diminish U.S. power in foreign affairs. The constraints imposed by the debt problem are evident – the risks of possible financial disruption, loss of export markets, souring of political relations, or instability or disorder in areas of vital strategic importance. But opportunities to promote U.S. policy preferences may be generated as well. The key is whether debt-related concessions may be regarded as advantageous *outside the immediate area of financial relations*. Do the concessions, while effectively underwriting debt, also serve to reinforce other U.S. policy interests? Or do they work at cross-purposes, demanding trade-offs among interests? Concessions will be disadvantageous only when inconsistent with other foreign-policy objectives.

Of crucial importance in this connection is whether U.S. relations with troubled debtors are adversarial or not. Where relations are adversarial, as they were in the case of Poland, efforts to cope with debt-service difficulties may actually undermine the effectiveness or credibility of other policy measures, weakening U.S. power in foreign affairs. Concessions in such instances may be regarded as disadvantageous. But where relations are nonconflictual, as in Latin America, helping others can, under appropriate circumstances, also help ourselves. Concessions may be of mutual benefit and may even lead to matching political or economic concessions from debtor governments. In such instances a potential certainly exists for promoting foreign-policy preferences.

A second consideration bearing on policy linkages is whether, or to what extent, the government may be able to supplement its own power resources by relating bank decisions, directly or indirectly, to foreign-policy considerations. Insofar as bank behavior has a significant influence on the general foreign-policy environment, public officials could, hypothetically at least, try to alter that behavior to conform more closely to policy objectives – in effect, to deploy the banks as part of the government's broader linkage strategies. How effective are such attempts likely to be in reality?

In principle the international activities of American banks are supposed to be independent of politics. But in practice political considerations are rarely absent, even if in most instances they remain fairly subtle. At times they become overt. The U.S. government has long had an arsenal of policy instruments available in order, when deemed appropriate, to relate the commercial activities of U.S. banks to foreign-policy questions: among those instruments are loan guaranty programs, restrictions, and outright prohibitions as well as prudential supervision, general monetary policy, and "moral suasion." During the years of the Cold War, for instance, loans to communist governments were strictly prohibited on political grounds (as they still are to Cambodia, Cuba, North Korea, and Vietnam). The prohibitions were reversed with the coming of detente. At their summit conference in 1972 Leonid Brezhnev and Richard Nixon declared that "the USA and the USSR regard commercial and economic ties as an important and necessary element in the strengthening of their bilateral relations and thus will actively promote the growth of such ties." Quite clearly the activity was to include promotion of credits from American and other Western banks. By mid-1982 U.S. banks alone had built up an exposure in Soviet-bloc countries in excess of $7 billion. The exposure of all Western (including Japanese) banks was in excess of $60 billion.

Other examples can also be cited. Prohibitions on lending were employed in support of UN sanctions against Rhodesia, for instance, in the years following that colony's unilateral declaration of independence as well as in support of Washington's economic sanctions against the revolutionary government of Iran during the months of the hostage crisis. Conversely, in early 1982 the State Department went out of its way to make plain its hope that banks would keep open their credit lines to Yugoslavia, lest that nation be driven closer to the Soviet Union.[13]

But the fact that such efforts are not unprecedented does not mean that they are uncontroversial. On the contrary, any attempts by Washington to influence bank behavior on foreign-policy grounds – either to encourage or discourage lending, to individual debtor countries or in general – have tended to generate lively public debate. Some observers, indeed, feel that the only problem is that the U.S. government has not gone far enough to link foreign policy and the commercial decisions of American banks. As Zwick and Goeltz argue, "This step must be taken to preserve not only the financial integrity of the banking system but also the discretion of the Government in the formulation of foreign policy."[14] For others, Robert Russell among them, the problem is precisely the opposite: "It would seem better to keep public policy and private investment at arm's length to the extent possible.... Injecting foreign policy considerations into private bank decision making... seems likely to exacerbate both the problems of foreign policy and bank soundness."[15]

The key issue here is effectiveness. *Can* public officials effectively influence the commercial decisions of banks? In an era when much of the international activity of American banks takes place beyond Washington's direct jurisdictional reach in an almost totally unregulated environment (the Eurocurrency market), the answer is no simple matter. Today most foreign lending takes the form of bank credits booked through financial centers where official supervision is by definition minimal. Moreover, with the evolution of the Eurocurrency market has come a blurring of the strictly national identity of banking institutions. The largest part of bank credits is now the product of syndicates of mixed nationality. The ease and intimacy with which financiers from different countries work together today would have seemed unthinkable, if not treasonous, three-quarters of a century ago. As a result it is difficult indeed for Washington effectively to control or manipulate bank behavior on foreign-policy grounds.

But it is not impossible; government officials are not entirely without leverage. In the first place, while national identity may have become blurred, it has certainly not been forgotten. As Herbert Feis wrote half a century ago, "Bankers are subject to the forces of national feeling as are their fellow men."[16] The men and women who run America's largest banks can still be moved by "moral suasion" when the national interest appears to be at stake. Furthermore, despite the extent of their overseas operations, the banks are still ultimately dependent on a domestic financial base and subject to the influence of domestic monetary policy and prudential supervision. What is implied, however, is that any government attempts at leverage are likely to be effective only within rather broad limits – that is, control is likely to be "loose" rather than "tight." As we shall see, control is especially likely to be loose when the government aims in individual instances to encourage rather than to discourage lending.

The third and final consideration bearing on the question of policy linkages is whether, or to what extent, Washington might be able to supplement its power resources by pursuing policy objectives through the intermediation of a multilateral agency such as the International Monetary Fund – in effect, to deploy the Fund as part of the government's broader linkage strategies. Because of the global debt problem, the IMF has gained considerable leverage over the behavior of both debtor governments and banks. But the Fund itself is subject to substantial leverage from the U.S. government, which still retains unparalleled influence over IMF decision making. In effect, therefore, an opportunity seems to have been created for U.S. policy makers to accomplish indirectly, via the IMF, what they cannot accomplish (or can accomplish only at a higher economic or political cost) on a direct, bilateral basis.

Solidarity suppressed

The Polish debt crisis of 1981–82 provides a particularly apt case for empirical investigation. Rarely in recent American experience have the complex connections between high finance and high politics been quite so manifest. After the rise of the Solidarity trade union movement in 1980, Poland became the touchstone for U.S. foreign policy in Eastern Europe. Yet Washington's ability to exercise leverage over the course of events in that troubled country was plainly compromised by the high level of Western bank exposure in Poland. Polish debt added to the difficulties experienced by the United States in trying to prevent suppression of Solidarity after martial law was declared in December 1981.

Even before December 1981 Polish debt was becoming a problem. As early as 1979 Poland's economy had stopped growing, in good part because of a deterioration of export revenues; and in 1980 and 1981 national income actually dropped at a rate of 5 percent a year. To maintain imports, Warsaw resorted to accelerated borrowing from the West. As a result, between 1978 and 1981 Polish foreign debt increased by nearly half, from under $18 billion to an estimated $26 billion; and its debt-service ratio (the ratio of interest and amortization to export revenues) more than doubled, from an already high 79 percent to an incredible 173 percent.[17] By the start of 1981 it was an open secret that Poland could not meet its scheduled obligations. Warsaw formally notified its creditors in March that it would no longer be able to guarantee debt service.

At the time the attitude of the U.S. government was clear: do everything possible to avoid destabilizing the situation inside Poland, and do nothing to jeopardize the achievements of Solidarity. Throughout 1981, therefore, Washington maintained an essentially benevolent posture toward the Polish debt problem. While it contemplated no massive new credits, it did undertake several actions to ease Warsaw's financial difficulties. As early as the previous summer, in an obvious attempt at a linkage strategy, Washington had openly pressured American banks to keep a substantial refinancing loan from failing. (Washington was not alone in this instance: in Bonn the West German chancellor, Helmut Schmidt, personally telephoned the presidents of the three largest German banks to back a similar Polish loan.) And in April 1981 the United States joined with fourteen other industrial nations (later fifteen) in agreeing to postpone for four years $2.3 billion of Polish debt payments due in 1981 to official creditors. In the first week of December, after some difficult negotiations, there followed an agreement among Western banks to reschedule $2.4 billion of commercial debt due in 1981 as well. The concurrence of Western banks was crucial inasmuch as almost two-thirds of Poland's debt–some $16 billion–was owed to private lenders, reflecting a decade's growth in Western bank lending to the East. West German banks held the largest amount–about $6 billion. American banks accounted for about $3 billion.[18] The December 1981 rescheduling was made contingent on Poland's payment of $500 million in interest obligations for the last three months of 1981.

In addition, in the spring of 1981 the Commodity Credit Corporation (CCC) of the U.S. Department of Agriculture raised the interest-rate guarantee for private agricultural export credits to Poland (used to finance grain sales) from 8 percent to 12 percent; this exceptional provision for the Poles was not generalized to any other country. And even as late as early December plans were going forward for $100 million of new CCC credits that would have fully guaranteed, for the first time and for any country, all interest payments as well as principal.[19]

But then came General Jaruzelski's declaration of martial law on 13 December 1981, followed by suppression of Solidarity. Washington's attitude quickly hardened. Western governments immediately suspended talks with the Jaruzelski regime about a possible rescheduling of Poland's 1982 debt to official creditors, at Washington's behest, and numerous other economic sanctions were levied against both Poland and the Soviet Union, including termination of all subsidized food shipments and most U.S. government-guaranteed bank credits to Poland (including the planned new CCC credits), restrictions on Polish fishing rights in American waters, suspension of talks (due to have begun in February 1982) with the Soviet Union on a new long-term grain agreement, and an embargo on materials for Russia's natural gas pipeline from Siberia to Western Europe. The aims of the sanctions were clear – to persuade Poland and its patron the Soviet Union to end martial law, free all political prisoners, and restore Solidarity to its previous domestic status. Pressure would be maintained, the Reagan administration insisted, until these goals were achieved. In the words of the assistant secretary of state at the time. Robert Hormats,

> In these circumstances, our continuing objective is to apply sustained pressure on both Poland and the Soviet Union to have martial law lifted, the prisoners released, and the dialog between the government, the church and Solidarity begun in earnest in a free atmosphere. In short, our goal is the restoration of the process of reform and renewal in Poland.[20]

The impact of the sanctions, however, was diluted by the continuing problem of Poland's debt. For 1982 alone the country was estimated to owe Western creditors a total of $10.4 billion in principal and interest – yet Warsaw had still not even gotten current on the interest due for its rescheduled 1981 debt.[21] Clearly, some additional relief would be required if default were to be avoided, and Washington had no desire to precipitate a Western banking crisis. It was recognized, of course, that the direct exposure of Western banks was not large (certainly not as compared with their exposure in Latin America or the Far East). Of the $16 billion of outstanding bank claims on Poland, almost half (about $7 billion) was guaranteed by creditor governments. Of the $3 billion owed to American banks, the CCC guaranteed $1.6 billion, and the remainder was spread so thinly among some sixty institutions that for most American banks guarantee-adjusted exposure amounted to less than 5 percent of capital.[22] The fear of financial disruption was nevertheless genuine. Who knew what might happen if a major debtor like Poland were compelled to default?

The biggest question was whether a default could be contained. Many U.S. officials were concerned about the possibility of a "domino effect"–a scramble by banks to reduce their exposure elsewhere in Eastern Europe, which might lead to a chain reaction of defaults throughout the region, and perhaps in other areas of the world as well, endangering the entire Western banking structure. The flow of new bank credits to other Soviet bloc countries, as well as to Yugoslavia, had already started drying up as a result of Poland's debt-service difficulties.[23] American policy makers were convinced by their conversations with bankers that their fears of a regional "contagion" were not unfounded.[24] Banks, after all, had their own interests to protect.

Indeed, Washington's concern was such that despite its tough rhetoric, it even started servicing some of Poland's debt itself when Warsaw failed to meet payments due on part of its $1.6 billion of CCC-guaranteed credits beginning in January 1982.[25] In such an instance creditor banks would ordinarily have been required to declare the debtor formally in default in order to qualify for CCC payments. But in this case, for the first time ever, the Reagan administration circumvented the legal requirement by quietly adopting an emergency waiver to avoid triggering cross-default clauses in other bank loans to Poland. In effect, by meeting the CCC's guarantees and then transferring the overdue credits to its own books, the U.S. government unilaterally rescheduled a portion of Poland's debt. Most importantly, it did so *unconditionally*, without extracting any price from Warsaw – no formal default, no attempt to attach Polish assets, not even a public announcement. From a foreign-policy point of view this action was undoubtedly the turning point of the whole affair.

The CCC decision did not go unopposed within the administration. Defense Department officials in particular, led by Under Secretary for Policy Fred Iklé, argued vigorously for maintaining the hardest possible line vis-à-vis Poland, up to and including a formal declaration of default. But the prevailing view among policy makers, reflecting a de facto coalition of the Treasury and State departments, ruled out default under almost any circumstance, for three principal reasons. First was the fear of financial disruption, described above. Second was a fear of political disruption in the Western alliance, reflecting Western Europe's far greater loan exposure in Poland (amounting, in fact, to about three-quarters of all Polish debt). Given that West European banks and governments had so much more of an investment to protect, there was a considerable risk that they might respond favorably to any Polish overture to negotiate a separate deal. American bankers were especially concerned about the prospect. As a confidential working document prepared by one large U.S. bank warned, "There is every reason to believe that European banks and governments would cooperate with the Poles.... There is [therefore] not only a significant probability that such a default action would fail, but it would also impose massive costs on the alliance."[26]

Finally, there was a fear of losing a possible instrument of leverage over the Poles. Policy makers reasoned that by taking over the debt itself, Washington could actually hope to reinforce its pressure on the Jaruzelski regime–"keep Poland's feet to the fire," to quote a leaked State Department memorandum. With new lending at a standstill, Warsaw's interest payments represented a net transfer of financial resources *to the West*. A formal declaration of default, however satisfying to the emotions, would only have relieved the Poles of that burden. The Jaruzelski regime would no longer have had to find precious foreign exchange to meet debt-service obligations to Western banks. Instead, the martial-law regime would have been freed to consolidate its authority with even greater force and harshness. According to one administration official, "keeping the pressure on this way is the real hard line."[27] The view was summarized by Assistant Treasury Secretary Marc Leland:

> What should we do about the debt? Our feeling is that we should try to collect it. The more pressure we can thereby put on the East Europeans, particularly on the Soviet Union, to come up with the funds to help Poland, the better....
>
> To maintain maximum leverage...they should be held to the normal commercial concept that they owe us this money, so they should come up with it....
>
> In this way we hope to maintain the maximum amount of pressure on them to try to roll back the actions of December 13th and to enter into an internal political dialog.[28]

The proof of the pudding, however, is not to be found in the chef's fine words. In practice this "real hard line" proved scarcely effective at all, and it may even have been counterproductive in Washington's attempt to exercise leverage over the Poles. For once having signaled the depth of its apprehensions about default in its decision to pay off CCC-guaranteed credits unconditionally, the U.S. administration actually made itself *more* vulnerable to the threat of financial disruption; and the Jaruzelski regime was not above making veiled hints about possible default as a form of policy leverage of its own.[29] Washington's constraint, in effect, became Warsaw's opportunity. Western bank assets could be held as a sort of hostage, and perhaps a wedge could be driven between the U.S. government and its West European allies. The CCC decision handed the Poles, despite their desperate economic straits, some additional room for maneuver.

At a minimum, the action strained the credibility of the Reagan administration's commitment to sanctions. The key question at the time was why the CCC guarantees were paid off unconditionally. Observers were entitled to ask why no quid pro quo of any kind was demanded of the Poles, for instance, by attaching some of their foreign assets as collateral for eventual repayment. Officials argued that few such assets were available: perhaps a few airplanes and ships plus some meager hard-currency reserves. But their response missed the symbolic value of the opportunity thus lost. Psychologically, the appearance of vacillation by policy makers quickly dissipated the impact of Washington's sanctions. What was left was an impression – right or wrong – that the administration, simply put, was more concerned about a Western banking crisis than it was about the future of Solidarity. Public perceptions at the time were accurately, if colorfully, summarized by columnist William Safire:

> The secret regulation giving the junta extraordinarily lenient treatment makes a mockery of pretensions of pressure.
> In an eyeball-to-eyeball confrontation, the Reagan administration has just blinked. Poland's rulers can afford to dismiss the Reagan rhetoric because they have seen that the U.S. is ready to do regulatory nip-ups to save them from default.[30]

In the end, of course, as we know, the administration achieved few of its goals. Poland neither "came up with the money" nor "rolled back" the actions of 13 December. Martial law was formally lifted after two years, to be sure, but many of its key features still remain, now incorporated into Polish civil law. And while most political prisoners were released in 1984, Solidarity still remains an outlawed organization, replaced by tame government-sponsored trade unions. In short, the process of "reform and renewal" was not restored. Yet, one by one, most of the sanctions imposed so dramatically in 1981 were either eased or eliminated. In July 1983 a new long-term grain agreement with the Soviet Union was announced. In November 1983 the most stringent sanctions directed against the Soviet gas pipeline were lifted, and restrictions on Polish fishing rights were relaxed. And the following month Washington joined other Western governments in reopening the suspended talks with Poland on rescheduling some of its debt to official creditors.

Admittedly, apprehensions about default were by no means the only – or even the most important – reason for such seemingly conciliatory behavior. The Soviet grain agreement, for example, was best understood in terms of President Reagan's 1980 campaign promises to American farmers. Similarly, the easing of sanctions against the Soviet pipeline was most evidently motivated by a desire to improve roiled relations with Western European allies. Even the reopening of debt negotiations was a response, at least in part, to growing discontent on the part of other Western governments that viewed Washington's continued refusal to talk as essentially self-defeating. From the time discussions were first cut off, following the declaration of martial law, Warsaw had suspended all payments of interest as well as principal on its official debt (although interest payments to banks were maintained, albeit with delays). As a result, U.S. allies began to argue, Poland was actually able to save precious foreign exchange, in effect at the expense of Western taxpayers. Other Western governments had initially gone along with the suspension of negotiations.[31] But as the situation dragged on, they eventually started to lobby the Reagan administration vigorously for agreement to an early resumption of talks.[32]

It must also be admitted that the easing of sanctions might have occurred even *without* apprehensions about default. The use of economic sanctions in pursuit of foreign-policy goals is a tricky business in the best of circumstances. The success rate of sanctions varies greatly, depending among other factors on the type of goals being pursued.[33] The more modest the policy changes targeted, the greater is the probability of success. Conversely, in instances where "major" policy changes have been sought, as in the Polish case, the evidence suggests that economic sanctions have rarely been effective. Washington was fighting an uphill battle. Even with *no* Western bank exposure in Poland, the Reagan administration would have experienced difficulties in trying to prevent the suppression of Solidarity.

Poland's debt, therefore, cannot be blamed per se for the evident failure of the administration's policies. Washington's leverage in the situation was at best limited. But debt can be blamed for adding to the administration's difficulties, by undermining the effectiveness and credibility of its other policy initiatives. The effort to avoid Polish default worked at cross-purposes with other policy interests. I would not go so far as to argue with John Van Meer that the default issue thus "allowed the tyranny of the debtor to replace the tyranny of police-state Communism as the key to Western calculations."[34] But I would contend that debt helped to undercut whatever power the U.S. government might otherwise have had in its confrontation with Warsaw. The negative effect of the linkage may have been only marginal, but it was not trivial. Foreign-policy capabilities were indeed diminished.

The debt storm in Latin America

In Latin America the situation was different. Although here too Washington feared financial disruption – indeed, such fears were rampant – the U.S. government's foreign-policy capabilities in the region were, for a time at least, enhanced rather than diminished by the sudden explosion of a debt crisis in 1982. The principal reason seems to have been that U.S. relations with the major Latin borrowers were at the time not adversarial, as they had been with Poland. Initially, this general sense of cooperation created an opportunity for Washington, through a series of financial concessions, to win considerable goodwill and influence for itself at comparatively little economic or political cost. Over time, however, these gains proved essentially transient. As the region's debt crisis wore on, and particularly as Washington's efforts to revive private lending to Latin America proved largely ineffective, relations grew gradually more strained. Two years after the crisis began, in mid-1984, the continued goodwill of our hemispheric neighbors appeared to depend on new concessions of some kind from Washington. Foreign-policy leverage, it seemed, needed nourishment to remain effective.

The roots of the Latin American crisis go back at least to the late 1960s, when a number of governments made a deliberate decision to finance accelerated domestic investment with borrowing from private and public institutions abroad – "indebted industrialization," in Jeff Frieden's phrase.[35] Then came the first oil shock, which spurred further borrowing to pay for higher-priced oil imports, and after 1976 a trend toward negative real interest rates in global financial markets, which whetted appetites even further. By the time of the second oil shock, at the end of the decade, many Latin governments had seemingly become addicted to foreign finance, and debt was piling up at a dizzying pace. By mid-1982 total debt in the region had swollen to an estimated $295 billion, including $90 billion in Mexico, $75 billion in Brazil, $30 billion each in Argentina and Venezuela, and $15 billion in Chile.[36] Two-thirds of the total was owed to private banks.

The banks, not surprisingly, were getting worried. Two years earlier they had already begun to shorten the maturities of new credits, hoping to position themselves to get their money out quickly should something go wrong. The policy would have been rational for any one creditor acting alone. With all banks doing the same thing, however, the practice merely added to the risks of lending in the region by greatly increasing the aggregate amount of debt that repeatedly had to be rolled over. By mid-1982, according to Morgan Guaranty Bank, the debt-service ratio (including amortization) of the five largest debtors had grown to 179 percent for Argentina, 129 percent for Mexico, 122 percent for Brazil, 116 percent for Chile, and 95 percent for Venezuela.[37] Interest payments alone for these five were expected to eat up from 35 to 45 percent of export revenues. Clearly, a storm was brewing.

The first threatening clouds appeared in early 1982, during the Falklands/Malvinas conflict, when Argentina began to fall behind on its debt service because of the British government's freeze of Argentinian assets in London. But the really rough weather did not set in until the middle of the year, when political and economic uncertainties in Mexico sparked a major capital flight. In June 1982 the Mexicans had still been able to raise $2.5 billion in the Eurocurrency market, albeit with considerable difficulty. By August, new private lending had ceased, the peso had to be devalued, and the government was forced to announce that it could no longer meet its scheduled repayments of principal on external public debt. Suddenly, one of the Third World's two largest debtors seemed on the edge of default, and the tempest had broken.

Like the cavalry of old the U.S. government rushed to the rescue (but this time *on behalf* of the Mexicans), quickly providing more than $2.5 billion of emergency assistance – $700 million via the Federal Reserve's swap arrangement with the Bank of Mexico, $1 billion from the Commodity Credit Corporation, and an advance payment of $1 billion on oil purchases by the Department of Energy for the U.S. Strategic Petroleum Reserve. In addition, the Treasury Department's

Exchange Stabilization Fund (ESF) and the Federal Reserve together contributed about half of a $1.85 billion bridging facility provided through the Bank for International Settlements. And Washington also backed a proposed $3.9 billion credit from the International Monetary Fund.[38] By September the Mexican situation seemed, for the moment at least, in hand.

But the storm kept spreading. Largely because of the Mexican crisis, bank confidence sagged, new private lending dried up throughout Latin America, and soon other debtors in the region were finding themselves deep in trouble too. More rescue packages had to be organized. In the latter part of 1982 the ESF made some $1.23 billion available to Brazil. And in December and January bridging loans were arranged through the Bank for International Settlements, with substantial U.S. participation, for both Brazil and Argentina.[39] In addition banks were constantly exhorted by Treasury and Federal Reserve officials, in the name of the public interest, to resume their lending in the region despite already high exposure levels. Typical was a well-publicized speech by Federal Reserve chairman Paul Volcker in November 1982, in which he laid great stress on easing the difficulties of major Latin borrowers. "In such cases," he said, "new credits should not be subject to supervisory criticism."[40] Translated, his message was that considerations of banking prudence would not be allowed to prevail over the objective of keeping key debtors afloat. On the contrary, banks were reportedly threatened with closer scrutiny of their books if they did *not* go along with fresh loans for countries like Mexico.[41] The pressures on the banks were not inconsiderable.

Nonetheless, they proved largely ineffective. Banks simply did not regard it as in their own interest to increase their exposure in the region significantly. In 1980 and 1981 total bank claims in Latin America had risen by some $30 billion a year. In the eighteen months from June 1982 to December 1983, by contrast, they increased by no more than $9 billion in all, less than the total of so-called "involuntary" lending arranged in connection with parallel IMF credits (discussed below), meaning that there was absolutely no "spontaneous" new lending at all.[42] Accordingly, no important borrower in the region was able to maintain debt service without some difficulty. All had to enter into protracted and difficult negotiations with private and public creditors, and most were forced to initiate painful – as well as politically risky – domestic austerity measures. In the words of Pedro-Pablo Kuczynski, "Undoubtedly, the interruption of significant new lending by commercial banks has been the major stimulus for such measures."[43]

Still, Washington continued to press the banks for a more accommodating attitude. One example was Argentina in late 1983 after that country's presidential election. According to the *New York Times*,

The bankers ... said that they were already coming under pressure from the United States ... to aid the country's new democracy after nearly eight years of military rule. Many are resigned to making some concessions.

"We don't want to look like the bad guys," one American banker said.[44]

Officials also urged the banks to consider limiting the interest rates they charged on loans to hard-pressed debtors. In another well-publicized speech in early 1984 Federal Reserve chairman Volcker suggested that "one of the things certainly worth looking at is what arrangements could be made so that one particular important threat to their financial stability, the continued rise in interest rates, could be dealt with."[45] What he had in mind was some kind of a cap on interest payments, with any excess of market rates over the cap being added to loan principal ("capitalization"). A specific proposal along these lines, for a cap tied to real interest rates, was floated by the Federal Reserve Bank of New York at a meeting of central bankers in May 1984, though nothing ever came of the idea.[46]

Moreover, to encourage the banks Washington continued to put its own money where its mouth was, for example in the U.S. contribution to the IMF quota increase, finally approved by Congress in late 1983. Another example was the decision of the Export-Import Bank in the summer of 1983 to extend new loan guarantees of up to $1.5 billion to Brazil and $500 million to Mexico – the largest such package ever proposed by the Bank. William Draper, the Bank's president, made no secret of official intentions to prompt further private lending in these and other Latin countries. "We expect the proposed financing will strengthen the Mexican and Brazilian recovery," he said, "by acting as a catalyst for continuing support by the international financial community."[47] What was highly unusual about this initiative was that, unlike most guarantee proposals, these guarantees were not tied to specific projects. Clearly, the U.S. government wanted to send a signal.

It is not difficult to discern why the government took such an active role in the crisis. Latin America has always been regarded on broad foreign policy grounds as a region vital to U.S. national interests. From the moment Mexico's difficulties began, there was never any doubt among policy makers that America's own security, not just Mexico's, was at stake – that the United States too would be threatened by serious economic or political instabilities south of its border. Nor was there any doubt that the contagion might spread to other Latin American nations as well. Washington simply could not ignore the potential for disorder in its own backyard that financial default might have sparked. As the *Economist* commented at the time,

> How to resolve these difficulties is one of the biggest foreign policy questions facing Washington, for behind Mexico there stretches a line of other burrodollar [sic] debtors. Brazil, Argentina and Venezuela between them owe $140 billion. The United States dare not risk the political consequences of calling default on any of them.... Those in the Reagan administration who have calmly contemplated pulling the plug on Poland's debt, which is only a third of Mexico's, have to recognize that the problem facing them in Latin America is far bigger.[48]

More narrowly, of course, policy makers were also worried about the direct risks to American banks, particularly the large money-center banks, whose loan exposure in Latin America far exceeded that in Poland. For Mexico alone, at the end of 1982, exposure in relation to capital exceeded 40 percent in nine of the twelve largest U.S. banks; taking Latin America's five biggest borrowers (Argentina, Brazil, Chile, Mexico, and Venezuela) together, the exposure of these same dozen banks ranged from a low of 82.5 percent of capital (Security Pacific) to a high of 262.8 percent (Manufacturers Hanover); most banks fell in a range of 140 to 180 percent.[49] The banking system was clearly vulnerable. If Poland had provoked fears of financial disruption, Latin America triggered nightmares.

Finally, there was also concern about U.S. trade interests in Latin America. By 1982 the region had surpassed all but Western Europe as a market for U.S. goods; Mexico alone was America's third-largest customer. Once the Mexican crisis broke, commerce and real-estate markets throughout the American Southwest were seriously damaged.[50] U.S. government officials never tired of stressing how many exports, and hence jobs, would be lost if something were not done for troubled debtors. Washington's motives were neatly summarized by Paul Volcker: "The effort to manage the international debt problem goes beyond vague and generalized concerns about political and economic stability of borrowing countries.... The effort encompasses also the protection of our own financial stability and the markets for what we produce best."[51]

It is hardly surprising, then, that the government would take so active a role. Nor is it surprising, given the reluctance of private banks to resume lending in the region, that Washington's concerns might give debtors the leverage to extract official concessions of some sort. What is striking is how much goodwill and influence were initially generated for the United States, and therefore how much easier it became to realize U.S. foreign-policy preferences. Officials in Washington reported a marked shift on the part of Latin governments toward a more accommodating spirit on various international issues.[52] The United States was now in a position to say, when looking for cooperation, that "we were there when you needed us, now we need you." In Brazil, Washington's efforts to help out financially were reported to have given the United States "more leverage ... than it has enjoyed in more than a decade."[53] Suddenly the Brazilians were willing to talk about problems that had been roiling relations with the United States for years, most important among them nuclear policy and military cooperation. Likewise diplomats noted that Mexico toned down criticisms of U.S. policy in Central America; and also the Department of Energy was given permission to buy even more oil than originally agreed, at attractive prices, for the U.S. Strategic Petroleum Reserve.[54] In the short run Washington's investment in these countries' financial stability seemed to yield significant foreign-policy dividends.

But it did so only in the short run. As the debt crisis wore on, and domestic resistance to prolonged austerity measures grew, Latin governments were bound to grow more impatient. Riots and street demonstrations, as well as election results, suggested a decreasing tolerance for belt tightening in the region. Latin governments increasingly asked why the burden of adjustment should fall entirely on the shoulders of the debtors. What was first perceived as generosity on Washington's part came to be viewed more as miserliness and insensitivity.

U.S. concessions, it was noted, had been strictly financial and, for the most part, strictly short-term. (All of the loans included in the emergency packages for Argentina, Brazil, and Mexico, for example, had to be repaid within one year.) No trade concessions had been forthcoming at all – indeed barriers to key imports from Latin America, such as copper and steel, were on the rise – while at the same time rising U.S. interest rates, universally blamed on the Reagan administration's huge budget deficits, were adding to current debt-service burdens. Washington's emphasis on domestic "stabilization" translated, to Latin observers, into nothing more than retarded development, increased unemployment, and declining living standards. The risk was that this changing mood might eventually push Latin American governments toward alienation and confrontation with the United States. It could even lead to their replacement by regimes far less friendly to U.S. economic or security interests.

By 1984 the straws were in the wind. In May the presidents of four of the region's largest debtors – Argentina, Brazil, Colombia, and Mexico – meeting in Buenos Aires issued a joint statement warning that they "cannot indefinitely" accept the "hazards" of current approaches to the debt crisis. Expressing concern over the effects of "successive interest rate increases, prospects of new hikes and the proliferation and intensity of protectionist measures," they cautioned that "their peoples' yearning for development, the progress of democracy in their region and the economic security of their continent are seriously jeopardized." [55] Such sentiments were emphasized when eleven Latin debtors met in Cartagena, Colombia, in June and concluded with a plea to the United States and other creditor countries, as well as to the banks, to accept a greater share of the burden of adjustment. The dramas of Argentina and Venezuela, both of which had deliberately chosen to go into arrears on their debt rather than submit to harsh austerity programs, attested to the decline of patience in the region. And other regional governments were also considering a reordering of their domestic and foreign priorities. As a report of the Americas Society pointed out, "In virtually every Latin American and Caribbean country, there are major pressures to turn inward, . . . to turn their backs on existing obligations, and to look to solutions which stress a higher degree of protection and greater state control." [56] Washington's initial foreign-policy dividends in the region seemed after two years of crisis in danger of evaporating without a new investment of financial or trade concessions.

The role of the IMF

One issue raised by the gradual erosion of Washington's early gains in Latin America was whether the government's power resources, in the context of the global debt problem, could be supplemented through the intermediation of the International Monetary Fund – in effect, by using the IMF as an instrument of U.S. linkage strategy. The U.S. government's attitude toward the IMF changed dramatically over the first years of Ronald Reagan's presidency. Initially cool to any significant or rapid enlargement of Fund resources, the Reagan administration eventually became one of its strongest advocates. This policy shift appears to have reflected, at least in part, an altered perception of how a strong IMF might serve U.S. interests. Yet here too, as the crisis wore on, Washington's short-run gains in foreign policy came to be significantly eroded.

During its first year and a half the administration actively sought to discourage any early increase of Fund quotas (which determine a member country's borrowing privileges). The Seventh General Review of Quotas, which raised quotas by half, from approximately SDR 40 billion to SDR 59.6 billion (the value of the SDR in recent years has ranged from $0.95 to $1.05), had just been completed in November 1980, and another review was not formally required before 1983. Yet it was clear that the IMF's usable resources would soon be running low. Mostly as a result of the second oil shock and the subsequent recession in the industrial world, deficits of non-oil developing countries grew enormously, from $41 billion in 1978 to $89 billion in 1980 and $108 billion in 1981. Net borrowing from the Fund rose quickly, from under SDR 1 billion in 1978 (new loan commitments less repayments) to SDR 6.5 billion in 1980 and SDR 12 billion in 1981.[57] As early as the spring of 1981 the Fund's managing director, Jacques de Larosiere, was warning of an impending threat to the Fund's own liquidity position. Without a new quota increase, he insisted, the Fund itself would need to borrow as much as SDR 6–7 billion annually to meet all of its prospective commitments.[58]

Nonetheless, the Reagan administration remained adamant. Its opposition was to a large extent rooted in a critical view of IMF lending practices as they had developed during the presidency of Reagan's predecessor, Jimmy Carter, particularly after the second oil shock. In early 1979 the Fund's Executive Board had issued a revised set of guidelines on conditionality that put new emphasis on the presumed "structural" nature of many members' balance-of-payments difficulties. The traditional period for a Fund standby arrangement had been one year. But the revised guidelines extended standbys for up to three years if considered "necessary," confirming the trend toward longer adjustment periods already evident in programs financed through the Extended Fund Facility, first introduced in 1974, and the Supplementary Financing Facility (Witteveen Facility) established in 1977.[59] To the Reagan administration these changes smacked of development lending in disguise totally inconsistent with the Fund's intended role as a limited revolving fund for strictly short-term assistance for balance-of-payments problems. The administration was especially critical of large, low-conditionality loans, such as the SDR 5 billion credit arranged for India in late 1981, and was not at all eager to facilitate more such loans in the future.[60] At most, the administration stated, it might be prepared to contemplate a quota increase of perhaps 25 percent, and even for that there was no particular hurry.

But then came the Mexican crisis–and with it the dramatic shift in U.S. policy. Suddenly the administration *was* in a hurry. Not only did it now pronounce itself in favor of an accelerated increase of quotas (and a more sizable one at that), it wanted to go even further. At the Fund's annual meeting in Toronto, in September 1982, Treasury Secretary Donald Regan suggested "establishment of an additional permanent borrowing arrangement, which would be available to the IMF on a contingency basis for use in extraordinary circumstances."[61] And in the following months the secretary pushed hard for formal consideration of such a proposal, surprising observers who had become accustomed to administration recalcitrance on the size and timing of any new IMF funding. Said one private banker, "Maybe there's a problem out there that we don't know about."[62]

With Washington no longer dragging its heels, the details did not take long to work out. In February 1983 the IMF announced agreement on an increase of quotas from approximately SDR 61 billion to SDR 90 billion–a rise of 47.5 percent. Furthermore, the Fund's General Arrangements to Borrow (GAB) were to be tripled, from approximately SDR 6.4 billion to SDR 17 billion, and for the first time made available to finance loans to countries outside the Group of Ten – thus converting the GAB into precisely the sort of emergency fund that Secretary Regan had earlier suggested.[63] The U.S. share of these increases, which at prevailing exchange rates came to a total of some $8.5 billion ($5.8 billion for a quota increase, $2.7 billion for the GAB expansion), was finally approved by Congress, after protracted lobbying by the administration, in November 1983. In the following month the enlargement of Fund resources formally came into effect.

A policy shift of this magnitude demands some explanation. At one level the explanation was simple: there really *was* a problem "out there" – the threat of a chain reaction of defaults in Latin America and elsewhere that could have plunged the whole world into the abyss of another Great Depression. The Reagan administration did not want to go down in history alongside the Hoover administration; in any event, there was a presidential election coming up in 1984. It had to do *something*, and the IMF was there. It seemed only natural to use what was already available.

At a deeper level, however, the explanation was more complex. Use of the IMF, some administration officials began to believe, might actually serve U.S. policy interests more effectively than attempts to deal with debt problems on a direct, bilateral basis. "A convenient conduit for U.S. influence," one high-level policy maker called it.[64] Any effort by Washington itself to impose unpopular policy conditions on troubled debtors would undoubtedly have fanned the flames of nationalism, if not revolution, in many countries. But what would be intolerable when demanded by a major foreign power might, it seemed, be rather more acceptable if administered by an impartial international agency with no ostensible interests other than the maintenance of international monetary stability. Likewise, the Fund could apply pressures to banks, to maintain or increase lending exposure in debtor countries, that the banks might have resisted had they come from national officials. As the country with the largest share of votes in the Fund (just under 20%), and as the source of the world's preeminent international currency, the United States still enjoys unparalleled influence over IMF decision making – in effect, an implicit veto on all matters of substantive importance. Through its ability to shape attitudes at the Fund, therefore, Washington could hope to exercise more leverage over debtors and banks indirectly than seemed feasible directly, and at a lower political cost.

On the issue of policy conditions the Fund had begun to tighten its standards even before the Mexican crisis, owing in good part to the Reagan administration's active disapproval of earlier lending practices. By the summer of 1982 its institutional attitude had already shifted back toward more rigorous enforcement of domestic austerity measures. Thus once the storm hit, Fund officials needed no persuasion to take on the role, in effect, of the "cop on the beat" – setting policy conditions for new or renewed credits and ensuring strict compliance with their terms. Following the Mexican crisis nearly three dozen countries fell into arrears on their foreign loans; and over the next year nearly two dozen of them found it necessary to negotiate debt relief of some sort with private or official creditors, or both. In all of these negotiations the Fund became a central arbiter of access to, as well as of the terms of, new external financing. Creditors began to insist formally that a debtor country, as a precondition to their own financial assistance, first conclude a standby arrangement with the IMF subject to upper-credit-tranche conditionality. Many restructurings were also made conditional upon continued compliance with Fund performance criteria; and on occasion disbursements of new loans were even timed to coincide with drawings scheduled under Fund stabilization programs.[65] The IMF spelled financial relief and, as such, exercised considerable leverage over the policies of troubled debtors.

That leverage, however, was clearly resented. Throughout the Third World the IMF became a dirty word. And the hand of the United States behind the IMF was increasingly evident to many. In this respect, too, Washington's gains proved essentially transient. Initially, U.S. interests were served by letting the Fund get out in front. But as the crisis persisted the veil tended to wear thin, and criticism came to be focused more and more on the perceived power behind the throne – the United States. This criticism helped stimulate the widespread and growing dissatisfaction with what was viewed as Washington's miserliness and insensitivity toward the problems of debtor countries.

The story is similar in the IMF's relationship with the banks. Initially, it seemed, U.S. interests might also be served by the Fund's ability to apply effective pressure on banks. Washington's own exhortations to banks to resume lending in Latin America or elsewhere fell, as already indicated, largely on deaf ears. Not so, however, with the Fund, which in several key instances successfully demanded specific commercial commitments as a precondition for its own financial assistance. In connection with its $3.9 billion arrangement for Mexico, for instance, which took some four months to negotiate, the Fund refused to go ahead until each of the country's fourteen hundred creditor banks first agreed to extend additional credit amounting to 7 percent of their existing loan exposure (amounting overall to some $5 billion in new bank money for Mexico).[66] Likewise before approving a loan of $5.5 billion for Brazil, in February 1983, the IMF laid down a number of requirements for the banks: restoration of interbank credit lines to $7.5 billion; new loans of $4.4 billion; rollover for eight years of $4 billion in principal due in 1983; and maintenance of short-term trade credits at $8.8 billion.[67] Similar conditions were attached to agreements with other countries as well, most notably Argentina and Yugoslavia.[68] The IMF's message to the banks was clear. In the words of de Larosière, "Banks will have to continue to increase their exposures . . . if widespread debt financing problems are to be avoided."[69]

Not that all the banks were eager to cooperate – not at first, at least. Many, pursuing their private interests, simply wanted to get their money out as quickly as possible. Managing Director de Larosière had to "knock heads together," as one official phrased it.[70] But eventually the banks themselves came to recognize the crucial public interest in such "involuntary" lending in critical cases. Said one prominent U.S. banker: "It was clear that somebody had to step in and play a leadership role." [71] Said another: "The IMF sensed a vacuum and properly stepped into it."[72] Could anyone imagine the U.S. government taking such interventionist initiatives? In the first place, Washington had no jurisdiction over the banks of other countries (which accounted for well over half of total loan exposure). And second, even American banks would have been highly reluctant to take such direction straight from government officials. U.S. banks have traditionally placed great store in their arm's-length relationship with authorities, insisting vehemently on their right as competitors in the marketplace to make their own commercial decisions. In this respect, too, U.S. interests seemed to be served by letting the Fund get out in front.

But this gain also proved to be essentially transient. What the banks were willing to tolerate in certain critical cases, they would not accept as a general rule. Certainly they might again be prepared, should similar emergencies arise in the future, to surrender temporarily some of their traditional operating autonomy. But they would not accept a permanent role for the IMF in the management of private international credit flows, and increasingly they reasserted their right to go their own way. Washington could not long rely on Fund intermediation with the banks either.

Conclusion

The limited selection of experiences that I have briefly examined suggest some interesting insights into the foreign-policy implications of international debt for the United States as a major creditor country.

In the first place, it is evident that America's foreign-policy capabilities are indeed affected, and that the influence is in fact significant. In Poland and Latin America alike, bank priorities turned out to be substantially at variance with the goals of public officials in Washington; and as a result the effectiveness of existing policy instruments in each region was to some extent compromised. For banks, the main goal was simply to avoid default while limiting the extent of any new loan exposure. In Poland this attitude made it more difficult for the Reagan administration to make its economic sanctions stick. In Latin America it undercut efforts to keep friendly governments financially secure without new concessions from Washington. In neither case could the negative impacts on policy effectiveness be described as trivial. In both cases money did indeed "talk" – but not to U.S. advantage.

Moreover, it is evident that in the complex intersection of high finance and high politics the government had at best only limited influence over the behavior of banks, given the traditional arm's-length relationship of the public and private sectors in the United States. The limitation was most obvious in Latin America, where despite both carrots (e.g., new Export-Import Bank loan guarantees) and sticks (e.g., threatened closer scrutiny of books), banks could not be induced to resume significant new amounts of voluntary lending. Bank behavior in this instance was not difficult to understand: Why should bankers accept the risk of increasing exposure more than they themselves consider prudent? In fact, much more could have been expected only if bankers could have been persuaded that vital national interests were at stake.

Third, it is evident that policy linkages were indeed created, though their consequences for U.S. power differed in the two instances. In Poland debt acted marginally as a constraint limiting Washington's ability to influence the ultimate outcome of events. Despite its proclaimed opposition to martial law the Reagan administration felt compelled by its concern over default, when push came to shove, to make a key financial concession to Warsaw – namely, the unconditional decision to pay off CCC-guaranteed credits as they came due. As a result Washington's leverage over Poland was reduced. The United States may not have been "conquered." but it did not "win" either.

In Latin America, by contrast, foreign-policy capabilities were initially enhanced after the Reagan administration acted to help out some of the region's major debtors. The crises of Mexico and others offered Washington, at least for a time, an opportunity to gain considerable goodwill and influence for itself in return for only limited financial concessions. The difference between the two cases was that in one U.S. relations were nonconflictual while in the other they were adversarial. In both cases avoidance of default was treated as an important policy goal. When dealing with an enemy like the Jaruzelski regime, this goal tended to handicap the realization of U.S. foreign-policy preferences, since it undermined the credibility of other policy measures; when dealing with our friends in Latin America, on the other hand, it meant that we were able to help ourselves even as we helped others. The lesson seems clear. Linkage strategies bred by the debt issue are more apt to work when the interest we share with others in avoiding default is reinforced by other shared economic or political interests.

Even in Latin America, however, the initial foreign-policy gains proved essentially transient. As the region's debt crisis wore on, Washington's ability to determine the course of events there declined. Additional concessions, it appeared, would be necessary if the U.S. government wished to retain its newly won leverage. Power in such situations seems to be a wasting asset. Repeated investment is needed to avoid the depletion of goodwill and influence.

Finally, it is evident that any tendency toward power depletion in such situations can only for a time be countered by reliance on the intermediation of a multilateral agency. In the immediate aftermath of the Mexican and other Latin rescues, the IMF gained considerable leverage over the behavior of both debtor governments and banks; and insofar as Washington still retained paramount influence over IMF decision making, U.S. interests, it seemed, could be served more effectively via the Fund than on a direct, bilateral basis. This realization helps to explain the sudden policy shift by the Reagan administration in mid-1982 in favor of a strong, well-endowed IMF. Money seemed to talk best indirectly. But this too, in time, proved to be an essentially transient opportunity.

All of these considerations have very serious implications for the politics of stabilization of the international financial system. The global debt problem appears to suggest an urgent need for some actor, or set of actors, to provide the "collective good" of stability. According to the popular "theory of hegemonic stability," that stabilizing role can be played only by a hegemonic power – meaning, in the contemporary era, the United States. But if my analysis is correct, America does not seem to have the capacity to play that role. Only at the outset of the series of crises in Latin America was the United States able to exercise significant influence over the course of events. The financial collapse of Mexico and others in effect threw those nations willy-nilly into the arms of the only country capable of organizing rescue packages on short notice (just as Poland's financial difficulties pushed it more under the influence of its patron, the Soviet Union). Emergency conditions gave Washington leverage. But once the emergency was past, even this gain was eroded. American power has been insufficient to stabilize the system.

In part, this insufficiency explains why Washington was prepared to try relying to the extent it did on the intermediation of the IMF. Why accept the constraints of operating indirectly through a multilateral agency unless power resources to act directly are inadequate? Unfortunately, even this tactic proved effective only in emergency conditions.

The key to the dilemma lies in the U.S. government's limited influence over the banks, which can best be understood in terms of the continuing dialectic between the "market" and the "state." At Bretton Woods, in 1944, an international monetary regime was designed that in principle excluded private markets from decisions affecting the creation of international liquidity. But the gradual emergence of the Eurocurrency market as a major souce of balance-of-payments financing to a significant extent "privatized" the creation of liquidity.[73] In effect, the market moved beyond the influence of any one state, even that of the former hegemonic power. The pendulum can swing back only if the jurisdiction of states catches up once more with the domain of the market – which means *collective* action by governments in lieu of reliance on a single stabilizer. The United States, it would appear, can no longer win the game on its own.

Notes

1 Karin Lissakers. "Money and Manipulation," *Foreign Policy* no. 44 (Autumn 1981), p. 123.
2 Meyer Rashish, "Bank Lending Overseas Has Become Intertwined with Politics." *American Banker*, 15 January 1982, pp. 4–5.
3 Robert O. Keohane and Joseph S. Nye, *Power and Interdependence: World Politics in Transition* (Boston: Little, Brown, 1977), p. 26.
4 Ibid., pp. 30–32.
5 Surprisingly, there have been few formal attempts by scholars to explore systematically, in a foreign-policy context, the question of reciprocal influences between governments and banks. But see Jonathan David Aronson, *Money and Power: Banks and the World*

Monetary System (Beverly Hills: Sage, 1977); Janet Kelly, "International Capital Markets: Power and Security in the International System," *Orbis* 21 (Winter 1978), pp. 843–74; and J. Andrew Spindler, *The Politics of International Credit* (Washington, D.C.: Brookings, 1984).

6 As quoted in *New York Times*, 11 November 1982, p. D3.
7 "The Politics of Banking," *Banker*, September 1977, p. 21.
8 Jack Zwick and Richard K. Goeltz, "U.S. Banks Are Making Foreign Policy," *New York Times*, 18 March 1979.
9 U.S. Senate, Committee on Foreign Relations, *International Debt, the Banks, and U.S. Foreign Policy*, A Staff Report (Washington, D.C., 1977), p. 7.
10 *IMF Survey*, 18 May 1981, p. 162.
11 Rashish, "Bank Lending Overseas," p. 6.
12 Committee on Foreign Relations, *International Debt*, p. 7.
13 "State Department Calls in U.S. Bankers to Warn against Cutting off Yugoslavia," *Wall Street Journal*, 22 April 1982, p. 33.
14 Zwick and Goeltz, "U.S. Banks Are Making."
15 Robert W. Russell, "Three Windows on LDC Debt: LDCs, the Banks, and the United States National Interest." in Lawrence G. Franko and Marilyn G. Seiber, eds., *Developing Country Debt* (Elmsford, N.Y.: Pergamon, 1979), pp. 263–264.
16 Herbert Feis, *Europe, the World's Banker, 1870–1914* (1930; rpt. New York: Norton, 1965), p. 468.
17 U.S. Treasury and State Department Fact Sheet on Polish Debt, in U.S. Senate. Committee on Foreign Relations, Subcommittee on European Affairs, *The Polish Economy*, Hearings, 17 January 1982 (hereafter *Polish Economy Hearings*), p. 12.
18 *New York Times*, 5 December 1981.
19 Interview, U.S. State Department, August 1984.
20 Robert Hormats, "Statement," *Polish Economy Hearings*, p. 4.
21 Treasury and State Department Fact Sheet, *Polish Economy Hearings*, p. 12.
22 Ibid., pp. 11–12. Bank capital is defined to include shareholders' equity, undistributed profits, and reserves for contingencies and other capital reserves – in essence, what a bank would have after paying off depositors and creditors.
23 See, for example, *New York Times*, 26 May 1982. p. D1.
24 Interview, U.S. State Department, August 1984.
25 *New York Times*, 1 February 1982, p. 1.
26 "Polish Default: Bankers' Perspectives on the Issues," 22 March 1982, p. 4.
27 As quoted in *New York Times*, 1 February 1982, p. 1.
28 Marc Leland, "Statement," *Polish Economy Hearings*, p. 7.
29 See, for example, *New York Times*, 8 June 1982, p. Dl.
30 William Safire, "Payoff for Repression," *New York Times*, 1 February 1982.
31 Interview, U.S. State Department, August 1984.
32 See, for example. *New York Times*, 30 July 1983, p. 34.
33 Gary Clyde Hufbauer and Jeffrey J. Schott, *Economic Sanctions in Support of Foreign Policy Goals* (Washington: Institute for International Economics, 1983). pp. 73–75.
34 John Van Meer, "Banks, Tanks and Freedom," *Commentary*, December 1982, p. 17.
35 Jeff Frieden, "Third World Indebted Industrialization: International Finance and State Capitalism in Mexico, Brazil, Algeria, and South Korea," *International Organization* 35 (Summer 1981), pp. 407–31.
36 Pedro-Pablo Kuczynski, "Latin American Debt," *Foreign Affairs* 61 (Winter 1982–83), p. 349.
37 Morgan Guaranty Trust Company, *World Financial Markets*, October 1982, p. 5.
38 For detail, see Paul A. Volcker, "Statement." in U.S. House, Committee on Banking, Finance and Urban Affairs, *International Financial Markets and Related Problems*, Hearings, 2 February 1983, Appendix I, pp. 80–81.
39 Ibid., pp. 81–83.

40 Paul A. Volcker, "Sustainable Recovery: Setting the Stage," Remarks before the New England Council, Boston, 16 November 1982 (processed), p. 17.
41 *New York Times*, 14 January 1983, p. D1.
42 Bank for International Settlements, *International Banking Developments, Fourth Quarter 1983* (Basle, April 1984).
43 Pedro-Pablo Kuczynski, "Latin American Debt: Act Two," *Foreign Affairs* 62 (Autumn 1983), p. 24.
44 *New York Times*, 5 November 1983, p. 46.
45 As quoted in ibid., 13 May 1984, p. 1.
46 Ibid., 11 May 1984, p. D2.
47 As quoted in ibid., 18 August 1983, p. 1.
48 *Economist*, 21 August 1982, p. 11.
49 William R. Cline, *International Debt and the Stability of the World Economy*, Policy Analyses in International Economics no. 4 (Washington, D.C.: Institute for International Economics, September 1983), p. 34.
50 *New York Times*, 6 December 1982, p. D9.
51 As quoted in ibid., 4 June 1983, p. 29.
52 Interviews, U.S. Treasury. November 1983 and January 1984.
53 *New York Times*, 15 November 1982, p. D1.
54 *Miami Herald*, 30 August 1982.
55 *New York Times*, 21 May 1984, p. D1.
56 Western Hemisphere Commission on Public Policy Implications of Foreign Debt, *Report* (New York: Americas Society, February 1984), pp. 19–20.
57 *IMF Survey*, 6 February 1984, p. 40.
58 See, for example, ibid., 18 May 1981, p. 152.
59 Ibid., 19 March 1979. pp. 82–83.
60 Ibid., 23 November 1981, p. 365, for the India loan.
61 As quoted in ibid., 4 October 1982. p. 327.
62 As quoted in *New York Times*, 12 December 1982, sec. 3, p. 1.
63 The United States for a time held out for a slightly smaller quota increase, to only SDR 85 billion, but was unsuccessful. It *was* successful in preventing expansion of the General Arrangements to Borrow to the figure of SDR 20 billion favored by European governments. See *Economist*, 22 January 1983, pp. 62–63.
64 Interview, U.S. Treasury, January 1984.
65 *Recent Multilateral Debt Restructurings with Official and Bank Creditors*, IMF Occasional Paper no. 25 (Washington. D.C., December 1983), pp. 10, 26.
66 *Economist*, 19 February 1983, p. 89.
67 *New York Times*, 1 March 1983, p. Dl.
68 Ibid., 22 January 1983.
69 As quoted in *New York Times*, 9 January 1983, sec. 3, p. 10.
70 Ibid.
71 Ibid.
72 Ibid.
73 Benjamin J. Cohen, "Balance-of-Payments Financing: Evolution of a Regime," in Stephen D. Krasner, ed., *International Regimes* (Ithaca: Cornell University Press, 1983), pp. 315–36.

7   Developing-country debt[*]

A middle way

Source: *Princeton Essays in International Finance*, No. 173, May 1989.

Introduction

More than half a decade after Mexico's dramatic financial collapse in the summer of 1982, the debt problem of developing countries remains as intractable as ever. The good news is that the threat of a global banking crisis appears to have been successfully contained – at least until now – by the multilateral strategy quickly put together under U.S. leadership in the first months after the Mexican rescue. The bad news is that many third-world countries continue to stagnate, frustrated and resentful, under the burden of their outstanding contractual obligations. It is now widely acknowledged by scholars and practitioners alike that the LDC debt dilemma will not be truly resolved until the severe cash-flow strains on debtors can be durably eased in a context of renewed economic development. And that, everyone seems increasingly prepared to agree, will require reform of the prevailing strategy to reduce in some way the large sums now owed to creditors. At the International Monetary Fund's most recent meeting in Berlin in September 1988, even as authoritative a body as the Fund's Interim Committee "expressed concern that many countries continue to face severe financing and adjustment difficulties" and called for "more forceful actions . . . to reduce the stock of debt" (Interim Committee, 1988, par. 4). The core question is: how can reform of the prevailing strategy best be accomplished?

Among advocates of debt reform, two main schools of thought have emerged over time. On one side are the "evolutionists," who argue that reform can best be promoted through extension and refinement, rather than replacement, of the prevailing case-by-case strategy, retaining in particular its emphasis on initiatives that are both voluntary and market-oriented. The original 1982 strategy has already evolved substantially, they point out, first with the celebrated Baker Plan of 1985, then with the so-called "menu approach" initially introduced in 1987. A smorgasbord of imaginative schemes for debt reduction has already been developed through direct negotiations between creditors and individual debtors and, in

---

* This essay has benefited from the comments and suggestions of Sheldon Boege, Norman Fieleke, Alvin Goldman, Joanne Gowa, Gerald Helleiner, J. David Richardson, Jeswald Salacuse, and an anonymous referee. All the usual disclaimers of course apply.

selected instances, implemented. These schemes may or may not include elements of outright debt relief, which is understood here to entail measures that effectively reduce not only the nominal stock of conventional debt in the present but also the discounted value of total contractual obligations in the future. They encompass direct or indirect conversions of various kinds (debt-for-equity, debt-for-debt, even debt-for-nature), as in the major package negotiated with Brazil in 1988, as well as straight debt buybacks, as in the deal worked out for Bolivia in 1987. The evolutionist approach, not surprisingly, attracts most bankers and public officials. It was commended by the Interim Committee in September 1988. It has also been endorsed by such scholars as William Cline (1987) and John Williamson (1988), as well as by blue-ribbon panels such as the Economic Policy Council of the United Nations Association of the United States (1988) and the Inter-American Dialogue (1989). And it forms the basis for the debt program of the new Bush administration, first outlined by Treasury Secretary Nicholas Brady in March 1989 (Kilborn, 1989).

On the other side are the "creationists," who by contrast plead for more comprehensive and if necessary mandatory solutions, usually involving establishment or designation of some public institution to implement a concerted approach to the problem. Creationists do not believe that serious progress on debt is likely to occur in the absence of organized collective action. Creationists also put more emphasis than do evolutionists on measures of outright relief rather than merely conventional reduction of debt. The school originated after 1982 with the early plans of Peter Kenen (1983) and Felix Rohatyn (1983), each proposing the launching of a new multilateral facility to aid in consolidating LDC obligations. More recently, there has been a flood of ideas along this line – not just from scholars and academics (e.g., Sachs and Huizinga, 1987; Islam, 1988), as might be expected, but also from present and former international officials (Sengupta, 1988; Rotberg, 1988), members of the U.S. Congress (LaFalce, 1987; Pease, 1988), commercial bankers (Robinson, 1988), and even the finance ministry of Japan (Sumita, 1988). Few of these schemes, with their emphasis on institutional innovation by the public sector, have much in common with the laissez-faire tone of the private-market initiatives favored by evolutionists.

Is there any middle ground between these two contending schools of thought?[1] The purpose of this essay is to suggest that there is indeed a middle way to debt reform – a practical approach that retains the creationists' stress on the need for collective action while not abandoning the evolutionists' preference for voluntary and market-oriented solutions. Like other advocates of reform, I start from the premise that creditor-debtor relations today amount to something akin to a non-zero-sum game – a strategic interaction among many players with an unexploited opportunity for joint gain. The now standard argument for this premise is summarized briefly in section 2. The remainder of the essay is concerned with the question of how to realize that joint gain.

Section 3 opens the discussion with an explanation for the unsatisfactory outcome of the current strategy, contending that it is a direct result of underlying configurations of economic and political power in creditor-debtor relations.

Section 4 suggests reasons why creationists are correct in insisting that no significant change in the current outcome can be expected without organized collective action to promote revision of the prevailing approach. Imaginative institutional innovation does appear to be required to achieve genuine debt reform. Yet a concerted approach need not be inconsistent with differentiated solutions that remain voluntary and market-oriented, as advocated by evolutionists. Section 5 spells out what a reformed strategy might look like, arguing that a middle way between the evolutionists and the creationists can best be found in an international mechanism for debt relief organized on the model of Chapter 11 of the U.S. Bankruptcy Code. The essential feature would be a new agency – the International Debt Restructuring Agency – established to provide a framework for the negotiated resolution of LDC debt-service difficulties on a flexible case-by-case basis consistent with the interests of all the parties concerned. The approach would be comprehensive, but individual arrangements would remain to be worked out through direct bargaining by creditors and debtors.

An unexploited opportunity for joint gain

The argument that there is an unexploited opportunity for joint gain proceeds from the obviously skewed distribution of the burden of adjustment that has resulted from creditor-debtor bargaining until now. For the most part, debtors rather than creditors have borne the bulk of losses under the prevailing strategy, through stunted growth and reverse resource transfers. While in principle all parties involved are supposed to share the burden, in practice most attention has been given to IMF-sponsored or -monitored domestic "stabilization" programs for the debtor nations, complete with tough policy conditionality and rigorous enforcement of internal and external performance criteria. The capital-market countries have done little to ease developing-country debt-service burdens, apart from agreeing at the June 1988 Group of 7 economic summit to consider some mild relief measures for the poor countries of sub-Saharan Africa, where most debts are owed to official creditors. Nor have commercial banks yet made many direct concessions of any significance to the middle-income debtors in Latin America or elsewhere, apart from frequent reschedulings of maturities as they come due, occasionally accompanied by limited amounts of so-called "concerted" (involuntary) new lending and some modest reductions of interest margins. A number of smaller banks, it is true, have formally accepted losses via write-offs or sales at discount in the growing secondary market for LDC paper. In most cases, however, bankers still insist on holding debtors to their full contractual obligations while continuing to carry loans on their books at 100 percent of face value.

It can be argued that the banks have paid a price indirectly: the financial markets have effectively discounted their LDC paper for them by bidding down the value of bank equity instead. The persistently low quotations for the shares of America's big money-center institutions – despite a five-year boom in the stock market up to October 1987 – have been widely attributed to their heavy third-world exposure, especially in Latin America (Makin, 1987; Sachs and Huizinga, 1987). That price was finally implicitly acknowledged in the spring of 1987 when U.S. banks, led by Citicorp, began a massive buildup of their previously meager loan-loss reserves. But it must be remembered that, even with these additional provisions (mostly created via transfers from bank equity), there has been no substantial forgiveness of third-world debts. As David Rockefeller wrote in the summer of 1987, "This transfer of funds – and that is all it is – has not cost the banks a penny. It does not reduce the obligations of the debtor nations, nor will it diminish the efforts by the banks to recover all the interest and principal represented by their current loans." Developing countries are still expected to do most of the adjusting, whatever the prospects for their future debt-service capacity.

Creditors therefore continue to treat most debtors as effectively illiquid rather than in any sense insolvent. That is, no matter how severe the debtors' present cash-flow strains may be, their longer-term ability to service debt is assumed to be fundamentally unimpaired. Debtor nations may have borne a heavy burden until now, it is argued, but that is part of the adjustment of policies and performance necessary for the improvement of their economies. The key, these countries are told, continues to be patience: ultimately their development will resume if only they keep playing by the rules. Given time, domestic-policy reforms will lead to higher levels of exports and output growth, gradually shrinking the *relative* weight of their external debt obligations and sparking, it is hoped, some "spontaneous" new foreign financing as well. With perseverance, in other words, their efforts to restore creditworthiness and reverse the net outward transfer of resources will sooner or later pay off.[1]

More than half a decade onward, however, as even some of the most determined debtors find themselves caught in what Krueger (1987, p. 163) has labeled a "low-growth, high-debt-service trap," this argument is beginning to wear thin. The real tragedy of the prevailing strategy, as Krueger and others (Sachs, 1986; Dornbusch, 1987) have pointed out, is the extent to which it discourages investment in debtor countries, thereby depriving them of the very means they need – an expansion of productive capacity – to help them earn their way out of their difficulties. In macroeconomic terms, the obligation to pay full debt service requires a corresponding reduction of domestic expenditures in order to release real resources for transfer abroad. In budgetary terms, the obligation requires extra public revenues in order to pay foreign interest costs. In practice, therefore, debtor governments must undertake some combination of spending cuts and tax increases, both of which fall especially hard on domestic capital formation. The result has been a cut in investment rates in highly indebted countries from above 25 percent of gross domestic product before 1982 to under 15 percent in more recent years – in some cases barely enough, at the present pace, to maintain the existing capital stock (American Express Bank, 1987, pp. 6–7). Is it any surprise, then, that the debt problem has proved so intractable? The prevailing strategy virtually condemns debtor countries – even those committed to serious policy reforms – to frustration and failure. For many if not most debtors, it may fairly be contended, we are really talking about something closer to insolvency – call it de facto insolvency – than to mere illiquidity.[2]

In such circumstances, a strong case can be made that at least in some situations creditors as well as debtors would be significantly better off with a

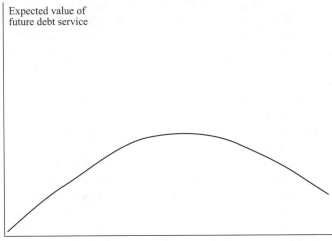

Figure 7.1 The debt relief Laffer curve.

cooperative strategy of debt relief. The logic of the case has been most elegantly summarized by Krugman (1988), using what he calls the "debt relief Laffer curve," which relates the expected value of a country's future debt service to the nominal value of its present foreign debt (see the accompanying figure). At relatively low levels of debt, nominal claims can be expected to be fully repaid. But as liabilities accumulate, the possibility of nonpayment is likely to grow, owing in particular to the exigencies of the low-growth, high-debt-service trap, to the point where any further additions to a country's debt stock could reduce its capacity to meet all future contractual obligations. In Krugman's words:

> Just as governments may sometimes actually increase tax revenue by reducing tax rates, creditors may sometimes increase expected payment by forgiving part of a country's debt. . . . Arguments that debt relief is in everyone's interest are, in effect, arguments that countries are on the wrong side of the debt relief Laffer curve (Krugman, 1988, pp. 11–12).

In view of the persistence of the cash-flow strains of so many LDC debtors since 1982, it seems reasonable to conclude that a good number of them are indeed on the wrong side of the debt relief Laffer curve.

Explaining the current outcome

In learn how debtors can get back on the correct side of the debt relief Laffer curve, we must begin by asking what *explains* the decidedly uneven distribution of the burden of adjustment that has been evident until now. This means asking why debtors have, in effect, consented to playing the game on creditors terms. Why have they chosen not to "defect" by repudiating their liabilities or otherwise refusing to acknowledge their outstanding contractual obligations? Most developing countries have been careful, no matter how hard-pressed, to preserve their lines of communication with other major players and, as much as possible, abide by the results of creditor-debtor negotiations, however unfavorable. Dornbusch (1987, p. 15) likens the outcome to a mugging. If so, debtors have collaborated fully with their muggers.

But collaboration is not cooperation, whatever lip service is paid on the creditor side to multilateralism in the current strategy. Collaboration implies acquiescence at best, coercion and threat at worst – hardly the same as a voluntary process of reciprocal adjustment in pursuit of mutual benefit. For this reason, I regard characterizations of the outcome that use the word "cooperation" – even with qualifiers – as misleading. For one example, see Kahler (1986, p. 26), who proposes the phrase "cooperation without reform." For another, see *The Economist* (1987, p. 46), where the debt problem, among all international economic-policy issues, is described as "the best example of successful cooperation," albeit "of course, at the expense of the debtor countries." The point is aptly, if inadvertently, captured by the official historian of the IMF (De Vries, 1987, p. 220) when she remarks that the "cooperative" strategy adopted in 1982 "was worked out in conjunction with officials of the governments of industrial members ... of other major institutions ... with private commercial bankers, and *with the acceptance* of the authorities of the debtor members concerned" (emphasis supplied).

Three hypotheses, not mutually exclusive, may explain debtor behavior:

a. At the subjective level of "cognitive dynamics," an explanation might be found in the perceptions and values of key players. Debtors may share with creditors a commitment to certain essential norms (standards of behavior defined in terms of mutually accepted rights and obligations).

b. Within debtor countries, an explanation might be found in the demands of domestic politics. Home governments may acquiesce in the prevailing strategy because collaboration with creditors abroad corresponds most closely to (or conflicts least sharply with) the interests of currently dominant political elites.

c. At the international level, an explanation might be found in the distribution of bargaining power among the key players arrayed around the negotiating table. Debtors may play the game on creditors' terms because, in effect, they are coerced or bribed to do so.

Of these hypotheses, the least persuasive is the first. Clearly, belief systems are important in shaping attitudes toward transactions conducted in the marketplace, where standards of behavior and property rights are well established in practice and law. Policymakers in debtor countries, especially the more technically minded officials in the central banks and finance ministries, are undoubtedly influenced by an economic culture that puts a high premium on market-based norms – particularly sanctity of contract and nonpoliticization of commercial relations.

But *how much* do such ideas matter in determining the ordering of LDC preferences? The evidence does not permit us to infer that the prevailing economic culture plays more than a marginal role in shaping debtors' perceptions of their interests.

The principal evidence is the obvious dissonance between the words and the deeds of LDC policymakers, which hardly suggests that they have been motivated by a sincere belief in the essential rightness of creditor demands for full satisfaction of contractual obligations. Quite the contrary. Virtually from the moment Mexico's crisis broke in 1982, LDC leaders have made a point of proclaiming their opposition to the prevailing rules of the game, which they clearly feel are biased against their interests. While initially there may have been inertia in at least some debtors' perceptions – much in the manner of cartoon figures who, running off a cliff, hang suspended in midair before finally plummeting downward – it took little time for a different *gestalt* to dominate the public utterances of policy-makers. Debtor governments denounce market norms as unfair or even iniquitous with such vigor and persistence that it is difficult to believe these utterances represent mere posturing for domestic or international advantage.

Yet even as debtor governments protest the rules as a matter of principle, in practice they uphold the norms of sanctity of contract and nonpoliticization of exchanges. They seek more rights, but they do not deny the fact of obligation. Established values do appear to have some operative force. The question is: how independent is that force from other, more objective factors?

One view, following the political scientist Charles Lipson (1981), attributes genuinely independent influence to market norms, institutionalized in what amounts to an international "regime." The standard definition of a regime among international-relations scholars is a set of "implicit or explicit principles, norms, rules, and decisionmaking procedures around which actors' expectations converge in a given area of international relations" (Krasner, 1983, p. 2). Even before the Mexican crisis, according to Lipson, a distinctive and reasonably well articulated regime had evolved for dealing with LDC debt problems that embodied most of the elements of what later became known as the multilateral debt strategy. But, as Lipson (1986a, 1986b) himself concedes, most of the cooperation has taken place on the creditor side, among commercial banks and between them and public institutions. On the debtor side, a considerable amount of leverage has had to be exercised by the governments of capital-market countries and especially the IMF to gain LDC compliance with creditor terms. This does not suggest that debtors have really operated from the same premises as creditors or shared the same expectations.

The alternative view is more likely, that the influence of market norms is more instrumental than independent; it derives from other factors rather than operating separately from them. Generally, where there is no normative consensus, under-lying power configurations will emerge. Norms become merely one means for the strong to legitimate their dominance over the weak – a rationale, in effect, for vested interests. The advantage to the strong of established values is that they put the burden of proof on those who would change them. For countries without the resources to alter outcomes unilaterally, the result is a Catch 22. To be persuasive they must establish credentials (a good reputation), but to establish credentials they must conform, or at least appear to conform or to wish to conform, to the very values they are committed to changing. Hence the illusion that market norms have independent operative force. The reality, it seems evident, is that they function mostly as a reflection of fundamental power relationships in the political game at home and between debtors and creditors abroad, supporting the second and third of the hypotheses suggested above.

Studies of the politics of adjustment within debtor countries show the importance of domestic distributional struggles in determining the "will and capacity" of governments to play the game on creditors' terms (for a survey, see Haggard and Kaufman, 1989). Stabilization programs generate conflicts among societal forces. As the political scientist, Robert Kaufman (1986, p. 193), has written, "In a world composed of many interest-maximizing economic groups...attempts to transfer the costs of stabilization onto others will be the norm rather than the exception." The acquiescence of many developing nations to the multilateral debt strategy can be traced directly to the ability of locally dominant elites to accomplish just such transfers, thereby evading most of the pain of austerity. By insisting on upholding basic market norms in relations with creditors abroad, these nations hope to avert any radicalization of the politics of income distribution at home.

It is no accident that the heaviest burden of adjustment in most debtor countries has fallen on the groups that are least well positioned to influence the course of government – unorganized laborers, peasant farmers, small businessmen, civil servants, and urban or rural marginals. They lack the options usually available to more powerful domestic interests. Private industrialists, large landowners, managers of parastatal enterprises, and the military can often use their influential voices to extract special treatment from policymakers at home or to win exemption from taxation or repressive economic policies. Many are also able, *in extremis*, to take their movable assets elsewhere – otherwise known as capital flight. The more successful the elites have been in exercising these options, the less pressure they have put on debtor governments to seek a change in the rules of the game.

At the international level, too, the practical importance of power has been abundantly clear. Ever since the third world's recent debt difficulties began, commercial bankers (often backed by their home governments and the IMF) have not hesitated whenever possible to exploit the potential for side payments or sanctions to shape outcomes to their advantage. Creditors have encouraged LDC acquiescence in the multilateral strategy by holding out the prospect of more generous rescheduling terms (e.g., longer grace periods, lower interest margins, relaxed policy conditions) and perhaps even "spontaneous" new financing somewhere down the road. They have discouraged defection by implicitly or explicitly threatening retaliation. Penalties might include not just a cessation of medium- or long-term lending or an interruption of shorter-term trade credits but also the seizure of exports or even the attachment of a debtor's foreign assets, such as commercial airliners, ships, and bank accounts. In Mexico in 1982, creditors used the offer of emergency assistance quite skillfully to strengthen the hand of those in the Mexican government who were opposed to outright default, an option then under serious consideration (Kraft, 1984, p. 4). By 1985, a coherent strategy of "divide and rule" had unashamedly taken hold in the banking community. Carrots, such as multiyear reschedulings or liberalized terms, were dangled before debtor countries as a reward for good behavior; the stick of tough bargaining (or, in the background, damaging punishments) was held over the heads of stubborn recalcitrants (Cohen, 1986, pp. 221–222; Kahler, 1986, p. 29). The investment banker, Pedro-Pablo Kuczynski (1987), accurately describes this as a "containment" strategy. The more successful creditors have been in using the tactics of bribery or coercion, the more pressure there has been on debtor governments *not* to seek a change in the rules of the game.

In short, it is *realpolitik*, not cognitive dynamics, that best explains the behavior of debtor countries. Domestic politics have made it easier for most of these governments to eschew defection, while the international influence of creditors has reinforced rational fears of the consequences of defection. In other words, underlying configurations of power at the domestic and international levels have intersected to make acquiescence appear by far the least-cost choice for policy-makers. Is it any wonder, then, that debtors have collaborated so fully with their muggers? As refracted through the lens of power relationships, collaboration has appeared to be in their best interests, frustrated though they may be.

The need for collective action

Can LDC frustrations be relieved without the organized collective action that creationists advocate to revise the prevailing strategy? Evolutionists argue that genuine debt reform can be attained simply by continuing to rely on direct bargaining between creditors and debtors. But this implies the possibility of a significant shift in the power relationships that have determined the outcome of creditor-debtor negotiations until now. Creditor resistance to major changes in the status quo, particularly if they involve a substantial degree of debt relief, will not be abandoned lightly. The evolutionists' faith in voluntary market solutions is justified only if a new political equation considerably more favorable to debt reform can be expected to emerge more or less naturally over time to replace previous power relationships.

In point of fact, signs of a changing political equation can be found everywhere today – within debtor countries, in the broad balance of power between debtors and creditors, and among those on the creditor side. The dynamics of the strategic interaction are apparently gradually producing "endogenous" alterations of relevant power relationships. However, in none of these relationships do the changes underway seem sufficient on their own to fundamentally alleviate the de facto insolvency of many debtor countries. Hence a case can be made that supplementary "exogenous" efforts will be required to facilitate further progress in negotiations. There is little evidence to support the view that genuine reform can be expected to emerge spontaneously.

Domestic politics in debtor countries

Within debtor countries, the possibility of a shift in power relationships looks especially good. Influential economic and social forces at home are becoming increasingly sensitive to the heavy costs of maintaining full debt service abroad. Local elites may so far have been able to evade the bulk of the burden of adjustment, but as long as domestic economic stagnation persists there are likely to be increasing pressures on debtor governments to seek a change in the rules. The debt trap acts like a pressure cooker to heat up conflicts of interest among societal forces at home, gradually eroding the political basis for continued acquiescence abroad. Privileges and exemptions that can be quietly arranged for favored groups in the short term, despite the need for extra public revenues to pay foreign interest, become steadily harder to preserve in an environment of prolonged austerity and fiscal stringency. Meanwhile, those whose living standards suffer the most from stabilization programs understandably grow more and more resistant to repeated calls for patience and perseverance. The danger of continuing economic stagnation is that the domestic political pot could reach the boiling point, as occurred in Venezuela earlier this year. The specter of disorder or worse may compel debtor governments, whether they like it or not, to look for other more radical solutions to their difficulties – up to and including a unilateral moratorium on all outstanding contractual obligations.

Thus, complacency is not in order. As Putnam (1988, pp. 438–439) has pointed out, national policymakers not otherwise disposed to "voluntary" defection in international relations may nonetheless be forced into "involuntary" defection by politics closer to home. They may not regard defiance of their foreign creditors as rational, but personal and political considerations may leave them little choice, as recent events in a number of developing countries have already demonstrated. A notable example was provided during the 1988 presidential election in Mexico, where ruling-party candidate Carlos Salinas de Gortari, despite his past record of close cooperation with foreign creditors, apparently felt impelled by the pressure of domestic opposition to adopt a strikingly tougher stand on the issue of future debt negotiations.

Nevertheless, however plausible the prospect of involuntary defection, the danger ought not be exaggerated. The pot has *not* boiled over in many debtor countries, despite rising public dissatisfaction with prevailing policies. Debtor governments will undoubtedly continue to feel the heat from their constituents; it is even possible that a growing number will be driven to adopt a more confrontational posture vis-à-vis creditors, like Peru in 1985 and Brazil in 1987. But experience to date does not indicate that enough governments will go this route to produce an "endogenous" shift in bargaining power sufficient on its own to achieve genuine debt reform. Even in Brazil, with its considerable international negotiating leverage, domestic political discontent did not prevent an eventual return to more orthodox policies in 1988 after an eleven-month moratorium on commercial debt service.

The balance of power between debtors and creditors

What about the broad balance of bargaining power between debtors and creditors? Until now, creditors have been remarkably successful in maneuvering most debtors into a policy of acquiescence. The main reason, obviously, is the wide range of financial and legal resources available to creditors, providing them with ample ammunition for their tactics of bribery and coercion. But debtors are not without their own resources to put to work as possible carrots or sticks. Debtors can tempt creditors into concessions by offering side payments – for example, generous debt-equity conversion programs or improved access to domestic lending markets. They can also threaten creditors with some sort of abrogation of full contractual obligations, reflecting one of the most fundamental characteristics of international financial markets: the inability of lenders to directly enforce repayment. Abrogation could mean formal repudiation of all outstanding debts – de jure default, the ultimate weapon. Or it could mean something less dramatic, such as a temporary postponement of amortization or just a short-term moratorium on some or all interest payments. These intermediate actions between full compliance and de jure default are variously described as "partial," "de facto," or, in the phrase of the financial journalist Anatole Kaletsky (1985), "conciliatory" default. As all concerned have long understood, *both* creditors and debtors are constrained to some extent by the potential negotiating leverage of the other – mutual hostages, as it were, to their strategic interaction.[3] As should also be understood, there is no reason to assume that the broad balance of leverage between the two sides will always be the same.

It can be argued that to some extent the balance of leverage has already shifted, despite the past effectiveness of the carrot-and-stick "containment" approach of creditors. The issue here is credibility. Over time, promises of rewards or threats of punishment will almost certainly become less and less persuasive to debtors. Strenuous LDC exertions to improve trade balances have yet to earn a renewal of spontaneous lending by the markets. Even Colombia, the one nation in Latin America that since 1982 has never requested a rescheduling, has experienced great difficulties arranging fresh financing from Western banks. Meanwhile, recent involuntary – or even voluntary – defections by several LDC governments have failed to provoke many damaging penalties from creditors. Not even Peru, which under its Socialist president Alan Garcia has been perhaps the most confrontational of third-world debtors, has seen its exports seized or its foreign assets attached. While there has been a sizable falloff of short-term trade credits for Peru, it began as early as 1982 and was largely completed by the time Garcia took office in mid-1985 (Alexander, 1987, p. 46). Reportedly, the Peruvians can still raise enough trade financing when needed simply by paying slightly more than standard market rates. Many debtors are becoming increasingly skeptical that they have much to fear from creditors.

Two major factors appear to be responsible. One is juridical uncertainty: the limited, not to say dubious, basis in law for the usual list of legal sanctions threatened by creditors against recalcitrant debtors. There are few court precedents establishing the right of international lenders to seize exports or attach the assets of a sovereign borrower. Despite much discussion in recent years, lawyers are still unable to agree on what forms of legal redress, if any, are applicable, or even on whether court judgments could actually be enforced.[4] Awareness has grown, therefore, that the range of resources truly available to creditors may be more restricted than first thought, justifying increasing skepticism on the part of many debtors.

The second factor is the sheer number of debtors that must be induced or pressured into acquiescence in order to preserve the credibility of creditors. When only one or two countries appear to be on the verge of defection – whether involuntary or voluntary – it is not difficult for creditors to make believable promises of rewards or threats of sanctions. Indeed, it is plainly to their advantage to do all they can to cultivate a reputation for toughness. But neither bribery nor coercion is without cost. As the ranks of potential defaulters grow, so too do the potential losses for creditors, should push come to shove. Just as in the so-called "chain-store paradox" of game theory, the benefits of investing in a reputation for toughness may disappear altogether in a scenario of many simultaneous defections (see, e.g., Ordeshook, 1986, p. 453). The historical record, as Lindert and Morton (1989) recently noted, demonstrates an inverse relationship between the number of countries that have been in trouble at any given moment and the willingness of creditors in effect to put their money where their mouth is. Prior to World War 1, the only debtors ever subjected to sanctions were those that defaulted more or less in isolation. During global crises, by contrast, in the nineteenth century and in the interwar period, most nonpayers escaped significant retribution by creditors. Debtor countries today may be forgiven for seeing in this experience a lesson for their own time.

The trouble with bribery is its "demonstration effect." Each debtor country keeps a close watch on creditor negotiations with all other debtors, and any concessions made to one are soon demanded by all. Thus creditors understandably hesitate to spark the process by making concessions in the first place. The trouble with coercion, conversely, is a kind of reverse demonstration effect: to be credible, sanctions imposed on one recalcitrant debtor must be imposed on all. Otherwise, individual debtors will always hope to be treated as the exception rather than the rule, and incentives to defect may actually increase rather than fall. Creditors are not eager to spark this process either, given the number of potential defaulters to be kept in line.

Creditors are not unaware of the erosion of their credibility, and to the extent possible have acted decisively to maintain or reinforce their leverage vis-à-vis debtors. Almost from the first moments following Mexico's crisis in 1982, banks have sought to reduce their vulnerability by gradually bolstering general capital ratios. Even more dramatic was the sudden and massive buildup of loan-loss reserves in the spring of 1987 by banks in the United States, Canada, and Great Britain, triggered by Citicorp, America's biggest bank. Citicorp set a new standard for American lenders, a minimum provision of 25 percent against overall LDC exposure. Subsequently, even higher levels were established by a number of important U.S. intermediaries.

Whatever Citicorp's motivations in triggering this historic round of reserve increases,[5] and whatever the ultimate results of the initiative, the immediate effect in the opinion of many observers was to improve the banking community's strategic position in negotiations with debtors. The fact that the provisions had to be deducted from current earnings under U.S. accounting conventions gave the appearance of record losses for many banks in their 1987 income statements. But these were paper losses only, as indicated earlier, since most of the reserves were created by setting aside a portion of already-existing shareholder equity. In bargaining terms, the main importance of the provisions was that they further insulated future earnings from the impact of possible LDC defections, signaling to debtors that banks could now afford to take some hits, if necessary.

In the opinion of other observers, however, the effect was less salutory for banks, for several reasons. In the first place, a 25 percent provision is still considerably smaller than the discounts that have recently prevailed in the secondary market for LDC debts, suggesting that yet more reserves will be required to fully insulate future bank earnings against all possible losses.[6] Furthermore, even though future *earnings* may now be better protected, bank *capital* is not. Charges against the banks' new reserves will automatically reduce their capital, as currently measured, requiring them either to market additional equity and sell off existing loans or to apply to the regulators for an exemption from minimum capital requirements. Finally, the possible impact on debtor incentives must be considered. Plainly, one consequence of the 1987 provisions will be to discourage banks from future third-world financing. A higher standard for reserves acts as a tax on new lending by requiring a larger charge against current earnings for each additional credit extended. It will now be harder for bank managers to justify new LDC loans to their shareholders. This, in turn, removes one of the most important bribes that creditors have traditionally dangled before debtors. If the carrot of new money is taken away, LDC policymakers may become even more intransigent.

It is therefore not at all clear that creditors have really been successful in their efforts to reverse the erosion of their bargaining power. Indeed, the ambiguity inherent in this already complex setting is probably becoming greater, not less. Can debtor countries seize the opportunity afforded by this increased ambiguity to gain the upper hand? Do they now have the power to diminish or overcome creditor resistance to major debt reform?

Most potent, of course, would be some form of *collective action* by LDC governments to extract concessions from creditors – some variant of the long-dreaded debtors' cartel. A common front would certainly improve the debtor side's capacity to proffer credible carrots or sticks of its own in future negotiations. If the creditor side did not have to worry about competition among debtors for the most favorable treatment (the demonstration effect), attractive new money packages could more easily be agreed upon. These might include generous exit options or debt-conversion schemes for banks that want "out," or flexible "onlending" or "relending" arrangements for those willing to stay in.[7] Even more to the point, any threat of de jure or de facto default would be far more persuasive if made jointly rather than individually.

Potent as a debtors' cartel might be, however, its likelihood is still remote. Recent experience, particularly in Latin America, demonstrates that serious obstacles block effective coordination among debtors, whatever the rhetoric. The two most fundamental obstacles are (a) the extraordinary diversity of economic conditions and prospects among debtors, which tends to overshadow their common interest in debt relief, and (b) the fact of national sovereignty, which encourages each government to seek the best possible deal for itself. Differences in the timing of financial crises, in foreign strategic relationships, in domestic political systems, and even in the personalities and values of key decisionmakers have presented additional obstacles.

Perhaps the most important obstacle to a debtors' cartel is that from the debtors' point of view formal coordination may not even be necessary and could well be counterproductive. As Kaletsky (1985, p. 63) has written, "The main objection to a debtors' cartel is the same as the one against flagrant repudiation: it would needlessly provoke governmental and public opinion in creditor countries." The cumulative effect of a series of individual initiatives by troubled debtors would be far less provocative but might be almost as potent. Just this has occurred lately, for one reason or another, in both Latin America and sub-Saharan Africa. One by one, more than a dozen governments, including eight of the fifteen classified by the IMF as "heavily indebted," have unilaterally ceased debt service or fallen into serious arrears, thereby saving valuable foreign exchange. Moreover, once in arrears, few of these debtors have managed to find both the will and the means to catch up on their interest payments. Yet creditors have become increasingly reluctant to engage in costly reprisals because of the considerable number of countries involved. Who needs a debtors' cartel when much the same impact can be achieved without the difficulties and risks of formal coordination?

Perhaps the most likely scenario, therefore, at least for the near term, is a continuation of the trend already discernible – collective *inaction* (nonpayment) rather than collective action. And the more the trend persists, *ceteris paribus*, the greater will be the ultimate erosion in the bargaining power of creditors. To that extent, momentum would appear to be flowing to the debtor side. The political equation does seem to be changing.

But is it changing enough? The answer remains in considerable doubt. An ebbing of creditor leverage is one thing; momentum sufficient to compel a fundamental reform of the prevailing containment strategy is quite another. The outcome will depend in good part on which, if any, debtor countries choose to join the ranks of nonpayers. Sustained defaults by three or four of the largest debtor nations would do more to concentrate minds on the creditor side than several times that many individual initiatives by smaller countries. But since we cannot foresee who among the debtors will in time defect, and who not, we cannot be sure that this trend will suffice to alter the broad balance of power in creditor-debtor relations. Realistically, we must admit that the probabilities involved are simply too low to inspire confidence in such a spontaneous solution to the problem. The odds in favor of debtors may now have shortened somewhat, but hardly enough for us to be able to declare *les jeux sont faits*.

The dynamics of creditor preference formation

The scenario of collective inaction affects only the debtor side of the political equation. Much also depends on the creditor side. Can concurrent endogenous changes be expected in creditor perceptions of their interests? If so, are these likely to complement or counteract the accumulating tide of pressures from debtor nations? To answer these questions, we must take a closer look at the internal dynamics of preference formation on the part of creditors. Specifically, we must look at alignments among creditor groups – among banks and between banks and public institutions – and at how these shape or alter the collective strategic interaction of creditors and debtors. How are creditor alignments likely to evolve, given current and prospective developments in broader creditor-debtor relations?

The creditor side is not a monolith. On the contrary, there is tremendous heterogeneity among the hundreds of creditors. Nevertheless, lenders have been remarkably successful in maintaining enough solidarity in debt negotiations to shape outcomes largely to their advantage. What accounts for their success?

At first glance, the answer seems obvious: an instinct for self-preservation. Had LDC debtors not been held to their full contractual obligations back in 1982, widespread defaults might have triggered a wave of bank failures, possibly even a repetition of the financial collapse of the 1930s. But a closer look raises doubt about this simple explanation, since it is evident that not all creditors have been equally threatened by the debt problem. Public creditors can certainly survive a hit on their third-world loans. The viability of national governments is a matter of politics, not mere financial profit and loss, and the same is ultimately true of the IMF and multilateral development banks because of their legal backing by the "full faith and credit" of their respective sovereign members. Only private creditors have been directly at risk, and of these the only truly threatened institutions have been those whose exposure was and continues to be high relative to their capital – which means only the biggest of the commercial banks active in LDC lending. For the large number of smaller institutions with loans well below the level of their own capital, widespread defaults would be painful but not disastrous. For the major international commercial lenders, however – the two or three dozen giants at the peak of the global banking industry – the result could be technical insolvency (unless abridged by a modification of traditional accounting regulations). In reality, then, only these giants have had any serious reason to worry about self-preservation.

This suggests that there is more at work here than appears at first glance. Since it is the giants that have stood to lose the most from concessions to debtors, it is their interests that have been served most directly by the containment strategy in force since 1982. In effect, they have called the tune, even when other creditors with other interests might have preferred a different drummer. Creditor solidarity has been maintained by a decision-making process dominated, however imperfectly, by the needs and preferences of the biggest commercial lenders.

By exploiting two features of their institutional environment, the giants have been strikingly effective. One feature is the oligopolistic and hierarchical structure of the international banking community, which gives larger intermediaries in the banking industry disproportionate influence over their smaller rivals. The other feature is the fragmented and dispersed structure of policy assignments within the governments of the capital-market countries, which generally gives banks disproportionate influence over official attitudes on debt matters. Coordination problems have been suppressed to the extent possible by forming informal transnational coalitions. Diversity of interests has been accommodated, again to the extent possible, by the usual tactics of side payments or sanctions.

Diversity of interests within the industry is only to be expected, given the nature of the LDC loan market. There are differences among banks not only in terms of exposure (absolute or relative to capital) but in a variety of other key respects. They differ, for example, in their commitment to foreign business in general, in the extent of their commercial ties to developing nations in particular, and in the geographic distribution of their third-world activity. As numerous studies have shown (see especially Lipson, 1986a, 1986b; Aggarwal, 1987, Chap. 3), gaining the cooperation of all these contenders, with their diverse interests, on a common strategy vis-à-vis debtors has by no means been easy. For the most part, the industry's giants have successfully suppressed divergences by exploiting competitive advantages. They negotiate terms with each other and with debtors and then seek the ratification of smaller institutions, exploiting the latter's dependence on their bigger brethren for correspondent relationships or other financial services. In effect, bankers play a parallel game among themselves, employing their own separate side payments and sanctions to accommodate industry differences. Local and regional banks can be bribed, for example, by offers of privileged access to interbank credit lines or possible participation in lucrative new lending syndicates. They can be coerced by threats of exclusion from traditional industry networks – "peer pressure," as it is politely known in the trade.

The banking giants' dominance has been reinforced by the fragmented nature of governmental policy assignments in the capital-market countries, which biases official attitudes toward debt in their favor. In all the capital-market countries, primary responsibility for LDC debt issues has been entrusted to finance ministries or central banks rather than to foreign ministries or industry- or trade-oriented agencies. As a result, not surprisingly, highest priority has been accorded to the purely financial aspects of the problem rather than to diplomatic or commercial implications. Relatively little weight has been attached to threats of political disruption or to lost export opportunities in the third world. Public policy has been conditioned most directly by concerns for the safety and soundness of financial institutions; since the largest institutions have been most at risk, their interests have received the most attention. There is no need to invoke conspiracy theory to account for the tacit alliances that have been formed between the big international lenders and their home governments.

Thus, despite differences and coordination problems within the banking industry, creditor solidarity has been maintained by a singular alignment of political forces. Power has centered on the joint preferences of a small number of large banks backed by an equally small number of public institutions. And within this configuration of power, no players have been more influential in shaping creditors' collective behavior than those of the United States – the major money-center banks of New York, Chicago, and California, together with the Federal Reserve and, most important, the Department of the Treasury. Other players on the creditor side generally defer to U.S. leadership in dealing with third-world debt problems (Aggarwal, 1987, Chap. 3). This reflects not only the key role of the dollar as the currency in which most LDC paper is denominated (making the Federal Reserve the de facto lender of last resort in the event of a debt-induced banking crisis) but, even more to the point, the dominant market share of U.S. lenders in the most prominent of the troubled debtor nations, Latin American countries and the Philippines. The bank advisory committees that negotiate with LDC governments traditionally comprise no more than a dozen of a country's largest creditors. This has given America's big money-center intermediaries, backed by the Federal Reserve and Treasury, by far the greatest influence in formulating and managing the prevailing containment strategy (Holley, 1987, pp. 25–26). It is no accident that the strategy was first developed at the Federal Reserve and Treasury Department back in 1982. Nor is it an accident that all the major adjustments in the strategy since then – including especially the Baker Plan, the menu approach, and the new Brady program – have also emanated from Washington. The tune that has been called since 1982 has had a distinctly American ring to it.

The key question is: will other players on the creditor side continue to follow this tune, or could there be changes in political alignments that will significantly revise the ordering of creditor preferences? The answer is not immediately apparent. On the one hand, growing distributional struggles among banks and between them and other interested parties in the capital-market countries are exacerbating strains and coordination problems within the banking industry. Creditor-side alignments are becoming more fluid. On the other hand, it is not clear that this increased fluidity will lead soon to a powerful new coalition that will challenge the dominance of the largest commercial lenders, led by the United States. Here too, as on the debtor side of the equation, change is indeed occurring – but, once again, not necessarily enough to cause fundamental alterations in the rules of the game.

The signs of increasing strains on the creditor side are everywhere. Consider first relations between the big banks and their smaller brethren in the capital-market countries. Local and regional banks have always resented the strong-arm tactics of the giants of the industry. They have been compelled to go along with each successive rescheduling of outstanding syndicated loans and even to participate on a pro rata basis in concerted new credits to troubled debtors. But, as the prospect of de facto insolvency rises for many of these debtors, more and more smaller creditors seem prepared to ignore peer pressure and break ranks. Many, especially those with limited third-world exposure and few other commercial ties to developing countries, are simply getting out. They are selling off their paper in the secondary market or refusing to participate in new reschedulings, forcing larger banks to take over their shares. Others, more dramatically, are writing off substantial portions of their portfolios or working out separate deals with debtor governments. The ability of the major banks to suppress intra-industry differences is clearly in decline.

Even among the majors themselves, disparities in interests and priorities appear to be widening. The Continental European banks have long chafed under the current strategy of rescheduling-plus-concerted-lending favored by the big U.S. banks and the Federal Reserve and Treasury. Under their different regulations, the Europeans would find it less costly to capitalize interest arrears than to keep lending debtors new money with which to service old debt. With their more substantial provisions (mostly well hidden), the Europeans are also more willing to contemplate the idea of outright debt relief. More and more, they too seem prepared to break ranks with the Americans, or at least to talk publicly about the possibility of new approaches. American leadership no longer receives quite the degree of deference that it once did.

Furthermore, divergences are evident in the ranks of the major banks *within* the United States. Citicorp's dramatic, unilateral, and unexpected decision to add to its loan-loss reserves in 1987 provides one example. While other U.S. lenders soon emulated Citicorp, its action was resented by money-center banks less well positioned (because of either lower profitability or greater exposure) to meet what from that time became the 25 percent minimum standard for provisions. Tensions over the issue were exacerbated near the end of 1987 when the Bank of Boston and some other large regionals initiated a second round of increases in reserves to an even higher standard of 50 percent or more of exposure. By early 1988, a distinct cleavage had developed between the big New York institutions (together with the Bank of America), which refused to add yet again to their LDC provisions and the remaining money-center banks of California and Chicago, as well as most regional institutions, which opted for the new higher standard. There is evidence that at least some of big New York banks would have been extremely hard-pressed to find the requisite resources had they tried to go along.

Another example of divergence within the American ranks was the deal Morgan Guaranty Bank negotiated secretly with the Mexican government and announced at the end of December 1987. Under that proposal, Mexico hoped to swap a sizable portion of its bank debt at a discount for newly issued marketable Mexican securities, which were to be backed by U.S. Treasury bonds bought with cash reserves by the Mexican government. Initially, many hailed the deal as a breakthrough in coping with third-world debt problems, because it enabled Mexico (and possibly other countries) to retire some of its bank credits at less than par – in effect "capturing the discount" prevailing in the secondary market. For precisely that reason, however, Morgan Guaranty's plan was greeted with little enthusiasm by most other U.S. money-center institutions, still reluctant to accept formal losses on their LDC portfolios. When the plan was implemented two months later, none of them chose to participate, and the final results fell far short of aspirations. Increasingly, relations among America's major banks appear to be dominated less by thoughts of preserving industry solidarity than by sentiments of *sauve qui peut*.

Finally, sectors *outside* the financial community with their own interests in debtor countries are beginning to express opposition to the prevailing containment strategy. This is especially true of key constituencies in the export sector in the United States and elsewhere as they realize the extent to which the debt trap has cut traditional sales to developing nations. Exporters have had their consciousness raised in recent years. Their anger is directed particularly at the Federal Reserve and Treasury for their apparent bias in favor of financial interests. More and more, exporters are asking that framers of public policy on LDC debt accord higher priority to commercial and even diplomatic considerations, instead of focusing mainly on financial concerns. Pressures are clearly growing to loosen the close, albeit tacit, bank-government alliances that have previously dominated decisionmaking in this area.

Despite all these signs of strain on the creditor side, however, no change can be expected in the effective ordering of creditor preferences unless existing coalitions in the capital-market countries are supplanted by new and even stronger alignments, whether implicit or explicit. Increased fluidity among the players is not enough to alter the political equation significantly: resentments and frustrations must be translated into practical action. The big banks, backed by finance ministries and central banks, are unlikely to abandon their resistance to the idea of major debt reform without a struggle, since it is they who stand to lose the most. In the absence of sufficient leverage on the debtor side, their resistance can be diminished or overcome only with superior use of power from within the creditor side, by means of new tactics of side payments or sanctions to replace those exercised at present by the industry giants. Since such organization is unlikely to occur spontaneously, it can be accomplished only by deliberate political organization amoung other players inside or outside the financial community.

Unfortunately, efforts along these lines to date have not been very fruitful. An early case in point was the so-called Bradley Plan, the well-publicized debt-relief scheme proposed by Senator Bill Bradley of New Jersey in 1986. Under the Bradley Plan, all outstanding loans to eligible countries would have been written down by 3 percent a year for three years, and interest rates would have been reduced by 3 percentage points (300 basis points) over the same period. Eligibility would have been tied to a debtor government's commitment to a program of trade liberalization designed to promote imports from the United States and other industrialized nations (Bradley, 1986). By linking trade and debt so explicitly, Senator Bradley plainly hoped to draw export interests into the policymaking process as a counter weight to the influence of the money-center banks. Despite some initially favorable reactions, however (see e.g., AFL-CIO, 1986), his plan soon faded into oblivion under the persistent and determined opposition of the Treasury and Federal Reserve. Much the same fate has awaited similar proposals promoted more recently by other members of Congress, such as Representatives John LaFalce of New York (1987) or Don Pease of Ohio (1988).

Nor is the failure of such efforts surprising, given the considerable difficulties involved. Inside the financial community, barriers to alternative alignments are high and undoubtedly will remain so as long as the industry remains as oligopolistic and hierarchical as it is. Outside, other interested parties will continue to have difficulty influencing official attitudes as long as finance ministries and central banks retain primary policy responsibility for the debt issue. And any forging of links between selected elements of the financial community and other parties, for example between the smaller banks and exporters, will continue to be hampered by the absence of either a tradition or an institutional base for effective joint political action. We must therefore admit that here too, as on the debtor side, the probabilities are simply too low to inspire confidence in such an endogenous solution to the problem. Again, the odds are unlikely to shorten sufficiently for us to declare categorically *les jeux sont faits*.

Correcting for market failure

If it is unrealistic to expect an endogenous change in power relationships sufficient to alleviate the de facto insolvency of many developing countries, it follows that supplementary exogenous efforts will be required to promote genuine debt reform. This means that effective collective action will have to be organized in order to bring about appropriate agreements among all the parties concerned. Serious progress on the debt front is simply not likely to be achieved if we continue to rely solely on the laissez-faire approach favored by evolutionists.

The point can be put more formally. Earlier, the strategic interaction between creditors and debtors was likened to a multiplayer game with an unexploited opportunity for joint gain. Alternatively, the situation can be described as an example of market failure caused by the unwillingness of any player or group of players to take responsibility for the needed "collective good" of a genuinely durable solution. All recognize their common interest in easing the severe cash-flow strains on debtors, but none wants to pay any of the costs if they can be avoided. Everyone, in short, would like to be a "free rider." And so there is a tendency for each player to concentrate principally on avoiding losses or deflecting them as much as possible onto others – equivalent, in game-theoretic terms, to saying that any potential for joint gain tends to be lost because of the individual temptation to defect. Reliance solely on the market in such circumstances will not achieve the optimal outcome.

This free-rider problem is by now widely recognized, especially as it affects relations within the banking industry. As scholars like Williamson (1988) and Krugman (1988) have noted, broad agreement on significant debt-reform measures is difficult to achieve, particularly if these measures contain some degree of outright relief, because of the ever-present risk of widespread nonparticipation. Most individual lenders have an incentive to avoid any share of the costs of concessions while hoping to reap the benefit of any ensuing gain in the value of their claims. Hence the signs of increasing strains on the creditor side come as no surprise. Collective market failure derives directly from the myopia of individual self-interest.

It is precisely in such circumstances that economic theory recommends concerted action to correct for market failures. As Sachs (1988, pp. 22–23) has commented:

> Fundamentally, we face here the so-called collective action problem: each
> individual bank sees its self-interest in getting the best possible terms, while

it would be in the collective interest of all banks to moderate the terms. It's very hard to maintain the collective interest in this world when nobody is managing the overall strategy properly. .... it's a myth to believe that the market can do this on its own.

What is needed instead is deliberate organization of the common effort to exploit opportunities for joint gain.

Toward genuine debt reform

The creationists press for active institutional innovation to achieve genuine debt reform. Institutional innovation, however, does not have to mean imposed or mandatory solutions to the debt problem. To say that markets may fail is not to say that they must be replaced. It might be enough simply to provide a third party to facilitate mutually beneficial agreements that will help participants avoid the costs of their own imperfections. Accords may continue to be negotiated on a case-by-case basis. The point has been put most succinctly by Krugman (1989):

> The costs incurred by a failure to reach agreement represent a real social cost (e.g., through disruption of trade, financial flows, political stability, etc.). It may be worthwhile for the [debtors] and their bankers to accept this cost in order to demonstrate their toughness, but it is preferable from the world's point of view, and possibly from the point of view of the parties themselves, if agreement can be reached more quickly. Thus there is a potential albeit problematic role for [third parties] as facilitators of agreement.

Who should that third party he and how would its role be defined? Can a middle way to debt reform be found that retains the creationists' stress on collective action without abandoning the evolutionists' preference for voluntary and market-oriented solutions?

Creditor objections to debt relief

If large commercial lenders are to be persuaded to abandon the status quo, they will have to be offered sufficient incentives. No collective approach that is not genuinely responsive to their legitimate concerns could possibly work. What might such incentives look like? What concessions from others would be most likely to draw these creditors into voluntary concessions of their own?

Clues are provided by what large creditors themselves have to say about the idea of comprehensive debt reform, and in particular about the possibility of debt relief. Mostly they object. In spite of the evidence of changing attitudes in the financial community, large creditors' resistance to any substantial reduction of obligations remains strong and vocal. But an analysis of *why* they object can help us understand what safeguards or side payments might make the idea of debt reform more palatable. In this way, we can learn what revisions of the prevailing strategy they might realistically regard as a fair price to be paid for their cooperation. The goal is to identify a set of practical working principles for a new concerted approach to the debt problem.

Creditor objections to debt relief encompass a wide range of arguments of varying degrees of intellectual sophistication and rigor. For analytical purposes, it is convenient to group them under six major headings: (a) contagion, (b) loss of creditworthiness, (c) weakening of discipline, (d) moral hazard, (e) legal problems, and (f) politicization. All of these arguments have self-serving elements: lenders are not disinterested bystanders, after all. But all the objections are legitimate and, when placed in perspective and shorn of exaggeration, deserve to be taken seriously for what they can tell us about the perceptions and motivations of creditors.

a. Contagion. Perhaps the most self-serving of all these arguments stresses the possible "contagion effects" of a widespread markdown of third-world debt obligations. Heavily exposed creditors express concern not only about what such a step might mean for their own safety and soundness but, more broadly, what it could do to the banking industry and world financial markets in general. Given the manifold links among lending institutions, they say, even a single major insolvency could produce potentially disastrous ripples and feedbacks. At a minimum, a good number of intermediaries could be seriously weakened. At worst, a full-blown financial crisis might occur.

Contentions of this kind are bound to exaggerate to some extent the dangers involved. Vulnerable though they may be, banks have been remarkably successful in reinforcing their defenses against any threat of loss on their third-world exposure. Moreover, talk of a possible financial crisis discounts the effectiveness of present prudential supervisory practices, as well as the powerful role of central banks as lenders of last resort. And it overlooks the positive impact that debt relief might have on the equity prices and credit ratings of major banks. In fact, the risk of contagion effects is just not as serious as is sometimes suggested.

Nonetheless, some residual risk undoubtedly remains. The question is whether safeguards can be developed to help ease the legitimate concerns expressed by creditors on this score. At least two safeguards can be imagined. One possibility would be to insist on *selectivity:* make debt relief selective rather than general, limiting reductions of contractual obligations to those countries that, by objective analysis, really do appear to face something approximating insolvency rather than mere illiquidity. A differentiated, case-by-case approach is already employed as part of the debt strategy. An equivalent approach to debt relief would substantially diminish potential hits to bank earnings and balance sheets.

A second possibility would involve greater *flexibility* in accounting for all such hits: design regulatory changes or reinterpretations to permit banks to avoid an immediate write-down of existing capital assets when obligations are reduced. Such reforms are within the scope of supervisors' present authority in most of the capital-market countries. In the United States, for instance, ample precedent exists under current accounting rules for stretching out lenders' capital losses in selected instances. One example is the system of so-called Allocated Transfer Risk Reserves for LDC loans that have been classified as "value impaired."

Why not authorize banks to spread out the costs of debt relief in the same way? Neither of these safeguards would remove all the pain for creditors, of course. But they would certainly help to reduce discomfort levels significantly,[8] and so contain the threat of contagion spreading through the interbank market from one financial institution to another.

b. Loss of creditworthiness. The second line of argument, also somewhat self-serving, stresses possible consequences for debtors rather than creditors – specifically, the damage debt relief could do to the long-term credit standing of developing nations. Like any bankrupt enterprise or individual, we are told, debtor countries could find access to market financing severely curtailed, perhaps even totally blocked, for an indefinite period should their creditors be obliged to cancel some fraction of outstanding contractual obligations. The result could be an even longer delay in the return to healthy economic growth.

This argument might be persuasive but for a simple fact: troubled countries already have suffered severe damage to their credit standing. No new money is going to debtors even now, apart from occasional concerted lending agreements. Even in those instances, a perverse relationship has developed between debtor performance and credit availability, as Krugman (1989) has noted. Any improvement in a debtor's economic health tends to be reflected in a reduction rather than an increase in capital inflows as concerted lending is cut back; in effect, success in complying with the prevailing debt strategy is punished rather than rewarded by creditors. The pattern amounts to a tax on a country's efforts to adjust its economy. Seen in this light, creditor expressions of concern for LDC creditworthiness seem disingenuous at best.

Indeed, the logic of the argument could be stood on its head: debt relief might actually enhance the capacity of these countries to service their remaining obligations – the debt relief Laffer curve again. Foreign earnings currently absorbed by interest payments abroad could instead be used to promote accelerated investment and economic reforms at home, and creditworthiness might ultimately improve as a result. Much depends, of course, on what debtor governments do with their new-found degrees of freedom. From the creditors' point of view, the pain associated with debt relief would surely seem more tolerable if they could be assured that developing countries would not waste the additional resources made available to them.[9] This suggests yet a third, rather obvious safeguard, *conditionality*, which is also already well established in the prevailing debt strategy. To lower the risks of an alternative approach, relief could be made contingent upon pursuit of appropriate policies by debtor governments. That leads directly to the third line of argument traditionally advanced by creditors to oppose any reduction of debtors' contractual obligations.

c. Weakening of discipline. The third line of argument stresses possible deleterious effects on the policies pursued by debtors – the risk that debt relief will remove incentives to adopt tough domestic adjustment measures and reforms. The advantage of the prevailing strategy, creditors insist, is that it encourages responsible economic management; the disadvantage of an alternative approach, that it would weaken discipline over future policy and performance.

Here, too, the logic of the argument could be stood on its head: incentives are already diluted by the perverse relationship that has developed between debtor performance and credit availability. The effective tax on successful adjustment actually discourages rather than encourages a continued commitment to the current strategy. Moreover, there is the reverse question of incentives for banks, which until now have been obliged to pay little direct price for their own past imprudence. By some measures, commercial lending to developing countries was excessive in the period up to 1982. Lacking an explicit loss on the resulting claims, what discipline are banks under to ensure appropriate caution on their part in the future?

Nonetheless, given the intense distributional struggles that underlie economic policymaking in any country, it must be conceded that the discipline argument makes a point. Any government – debtor or not – is apt to act like an irresponsible child if presented with a free good. But why should we assume that debt relief must be granted with no strings attached? To the contrary, the discipline argument reinforces the case for retaining conditionality as an integral part of such an approach. Incentives for responsible management could actually be increased if linked to a reduction of outstanding contractual obligations.

d. Moral hazard. Parallel to the discipline argument is the so-called "moral hazard" issue – the risk that some developing nations might deliberately take steps to lower their economic performance in order to qualify for debt relief. Any compromise of the prevailing strategy, we are told, would appear to reward wasteful or inefficient policies at the expense of debtor countries that have done everything possible to keep up with their contractual obligations, making a mockery of their sacrifices. The danger is that these well-managed countries will therefore be tempted to relax their domestic discipline.

The answer to this argument, plainly, is the same as before: continue to make any approach contingent upon pursuit of appropriate policies. Moral hazard might indeed be a problem if the strings attached to debt relief were too loose or flimsy. With a real price to be paid, however, governments would be deterred to the extent that the costs of qualifying for relief appeared to exceed the benefits. The trick, of course, would be to determine just how high that price should be. It would have to be high enough to be effective as a deterrent to moral hazard, yet not too high to drive away those truly in need. We return to this point below.

e. Legal problems. The fifth line of argument stresses the many legal issues that would have to be surmounted by any plan for debt relief. These issues would involve everything from the definition of obligations and the identity of obligors to be covered in each country to the relationships and priorities to be established among various foreign claimants. Underlying all these issues is an even more fundamental objection concerning sanctity of contract: the fear that any abrogation of contracts voluntarily entered into in the past would severely, if not permanently, undermine the basis for further commercial lending in the future. Why should creditors ever again put money into the third world if full repayment cannot be assured?

These are not inconsequential issues and clearly must be confronted head on. It is also clear that they are within the wit of humans to resolve, as most nations have already demonstrated in their domestic arrangements for dealing with the challenge of insolvency. Basic legal theory has long held that there may be occasions when contracts should not be enforced but instead rewritten, particularly when unforeseen low-probability contingencies place extreme and unexpected burdens on debtors (see, e.g., Posner and Rosenfield, 1977). The issue is whether rigid insistence by creditors on full adherence to contractual obligations could so endanger a debtor's capacity to pay that both sides would be better off with some form of relief. The means for resolving the issue at the national level are already well developed in mechanisms such as Chapter 11 of the U.S. Bankruptcy Code or analogous regulations elsewhere. There seems to be little reason in principle why such mechanisms could not be used as a model for resolving the relevant legal issues at the international level as well. From the creditors' point of view, the key safeguard here would appear to be a need for *mutuality:* explicit recognition of rights and obligations on both sides. We return to this point as well.

f. Politicization. The final line of argument is that any scheme for debt relief would surely inject politics into the creditor-debtor relationship. But is this necessarily so? One could argue just the opposite, that the issue is obviously already highly politicized and could actually be defused by an orderly procedure that promises to ease the cash-flow strains of debtor countries in a context of renewed development and continued stability in financial markets. Much depends on the degree to which a third party would be directly interposed between creditors and debtors in setting the terms of relief. Commercial lenders, understandably, are happiest with a minimum of political intervention, preferring to preserve to the extent possible the formally voluntary and market-oriented character of today's negotiating framework. A final safeguard, therefore, would be to reaffirm the basic *autonomy* of participants on both sides. Indeed, in practical terms this could prove to be the most important incentive of all from the creditors' point of view.

A new design

This analysis of creditor objections has suggested five crucial safeguards that could reduce creditor resistance to the idea of debt reform, with or without outright relief:

a. *Selectivity:* a differentiated case-by-case approach.
b. *Flexibility:* rules changes to stretch out costs to creditors.
c. *Conditionality:* a direct link between creditor concessions and appropriate policy commitments by debtors.
d. *Mutuality:* explicit recognition of rights and obligations on both sides.
e. *Autonomy:* preservation of an essentially voluntary and market-oriented negotiating framework.

These five safeguards can be understood as the working principles needed for a new concerted approach to the debt problem. The challenge is to translate them into a practical and effective design for reform.

A useful model is provided by Chapter 11 of the U.S. Bankruptcy Code or analogous mechanisms established elsewhere to deal with problems of insolvency at the national level. Under Chapter 11, debtors unable to meet their contractual obligations can appeal for protection from creditors while they reorganize their affairs, under the supervision of a bankruptcy court, and work out mutually satisfactory terms for a resolution of their difficulties. Settlement terms may or may not include elements of outright debt relief. Indeed, subject to certain conditions, they may include just about anything to which debtors and a qualified majority of creditors can agree through direct negotiation – deferral of principle, reduction of interest rates, conversion of debt into alternative claims, etc. The role of the court, in the first instance, is to facilitate negotiations with creditors (e.g., by establishing representative committees for each class of claimant, setting timetables for discussions, and acting as a conduit of communication) while exercising general surveillance over the relevant managerial decisions of the debtor. More broadly, the court's responsibility is to use its adjudicatory powers to ensure that creditors receive equitable treatment at the same time that debtors are given the breathing space needed to put their affairs back in order.[10]

The attractions of a Chapter 11 procedure are obvious, in that it embodies all five of the working principles that seem appropriate to promote durable solutions to debt problems. While the approach is comprehensive, mutuality and autonomy are preserved by an essentially voluntary and market-oriented negotiating framework based on explicit recognition of respective rights and obligations. Selectivity is embodied in the right of the debtor to make the initial decision to seek protection, while flexibility is inherent in the virtually unlimited scope provided for final terms of settlement. Finally, conditionality is respected in the assignment of a supervisory role to the court over the debtor's continuing operations. Debtors benefit from the opportunity to get back on their feet without being driven to the wall, but creditors are safeguarded by the conditions attached to the assistance provided obligors. Relief does not come without a price.

Those interested in the problem of third-world debt have long lamented the absence of something like Chapter 11 at the international level (see, e.g., Suratgar, 1984; Dell, 1985; Williamson, 1985; UNCTAD, 1986, Chap. 6). Until now, imaginative institutional innovation along these lines has been effectively blocked by the determined opposition of creditors. But with attitudes on LDC debt now changing in the financial community, the time may at last be ripe for serious consideration of just such an alternative approach. What shape might it take?

As a first step, it would be necessary to establish an appropriate institution – some entity authorized to play a role comparable to that of the bankruptcy court, which is the core of the Chapter 11 procedure. Negotiations between creditors and debtors may be direct and voluntary, but if the two sides are ultimately to be persuaded to take responsibility for the needed "collective good" of a durable solution, there must be some neutral intermediary capable of assuring them both that their rights and needs will be respected. A comprehensive new set of rules of the game would not be enough to overcome the misgivings over motives and commitments inherent in any such strategic interaction. Players must also be confident that the rules will be interpreted and implemented objectively, assuring creditors that moral hazard will be deterred and assuring debtors that the price paid for relief will not be punitive. In short, the two sides need a referee.

Fortunately, there are precedents for such an institution, even at the international level. One example is the Iran–U.S. Claims Tribunal established in 1981 as part of the agreement negotiated between Washington and Tehran to unblock Iran's frozen assets in exchange for the release of American hostages held since 1979 (Cohen, 1986, Chap. 4; Riesenfeld, 1982). Another is the little-known but influential International Centre for Settlement of Investment Disputes (ICSID), an affiliate of the World Bank created by a multilateral convention over two decades ago to provide a forum for resolving conflicts between national governments and foreign investors (Soley, 1985; Shihata, 1986). ICSID functions as an arbitrator for investment disputes submitted to it. The process is voluntary in that the interested parties decide whether to consent to use of the ICSID machinery; it is binding in that once consent is given it cannot be revoked and all judgments are final. Disputes covered by ICSID concern every possible type of foreign direct investment, from wholly owned or joint ventures to technical and licensing agreements. Specifically excluded are conflicts relating to purely financial transactions of the sort we are considering here.

For our purposes, however, there is one key problem with these precedents, whether at the international level or as represented in national arrangements like Chapter 11 – the extent of the powers to be conferred on the referee. Alternative models for conflict resolution display a wide range in the degree of authority accorded a designated third party to fix settlement terms between disputants (Goldman, 1985). At one extreme are procedures based on governmental fiat or its equivalent – models that are clearly incompatible with the principle of autonomy that seems needed for a new concerted approach to LDC debt. At the other extreme are procedures relying exclusively on direct negotiations between the parties involved, formally independent of explicit intervention by third parties – essentially the method embodied in the prevailing debt strategy, with all its attendant disadvantages. In between are yet other models that attempt to compromise between the two extremes, for example, adjudication or arbitration, where neutral third parties are empowered in some degree to resolve differences on the basis of settled principles, or mediation or conciliation, where the role of third parties is limited to facilitating negotiations by one means or another. Adjudication and arbitration are obviously nearer the government-fiat end of the range, and mediation and conciliation nearer the direct-negotiation end.

The problem is that all the precedents are placed closer to the government fiat end of the range than is likely to prove acceptable to either sovereign borrowers or commercial lenders. Chapter 11 depends on the broad adjudicatory authority of the bankruptcy court; both the Iran–U.S. Tribunal and ICSID act in an arbitrational capacity. Precedents though they may be, therefore, they are not directly replicable for our purposes; they are imperfect analogies for the design of a new institution to deal specifically with the problem of third-world debt. If political intervention in the creditor-debtor relationship is to be kept to a minimum, consistent with the other working principles of a comprehensive reform strategy, the powers of the referee will have to be more restricted than in any of these arrangements. The new approach must rely most on the model of mediation or conciliated negotiation if it is to be workable in practical terms.

An effective alternative to the prevailing debt strategy might thus be designed along the following lines:

a. A new institution. An appropriate institution would be established by multilateral convention to set the framework for a negotiated resolution of LDC debt-service difficulties on a case-by-case basis consistent with the interests of both creditors and debtors. The institution could be called the International Debt Restructuring Agency (IDRA). Ideally, it would be organized as a wholly new and independent entity in order to underscore its neutrality and objectivity. In practice, it might be more feasible – and certainly would be quicker – to get IDRA started as a joint subsidiary of the two multilateral agencies most involved with the problem now, the IMF and the World Bank, relying on the expertise and experience of existing staff, who would be seconded for this specific project.

b. Basic procedures. LDC debtors would have the right to apply to IDRA if they believed their circumstances warranted some degree of debt relief. However, by doing so they would commit themselves irrevocably to a process of conciliated negotiation with their creditors, as well as to some surveillance of their policies by IDRA. Relief would be provided only where all the parties concerned concurred that it was justified. The terms of relief would be anything to which the debtor and a qualified majority of creditors could agree. Following agreement, terms would be supervised by IDRA until such time as the country was back on its feet and, if possible, its external creditworthiness was restored.

c. Responsibilities of the new institution. The general role of IDRA would be to facilitate negotiations between creditors and debtors on a fair and equitable basis. Specifically, its functions might include the following:

(1) Creditor committees. Following application by a debtor, IDRA would establish or, where such negotiating groups already exist (as in the standard advisory committees for medium-term bank debts), certify representative committees for each class of claimant.

(2) Timetables for discussion. Once creditor committees were established or certified, IDRA would set timetables for submission of initial negotiating positions, responses, counterproposals, and so on.

(3) Conduit of communication. IDRA would investigate the policies and financial conditions of the debtor in order to provide a common factual basis for negotiators on both sides.

(4) Analysis and evaluation. More controversially, IDRA might be authorized to go beyond mere fact finding to undertake formal evaluation of the policies and financial condition of the debtor, with the aim of providing an objective analysis of its economic circumstances and prospects. The purpose would be to determine, in as neutral a manner as possible, whether the country really appears to be facing something approximating insolvency rather than mere illiquidity and, if so, to what extent.

(5) Formulas for settlement. Even more controversially, IDRA could be authorized to propose its own formulas and terms for settlement, as a means to bridge gaps between positions and identify areas of potential agreement.

(6) Breaking deadlocks. Most controversially of all, IDRA could conceivably be authorized to compel agreement in the event of deadlock, in order to suppress any remaining temptation among lenders to free ride. For example, dissenting creditors might be obliged to accept terms agreed by a qualified majority if IDRA declared the proposed settlement to be "fair and equitable" and in the best interests of all concerned.[11] Or both sides might be obliged to accept a settlement proposed by IDRA if agreement could not be attained within the limits of a specified timetable. Obviously, this function would push IDRA's conciliator role quite distinctly into the area of arbitration and could thus prove too much for either lenders or borrowers to accept. On the other hand, if included strictly as a last-resort element in an otherwise flexible and unencumbered negotiating process, it might have some appeal to all concerned.

(7) Monitoring debtor behavior. Finally, as part of any settlement, IDRA (or another agency designated by IDRA, such as the IMF or the World Bank) would have the responsibility of monitoring the debtor's economic performance in order to ensure that all terms were being faithfully met. The specific content of conditionality would be defined by the parties themselves on the basis of an agreed understanding of the adjustments or reforms needed to restore the country's capacity to service obligations on a sustained basis. Creditors would be permitted to withdraw all concessions on such matters as interest rates if IDRA determined that a debtor was not complying with its policy commitments.

Would such a design be politically feasible? Both commercial banks and developing countries ought to find it attractive, since like the Chapter 11 procedure it embodies all five of the working principles needed to make an alternative strategy workable. The banks' home governments should also find it appealing since it puts little demand on scarce public revenues. In this respect, the design stands in stark contrast to most of the previous proposals for institutional innovation. The distinguishing characteristic of these earlier plans is usually that a sizable financial liability, outright or contingent, would have to be assumed by a public entity as part of a multilaterally negotiated program of debt reform. As Corden (1988) has pointed out, creationist schemes for an international debt facility inevitably depend on some level of funding or financial risk on the part of the governments of the capital-market countries in order to be effective. By contrast, IDRA calls for mediation, not intermediation. Hence it would entail no explicit new financial commitment beyond the comparatively trivial amounts needed for its own operating expenses. This would surely count as a plus from a political point of view.

Implicitly, to be sure, there would be some cost to taxpayers: they would be obligated to compensate for any tax deductions or credits legitimately taken by banks if LDC obligations were marked down. This could give rise to charges that public money was being used to "bail out" private lenders. But that would be true only to the extent that the loss of taxable bank earnings implied by a settlement negotiated under IDRA could otherwise be averted – a dubious proposition if the discounts in the secondary market and other signs of de facto insolvency in the third world are to be believed. In any event, the pain for taxpayers would be eased as much as for banks by regulatory changes to stretch out the costs of debt relief. Any discomfort remaining should not be politically intolerable – a small price to be paid, really, for a durable solution to the debt problem.

One could argue that the proposed IDRA mechanism does not actually add much. After all, creditors and debtors already negotiate directly, case-by-case, on a formally voluntary and market-oriented basis, and even now many bankers seem ready to acknowledge the need for selective concessions in appropriate circumstances to help ease the plight of troubled debtors. Why interpose a new player in a game where the old players already know all the rules? The answer should be obvious: because of the unsatisfactory outcome of the prevailing strategy – the "market failure" of an unexploited opportunity for joint gain. Today's approach is costly because, by relying on the continued ability of creditors to bribe or coerce debtors into acquiescence, it inevitably generates frustration, confrontation, and conflict. The great advantage of the IDRA approach is that it would structure incentives in a far more positive way for all concerned.

In the end, of course, an IDRA mechanism would be only as effective as creditors and debtors wanted it to be. However, in a situation where both sides could benefit compared with the prevailing strategy, good will ought not to be in short supply. The presence of IDRA could help greatly to reduce or eliminate existing obstacles to debt reform. With the stakes as high as they are, that would certainly be no mean accomplishment.

Notes

1 The distinction drawn here between these two schools of thought is a practical one, based on the state of current debate rather than derived from formal economic logic. In principle, voluntary and market-oriented solutions are not necessarily synonymous, nor (as we shall see) are they necessarily inconsistent with approaches that are comprehensive and involve a degree of collective action. But that tends to be the way the choice is framed in public discussion today (see, e.g., Williamson, 1988; Krugman, 1988).

2 Other more formal and cumbersome circumlocutions have been invented to describe what I call de facto insolvency – for example, "structural indebtedness" (Bailey and Cohen, 1987, p. 2) or "hysteresis of solvency" (Islam, 1988, p. 16). I prefer to call a spade a spade.

3 A considerable literature has developed in recent years attempting to model formally the complex bargaining relationship between international creditors and debtors. For useful surveys, see Eaton, Gersovitz, and Stiglitz (1986), Glick (1986), and Crawford (1987).

4 Central to the debate among lawyers are two traditional tenets of international law – the principle of foreign sovereign immunity and the act of state doctrine – and the extent to which either, or both, may constrain the legal remedies available to lenders to foreign sovereigns. Neither recent legislation (e.g., the U.S. Foreign Sovereign Immunities Act of 1976) nor court rulings (involving countries as diverse as Costa Rica, Cuba, and Iran) have succeeded in clarifying the juridical issues or risks involved. For a sample of opinion, see Nichols (1984), McCormick (1984), and Alexander (1987, Chap. 2).

5 Various commentators have suggested at least four motivations for Citicorp's action in addition to a desire to strengthen its bargaining position vis-à-vis debtors: (a) to position the bank to "reliquify" its LDC portfolio by enabling it to take future selective charges against its new reserves: (b) to improve its competitive position in relation to less profitable or more heavily exposed commercial-banking rivals; (c) to exploit certain tax advantages before their termination under the tax-reform law passed in 1986; or (d) to provide its recently appointed chairman, John Reed, with a dramatic opportunity to distinguish his leadership of the bank from the policies of his well-known predecessor and patron, Walter Wriston. The five motivations are not mutually exclusive, of course.

6 This does not apply to banks in Continental European countries such as Germany or Switzerland, where loan-loss reserves have customarily been maintained at levels well above the 25 percent figure; it does apply to banks in Britain and Canada as well as the United States, and above all to banks in Japan, where provisions still amount to less than 5 percent of LDC exposure.

  Many bankers object to the use of quotations in the secondary market as a guide to the true long-term value of LDC paper: it is an extremely thin market where discounts in effect reflect fire-sale prices. The secondary market is, however, the best guide available and is certainly a better indicator of true value than the bankers' formal valuation of most of these loans on their books at 100 cents on the dollar.

7 For more on these and other possible technical innovations, see Cline (1987) and Regling (1998).

8 According to one estimate based on financial results in recent years (Pease, 1988, p. 101), a five-year write-down cumulating to 25 percent of third-world exposure (beyond the write-down that would already be permitted by previous loan-loss provisions) would require America's large money-center banks, on average, to allocate no more than half their annual pre-tax earnings – painful, clearly, but hardly devastating.

9 As one New York banker said to me in private conversation in September 1987, "Banks are not opposed to pain, but to pain with no purpose."

10 For a useful guide to the intricacies of Chapter 11, see Weintraub (1980).

11 This authority would parallel the so-called "cramdown" rule that is an integral part of the Chapter 11 procedure (Weintraub, 1980, Chap. 16). An alternative possibility, more consistent with voluntary market-oriented solutions, would be to allow dissenting creditors to reject proposed IDRA settlements – but only at a price, such as forfeiture of some or all of any ensuing gain in the value of their claims.

References

AFL-CIO, "The International Debt Problem," statement by the AFL-CIO Executive Council, Aug. 5, 1986.

Aggarwal, Vinod, *International Debt Threat: Bargaining among Creditors and Debtors in the 1980s*, Policy Papers in International Affairs No. 29, Berkeley, University of California, Institute of International Studies, 1987.

Alexander, Lewis S., "Three Essays on Sovereign Default and International Lending," Yale University, May 1987, dissertation.

American Express Bank, "Business Investment: Time for a 'Second Wave,' " *The AMEX Bank Review*, 14 (Sept. 28, 1987), pp. 1–8.

Bailey, Norman A., and Richard Cohen, *The Mexican Time Bomb*, New York, Twentieth Century Fund, 1987.

Bradley, Bill, "A Proposal for Third World Debt Management," speech presented in Zurich, Switzerland, June 29, 1986.

Cline, William R., *Mobilizing Bank Lending to Debtor Countries*, Policy Analyses in International Economics No. 18, Washington, Institute for International Economics, June 1987.

Cohen, Benjamin J., *In Whose Interest? International Banking and American Foreign Policy*, New Haven, Conn., Yale University Press for the Council on Foreign Relations, 1986.

Corden, W. Max, "An International Debt Facility?" *International Monetary Fund Staff Papers*, 35 (September 1988), pp. 401–421.

Crawford, Vincent P., *International Lending, Long-Term Credit Relationships, and Dynamic Contract Theory*, Princeton Studies in International Finance No. 59, Princeton, N.J., Princeton University, International Finance Section, March 1987.

Dell, Sidney, "Crisis Management and the International Debt Problem," *International Journal*, 40 (Autumn 1985), pp. 655–688.

De Vries, Margaret Garritsen, *Balance of Payments Adjustment, 1945 to 1986: The IMF Experience*, Washington, International Monetary Fund, 1987.

Dornbusch, Rudiger, "International Debt and Economic Instability," *Federal Reserve Bank of Kansas City Economic Review*, January 1987, pp. 15–32.

Eaton, Jonathan, Mark Gersovitz, and Joseph E. Stiglitz, "The Pure Theory of Country Risk," *European Economic Review*, 30 (June 1986), pp. 481–513.

Economic Policy Council of the United Nations Association of the United States of America, *Third World Debt: A Reexamination of Long-Term Management*, report of the Third World Debt Panel, New York, Sept. 7, 1988.

The Economist, "The Limits of Cooperation," Survey of the World Economy, Sept. 26, 1987.

Glick, Reuven, *Economic Perspectives on Foreign Borrowing and Debt Repudiation: An Analytical Literature Review*, Monograph Series in Finance and Economics No. 4, New York, New York University Graduate School of Business Administration, 1986.

Goldman, Alvin, "Settlement of Disputes over Interests," in R. Blanpain, ed., *Comparative Labour Law and Industrial Relations*, 2nd rev. ed,, Deventer, Netherlands, Kluwer, 1985, pp. 359–380.

Haggard, Stephan, and Robert R. Kaufman, "The Polities of Stabilization and Structural Adjustment," in Sachs, ed. (1989).

Holley, H. A., *Developing Country Debt: The Role of the Commercial Banks*, Chatham House Papers No. 35, London, Routledge and Kegan Paul, 1987.

Inter-American Dialogue, *The Americas in 1989: Consensus for Action*, Washington, 1989.

Interim Committee of the Board of Governors of the International Monetary Fund, Communiqué, Press Release No. 88/33, Sept. 26, 1988.

Islam, Shafiqul, *Breaking the International Debt Deadlock*, Critical Issues Series No. 2, New York, Council on Foreign Relations, February 1988.

Kahler, Miles, "Politics and International Debt: Explaining the Crisis," in Kahler, ed. (1986, pp. 11–36).

——, ed., *The Politics of International Debt*, Ithaca, N.Y., Cornell University Press, 1986.

Kaletsky, Anatole, *The Costs of Default*, New York, Twentieth Century Fund, 1985.

Kaufman, Robert R., "Democratic and Authoritarian Responses to the Debt Issue: Argentina, Brazil, Mexico," in Kahler, ed. (1986, pp. 187–217).

Kenen, Peter B., "Third World Debt: Sharing the Burden, A Bailout Plan for the Banks," *The New York Times*, Mar. 6, 1983, Sec. 3, p. F 3.

Kilborn, Peter T., "Debt Policy Shift Set on Third World," *New York Times*, Mar, 11, 1989, National Ed., p. 17.

Kraft, Joseph, *The Mexican Rescue*, New York, Group of Thirty, 1984.

Krasner, Stephen D., ed., *International Regimes*, Ithaca, N. Y., Cornell University Press, 1983.

Krueger, Anne O., "Debt, Capital Flows, and LDC Growth," *American Economic Review*, 77 (May 1987), pp. 159–164.

Krugman, Paul R., "Market-Based Debt-Reduction Schemes," Working Paper Series No. 2587, Cambridge, Mass., National Bureau of Economic Research, May 1988.

——, "Private Capital Flows to Problem Debtors," in Sachs, ed. (1989).

Kuczynski, Pedro-Pablo, "The Outlook for Latin American Debt," *Foreign Affairs*, 66 (Fall 1987), pp. 129–149.

LaFalce, John, "Third World Debt Crisis: The Urgent Need to Confront Reality," statement presented in Washington, Mar. 5, 1987.

Lindert, Peter H., and Peter J. Morton, "How Sovereign Debt Has Worked," in Sachs, ed. (1989).

Lipson, Charles, "The International Organization of Third World Debt," *International Organization*, 35 (Autumn 1981), pp. 603–631.

——, "Bankers' Dilemmas: Private Cooperation in Rescheduling Sovereign Debts," in Kenneth A. Oye, ed., *Cooperation Under Anarchy*, Princeton, N.J., Princeton University Press, 1986a, pp. 200–225.

——, "International Debt and International Institutions," in Kahler, ed. (1986b, pp. 219–243).

Makin, John H., "The Third World Debt Crisis and the American Banking System," *AEI Economist*, May 1987, pp. 1–11.

McCormick, Caitlin, "The Commercial Activity Exception to Foreign Sovereign Immunity and the Act of State Doctrine," *Law and Policy in International Business*, 16 (November 1984), pp. 477–538.

Nichols, Bruce W., "Sovereign Debtors under U.S. Immunity Law," in Michael Gruson and Ralph Reisner, eds., *Sovereign Lending: Managing Legal Risk*, London, Euromoney Publications, 1984, pp. 81–87.

Ordeshook, Peter C., *Game Theory and Political Theory: An Introduction*, Cambridge and New York, Cambridge University Press, 1986.

Pease, Don, "A Congressional Plan to Solve the Debt Crisis," *The International Economy*, 2 (March / April 1988), pp. 98–105.

Posner, Richard A., and Andrew M. Rosenfield, "Impossibility and Related Doctrines in Contract Law: An Economic Analysis," *Journal of Legal Studies*, 6 (January 1977), pp. 83–118.

Putnam, Robert D., "Diplomacy and Domestic Politics: The Logic of Two-Level Games," *International Organization*, 42 (Summer 1988), pp. 427–460.

Regling, Klaus P., "New Financing Approaches in the Debt Strategy," *Finance and Development*, 25 (March 1988), pp. 6–9.

Riesenfeld, Stefan A., "The Powers of the Executive to Govern the Rights of Creditors in the Event of Defaults of Foreign Governments," *University of Illinois Law Review*, No, 1 (1982), pp. 319–331.

Robinson, James D., *A Comprehensive Agenda for LDC Debt and World Trade Growth*, Amex Bank Review Special Papers Series No. 13, London, American Express Bank, March 1988.

Rockefeller, David, "Let's Not Write Off Latin America," *The New York Times*, July 5, 1987, Sec. 4, p. E 15.

Rohatyn, Felix G., "A Plan for Stretching Out Global Debt," *Business Week*, Feb. 28, 1983, pp. 15–18.

Rotberg, Eugene H., "Toward a Solution to the Debt Crisis," *The International Economy*, 2 (May/June 1988), pp. 42–48.

Sachs, Jeffrey D., "Managing the LDC Debt Crisis," *Brookings Papers on Economic Activity*, No. 2 (1986), pp. 397–431.

——, "The Debt Crisis at a Turning Point," *Challenge* (May/June 1988), pp. 17–26.

——, ed., *Developing Country Debt and Economic Performance*, Vol. 1, *The International Financial System*, Chicago, University of Chicago Press for the National Bureau of Economic Research, 1989.

Sachs, Jeffrey D., and Harry Huizinga, "U.S. Commercial Banks and the Developing-Country Debt Crisis," *Brookings Papers on Economic Activity*, No. 2 (1987), pp. 555–601.

Sengupta, Arjun K., "A Proposal for a Debt Adjustment Facility," prepared for IMF Executive Board Seminar 88/3, Washington, Feb. 9, 1988.

Shihata, Ibrahim F. I., "Towards a Greater Depoliticization of Investment Disputes: The Roles of ICSID and MIGA," *ICSID Review*, 1 (Spring 1986), pp. 1–25.

Soley, David A., "ICSID Implementation: An Effective Alternative to International Conflict," *International Lawyer*, 19 (Spring 1985), pp. 521–544.

Sumita, Satoshi, Statement by the Alternate Governor of the IMF and World Bank for Japan, Press Release No. 12, Sept. 27, 1988.

Suratgar, David, "The International Financial System and the Management of the International Debt Crisis," in David Suratgar, ed., *Default and Rescheduling: Corporate and Sovereign Borrowers in Difficulty*, London, Euromoney Publications, 1984, pp. 151–160.

United Nations Conference on Trade and Development, *Trade and Development Report, 1986*, Geneva, Switzerland, 1986.

Weintraub, Benjamin, *What Every Credit Executive Should Know about Chapter 11 of the Bankruptcy Code*, New York, National Association of Credit Management, 1980.

Williamson, John, "On the Question of Debt Relief," Appendix to the Statement of the Roundtable on Money and Finance, New York, Dec. 13–14, 1985, Islamabad, Pakistan, North-South Roundtable.

——, *Voluntary Approaches to Debt Relief*, Policy Analyses in International Economics No. 25, Washington, Institute for International Economics, September 1988.

8 Taming the phoenix?

Monetary governance after the crisis[1]

Source: From G.W. Noble and J. Ravenhill (eds), *The Asian Financial Crisis and the Architecture of Global Finance*, 2000.

> Ideas, knowledge, art, hospitality, travel – these are the things which should of their nature be international. But let goods be homespun whenever it is reasonably and conveniently possible; and, above all, let finance be primarily national.
>
> *John Maynard Keynes*

Few observers doubt that the financial crisis that struck Asia in 1997–98 was a watershed event for the global monetary system. For years the tide had been running one way – toward ever closer integration of national financial and currency markets. Politically, governments were increasingly thrown on the defensive by the rapid growth of international capital mobility. As I wrote a few years ago: 'Like a phoenix risen from the ashes, global finance [has taken] flight and soared to new heights of power and influence in the affairs of nations' (Cohen 1996: 268). The only question, it seemed, was how much the traditional monetary authority of sovereign states had, as a result, been compromised. 'The phoenix has risen. Does it also rule the roost?' (Cohen 1996: 270).

Then came the fall of the Thai baht and all the contagion – the 'bahtulism' – that followed. For many, these events served to affirm the new power of markets to constrain policy. The phoenix did indeed rule the roost. Governments had no choice but to live with new limits on their authority. But for others, choice was precisely the issue. The crisis appeared to pose an opportunity to think again about the priority popularly attached to financial liberalisation. Why should governments meekly submit to the dictates of market forces? Perhaps the time had come to cage the wilder impulses of the phoenix – to tame it, if not slay it, by imposing limitations of some kind on the cross-border mobility of capital.

At issue is the governance of monetary relations in the global economy. The purpose of this chapter is to explore prospects for world monetary governance after the crisis, with particular emphasis on the management of international competition among national currencies. The chapter begins with a brief look at the gradual transformation of the global financial environment in the decades prior to the recent crisis, an epoch during which governments found it increasingly difficult to manage monetary affairs within their sovereign territories. As long as the tide was running toward greater mobility of capital, states assumed they had little choice but to learn to live with the consequences. Focusing on the countries of East Asia, the chapter then considers how policy calculations are being recalibrated as a result of the worst financial calamity since the Great Depression, bringing new respectability to the old case for capital controls. Once scorned as a relic of the past, limits on capital mobility suddenly looked as if they might become the wave of the future. The question, increasingly, was no longer whether capital mobility might be limited but rather when, how and under what rules controls might be implemented by sovereign national governments.[2]

The debate, however, is just beginning. The remainder of the chapter will probe the case for capital controls in more detail, in the hope of providing a useful roadmap of the main policy challenges involved. Three questions will be stressed: What kinds of capital movements, if any, should be subject to limitation? What kinds of controls might be most effective? What kinds of rules could be designed to avoid either economic inefficiencies or serious policy conflict? All three questions are essential to the effective governance of monetary relations. How they are answered will go far to determining the shape of the global financial system well into the twenty-first century.

The new geography of money[3]

That the global financial environment has been greatly transformed in recent decades is undeniable. The full significance of that change for monetary governance, however, has only lately begun to be widely appreciated. Prior to the recent crisis, policy-makers were just starting to learn how to cope with the rising challenge to their authority.

The postwar resurrection of global finance was truly phenomenal. Half a century ago, after the ravages of the Great Depression and World War II, financial markets everywhere – with the notable exception of the United States – were weak, insular and strictly controlled, reduced from their previously central role in international economic relations and offering little more than a negligible amount of trade financing. From the 1950s, however, deregulation and liberalisation began to combine with technological and institutional innovation to breach many of the barriers limiting cross-border activity. In a cumulative process driven by the pressures of domestic and international competition, the range of commercial opportunities gradually widened for lenders and borrowers alike. The result was a remarkable growth of capital mobility, reflected in a scale of financial flows unequalled since the glory days of the nineteenth-century gold standard.

Even more phenomenal were the implications of these changes for monetary governance and the long-standing convention of national monetary sovereignty. With the deepening integration of financial markets, strict dividing lines between separate national moneys became less and less distinct. No longer were economic actors restricted to a single currency – their own home money – as they went about their daily business. Cross-border circulation of currencies, which had been quite common prior to the emergence of the modern state system, dramatically re-emerged, with competition between national moneys gradually accelerating. This is what I have referred to elsewhere as the new geography of money – the new configuration of currency space (Cohen 1998a). The functional domain of each money no longer corresponded precisely with the formal jurisdiction of its issuing authority. Currencies became increasingly deterritorialised, their circulation determined not by law or politics but by the dynamics of supply and demand.

Currency deterritorialisation posed a new and critical challenge to governments, which had long relied upon the privileges derived from a formal monetary monopoly (in particular, the powers of seigniorage and macroeconomic control) to promote their concept of state interest. No longer able to exert the same degree of control over the use of their moneys by their citizens or others, governments felt driven to compete, inside and across borders, for the allegiance of market agents – in effect, to sustain or cultivate market share for their own brand of currency. Monopoly yielded to something more like oligopoly, and monetary governance was reduced to little more than a choice among marketing strategies designed to shape and manage demand.

Broadly speaking, four strategies were possible, depending on two key considerations: first, whether policy was defensive or offensive, aiming to preserve or promote market share; and second, whether policy was pursued unilaterally or collusively. The four strategies were:

- market leadership: an aggressive unilateralist policy intended to maximise use of the national currency, analogous to predatory price leadership in an oligopoly;
- market alliance: a collusive policy of sharing monetary sovereignty in a monetary or exchange rate union of some kind, analogous to a tacit or explicit cartel;
- market preservation: a status quo policy intended to defend, rather than augment, a previously acquired market position;
- market followership: an acquiescent policy of subordinating monetary sovereignty to a stronger foreign currency via some form of exchange rate rule, analogous to passive price followership in an oligopoly.

Strategies could involve tactics of persuasion or coercion. Persuasion involved investing in a money's reputation, acting to enhance confidence in the currency's continued usefulness and reliability – in effect, establishing or sustaining a successful brand name. Coercion could be exercised through a wide range of measures designed to regulate or prohibit diverse financial activities (in principle, up to and including the unfashionable option of capital controls). Though neither persuasion nor coercion was foolproof, each could be highly effective in influencing a currency's market position. In practice, most governments learned to use both in varying combinations, since they were not mutually exclusive.

Nothing demonstrated the challenge to monetary governance more than the financial crisis that hit East Asia in mid 1997. Governments that had taken pride in the competitiveness of their currencies suddenly found themselves unable to preserve user loyalty. Strategies that once seemed adequate to sustain market share had to be re-evaluated in the light of a worldwide 'flight to quality' by mobile capital. Inevitably, policymakers were forced to take a new look at the option of capital controls.

Shock and aftershock

As the first shockwaves of crisis swept over the region, the initial government impulse was to go on the defensive, investing expensively in determined efforts to reinforce confidence in their currencies – the 'confidence game', as Krugman ironically dubbed it (Krugman 1998a). The aim of the confidence game was market preservation, at almost any cost.[4] But as user preferences proved more resistant to tactics of persuasion than anticipated, a search for new approaches began. The question was whether anyone could think of an alternative.

Currency boards

To a few, the answer seemed obvious: abandon any pretence of national monetary sovereignty and adopt a strategy of strict market followership in the form of a currency board, as existed in Brunei and Hong Kong. Long promoted by a small coterie of specialists inspired by the writings of US economist Steve Hanke (see, for example, Hanke & Schuler 1994; Cohen 1998a: 52–5), the currency board idea enjoyed a brief vogue in Indonesia in early 1998 prior to the forced resignation of President Suharto in May. In February 1998, on Hanke's advice, the government announced it was moving ahead with plans to establish a currency board system linked to the US dollar. Suharto referred to the project as an 'IMF-plus' program (quoted in *Economist*, 7 March 1998: 43).

However, the idea was abandoned under pressure from the International Monetary Fund (IMF) and other foreign creditors, who – with very good reason – sensed a disaster in the making. Certainly a currency board had not protected Hong Kong from the relentless pressures of destabilising speculation. Given the level of uncertainty in Indonesia at the time, establishment of a currency board might well have led to a rush to buy dollars, generating sky-high interest rates that in turn could have crushed what was left of the country's banking system. The Indonesian government was persuaded that it first needed to strengthen financial markets, deal with foreign debts and bolster central bank reserves before it could think of embarking on such a risky experiment. The plan was formally abandoned in late March,[5] and no other country in the region has indicated any interest in moving in the same direction.

Monetary union

To others, the answer seemed to lie in abandoning monetary sovereignty not to a currency board but to a monetary union of some kind based on the model of

Europe's new Economic and Monetary Union (EMU) – to go on the offensive with a forceful strategy of market alliance. Union would offer the benefit of numbers and thus the hope that the whole might, in effect, be greater than the sum of the parts. Who could doubt that one joint money might be more attractive than a myriad of separate national currencies? Even before the crisis broke, the idea was being actively explored by prominent economists (for example, Eichengreen 1997). Once the region's troubles began, interest rapidly spread. An observer wrote: 'Some kind of monetary regionalism in the region is...inevitable' (Mundell 1997). And another: 'Asia should...create an Asian Monetary Union' (Walter 1998). Official responses, however, were mostly distinctly unenthusiastic.[6] For obvious reasons, political as well as economic, no government was prepared to completely forsake its own brand of money.

In fact, the political preconditions for monetary union in Asia are not yet in place. The lessons of history on this issue are clear (Cohen 1993, 1998a: 84–91). To be sustainable, a joint currency among sovereign states requires one of two prerequisites – a local hegemon to enforce discipline or a broad network of institutional linkages sufficient to neutralise the risks of free-riding or exit by any participant. Neither prerequisite seems to be in evidence in Asia today.

It is clear that, as yet, Asian countries lack a broad constellation of commitments of the sort that might make a full surrender of monetary sovereignty immediately acceptable to all partners. This is not for want of trying. Even before the crisis, regional central banks had begun to build institutional linkages in a series of low-profile forums designed to promote dialogue and mutual exchange of information.[7] Many hoped that such groupings might weave the sort of fabric of related ties that could one day support more ambitious strategies of monetary alliance. But despite such efforts there is still little tradition of true financial solidarity – to say nothing of political solidarity – across the region.

A yen bloc

However, there is a potential hegemon in the neighbourhood: Japan. Indeed, it is fair to say that no regional initiative toward monetary alliance would have much chance without the active participation of Asia's dominant financial power. Collusion to promote market share would require determined leadership from Tokyo to create a currency bloc based on an internationalised yen. But are Asians prepared to bury historical suspicions of Japanese motivations and interests? Japan might well aspire to a strategy of market leadership, but it is unclear whether others in the area would voluntarily follow. Nor, in view of Japan's own economic travails during the 1990s, is it evident that Tokyo can sustain an effective campaign to cultivate regional use of its currency. In fact, nothing approximating a formal yen bloc is likely to emerge soon.

That does not rule out less ambitious forms of collaboration with the Japanese, as long as Japan's hegemonic pretensions remain relatively muted and within the limits of its present capabilities. In early 1996, for example, as many as nine governments were happy to sign a series of agreements committing the Bank of

Japan to make yen credits available when needed to help stabilise exchange rates (*New York Times*, 27 April 1996: 20). In 1997, after the first shockwaves hit, they were even more enthusiastic about Tokyo's proposal for a new regional financial facility – the Asian Monetary Fund (AMF) – to help protect national currencies against speculative attack (Altbach 1997; Rowley 1997). The AMF proposal was by far Japan's most ambitious effort to implement a strategy of market leadership in Asian finance. Although successfully blocked by the United States, which publicly expressed concern about a possible threat to the central role of the IMF in monetary affairs,[8] the idea continues to attract interest (Bergsten 1998) and Tokyo has persisted in seeking new ways to promote its monetary role in the region.[9] The process, however, is likely to be evolutionary than revolutionary in nature. Was there an alternative way to deal with the immediate crisis?

Capital controls

Throughout 1998, attention began to focus on the option of capital controls – a strategy of market preservation conventionally based on coercion rather than persuasion, inspired by the obvious example of China. Though hardly without troubles of its own, including a near-bankrupt banking system, loss-making state industries and rising unemployment, China was spared the worst ravages of the crisis. When other economies were being pushed into recession China's growth barely faltered; when other regional currencies were being depreciated in value (from 10–20 per cent in Taiwan and Singapore to as much as 80 per cent in Indonesia), the yuan held steady. One of the main reasons, observers concurred, was China's vast panoply of exchange and capital restrictions, which made it virtually impossible for domestic or foreign users to bet heavily on a devaluation.

The most dramatic implementation came from Malaysia, which in early September 1999 imposed strict controls on the convertibility of the national currency, the ringgit, for both trade and investment uses. Kuala Lumpur's new strategy was adopted in emulation of the Chinese, as stated by one government minister: 'Malaysia's new currency controls are based on China's model'.[10]

In the first year of the crisis the Malaysian economy had shrunk by close to 7 per cent, the ringgit by 40 per cent and the Kuala Lumpur stock market by 75 per cent. By the end of August, the country's authoritarian leader, Prime Minister Mahathir Mohamad, was no longer prepared to tolerate the orthodox policies of his Finance Minister and heir apparent Anwar Ibrahim, who was fired and later jailed. The policies, the prime minister believed, were collaboration in a Western conspiracy to ruin the Malaysian economy. The time had come to regain control from international speculators, led by George Soros and 'the Jews'. Henceforth trading in the ringgit would be carefully controlled, the exchange rate would be rigidly fixed and capital invested in the country would have to remain for at least one year before it could be repatriated. The idea was to provide room for more expansionary domestic policies than had otherwise seemed possible. Monetary policy was immediately eased and interest rates cut sharply, and in October a new budget combined substantial tax cuts with heavy new public spending programs. 'The plan', Dr Mahathir told legislators, 'aims at freeing Malaysia from the grip of the Asian financial crisis and to place Malaysia's economy on a stronger footing' (quoted in *New York Times*, 24 October 1998: B15).

That the prime minister's radical controls would prove controversial was hardly surprising. Though easy to ridicule for his conspiratorial views, Dr Mahathir posed a difficult challenge for conventional views on international financial management, which assumed the primacy of capital mobility. For decades, emerging nations had been lectured on the virtues of financial market liberalisation—yet here was a government that was doing just the reverse. Early signs suggested that Malaysia's economy was responding positively to the regime's expansionary policies. Dr Mahathir's audacity could have a powerful demonstration effect. What if Malaysia recovered more quickly as a result of its new insulation from international speculation? The experiment was carefully watched, though the jury remains out on a final verdict. Within six months growth was restored, permitting the prime minister to claim victory for his strategy (*Economist*, 1 May 1999: 73). However, most neighbouring countries also recovered during the same period, some even more rapidly than Malaysia, suggesting that the controls might have done more harm than good (Lum 1999). During 1999 restrictions were gradually eased, though not eliminated.

Nor was Malaysia alone. Some countries in the region, including South Korea and Taiwan, have always maintained residual controls to limit the volatility of capital flows. Even before Dr Mahathir acted Taiwan and others had resorted to new restrictions, albeit none as draconian as Malaysia's. One example was the Philippines, which in mid 1998 reintroduced limits on selected transactions involving repatriation of capital or remittance of profits. Another example, rather more startling, was Hong Kong, long considered the region's last bastion of true *laissez-faire* capitalism, where in late summer a broad program of new regulations was instituted to limit speculation on the local stock and currency exchanges.

With these initiatives, capital controls were no longer a forbidden topic in policy circles. As one source commented, 'capital curbs are an idea whose time, in the minds of many Asian government officials, has come back' (Wade & Veneroso 1998: 23). A policy approach once dismissed as obsolete, left over from a more interventionist era, was back on the agenda.

Shifting the discourse

Capital controls are controversial. Critics oppose them as inefficient and unworkable. Advocates defend them as a tonic for stricken economies. For decades the burden of proof was on those who tried to block the seemingly irresistible tide of financial globalisation, but with the crisis in Asia came a new respectability for limits on the cross-border mobility of capital. Both theory and history suggest that the burden of proof has shifted to those who defend the conventional wisdom rather than those who attack it.

For and against controls

The traditional case against capital controls is simple: it is the case for free markets, based on an analogy with standard theoretical arguments for free trade in goods and services. Commercial liberalisation is assumed to be a mutual-gain phenomenon, so why not financial liberalisation? Like trade based on comparative advantage, capital mobility is assumed to lead to more productive employment of investment resources, as well as to increased opportunities for effective risk management and welfare-improving intertemporal consumption smoothing. We are all presumably better off as a result. In the words of Federal Reserve chairman Alan Greenspan, an authoritative representative of the conventional wisdom:

> The accelerating expansion of global finance . . . enhances cross-border trade in goods and services, facilitates cross-border portfolio investment strategies, enhances the lower-cost financing of real capital formation on a worldwide basis, and, hence, leads to an expansion of international trade and rising standards of living (Greenspan 1998: 246).

All these gains would be threatened by controls, which would almost certainly create economic distortions and inhibit socially desirable risktaking. Worse, given the inexorable advance of financial technology, restrictions might not even prove to be effective. 'We cannot turn back the clock on technology – and we should not try to do so' (Greenspan 1998: 249). Any government that prefers controls is, in effect, simply living in the past.

Against these arguments, which have long dominated thinking in policy circles, two broad lines of dissent may be found in the literature. One approach focuses on the assumptions necessary to support the conventional wisdom, which are as demanding for trade in financial assets as they are for exchanges of goods and services. Strictly speaking, as a matter of theoretical reasoning, we can be certain that free capital movements will optimise welfare only in an idealised world of pure competition and perfect foresight. In reality, economies are rife with distortions (such as asymmetric availability of information) that prevent attainment of 'first-best' equilibrium. 'It has long been established that capital mobility in the presence of significant distortions . . . will result in a misallocation of the world's capital, and indeed can even worsen the economic well-being of the capital-importing country (Cooper 1999: 105; see also Eichengreen, Mussa & Staff Team 1998; Lopez-Mejia 1999).

A plausible case for controls may be made on standard 'second-best' grounds. Judicious introduction of another distortion in the form of capital restrictions could actually raise rather than lower economic welfare on a net basis. For every possible form of market failure, there can be a corresponding form of optimal intervention.

The logic of this kind of argument is not disputed. An omniscient government dealing with one clear distortion could undoubtedly improve welfare with some form of capital market restriction. What is disputed is the value of such logic in the real world of multiple distortions and imperfect policy-making. As Dooley (1996) has noted in a comprehensive survey of the relevant literature, the issue is not theoretical but empirical. The assumptions necessary to support an argument based on second-best considerations are no less 'heroic' than those underlying the more conventional *laissez-faire* view.

The second line of dissent, much more relevant to today's circumstances, looks not at isolated economic distortions but at the very nature of financial markets, which even in the absence of other considerations are especially prone to crisis and flux. At issue are the interdependencies of expectations in the buying and selling of claims, which unavoidably lead to both herd behaviour and multiple possible equilibria. Financial markets are notoriously vulnerable to self-fulfilling speculative bubbles and attacks. They also have a disturbing tendency to react unpredictably slowly to changing fundamentals – and then to overreact, rapidly and often arbitrarily. The resulting flows of funds, which may be massive, can be highly disruptive to national economies owing to their amplified impact on real economic variables. A logical case may be made for judicious intervention by state authorities, this time to limit the excessive instabilities and contagion effects endemic to the everyday operation of financial markets. In the words of a former governor of the Bank of Mexico:

> Recent experiences of market instability in the new global, electronically linked markets...have made the potential costs of massive speculative flows difficult to ignore or underestimate...The assumed gains from free capital mobility will have to be balanced against the very real risks such mobility poses.
>
> Some form of regulation or control...seems necessary to protect emerging-market economies from the devastating financial crises caused by massive capital movements (Buira 1999: 8–10).

Admittedly the value of this sort of argument may be open to challenge on empirical grounds, but less so in the midst of a global emergency when the disadvantages of unconstrained mobility are obvious. In fact, the latest research demonstrates that financial liberalisation is almost always associated with serious systemic crisis (Williamson & Mahar 1998). It is the explosion of these costs that has been decisive in shifting the terms of discourse on capital controls. Increasingly the question is posed: why should freedom of capital movement be given absolute priority over all other considerations of policy? Why, in effect, should governments tie one hand behind their backs as they seek to shape and manage demand for their currency?

Perhaps most influential in this regard was a widely quoted article by economist Jagdish Bhagwati, which appeared in May 1998. After Asia's painful experience, could anyone remain persuaded by the 'myth' of capital mobility's benign beneficence?

> it has become apparent that crises attendant on capital mobility cannot be ignored...When a crisis hits, the downside of free capital mobility

arises . . . Thus, any nation contemplating the embrace of free capital mobility must reckon with these costs and also consider the probability of running into a crisis. The gains from economic efficiency that would flow from free capital mobility, in a hypothetical crisis-free world, must be set against this loss if a wise decision is to be made (Bhagwati 1998: 8–9).

In a similar vein, Krugman decried the failure of the confidence game – orthodox strategies of market preservation that he labelled Plan A. 'It is time to think seriously about Plan B', he contended, meaning controls. 'There is a virtual consensus among economists that exchange controls work badly. But when you face the kind of disaster now occurring in Asia, the question has to be: badly compared to what?' (Krugman 1998b; see also Krugman 1999: ch. 9). Within months, Soros wrote that 'some form of capital controls may . . . be preferable to instability even if it would not constitute good policy in an ideal world' (Soros 1998: 192–3). Even the World Bank joined the chorus, arguing that 'The benefits of capital account liberalisation and increased capital flows have to be weighed against the likelihood of crisis and its costs' (World Bank 1999: xxi).

By the fall of 1998, not much more than a year after the crisis began, the momentum had clearly shifted toward reappraisal of the conventional wisdom.[11] As Bhagwati concluded, 'despite the . . . assumption that the ideal world is indeed one of free capital flows . . . the weight of evidence and the force of logic point in the opposite direction, toward restraints on capital flows. It is time to shift the burden of proof from those who oppose to those who favor liberated capital' (Bhagwati 1998: 12).

Back to the future?

Reappraisal of the conventional wisdom could also be justified on historical grounds. Many people fail to remember that the IMF's original design did not call for free capital mobility. On the contrary. Reflecting an abhorrence for the sort of 'hot money' flows that destabilised monetary relations in the 1920s and 1930s, the charter drafted at Bretton Woods made explicit allowance for the preservation of capital controls. Virtually everyone involved in the negotiations agreed with the influential League of Nations study, *International Currency Experience*, that some form of protection was needed against the risk of 'mass movements of nervous flight capital' (Nurkse 1944: 188). The option of controls was explicitly reserved to the discretion of individual states, provided only that such restraints were not intended to restrict international commerce.[12] The idea was to afford governments sufficient autonomy to promote stability and prosperity at home without endangering the broader structure of multilateral trade and payments that was being constructed abroad. It was a deliberate compromise between the imperatives of domestic interventionism and international liberalism – the compromise of 'embedded liberalism', as Ruggie (1983) later called it.

Pivotal in promoting that compromise was none other than John Maynard Keynes, universally respected as the greatest economist of his day and intellectual leader of the British delegation at Bretton Woods. To Keynes, nothing was more damaging than the free movement of speculative capital, which he viewed as 'the major cause of instability... [Without] security against a repetition of this... the whereabouts of "the better 'ole" will shift with the speed of the magic carpet. Loose funds may sweep round the world disorganising all steady business. Nothing is more certain than that the movement of capital funds must be regulated'.[13] Keynes carefully distinguished between genuinely productive investment flows and footloose 'floating funds'. The former were vital to 'developing the world's resources' and should be encouraged. Only the latter should be controlled, preferably as a 'permanent feature of the postwar system'.[14] After Bretton Woods, Keynes expressed satisfaction that his objectives in that regard had been achieved: 'Not merely as a feature of the transition, but as a permanent arrangement, the plan accords to every member government the explicit right to control all capital movements. What used to be heresy is now endorsed as orthodox' (quoted in Pauly 1997: 94).[15]

However, that achievement did not last. Over the next half-century, as the phoenix of global finance rose from the ashes, Keynes' strictures were largely forgotten and what had been endorsed as orthodox again became heresy. Increasingly, controls came to be regarded as wrong-headed if not anachronistic. Less and less were states thought to have rights to resist the preferences of the financial marketplace. By the 1980s, financial liberalisation had become the goal of every self-respecting industrial or middle-income country. By the 1990s, the tide was moving toward free capital mobility as a universal norm. Perhaps the high-water mark was reached in early 1997 when the Interim Committee of the IMF approved a plan to begin preparing a new amendment to the organisation's charter to make the promotion of capital account liberalisation a specific IMF objective and responsibility.[16] Evidently insensitive to the irony, Camdessus asserted that the IMF's plan amounted to a mandate to add the 'unwritten chapter' of Bretton Woods (quoted in *IMF Survey*, 12 May 1997: 136).

Then came the fall of the Thai baht. Even the IMF changed its tune, dropping active discussion of a new amendment and talking instead of the possible efficacy of selective restraints (see, for example, Adams et al. 1998: 79, 150; Eichengreen, Mussa & Staff Team 1998: 2–3, 29) – a tentative step back to the future envisaged by Keynes and others when the IMF was created. Clearly, the pressure of events had conspired with a reawakened sense of history to put the case for capital controls in a new light. Limitations on capital mobility thus seemed to gain new legitimacy as an instrument of monetary governance.

Three critical questions

Shifting the burden of proof was only the start of the story, not the end. Even granting that a case for restraint might be made, important technical questions must be resolved if monetary governance is to be improved rather than disrupted. The three most critical questions are: What kinds of capital flows should be subject to limitation? What kinds of controls might be most effective? What kinds of rules might avoid major inefficiencies or serious policy conflict? The debate on these questions is just beginning (see, for example, Kahler 1998).

What kinds of flows?

Not all capital flows, to paraphrase the US Declaration of Independence, are created equal. In thinking about what flows might be limited, three key distinctions are important – differences involving the direction of capital movement, the type of capital movement and the identity of the actors.

Direction

The key distinction is between inflows and outflows of capital. In the midst of a currency crisis, when confidence in a nation's money suddenly collapses, attention naturally turns to the latter. The issue seems simple: how to stop the haemorrhaging. To many the solution seems equally simple: restrict the flight of funds in any or every way possible, as Malaysia has tried to do.

Capital outflows, however, are notoriously difficult to block, particularly at times of panic when the motivation to get out of a currency is highest. One of the more pernicious byproducts of financial globalisation has been the creation of a vast network of private institutions and intermediaries, backed by the latest in financial technology, that can be used – legally if possible, illegally when felt necessary – to evade even the most draconian public controls. As many governments have learned to their regret, restrictions may merely cause market actors to find new routes of escape. Cooper puts the point well: 'it is probably true that anyone determined to export private capital from a country can find a way, at a price, to do so' (Cooper 1998: 17).

A prime example occurred during the 1980s when several Latin American countries separately tried to suppress capital flight by imposing exchange controls, forcibly converting foreign currency accounts in domestic banks into local money. These included Bolivia and Mexico in 1982 and Peru in 1985. In all three cases, the immediate response was a decisive vote of no confidence, a clandestine flight of funds into accounts abroad that undermined rather than bolstered the market position of national money. Studies indicate that overall, taking into account deposits held in foreign as well as domestic banks, capital outflows increased rather than decreased after the restrictions were instituted (Savastano 1996). In all three countries, the failed measures were ultimately abandoned.

Experiences like these do not mean that such controls are inherently unworkable, as critics often charge. In practice restrictions may indeed work quite effectively, at least for a time, to limit flight from a currency. Much depends on institutional matters of policy design and administration – the degree to which governments can develop the technological sophistication and financial skills needed to beat the markets at their own game. Much depends on other policy initiatives that accompany the controls to restore confidence in the local money. Experience does suggest that, once imposed, limitations on outflows may have to be expanded if their impact is not to be gradually eroded.[17] The dyke must be built ever higher and wider to contain turbulent liquidity. It appears, therefore, that barriers to outflows might work best if imposed for relatively short periods to cope with temporary emergencies, rather than as a permanent element of a government's strategy of monetary governance.

Barriers to inflows, in contrast, might be sustainable for much longer periods, since it is easier to keep capital out than in. Restrictions on outflows drastically reduce the choices available to a currency's users, sowing frustration and creating incentives for evasion. Restrictions on inflows limit only one option among many, leaving foreign capital free to look for profitable outlets elsewhere. Champions of controls point to the example of Chile where, in the early 1990s, surging inflows generated growing conflict between the government's internal and external policy objectives. The problem was how to maintain a tight monetary policy without generating an exchange rate appreciation that might hinder export competitiveness. The solution was a program of administrative measures designed to discourage various forms of borrowing or portfolio investment from abroad – an approach that, with some caveats, apparently achieved its main goals before being largely dismantled in 1998 (see, for example, Adams et al. 1998: 176–9; Cooper 1999: 116–18). Similar measures have been implemented in a number of other countries, with varying degrees of success (Reinhart & Reinhart 1998: 117–19).

Limitations on inflows do little good in the midst of a panic, when the problem is too little interest in a currency rather than too much. In calmer times, however, much benefit might be derived if restrictions could succeed in reducing exposure to a reversal of sentiment. Most analyses of the current crisis in Asia concur that a key factor was a flood of capital into national financial systems that were unable to handle so much liquidity properly (Goldstein 1998; Radelet & Sachs 1998; Wade 1998). Perhaps some form of program to limit inflows, in emulation of the Chilean model, might help prevent history repeating itself.

Type

The key distinction is between varying degrees of volatility. If the challenge confronting governments is vulnerability to self-fulfilling bubbles and attacks, the solution can hardly lie in restricting something like foreign direct investment (FDI) in fixed assets, which can be assumed to be relatively unresponsive to transitory variations of market sentiment. A more appropriate target would be the more impatient categories of capital that are most liquid and prone to contagion and overreaction – those that are most easily reversed in a short time.

Reversibility is most characteristic of investments that focus on price rather than yield, seeking to maximise capital gain rather than accrue dividends and interest over time. These include purely speculative currency transactions that bear no direct relation to underlying trade or production decisions. That means not only the traditional spot and forward segments of the exchange market but also swaps, options and the exotic forms of currency derivatives that have become fashionable. Also included would be most other categories of purely portfolio investment – equities as well as marketable debt – that can be bought and sold at a moment's notice. In the light of Asia's recent experience, a compelling case can be made for imposing some kind of limit on any or all of these types of activity. In contrast, little would appear to be gained – and much might be lost – by restrictions on FDI or FDI-like flows such as long-term bank lending (World Bank 1998: ch. 3).[18]

What about short-term bank lending? A central cause of the Asian crisis was overreliance on foreign borrowing at short maturity – not a problem when creditors continued to refinance or roll over their claims, but very much a problem when expectations shifted. A sudden demand to make good on outstanding debts can be as damaging to a currency as sales of assets. A case could be made for some form of intervention or regulation to discourage excessive external exposure at short term.

Identity

The key distinction here is that of citizenship – whether the same rules should apply to all market actors or whether distinctions should be made between members of the national community and others. The argument cuts both ways.

Citizens are the only market actors that can legitimately hold a government accountable for its actions. Hence, one might reasonably conclude, citizens should be the only actors whose behaviour may be formally restricted by public authority. In practical terms, this would imply controls over borrowing or investments by nationals but freedom of action for non-nationals – a distinction sometimes rephrased in terms of residents versus non-residents. Foreigners (non-residents) would be allowed to move funds in and out at will; citizens (residents) would not.

Non-citizens are market actors with the least tenable claim to preferential treatment by a national government. Hence it might seem reasonable to limit the behaviour of foreigners (non-residents), if anyone, rather than one's own people (residents). Commentator Samuel Brittan (1998) evidently had that idea in mind: 'controls on inward movements are inherently less sinister than those on outward movements designed to prevent citizens from sending funds abroad'. It is certainly what Hale (1998: 11) means when he suggests that 'capital controls represent a form of command economy intervention which could have implications for a country's political freedom, not just its economic freedom'. Brittan (1998) puts the point most bluntly: 'The most basic argument against exchange control...is that it is one of the most potent weapons of tyranny which can be used to imprison citizens in their own country'.

Is the tyranny of free capital mobility any less sinister than that of intervention by the state? Might there not be some reasonable trade-off between support of the property rights of money's users, whether foreign or domestic, and defence of a government's sovereign right to act in the nation's interests? States have long since abandoned absolute *laissez-faire* as a proper guide to economic policy. In this sense, capital controls would be no different from any other form of intervention by public authorities intended to balance the desires and demands of the public and private sectors.

What kinds of controls?

Not all controls are created equal, either. In thinking about what kinds of controls might be the most effective, two key distinctions are important – duration and tactics.

Duration

The key distinction is between temporary and permanent. Controls that are imposed for unlimited duration, critics argue, are insidious for several reasons. Not only do they create powerful incentives for evasion, they might require an onerous amount of paperwork and an ever-expanding bureaucracy to administer them. Worst of all, they could invite corruption and cronyism, as market actors use bribery or political favours to obtain what is no longer legally available. Cooper (1998: 12) cites the risk that controls 'will favour scofflaws over law-abiding citizens, with corrosive effects on public morality'. The implication is that if restraints are to be used, they should be imposed only at times of emergency and then only temporarily, until more stable conditions return.

The force of such arguments has been acknowledged for measures designed to limit panicky capital flight. But are all other forms of restraint equally susceptible to the same kinds of risks? If that were so, states would have abandoned every kind of restriction or regulation of market activity – domestic business as well as international, commercial as well as financial – whereas the reverse is true. History amply demonstrates that permanent governmental interventions are not necessarily inconsistent with public morality, nor are they inevitably vitiated by widening leakage and circumvention. Again, much depends on policy design and administration as well as on the broader economic, political and social environment. There seems no reason to exclude the option of permanent controls in some circumstances.

Tactics

The issue here relates to the key distinction between persuasion and coercion. Most critics of capital controls seem to assume that restraints must be coercive in nature, involving strict quantitive limits on or outright prohibitions of specified transactions – borrowing or investment ceilings, exclusions, proscriptions and the like. Hale insisted that 'capital controls represent a form of *command economy* intervention' (1998: 11, emphasis added). But this assumption ignores the powerful role of persuasion as a tactic for preserving or promoting the market share of a currency. Much more market-friendly measures are also feasible, such as interventions that aim to alter actor incentives, via taxes or equivalent policy instruments, rather than formally suppress particular activities. That is obviously what Eichengreen (in IMF 1998) had in mind in commenting recently that 'capital account convertibility, while implying the removal of controls and prohibitions, need not mean abjuring taxes and tax-like levies on the underlying transactions' (see also Eichengreen, Mussa & Staff Team 1998). In principle, it ought to be possible to devise effective limits on capital mobility that do not involve overt coercion.

The classic example is Chile, whose oft-cited control program mainly comprised such market-based measures, the central of which was the so-called unremunerated reserve requirement (URR) on most forms of external financing other than FDI. Any investor or lender wishing to enter the Chilean market was required to leave a sum equal to a specified percentage of the transaction on deposit with the government for one year. (The percentage was raised to as high as 30 per cent then reduced to 10 per cent in 1998, before being phased out.) Since no interest was received on the deposit, the requirement acted like a tax to discourage short-term movements in and out of the country. But since no trans-actions were expressly prohibited, market actors could make decisions based on their assessment of potential risks and returns. Variations in the rate of the URR gave the government a convenient instrument for influencing flows through the capital account, thus demonstrating that a well-designed program of persuasion could work as well as more coercive currency strategies.

What kinds of rules?

The key question is the locus of authority, an inherently political issue. Where should ultimate jurisdiction over capital controls reside – at the national level or at a higher multilateral level? To some observers, there is no question. In a system of sovereign states responsibility must remain with national governments, which are presumably best placed to determine the needs and interests of their people. Cooper expressed the representative view in a recent public forum (IMF 1998): 'Each community should decide for itself the balance it wants to strike between corruption and scofflaws and so forth. Those are all legitimate national choices'. In effect, the trend toward oligopoly in monetary governance might be best resisted unilaterally. States should be free to limit capital mobility, if and as they wish, in an effort to restore some degree of monopoly control over their national currencies.

What of the risks of inefficiency and corruption that could result from an unrestrained use of controls? Worse, what about the risk of serious policy conflict if governments are tempted to retaliate in kind? In financial markets, as in markets for goods and services, no nation is an island. Actions in one place are bound to generate externalities that could invite damaging responses elsewhere, possibly leading to a vicious circle of beggar-thy-neighbour economic warfare on the model of the 1930s. The IMF was created to prevent a recurrence of that sad historical experience, forming the cornerstone of an edifice of norms and rules – an international regime – to govern monetary relations between sovereign states. National interest was not suppressed but, by common consent, international interests were to be taken into account. A strong case can be made for preserving the same principle as the debate over capital controls moves forward. As Mussa (in IMF 1998) remarked in responding to Cooper's proposition:

> Dick Cooper suggests that ... this issue should be viewed largely as a national issue, an issue of national economic policy, and the choice should be left to national governments ... and I think there is something to be said for that ... [But] I think there is [also] a broader systemic interest in having capital account liberalisation handled in a manner that maximises the benefits for the world economy as a whole and limits the risks as best as possible for the world economy as a whole ... There is not only a national interest, but there is also an international interest.

How might national and international interests be reconciled? Most desirable would be a broad set of guidelines negotiated multilaterally but applied unilaterally. The guidelines should include specifications on such questions as the sort of restraints on capital mobility that may be permitted, under what circumstances and using what procedures. Within the limits set by those guidelines, governments would have wide latitude to make their own choices, with a qualified international institution – logically the IMF – designated as referee in the event of conflict or dispute. In an early analysis of the challenges of financial globalisation for monetary governance, Kapstein (1994) labelled such an approach 'international cooperation based on home country control'. More recently, Rodrik (1998) has spoken of the need for a 'rule-based multilateral regime'. Whatever the terminology, the goal is clear – to achieve a workable compromise between national prerogatives and global considerations that will make the design and implementation of capital controls less controversial for all.

Conclusion

However, controversy is inevitable, given the distributional considerations. The Asian crisis provided one of those rare watershed moments when conventional wisdom could be seriously challenged. With economies seemingly brought to their knees by the vagaries of global finance, the time seemed ripe for reviving capital controls as a legitimate tool of public policy. Yet even if satisfactory answers are found to all the technical questions raised, there will be resistance from those most likely to be adversely affected by limitations on capital mobility. Prospective losers from controls include large industrial or commercial enterprises with sufficient creditworthiness to borrow internationally, who could be deprived of access to cheaper foreign sources of finance. They also include owners of mobile assets, typically financial service firms and high net worth individuals, who presently enjoy the privilege of investing wherever (risk-adjusted) returns promise to be highest. Potential winners include those who might benefit from a recovery of some degree of national monetary sovereignty, such as small and mediumsized businesses, retail trade, labour unions (representing worker interests) and local banks and borrowers. In practical terms, therefore, the most important question is political feasibility – how to mobilise effective support for restrictions of any kind.

Outcomes will depend on the lobbying and coalition strategies of interest groups on either side of the issue. It is difficult to predict which camp is likely to prevail in any given country, but it doesn't take much imagination to suppose that in most cases the balance of influence might tilt in favour of the bigger and wealthier anti-control constituencies, who are likely to have easier access to the corridors of power and to be better organised to articulate their interests and concerns. If governments are to reclaim any of the authority currently ceded to capital markets, it will require more than reasoned debate about market imperfections and multiple equilibria. Much more fundamentally, it will require active political engagement, both at home and abroad – the mobilisation of political constituencies everywhere, including foreign constituencies, with an interest in restoring the compromise of embedded liberalism written into the IMF charter at Bretton Woods. Otherwise the phoenix of global finance will continue to rule the roost untamed.

Notes

1 This chapter benefited from discussion at the Conference on the Asian Financial Crisis as well as the thoughtful comments of David Andrews, Michael Gordon, David McKay, Greg Noble and John Ravenhill. The assistance of Ben Pettit is also gratefully acknowledged.

2 The earliest example I can find of this change of tone was a column by *Financial Times* commentator Martin Wolf in March 1998. Ordinarily a firm champion of free markets, Wolf reluctantly concluded: 'After the crisis, the question can no longer be whether these flows should be regulated in some way. It can only be how' (Wolf 1998). Ten months later, at the annual World Economic Forum in Davos, Switzerland – always a useful means of tracking authoritative public- and private-sector opinion – it was clear that unrestricted capital mobility was no longer much in favour (see, for example, *New York Times*, 29 January 1999: C1).

3 The discussion in this section is based on arguments presented at greater length in Cohen (1998a).

4 In Krugman's words, in the confidence game economic policy 'must cater to the perceptions, the prejudices, the whims of the market. Or, rather, one must cater to what one *hopes* will be the perceptions of the market . . . . [Policy becomes] an exercise in amateur psychology' (1999: 113, original emphasis).

5 For a bitter post mortem, see Culp et al. (1999). Culp et al. dismiss the risk at the time of a rush to buy dollars as a 'nightmare scenario', suggesting that opposition to an Indonesian currency board, led by the US Treasury and the IMF, was motivated not by 'the fear that it would not have worked but rather that it would have worked too well – viz., saving Indonesia and postponing the end of the Suharto regime' (1999: 61, 64). This seems a bit strong in view of Washington's traditional support of Suharto.

6 A notable exception was the head of the Hong Kong Monetary Authority, Joseph Yam, who in early 1999 made a spirited plea for 'our own Asian currency' to reduce the region's vulnerability to speculative attack (quoted in *Financial Times*, 6 January 1999).

7 Perhaps most ambitious was EMEAP (Executive Meeting of East Asia and Pacific Central Banks), a self-described 'vehicle for regional cooperation among central banks' encompassing Australia, China, Hong Kong, Indonesia, Japan, Malaysia, New Zealand, the Philippines, Singapore, South Korea and Thailand. Other examples include

SEACEN (South-East Asian Central Banks) and SEANZA (South-East Asia, New Zealand and Australia), both of which provide for regular meetings of central bank officials as well as various training programs.

8 Privately, Washington feared a loss of political influence in the region since the AMF, if implemented, would obviously have been dominated by Tokyo. In economic terms, Washington's response to the AMF proposal was remarkably reminiscent of a similar episode a quarter-century earlier, when an agreement to create a Financial Support Fund in the OECD (based in Paris) was torpedoed by the US government on almost identical grounds (Cohen 1998b).

9 In October 1998, for example, Finance Minister Kiichi Miyazawa offered $US30 billion in fresh financial aid for Asia in a plan soon labelled the 'New Miyazawa initiative', and two months later made it clear that Japan intended to revive its AMF proposal when the time seemed right (*Financial Times*, 16 December 1998).

10 Special Functions Minister Diam Zainuddin, as quoted in Wade and Veneroso (1998b:20).

11 For an overview of recent debate, compare the contrasting views of Hale (1998) and Wade and Veneroso (1998b). A balanced analysis is provided by Cooper (1999).

12 Article VI, Sections 1 and 3 of the Articles of Agreement of the IMF.

13 'Post-war currency policy', a British Treasury memo dated September 1941, reprinted in Moggridge (1980: 31). For ''ole' read 'hole' – a handy place to hide money.

14 'Plan for an international currency (or clearing) union', January 1942, reprinted in Moggridge (1980: 129-30).

15 For more on Keynes' views and how they relate to the current crisis, see Cassidy (1998) and Kirshner (1999).

16 Interim Committee Communique, 28 April 1997: para. 7. Under the plan, two Articles were to be amended: Article I, where 'orderly liberalization of capital' would be added to the list of the IMF's formal purposes; and Article VIII, which would give the IMF the same jurisdiction over the capital account of its members as it already has over the current account. The language would require countries to commit themselves to capital liberalisation as a goal.

17 For a statement of the same point, see Cohen (1965). In my bolder and more dogmatic youth, I was even willing to raise this observation to the status of an economic law – what I ambitiously labelled the Iron Law of Economic Controls: 'to be effective, controls must reproduce at a rate faster than that at which means are found for avoiding them' (Cohen 1965: 174). Today I am less inclined to be quite so categorical.

18 Admittedly, the distinction between FDI-like flows and more impatient investment categories may be easier to draw in principle than in practice. For some discussion of the practical difficulties involved, see Maxfield (1998).

References

Adams, Charles, Donald J. Mathieson, Garry Schinasi & Bankim Chadha (1998), *International Capital Markets: Developments, Prospects and Key Policy Issues* (Washington DC: International Monetary Fund).

Altbach, Eric (1997), 'The Asian Monetary Fund proposal: a case study of Japanese regional leadership', *JEI Report*, 47A (December).

Bergsten, C. Fred (1998), 'Missed opportunity', *International Economy*, 12(6): 26–7.

Bhagwati, Jagdish (1998), 'The capital myth: the difference between trade in widgets and dollars, *Foreign Affairs*, 77(3): 7–12.

Brittan, Samuel (1998), 'Exchange controls: the economic trap', *Financial Times*, 1 October.

Buira, Ariel (1999), *An Alternative Approach to Financial Crises* (Princeton, NJ: Essays in International Finance No. 212, International Finance Section, Department of Economics, Princeton University).

Cassidy, John (1998), 'The new world disorder', *New Yorker*, 26 October: 198–207.

Cohen, Benjamin J. (1965), 'Capital controls and the U.S. balance of payments', *American Economic Review*, 55(1): 172–6.

Cohen, Benjamin J. (1993), 'Beyond EMU: the problem of sustainability', *Economics and Politics*, 5(2): 187–203.

Cohen, Benjamin J. (1996), 'Phoenix risen: the resurrection of global finance', *World Politics*, 48(2): 268–96.

Cohen, Benjamin J. (1998a), *The Geography of Money* (Ithaca, NY: Cornell University Press).

Cohen, Benjamin J. (1998b), 'When giants clash: the OECD Financial Support Fund and the IMF' in Vinod K. Aggarwal (ed.), *Institutional Designs for a Complex World: Bargaining, Linkages and Nesting* (Ithaca, NY: Cornell University Press).

Cooper, Richard N. (1998), 'Should capital-account convertibility be a world objective?' in Stanley Fischer et al., *Should the IMF Pursue Capital-Account Convertibility?* (Princeton, NJ: Essays in International Finance No. 207, International Finance Section, Department of Economics, Princeton University).

Cooper, Richard N. (1999), 'Should capital controls be banished?', *Brookings Papers on Economic Activity*, 1: 89–141.

Culp, Christopher L., Steve H. Hanke & Merton H. Miller (1999), 'The case for an Indonesian currency board', *Journal of Applied Corporate Finance*, 11(4): 57–65.

Dooley, Michael (1996), 'A survey of literature on controls over international capital transactions', *International Monetary Fund Staff Papers*, 43(4) (December): 639–87.

Eichengreen, Barry (1997), 'International monetary arrangements: is there a monetary union in Asia's future?', *Brookings Review*, 15(2): 33–5.

Eichengreen, Barry, Michael Mussa & Staff Team (1998), *Capital Account Liberalization: Theoretical and Practical Aspects* (Washington DC: International Monetary Fund, Occasional Paper No. 172).

Goldstein, Morris (1998), *The Asian Financial Crisis: Causes, Cures and Systemic Implications* (Washington DC: Institute for International Economics).

Greenspan, Alan (1998), 'The globalization of finance', *Cato Journal*, 17(3): 243–50.

Hale, David D. (1998), 'The hot money debate', *International Economy*, 12(6): 8–12, 66–9.

Hanke, Steve H. & Kurt Schuler (1994), *Currency Boards for Developing Countries: A Handbook* (San Francisco: Institute for Contemporary Studies).

IMF (International Monetary Fund) (1998), *Capital Account Liberalization: What's the Best Stance?*, IMF Economic Forum, 22 October (text available from the IMF website).

Kahler, Miles (ed.) (1998), *Capital Flows and Financial Crises* (Ithaca, NY: Cornell University Press).

Kapstein, Ethan B. (1994), *Governing the Global Economy: International Finance and the State* (Cambridge, Mass.: Harvard University Press).

Kirshner, Jonathan (1999), 'Keynes, capital mobility and the crisis of embedded liberalism', *Review of International Political Economy*, 6(3): 313–37.

Krugman, P. (1998a), 'The confidence game', *New Republic*, 5 October: 23–5 (see also http://web.mit.edu/krugman/www).

Krugman, Paul. (1998b), 'Saving Asia: it's time to get radical', *Fortune Magazine*, 138(5): 74–80.

Krugman, Paul. (1999), *The Return of Depression Economics* (New York: Norton).

Lopez-Mejia, Alejandro (1999), 'Large capital flows: a survey of the causes, consequences and policy responses' (Washington DC: IMF, Staff working Paper No. WP/99/17).

Lum, Linda (1999), 'Malaysia's response to the Asian financial crisis' (Washington DC: Testimony prepared for hearings before the Subcommittee on Asia and the Pacific of the House Committee on International Relations, US Congress, 16 June).

Maxfield, Sylvia (1998), 'Effects of international portfolio flows on government policy choice' in Miles Kahler (ed.), *Capital Flows and Financial Crises* (Ithaca, NY: Cornell University Press).

Moggridge, Donald (ed.) (1980), *The Collected Writings of John Maynard Keynes*, vol XXV (Cambridge: Cambridge University Press).

Mundell, Robert A. (1997), 'Forum on Asian fund', *Capital Trends*, 2(13).

Nurkse, Ragnar (1944), *International Currency Experience: Lessons from the Inter-war Period* (Geneva: League of Nations).

Pauly, Louis W. (1997), *Who Elected the Bankers? Surveillance and Control in the World Economy* (Ithaca, NY: Cornell University Press).

Radelet, Steven & Jeffrey D. Sachs (1998), 'The East Asian financial crisis: diagnosis, remedies, prospects', *Brookings Papers on Economic Activity*, 1: 1–90.

Reinhart, Carmen M. & Vincent Raymond Reinhart (1998), 'Some lessons for policy-makers who deal with the mixed blessing of capital inflows' in Miles Kahler (ed.), *Capital Flows and Financial Crises* (Ithaca, NY: Cornell University Press).

Rodrik, Dani (1998), 'The global fix', *New Republic,* 2 November: 17–19.

Rowley, Anthony (1997), 'International finance: Asian Fund, R.I.P.', *Capital Trends*, 2(14).

Ruggie, John G. (1983), International regimes, transactions and change: embedded liberalism in the postwar economic order' in Stephen D. Krasner (ed.), *International Regimes* (Ithaca, NY: Cornell University Press).

Savastano, M.A. (1996), 'Dollarization in Latin America: recent evidence and policy issues' in P.D. Mizen & E.J. Pentecost (eds), *The Macroeconomics of International Currencies: Theory, Policy and Evidence* (Brookfield, VT: Edward Elgar).

Soros, George (1998), *The Crisis of Global Capitalism* (New York: Public Affairs).

Wade, Robert (1998), 'The Asian crisis and the global economy: causes, consequences and cure', *Current History*, 97 (November): 361–73.

Wade, Robert & Frank Veneroso (1998), 'The gathering support for capital controls', *Challenge*, 41(6): 14–26.

Walter, Norbert (1998), 'An Asian prediction', *International Economy*, 12(3): 49.

Williamson, John & Molly Mahar (1998), *A Survey of Financial Liberalization* (Princeton, NJ: Essays in International Finance No. 211, International Finance Section, Department of Economics, Princeton University).

Wolf, Martin (1998), 'Flows and blows', *Financial Times*, 3 March.

World Bank (1998), *Global Economic Prospects and the Developing Countries 1998/99: Beyond Financial Crisis* (Washington DC: World Bank).

World Bank (1999), *Global Development Finance 1999* (Washington DC: World Bank).

9   Capital controls

The neglected option

Source: From G.R.D. Underhill and X. Zhang (eds), *International Financial Governance Under Stress: global structures versus national imperatives*, 2003.

Why don't emerging-market economies make more use of capital controls? Not long ago, in the wake of Asia's great financial crisis, limitations on capital mobility appeared about to make a comeback. At the intellectual level, scholars began to accord new respectability to the old case for controls as an instrument of monetary governance. At a more practical level, one country – Malaysia – imposed comprehensive restraints and, with seeming success, survived to tell the tale. As I wrote soon after the crisis broke: 'The tide... is starting to turn. Once scorned as a relic of the past, limits on capital mobility could soon become the wave of the future.'[1] Yet in reality governments in the newly industrialising economies still hesitate to raise or restore impediments to the free flow of capital. Controls remain the neglected option. The question is: why?

Elsewhere, I have suggested that the explanation has much to do with the prominent role of the United States, the still dominant power in international finance.[2] Washington, both directly and through the IMF, has brought its considerable power to bear to resist any significant revival of controls. Reflection suggests, however, that international politics is at best only part of the story; *domestic* politics too must be involved, in a mutually reinforcing interaction with the pressure of outside forces. The purpose of this chapter is to highlight the critical domestic side of the story. My focus is on the thirty or so newly industrialising countries, mostly located in east Asia and Latin America, that are commonly referred to as the 'emerging markets'.[3]

I begin in section one with a quick look back at the transformation of the global financial environment that gradually occurred in recent decades – an epochal change that has made it increasingly difficult for governments everywhere to manage monetary affairs within their own sovereign territories. Capital controls represent one possible response to the growing challenge that global financial markets pose for national monetary governance. The pros and cons of capital controls are evaluated in section two, highlighting the tidal shift that has occurred at the level of scholarly discourse. The analytical case for controls, it is now widely acknowledged, is actually a good deal stronger than conventionally supposed. Reasons for the continued opposition of the United States are briefly summarised in section three.

Section four then takes up the domestic side of the story, stressing the key role of powerful societal interests that, having benefited from liberalisation in the past, now share Washington's preference for keeping financial markets open in the future. In effect, a powerful transnational coalition would seem to be at work to ensure that capital restraints remain the neglected option. In section five I conclude by offering some brief thoughts on what, in practical terms, might be done to mobilise greater political support for controls as a legitimate tool of monetary governance.

The new geography of money[4]

That the global financial environment has been greatly transformed in recent decades is undeniable. The full significance of that change for monetary governance, however, has only lately begun to be widely appreciated. Prior to the Asian crisis in 1997–8, policy makers were only starting to learn how to cope with the rising challenge to their authority.

The postwar resurrection of global finance has been truly phenomenal. Half a century ago, after the ravages of the Great Depression and the Second World War, financial markets everywhere – with the notable exception of the United States – were generally weak, insular and strictly controlled, reduced from their previously central role in international economic relations to offer little more than a negligible amount of trade financing. Starting in the 1950s, however, deregulation and liberalisation began to combine with technological and institutional innovation to breach many of the barriers separating national currencies and monetary systems. In a cumulative process driven by the pressures of domestic and international competition, the range of market opportunities has gradually widened for borrowers and investors alike. The result has been a remarkable growth of capital mobility across political frontiers, reflected in a scale of financial flows unequalled since the glory days of the nineteenth-century gold standard.

Even more phenomenal have been the implications of these changes for monetary governance and the long-standing convention of national monetary sovereignty. With the deepening integration of financial markets, strict dividing lines between separate national monies have become less and less distinct. No longer are economic actors restricted to a single currency – their own home money – as they go about their daily business. Cross-border circulation of currencies, which was once quite common prior to the emergence of the modern state system, has dramatically re-emerged, with competition between national monies gradually accelerating. This is what I have referred to elsewhere as the new geography of money – the evolving configuration of currency space.[5] The functional domain of each money no longer corresponds precisely with the formal jurisdiction of its issuing authority. Currencies instead have become increasingly *deterritorialised*, their circulation determined not by law or politics but rather by the dynamics of supply and demand.

Currency deterritorialisation poses a new and critical challenge to governments, which have long relied upon the privileges derived from a formal monetary monopoly to promote their conception of state interest. These privileges include, in particular, the powers of seigniorage and macroeconomic management. No longer can governments exert the same degree of control over the use of their monies, either by their own citizens or others. Instead, policy makers have been driven to compete, inside and across borders, for the allegiance of market agents – in effect, to sustain or cultivate market share for their own brand of currency. Monopoly has yielded to something more like oligopoly, and monetary governance has been reduced to little more than a choice among marketing strategies designed to shape and manage demand.

Broadly speaking, four strategies are possible, depending on two key considerations – first, whether policy is defensive or offensive, aiming either to preserve or promote market share, and second, whether policy is pursued unilaterally or collusively. The four strategies are:

1. *Market leadership:* an aggressive unilateralist policy intended to maximise use of the national currency, analogous to predatory price leadership in an oligopoly.
2. *Market alliance:* a collusive policy of sharing monetary sovereignty in a monetary union of some kind, analogous to a tacit or explicit cartel.
3. *Market preservation:* a status-quo policy intended to defend, rather than augment, a previously acquired market position.
4. *Market followership:* an acquiescent policy of subordinating monetary sovereignty to a stronger foreign currency via some form of firm exchange rate rule (e.g., a currency board), analogous to passive price followership in an oligopoly. In extremis, followership may entail full replacement of the national currency by the stronger foreign currency (official dollarisation).

Of these four options, the first, market leadership, is generally available only to governments with the most widely circulated monies, such as America's dollar or Germany's mark (now replaced by the euro). Other countries, with less competitive currencies, must select from among the remaining three strategies. The basic question is plain. Should policy makers do what they can to sustain national monetary sovereignty (market preservation)? Or, alternatively, should they countenance delegating some or all of that authority either to a monetary union (market alliance) or to a dominant foreign power (market followership)? A former president of the Argentine central bank put the point bluntly: 'Should a [country] produce its own money, or should it buy it from a more efficient producer?'[6] For most countries today, the answer is equally plain. Most appear resolved, at least for now, to continue producing their own money – to keep the national currency alive, no matter how uncompetitive it may be. A sovereign money is still seen in most parts of the world as a natural extension of the principle of *political* sovereignty.

How can a national currency be kept alive? Market share can be defended by tactics of either persuasion or coercion. Most governments seek to sustain demand by buttressing their money's reputation, above all by publicly committing themselves to credible policies of 'sound' monetary management. The idea is to preserve market confidence in the value and usability of the nation's brand of currency – the 'confidence game', as Paul Krugman has ironically dubbed it.[7] But demand can also be managed by using the formal powers of the state to coerce rather than persuade. In fact, states regulate monetary use all the time. One way is by such means as legal-tender laws (specifying what currency private creditors must accept in payment of a debt) and public receivability provisions (specifying what currency the government itself will accept in payment of taxes or other public obligations). Another way may be by restraining the movement of funds into or out of the country – in a word, capital controls. Limitations on capital mobility are a logical corollary of any strategy of market preservation.

In practice, of course, the trend in recent decades has been all the other way, reflecting what has come to be known as the 'Washington consensus' – a triumphalist 'neo-liberal' economics emphasising the virtues of privatisation, deregulation and liberalisation wherever possible. The Washington consensus has been widely promoted by the US government together with the Washington-based IMF and World Bank. First the more advanced economies of Europe and Japan, then many emerging market economies, undertook to dismantle as many of their existing controls as possible. Restraints on capital mobility were frowned upon as a relic of an older, more *dirigiste* mentality – wrongheaded if not downright anachronistic. By the 1980s, financial liberalisation had become the goal of almost every self-respecting industrial or middle-income country. By the 1990s, the tide was clearly moving towards the consecration of free capital mobility as a universal norm. Perhaps the high-water mark was reached in early 1997 when the Interim Committee of the IMF approved a plan to begin preparing a new amendment to the Fund's charter to make the promotion of capital account liberalisation a specific IMF objective and responsibility.[8]

But then came Asia's financial crisis, which forced a fundamental reconsideration of the wisdom of financial liberalisation. Governments in east Asia which previously had taken pride in the competitiveness of their currencies suddenly found themselves unable to preserve user loyalty. Strategies that once seemed adequate to sustain market share now had to be re-evaluated in the light of a massive 'flight to quality' by mobile capital. Inevitably, policy makers were drawn to take a new look at the old case for capital controls. Observers could hardly fail to note that China, which had never abandoned its vast panoply of financial restraints, was able to avoid much of the distress afflicting its more liberalised neighbours. Nor could the actions of Malaysia be ignored, once its comprehensive control programme was announced in September 1998. As one source commented at the time, 'capital curbs are an idea whose time, in the minds of many Asian government officials, has come back'.[9] Like it or not, an approach once dismissed as obsolete – a leftover of a more interventionist era – was now back on the policy agenda.

The case for controls

Capital controls are controversial. Critics oppose them as inefficient and unworkable. Advocates justify them as a tonic for stricken economies. For decades the burden of proof was on those who would foolhardily try to block the seemingly irresistible tide of financial globalisation. With the crisis in Asia, however, came a new intellectual respectability for limits of some kind on the cross-border mobility of capital. Both theory and history suggest that the burden of proof has now shifted to those who would defend the conventional wisdom rather than those who attack it.[10]

Pros and cons

The traditional case against capital controls is simple. It is the case for free markets, based on an analogy with standard theoretical arguments for free trade in goods and services. Commercial liberalisation is assumed to be a mutual-gain phenomenon, so why not financial liberalisation too? Like trade based on comparative advantage, capital mobility is assumed to lead to a more productive employment of investment resources, as well as to increased opportunities for effective risk management and welfare-improving inter-temporal consumption smoothing. We arc all presumably better off as a result.[11] In the words of Federal Reserve Chairman Alan Greenspan, an authoritative representative of the conventional wisdom:

> The accelerating expansion of global finance ... enhances cross-border trade in goods and services, facilitates cross-border portfolio investment strategies, enhances the lower-cost financing of real capital formation on a world-wide basis, and, hence, leads to an expansion of international trade and rising standards of living.[12]

All these gains, conversely, would be threatened by controls, which it is assumed would almost certainly create economic distortions and inhibit socially desirable risk taking. Worse, given the inexorable advance of financial technology across the globe, restrictions in the end might not even prove to be effective. Again in Alan Greenspan's words: 'We cannot turn back the clock on technology – and we should not try to do so.[13] Any government that still preferred controls was, in effect, simply living in the past.

Against these arguments, which have long dominated thinking in policy circles, two broad lines of dissent may be found in the scholarly literature. One approach focuses on the assumptions necessary to support the conventional wisdom, which are as demanding for trade in financial assets as they are for trade in goods and services. Strictly speaking, as a matter of theoretical reasoning, we can be certain that free capital flows will optimise welfare only in an idealised world of pure competition and perfect foresight. In reality, economies are rife with distortions (such as asymmetries in the availability of information) that prevent attainment of 'first-best' equilibrium. As Richard Cooper has written:

> It has long been established that capital mobility in the presence of significant distortions ... will result in a misallocation of the world's capital and, indeed can even worsen the economic well-being of the capital-importing country.[14]

A plausible case for controls, therefore, may be made on standard 'second-best' grounds. Judicious introduction of another distortion in the form of capital restrictions could actually turn out to raise rather than lower economic welfare on a net basis. For every possible form of market failure, there is in principle a corresponding form of optimal intervention.

The logic of this kind of argument is not disputed. An omniscient government dealing with one clear distortion could undoubtedly improve welfare with some form of capital-market restriction. What is disputed is the value of such logic in the real world of multiple distortions and imperfect policy making. As Michael Dooley has noted in an oft-cited survey of the relevant literature, the issue is not theoretical but empirical.[15] The assumptions necessary to support an argument based on second-best considerations are no less 'heroic' than those underlying the more conventional laissez-faire view.

The second line of dissent, much more relevant to today's circumstances, looks not to marginal economic distortions but rather to the very nature of financial markets. Even in the absence of other considerations, financial markets tend to be especially prone to frequent crisis and flux. At issue here are the interdependencies of expectations inherent in the buying and selling of claims, which unavoidably lead to both herd behaviour and multiple equilibria. Financial markets are notoriously vulnerable to self-fulfilling speculative 'bubbles' and attacks. They also have a disturbing tendency to react with unpredictable lags to changing fundamentals – and then to overreact, rapidly and often arbitrarily. The resulting flows of funds, which may be massive, can be highly disruptive to national economies owing to their amplified impact on real economic variables. Hence here too a logical case may be made for judicious intervention by state authorities, in this case to limit the excessive instabilities and contagion effects endemic to the everyday operation of financial markets. Representative are the words of a former governor of the Bank of Mexico:

> Recent experiences of market instability in the new global, electronically linked markets...have made the potential costs of massive speculative flows difficult to ignore or underestimate...The assumed gains from free capital mobility will have to be balanced against the very real risks such mobility poses. Some form of regulation or control...seems necessary to protect emerging-market economies from the devastating financial crises caused by massive capital movements.[16]

Admittedly the value of this sort of argument too may be open to challenge on empirical grounds – but least so in the midst of a global emergency, when the disadvantages of unconstrained mobility are so obvious for everyone to see. In fact, recent research demonstrates that financial liberalisation is almost always associated, sooner or later, with serious systemic crisis.[17] It is precisely the explosion of these costs that was decisive in shifting the terms of discourse on capital controls. Increasingly the question is now posed: why should freedom of capital movement be given absolute priority over all other considerations of policy? Why, in effect, should governments tie one hand behind their back as they seek to shape and manage demand for their currency?

Perhaps most influential in shifting the discourse was a widely quoted article by the prominent trade economist Jagdish Bhagwati, which first appeared in May 1998.[18] Although other economists had been making the case for controls for some time,[19] Bhagwati's celebrity succeeded in bringing the issue to a new level of public awareness. After Asia's painful experience, Bhagwati asked, could anyone remain persuaded by the 'myth' of capital mobility's benign beneficence? In his words:

> It has become apparent that crises attendant on capital mobility cannot be ignored...When a crisis hits, the downside of free capital mobility arises...Thus, any nation contemplating the embrace of free capital mobility must reckon with these costs and also consider the probability of running into a crisis. The gains from economic efficiency that would flow from free capital mobility, in a hypothetical crisis-free world, must be set against this loss if a wise decision is to be made.[20]

In a similar vein, shortly afterwards, Krugman decried the failure of more conventional strategies of market preservation, which he labelled Plan A. 'It is time to think seriously about Plan B', he contended, meaning controls. 'There is a virtual consensus among economists that exchange controls work badly. But when you face the kind of disaster now occurring in Asia, the question has to be: badly compared to what?'[21] Likewise, within months, the financier George Soros was writing that 'some form of capital controls may...be preferable to instability even if it would not constitute good policy in an ideal world'.[22] By autumn 1998 the intellectual momentum had clearly shifted towards some manner of reappraisal of the conventional wisdom. As Bhagwati concluded: 'Despite the...assumption that the ideal world is indeed one of free capital flows...the weight of evidence and the force of logic point in the opposite direction, toward restraints on capital flows. It is time to shift the burden of proof from those who oppose to those who favour liberated capital.'[23]

Back to the future?

Reappraisal of the conventional wisdom could also be justified on historical grounds. Many people fail to remember that the original design of the IMF did not actually call for free capital mobility. Quite the contrary, in fact. Reflecting an abhorrence for the sort of 'hot-money' flows that had so destabilised monetary relations in the 1920s and 1930s, the charter drafted at Bretton Woods made explicit allowance for the preservation of capital controls. Virtually everyone involved in the negotiations agreed with the influential League of Nations study, *International Currency Experience*, that some form of protection was needed against the risk of 'mass movements of nervous flight capital'.[24] The option of controls, therefore, was explicitly reserved to the discretion of individual states, provided only that such restraints might not be intended to restrict international commerce.[25] The idea was to afford governments sufficient autonomy to promote stability and prosperity at home without endangering the broader structure of multilateral trade and payments that was being laboriously constructed abroad. It was a deliberate compromise between the imperatives of domestic interventionism and international liberalism – the compromise of 'embedded liberalism', as political scientist John Ruggie later called it.[26]

Pivotal in promoting that compromise was none other than John Maynard Keynes, universally respected as the greatest economist of his day and intellectual leader of the British delegation at Bretton Woods. For Keynes, nothing was more damaging than the free movement of speculative capital, which he viewed as 'the major cause of instability . . . [Without] security against a repetition of this . . . the whereabouts of "the better 'ole" will shift with the speed of the magic carpet. Loose funds may sweep round the world disorganising all steady business. Nothing is more certain than that the movement of capital funds must be regulated.'[27] Keynes carefully distinguished between genuinely productive investment flows and footloose 'floating funds'. The former, he concurred, were vital to 'developing the world's resources' and should be encouraged. It was only the latter that should be controlled, preferably as a 'permanent feature of the post-war system'.[28] Following Bretton Woods, Keynes expressed satisfaction that his objectives in this regard had been achieved:

> Not merely as a feature of the transition, but as a permanent arrangement, the plan accords to every member Government the explicit right to control all capital movements. What used to be heresy is now endorsed as orthodox.[29]

As we know, though, that achievement did not last. Over the course of the next half century, as the phoenix of global finance rose from the ashes, Keynes's strictures were largely forgotten. With the Washington consensus now increasingly dominant, what had been endorsed as orthodox once again became heresy – until the Asian crisis. Despite determined resistance from neo-liberal economists,[30] the tide has now decisively turned. Even the IMF has changed its tune, dropping active discussion of a new amendment to promote financial liberalisation and talking instead of the possible efficacy of financial restraints[31] – a tentative step back to the future envisaged by Keynes and others when the Fund was first created. Plainly, the pressure of events has conspired with a reawakened sense of history to cast the case for capital controls in a new light. Limitations on capital mobility, as a result, have gained new legitimacy as an instrument of monetary governance.

The role of the United States

Yet for all their new-found legitimacy, capital controls remain the neglected option. Can we understand why? Elsewhere, reviewing possible explanations, I have highlighted the key role of the United States, which continues as it has throughout most of the postwar period to dominate management of the international financial architecture.[32] Though somewhat eclipsed in the 1970s and 1980s, America's monetary hegemony was decisively reaffirmed by the long economic expansion of the 1990s – a record of success that stood in sharp contrast to lingering unemployment in Europe, stagnation in Japan and repeated crises elsewhere. Not for nothing do the French now call the United States the world's only hyperpower (*hyperpuissance*). Few governments today are inclined overtly to defy Washington's wishes on monetary and financial issues – and Washington has made no secret of its firm opposition to any significant reversal of financial liberalisation in emerging markets.

In fact, emerging market economies have been openly pressured to keep on playing the confidence game. Influence has been brought to bear both directly and through the policy conditionality imposed on hardest-hit countries by the IMF, which was once described to me by a high US Treasury official as 'a convenient conduit for US influence'.[33] Typical was the advice of the US Council of Economic Advisers following the 1997–8 crisis. For countries facing the prospect of volatile capital flows, the Council suggested, 'the need [is] to strengthen their domestic financial systems and adopt appropriate macroeconomic policies' – not a resort to capital controls.[34] On the contrary, the Council warned, 'many considerations argue against the use of capital controls'.[35] Similarly, Joseph Stiglitz, the World Bank's recently retired chief economist, has vividly described the close collaboration between the Treasury and the Fund that was instrumental in enforcing neo-liberal orthodoxy after the crisis broke.[36] We know that countries such as South Korea, which was willing to play the game by Washington's rules, were rewarded with generous financial assistance and other forms of support. Conversely, when Indonesia's newly elected president, Abdurrahman Wahid, briefly flirted with the idea of controls during a period of renewed currency pressure in June 2000, he was firmly discouraged by the IMF's Managing Director, who insisted that Indonesia must adhere strictly to the Fund's policy prescriptions.[37] We also know that Malaysia came in for much opprobrium after its rash break with the Washington consensus in 1998. In such an atmosphere, is it any wonder that most policy makers might hesitate to follow in Kuala Lumpur's footsteps?

Undoubtedly, one reason for Washington's determined opposition lay in ideological conviction. Most of the officials recently in charge of US policy, including Treasury Secretary Robert Rubin and his successor Lawrence Summers, were trained in neo-liberal economics and firmly persuaded of its essential merit; and the same can be said as well of their replacements following the presidential election of 2000. But that was hardly the only reason. Intellectual bias can explain only a predisposition towards some set of policies. It is unlikely to dominate hard-nosed political calculation. In practice, two other considerations clearly took precedence.

First was a concern for systemic stability, which obviously seemed jeopardised by the Asian crisis and its subsequent spread to Russia, Brazil and elsewhere. Not only did lending markets around the world threaten to seize up, risking a global credit crunch. There was also the possibility of crashing stock markets, worldwide depression and resurgent protectionism in international trade. Nightmare scenarios were a dime a dozen once the crisis started. As the dominant architect of the prevailing monetary structure, the United States is presumably also one of its principal beneficiaries. In that context America's leaders had every reason to seek to suppress any challenge to the status quo.

Second was domestic politics within the United States, which also favoured preservation of the status quo. Few American constituencies would be directly benefited by restraints on capital mobility in emerging markets. Many, however, could see their interests hurt, including especially major financial institutions and investors. Such powerful market actors are not the kind to keep their preferences under a bushel; nor are their elected representatives apt to be entirely insensitive to their pleas for support. This is not to suggest that Washington is merely the tool of an exploitative capitalist class. The world is rarely as simple as that. But it does imply a common interest in opposing controls. As political scientist Robert Wade has commented, in polemical but compelling terms:

> The United States has a powerful interest in maintaining and expanding the free world-wide movement of capital…Moreover, Wall Street banks and brokerage firms want to expand their sales by doing business in emerging markets…[Hence] there is a powerful confluence of interests between Wall Street and multinational corporations in favour of open capital accounts world-wide. In response, the US Treasury has been leading a campaign…to promote capital liberalisation.[38]

Elsewhere, Wade calls this the 'Wall Street–Treasury complex'.[39] Such a formidable coalition of forces is undoubtedly difficult to resist.

Domestic politics

Resistance, however, is not impossible – neither in principle nor in practice. Legally, there is nothing to prevent a sovereign government from limiting capital flows if it so chooses; politically, few emerging market countries are so supine as to knuckle under to the first whiff of pressure from Washington. Restraints on capital mobility, to repeat, are a logical corollary of a currency strategy of market preservation. Hence something else must be involved as well to explain why policy makers continue to hesitate to make more use of controls, effectively tying one hand behind their back even as they strive to maintain market share for their money. Reason suggests that the 'something else' is most likely to be found at home, in each country's own domestic politics and political institutions.

Significantly, formal analysis of the domestic politics of capital controls suggests that, if anything, governments should be biased *in favour of* restraints rather than hesitant.[40] In addition to their role in limiting the risk or damage of currency crises, controls can be highly useful to policy makers for both revenue and redistributive purposes. On the one hand, controls make it easier for governments to exploit the power of seigniorage, otherwise known as the 'inflation tax'. Seigniorage represents the capacity that a monetary monopoly gives policy makers to augment public expenditures at will. Resources can be extracted from the private sector via inflationary money creation. On the other hand, controls can be used to shift the tax burden towards capital owners by closing off opportunities for tax avoidance. The hesitancy of governments to make more use of capital restraints certainly cannot be attributed to a lack of plausible motivations.

Rather, one must look to the motivations of other domestic actors with a capacity to influence official policy. Such actors are not difficult to find. Numerous studies have analysed the politics of the wave of financial liberalisation that swept emerging market economies in the 1980s and 1990s.[41] All point to the key role played by powerful societal interests in helping to persuade policy makers to reduce or eliminate past restraints on capital mobility. Critical constituencies benefited measurably from the opening of a new range of market opportunities. These included, in particular, big tradable-goods producers, banks and other financial services firms, and large private asset holders. Exporters and importers, as well as domestic banks, gained improved access to loanable funds and lower borrowing costs; the owners and managers of financial wealth were freed to seek out more profitable investments or to develop new strategies for portfolio diversification. All these benefits, plainly, would be curtailed or lost if controls were now to be reimposed. It stands to reason, therefore, that these same constituencies would now do everything possible to ensure that governments sustain their commitment to the Washington consensus. These too are actors who are unlikely to keep their preferences under a bushel.

Details differ from country to country, of course, depending on the specific characteristics of each state's economic structure and political institutions. In Mexico, for instance, it was the banking industry that was most prominent in lobbying for liberalisation, acting in a de facto coalition with like-minded officials in the federal bureaucracy – what Sylvia Maxfield has called Mexico's 'bankers' alliance'.[42] According to Maxfield, the bankers' alliance was able to succeed as it did because of several key characteristics of the country's institutional structure. These included a relatively autonomous central bank, a finance ministry able to exercise hegemony over other state economic policy-making agencies, and a high degree of conglomeration between private industrial and financial enterprises. In countries like South Korea and Taiwan, by contrast, it was the industrial sector that was most directly involved – especially big manufacturers who, as they shifted towards more capital-intensive activities, sought to attain easier access to large-scale external financing.[43] Again, institutional factors, including in particular the relative strength of the central bank and allied agencies within the structure of government, were decisive in determining how much influence such sectoral interests could exercise over policy outcomes. And in yet other economies, such as Indonesia, it was large asset holders who were among the most influential, aided no doubt by close political (and even familial) ties to governmental authorities.[44]

Whatever the details, however, the broad implication is clear. Governments have been under pressure from not one but *two* directions. Opposition to controls comes not just from the United States and the IMF. on the outside, but also, undoubtedly, from key elements of the private sector at home, determined to preserve the benefits and privileges derived from liberalised financial markets. Interacting with the 'Wall Street–Treasury complex', in other words, is a comparably influential bank–industry–wealth-holder complex – in effect, a powerful transnational coalition that works in a mutually reinforcing fashion to bar any retreat from the Washington consensus. External pressure from the United States is amplified internally by the natural desire of influential societal actors to defend acquired privileges. In turn, the impact of those same domestic actors is strengthened and legitimised by the backing of the world's acknowledged monetary hegemon.

No evidence exists, of course, to suggest that this sort of coalition, which is informal at best, is in any way the result of deliberate design. No conspiracy is needed to explain a pattern of cooperation when there is so evident a confluence of interests. Premeditated or not, however, the coalition has certainly proved its effectiveness in constraining the actions of governments that might otherwise have been more partial to a revival of controls. Even the rashest of policy makers are bound to hesitate when faced by such a united front of opposition.

Conclusion

The Asian crisis provided one of those rare watershed moments when conventional wisdom could be seriously challenged. With the apparent failure of more orthodox strategies of market preservation – the confidence game – the time seemed ripe for a revival of capital controls as a legitimate tool of monetary governance. Yet governments in emerging markets still hesitate, despite the persuasiveness of both theoretical argument and historical precedent. That they do still hesitate is testament to the combined power of the United States and determined domestic interests, acting in tandem to preserve existing commitments to the Washington consensus.

In that case, what is to be done? Capital controls need not remain the neglected option. In practical terms, the critical issue is one of feasibility: how to fight fire with fire. Against foes of controls, whether at home or abroad, it is necessary to build an even more forceful coalition of proponents. The aim must be to mobilise political constituencies everywhere with an interest in restoring the compromise of embedded liberalism written into the Fund charter at Bretton Woods – to free governments to use the hand presently tied behind their back. To be effective, such a coalition could not rely on emerging market governments alone. Quite obviously, it would also have to draw in sympathetic and influential elements in the United States or elsewhere that until now have maintained a relatively low profile on the issue.

Potential allies are there. One source of support might be found in the World Bank, which has delicately suggested that 'The benefits of capital account liberalisation and increased capital flows have to be weighed against the likelihood of crisis and its costs.'[45] Stiglitz, while still at the Bank, was certainly well known for his opposition to Treasury views on capital controls. Other support might be found among the leadership of such elite organisations as America's Council on Foreign Relations, which recently published a task force report highly favourable to certain kinds of capital controls.[46] If elements like these could be recruited to the cause, governments might finally hesitate no longer.

Notes

1 Benjamin J. Cohen, 'Taming the Phoenix: Monetary Governance after the Crisis', in Gregory W. Noble and John Ravenhill (eds.), *The Asian Financial Crisis and the Architecture of Global Finance* (New York: Cambridge University Press), pp. 192–3. This paper was first prepared for a conference on the Asian financial crisis held in Melbourne, Australia, in December 1998.

2 Benjamin J. Cohen, 'Capital Controls: Why Do Governments Hesitate?' in Leslie Elliott Armijo (ed.), *Debating the Global Financial Architecture* (Albany, NY: SUNY Press, 2002).

3 See, for example, Michael Mussa, Paul Masson, Alexander Swoboda, Esteban Jadresic, Paolo Mauro and Andrew Berg, *Exchange Rate Regimes in an Increasingly Integrated World Economy* (Washington, DC: International Monetary Fund, 2000), p. 13. These countries are distinguished from the much larger number of poorer developing countries in sub-Saharan Africa and elsewhere, many with inconvertible currencies, that have long maintained significant restraints on capital flows.

4 The discussion in this section, which is necessarily condensed, is based on arguments presented at greater length in Benjamin J. Cohen, *The Geography of Money* (Ithaca, NY: Cornell University Press, 1998).

5 *Ibid.*

6 Pedro Pou, 'Is Globalisation Really to Blame?' in Jane Sneddon Little and Giovanni P. Olivei (eds.), *Rethinking the International Monetary System* (Boston, MA: Federal Reserve Bank of Boston, 1999), p. 244.

7 Paul Krugman, 'The Confidence Game', *The New Republic*, 5 October 1998, pp. 23–5; *The Return of Depression Economics* (New York: Norton, 1999).

8 Interim Committee Communiqué, 28 April 1997, para. 7. Under the plan, two Articles were to be amended – Article I, where 'orderly liberalisation of capital' would be added to the list of the Fund's formal purposes; and Article VIII, which would give the Fund the same jurisdiction over the capital account of its members as it already enjoys over the current account. The language would also have *required* countries to commit themselves to capital liberalisation as a goal.

9 Robert Wade and Frank Veneroso, 'The Gathering Support for Capital Controls', *Challenge*, vol. 41, no. 6 (1998), p. 23.

10 The earliest example I can find of this change of tone was a column by *Financial Times* commentator Martin Wolf in early March 1998. Ordinarily a firm champion of free markets, Wolf reluctantly concluded: 'After the crisis, the question can no longer be whether these flows should be regulated in some way. It can only be how.' Ten months later, at the annual World Economic Forum in Davos, Switzerland – always a useful means for tracking authoritative public- and private-sector opinion – it was clear from most remarks that absolutely unrestricted capital mobility was no longer much in favour. See, for example, *The New York Times*, 29 January 1999, p. C1.

11 Maurice Obstfeld and Kenneth Rogoff provide elegant theoretical arguments to demonstrate the potential for gains from inter-temporal trade through a free international market for securities, in *Foundations of International Finance* (Cambridge, MA: MIT Press, 1996).

12 Alan Greenspan, 'The Globalization of Finance', *Cato Journal*, vol. 17, no. 3 (Winter 1998), p. 246.

13 *Ibid.*, p. 249.
14 Richard N. Cooper, 'Should Capital Controls be Banished?' *Brookings Papers on Economic Activity*, no. 1 (1999), p. 105. See also Barry Eichengreen, Michael Mussa and a Staff Team, *Capital Account Liberalisation: Theoretical and Practical Aspects* (Washington, DC: International Monetary Fund, 1998); Alejandro López-Mejía, 'Large Capital Flows: A Survey of the Causes, Consequences, and Policy Responses', Working Paper WP/99/17 (Washington, DC: International Monetary Fund, 1999).
15 Michael P. Dooley, 'A Survey of Literature on Controls over International Capital Transactions', *International Monetary Fund Staff Papers*, vol. 43, no. 4 (1996), pp. 639–87.
16 Ariel Buira, *An Alternative Approach to Financial Crises* (Princeton, NJ: International Finance Section, 1999), pp. 8–10.
17 John Williamson and Molly Mahar, *A Survey of Financial Liberalisation* (Princeton, NJ: International Finance Section, 1998).
18 Jagdish Bhagwati, 'The Capital Myth', *Foreign Affairs*, vol. 77, no. 3 (1998), pp. 7–12.
19 See, for example, Ilene Grabel, 'Financial Markets, the State, and Economic Development: Controversies within Theory and Policy', *International Papers in Political Economy*, vol. 3, no. 1 (1996); 'Marketing the Third World: The Contradictions of Portfolio Investment in the Global Economy', *World Development*, vol. 24 (1996), pp. 1761–76.
20 Bhagwati, 'The Capital Myth', pp. 8–9.
21 Paul Krugman, 'Saving Asia: It's Time to Get Radical', *Fortune Magazine*, vol. 138, no. 5 (1998), p. 78. See also Paul Krugman, *The Return of Depression Economics* (New York: Norton, 1999), ch. 9.
22 George Soros, *The Crisis of Global Capitalism* (New York: Public Affairs, 1998), pp. 192–3.
23 Bhagwati, 'The Capital Myth', p. 12.
24 Ragnar Nurkse, *International Currency Experience: Lessons from the Inter-War Period* (Geneva: League of Nations, 1944), p. 188.
25 See Article VI, sections 1 and 3 of the Articles of Agreement of the International Monetary Fund.
26 John G. Ruggie, 'International Regimes, Transactions, and Change: Embedded Liberalism in the Postwar Economic Order', in Stephen D. Krasner (ed.), *International Regimes* (Ithaca, NY: Cornell University Press, 1983).
27 'Post-War Currency Policy', a British Treasury memorandum dated September 1941, reprinted in *The Collected Writings of John Maynard Keynes*, ed. Donald Moggridge, XXV (Cambridge: Cambridge University Press, 1980), p. 31.
28 'Plan for an International Currency (or Clearing) Union', January 1942, reprinted in *The Collected Writings*, pp. 129–30.
29 As quoted in Louis W. Pauly. *Who Elected the Bankers? Surveillance and Control in the World Economy* (Ithaca, NY: Cornell University Press, 1997), p. 94. For more on Keynes's views and how they relate to the contemporary scene, see John Cassidy, 'The New World Disorder', *The New Yorker*, 26 October 1998, pp. 198–207; and Jonathan Kirshner, 'Keynes, Capital Mobility and the Crisis of Embedded Liberalism', *Review of International Political Economy*, vol. 6, no. 3 (1999), pp. 313–37.
30 See, for example, Sebastian Edwards, 'How Effective are Capital Controls?' *Journal of Economic Perspectives*, vol. 13, no. 4 (1999), pp. 65–84; 'International Capital Flows and Emerging Markets: Amending the Rules of the Game?' in Little and Olivei, pp. 137–57; Günther G. Schulze, *The Political Economy of Capital Controls* (New York: Cambridge University Press, 2000).
31 See, for example, Charles Adams, Donald J. Mathieson, Garry Schinasi and Bankim Chadha, *International Capital Markets: Developments, Prospects, and Key Policy Issues* (Washington, DC: International Monetary Fund, 1998), p. 79; Charles Adams, Donald J. Mathieson and Garry Schinasi, *International Capital Markets: Developments, Prospects, and Key Policy Issues* (Washington, DC: IMF, 1999), pp. 92, 101; Akira Ariyoshi, Karl

Habermeíer, Bernard Laurens, Inci Otker-Robe, Jorge Iván Canales-Kriljenko and Andrei Kirilenko, *Country Experiences with the Use and Liberalisation of Capital Controls* (Washington, DC: IMF, 2000); Eichengreen *et al., Capital Account Liberalisation*, pp. 2–3, 29; Mussa *et al.*, pp. 30–1. The Fund's annual report for 1999 reports that its Board of Executíve Directors took up the issue of capital controls at a meeting in March 1999, when several directors were said to argue that, in a crisis, limitations on capital flows 'could play a useful role' (IMF, *Annual Report* 1999, p. 47).

32 Cohen, 'Capital Controls: Why Do Governments Hesitate?'.

33 As quoted in Benjamin J. Cohen, *In Whose Interest? International Banking and American Foreign Policy* (New Haven, CT: Yale University Press, 1986), p. 229.

34 Council of Economic Advisers, *Annual Report* (Washington, DC: US Government Printing Office, 2000), p. 226.

35 Council of Economic Advisers, *Annual Report* (Washington, DC: US Government Printing Office, 1999), p. 281.

36 Joseph Stiglitz, 'The Insider: What I Learned at the World Economic Crisis', *The New Republic*, 17 and 24 April 2000, pp. 56–60.

37 *New York Times*, 6 June 2000, p. C4.

38 Robert Wade, 'The Coming Fight Over Capital Controls', *Foreign Policy*, vol. 113 (1998–99), pp. 45–7.

39 Robert Wade, 'National Power, Coercive Liberalism and "Global" Finance', in Robert Art and Robert Jervis (eds.), *International Politics: Enduring Concepts and Contemporary Issues* (Ithaca, NY: Cornell University Press, 1999).

40 See, for example, Alberto Alesina, Vittorio Grilli and Gian Maria Milesi-Ferretti, 'The Political Economy of Capital Controls', in Leonardo Leiderman and Assaf Razin (eds.), *Capital Mobility: The Impact on Consumption, Investment and Growth* (New York: Cambridge University Press, 1994), ch. 11; Günther G. Schulze, *The Political Economy of Capital Controls* (New York: Cambridge University Press, 2000).

41 Among the most influential of these studies were Stephan Haggard, Chung H. Lee and Sylvia Maxfield (eds.), *The Politics of Finance in Developing Countries* (Ithaca, NY: Cornell University Press, 1993); Michael Loriaux, Meredith Woo-Cumings, Kent E. Calder, Sylvia Maxfield and Sofia A. Pérez, *Capital Ungoverned: Liberalising Finance in Interventionist States* (Ithaca, NY: Cornell University Press, 1997); Sylvia Maxfield, *Governing Capital: International Finance and Mexican Politics* (Ithaca, NY: Cornell University Press, 1990); Louis W. Pauly, *Opening Financial Markets: Banking Politics on the Pacific Rim* (Ithaca, NY: Cornell University Press, 1988).

42 Sylvia Maxfield, 'Bankers' Alliances and Economic Policy Patterns: Evidence from Mexico and Brazil', *Comparative Political Studies*, vol. 23, no. 4 (1991), pp. 419–58.

43 Stephan Haggard and Sylvia Maxfield, 'The Political Economy of Capital Account Liberalisation', in Helmut Reisen and Bernhard Fischer (eds.), *Financial Opening: Policy Issues and Experiences in Developing Countries* (Paris: Organization for Economic Co-operation and Development, 1993), pp. 65–91; 'Political Explanations of Financial Policy in Developing Countries', in Haggard *et al., The Politics of Finance*, ch. 10; Meredith Woo-Cumings, 'Slouching Toward the Market: The Politics of Liberalisation in South Korea', in Loriaux, *Capital Ungoverned*, ch. 3.

44 Stephan Haggard and Sylvia Maxfield, 'The Political Economy of Financial Internationalization in the Developing World', in Robert O. Keohane and Helen V. Milner (eds.), *Internationalisation and Domestic Politics* (New York: Cambridge University Press, 1996), ch. 9.

45 World Bank, *Global Economic Prospects and the Developing Countries, 1998/99: Beyond Financial Crisis* (Washington, DC: International Bank for Reconstruction and Development, 1999), p. xxi.

46 Council on Foreign Relations, *Safeguarding Prosperity in a Global Financial System: The Future International Financial Architecture*, Report of an Independent Task Force (New York: Council on Foreign Relations, 1999).

Part 3

The new geography of money

10 The new geography of money

Source: From E. Gilbert and E. Helleiner (eds), *Nation-States and Money: the past, present and future of national currencies*, 1999.

When addressing issues of global finance, we are accustomed to thinking of money as effectively insular: each currency sovereign within the territorial frontiers or a single country or monetary union. In fact, nothing could be further from the truth.

For a currency to be truly 'territorial', its functional domain would have to coincide precisely with the political jurisdiction of its issuing state – a very special case. The currency would have to exercise an exclusive claim to all the traditional roles of money within the domestic economy. There could be no other money accepted for transaction purposes or used for the denomination of contracts or financial assets. And the government would have to be able to maintain sole control over the operation of the monetary system, dominating market agents. In matters of commerce, the equivalent would be described as 'autarky'; national self-sufficiency. In truth, however, autarky is no more commonly achieved in monetary matters than it is in trade.

As a practical matter, a surprising number of moneys today have come to be employed widely outside their country of origin for transactions either between nations or within foreign states. The former is usually referred to as 'international' currency use (or currency 'internationalisation'); the latter is typically described by the term 'currency substitution' and may be referred to as 'foreign-domestic use'.[1] Reciprocally, an even larger number of moneys now routinely face growing competition at home from currencies originating abroad. It is simply wrong to assert, as did one economist recently, that 'several currencies rarely circulate within the same state' (Hansson 1993: 165). In fact, the phenomenon is increasingly prevalent.

Both currency internationalisation (CJ) and currency substitution (CS) are a product of intense market rivalry – a kind of Darwinian process of natural selection, driven by the force of demand, in which some moneys such as the US dollar or Deutschmark (DM) come to be viewed as more attractive than others for various commercial or financial purposes. As a growing body of historical research demonstrates, cross-border circulation of currencies was once quite common prior to the emergence of the modern state system. More recently the practice has re-emerged, as declining barriers to monetary exchange have greatly expanded the array of effective currency choice. Competition between national moneys is accelerating rapidly. As a result, the domains within which individual currencies serve the standard functions of money now diverge more and more sharply from the legal jurisdictions of issuing governments. Money has become effectively 'deterritorialised'.

What is the political significance of this new geography of money? Most fundamentally, money's deterritorialisation alters the structure of governance in global currency relations. Where national governments once, in principle, reigned supreme – each claiming the right to an absolute monopoly within its own borders – practical authority in monetary matters has now become more diffuse, incorporating key market actors as well as agents of the state. The primary advantage of this accelerating transformation is that it provides more of a check on the arbitrary exercise of governmental authority. The main disadvantage lies in the fact that market actors are less accountable than politicians to the general electorate, raising serious questions about legitimacy and representation in this critical realm of decision-making.

The purpose of this chapter is to explore the changing nature of monetary governance in a world of growing cross-border currency competition. After briefly outlining some of the key dimensions of today's new monetary geography in the first section below, I address first the role of the state and then that of markets in the following two sections. Deterritorialisation, I argue, has not totally deprived states of their capacity to act on behalf of their citizens. But it does oblige states now to *share* authority with key market agents, each side playing a critical endogenous role in an ongoing dialectical process. Governance today is exercised not by political sovereignty but rather by the 'invisible hand' of competition, states *interacting with* private societal forces in the functional spaces created by the Darwinian rivalry among moneys.

Mapping the new geography

Regrettably, the full dimensions of today's new geography of money cannot be mapped precisely. Since comprehensive statistics on global currency circulation do not exist, neither CI nor CS can be accurately or consistently documented with any degree of refinement. Partial indicators, however, may be gleaned from a variety of reliable sources.[2] Thought space limitations prevent their detailed reproduction here, some brief recapitulation can serve to underscore the impressive orders of magnitude involved.

The clearest signal of the accelerated pace of CI is sent by the global foreign-exchange market where, according to the Bank for International Settlements (1999), average daily turnover has accelerated from $620 million in 1989 (the first year for which such data are available) to close to $1.5 trillion nine years later – a rate of increase of nearly 30 per cent per annum. A parallel story also seems evident in international markets for other financial claims, including bank deposits and loans as well as bonds and stocks, all of which have grown at double-digit rates for years. Using data from a variety of sources. Thygesen *et al.* (1995) recently calculated what they call global financial wealth; the world's total portfolio of private international investments. From just over $1 trillion in 1981. aggregate cross-border holdings quadrupled to more than $4.5 trillion by 1993 – an expansion far faster than that of world output or trade in goods and services.

The clearest signal of the accelerated pace of CS is sent by the rapid increase in the physical circulation of several major currencies, including especially the US dollar, DM, and yen, outside their country of origin. For the dollar, an authoritative study by two Federal Reserve economists (Porter and Judson 1996) puts the value of US banknotes in circulation abroad at between 55 and 70 per cent of the total outstanding stock – equivalent to perhaps $250 billion in 1995. The same study also reckons that as much as three-quarters of the annual increase of notes in recent years has gone directly abroad, up from less than one-half in the 1980s and under one-third in the 1970s. Appetite for the greenback is obviously growing. Using a comparable approach, Germany's Bundesbank (1995) has estimated Deutschmark circulation outside Germany at about 30 to 40 per cent of total stock, equivalent to some DM 65–90 billion ($45–65 billion) at the end of 1994. In Asia, Bank of Japan officials are privately reported to believe that of the total supply of yen banknotes, amounting to some $370 billion in 1993, as much as 10 per cent may now be located outside Japan (Hale 1995: 164). Combining these diverse estimates suggests a minimum foreign circulation of the three big currencies of at least $300 billion in all – by no means an inconsiderable sum and, judging from available evidence, apparently growing rapidly.

The evidence also appears to suggest that a very wide range of countries is affected by the phenomenon, even if the precise numbers involved remain somewhat shrouded in mystery. According to one authoritative source, foreign banknotes account for 20 per cent or more of the local money stock in as many as three dozen nations inhabited by at least one-third of the world's population (Krueger and Ha 1996: 60–1). The same source also suggests that, in total, as much as one-quarter to one-third of the world's circulating currency is presently located outside its country of issue (Krueger and Ha 1996: 76).

These numbers clearly confirm the growing importance of both international and foreign-domestic use of money. Two main messages stand out. First, the scale of cross-border currency use is manifestly extensive, as well as growing rapidly, reflecting both the scope and intensity of market-driven competition. Monetary circulation really is no longer confined to the territories of issuing countries. Strict autarky in currency relations is indeed a special case.

Second, while the number of moneys actually employed for either international or foreign-domestic purposes tends to be rather small, the number of those routinely facing rivalry at home from currencies abroad appears to be remarkably large. Deterritorialisation also means that there is no longer a functional equivalence among national moneys. Even though all currencies of sovereign states enjoy nominally equal status as a matter of international law, some moneys – to paraphrase George Orwell – clearly are far more equal than others as a matter of practical reality. Many currencies, particularly in the developing world and so-called transition economics, face what amounts to a massive competitive invasion from abroad; others, especially those of the wealthiest industrial countries, are effectively immune from foreign rivalry at home. The population of the monetary universe is in fact distinctly stratified.

Topping the charts, quite obviously, is the dollar, which remains by far the world's most popular choice for both CI and CS. In effect, the dollar's functional domain spans the globe, from the Western Hemisphere (where the accepted synonym for currency substitution is 'dollarisation') to the former Soviet bloc and much of the Middle East (where dollars circulate widely as a *de facto* parallel currency). Next comes the DM, which clearly dominates currency relations within much of Europe, including East Central Europe and the Balkans. And not far behind are the yen and a handful of other elite international moneys, such as the pound sterling, Dutch guilder, and French and Swiss francs. Much lower ranked are the many currencies of poorer countries that are forced to struggle continuously for the loyalty of local users.

Add these two messages together and a picture emerges that is strikingly at variance with the conventional imagery of strictly territorial money – a universe of increasingly intense competition as well as distinct hierarchy among currencies. Individually, national moneys confront market forces that are increasingly indifferent to the barriers posed by political frontiers. Collectively, therefore, governments face a challenge to their monetary sovereignty that is unprecedented in modern times.

Role of the state

The tradition of monetary sovereignty is derived from the conventions of standard political geography which, ever since the seventeenth-century Peace of Westphalia, has celebrated the role of the nation-state, absolutely supreme within its own territory, as the basic unit of governance in world politics. Just as political space was conceived in terms of those fixed and mutually exclusive entities we call states, currency spaces came to be visualised in terms of the separate sovereign domains where each money originated. I label this the Westphalian model of monetary geography.

In the state-centric Westphalian model, national governments have been assumed to exercise monopoly control over the issue and management of their own money. As a result, power in monetary matters is conventionally thought to be concentrated decisively in the hands of the state. Not every government is expected always to be able to avail itself of all the advantages of a monetary monopoly. The need for frequent compromises is understood, leading often to either a subordination or a sharing of currency sovereignty among states. But even then, monetary governance is presumed to remain the privileged mandate of the government sector alone.

All that is now changed, however, by the deterritorialisation of money. In today's new monetary geography, the state is no longer automatically privileged in relation to societal actors. There can be little doubt, therefore, that governmental authority has been greatly eroded as a result. The only question is whether states retain any role at all in the governance of monetary affairs. The answer, I suggest, is that they do continue to play a vital role, but in a manner quite different from that assumed in the traditional Westphalian model.

The capital mobility hypothesis

That the monetary authority of governments is severely eroded today is hardly a novel proposition, of course. Students of international financial markets, noting the massive increase of cross-border capital flows in recent decades, have long stressed the resulting threat to national monetary sovereignty.[3] The conventional view, labelled by David Andrews (1994) the Capital Mobility Hypothesis, is that the growing world-wide integration of financial markets – financial globalisation, in the jargon – has effectively cost states their traditional monetary autonomy. As Andrews summarises the proposition:

> The degree of international capital mobility systematically constrains state behavior by rewarding some actions and punishing others…Consequently, the nature of the choice set available to states…becomes more constricted. (Andrews 1994: 193, 204)

But as Andrews himself cautions, this is only the beginning of the story, not the end.[4] In fact the Capital Mobility Hypothesis, for all its insight, borders on caricature, seriously misrepresenting both the scope and the severity of the challenge to contemporary government.

To be sure, there is nothing wrong with the logic of the proposition. Unless governments are willing to tolerate a virtually unlimited degree of currency instability, they must indeed tailor their policies to what is needed to avoid provoking massive or sudden capital movements. The challenge to state authority is real, neither easy to withstand nor, typically, amenable to formal negotiation. The constraint imposed by the globalised financial markets is not just a matter of individual constituencies with a self-interested axe to grind. Particularist pressures, exercised directly on government through lobbying or other 'rentseeking activities', have always been an integral part of the policy process in every national capital. What is different about financial globalisation is the more indirect role that markets can now play in inhibiting public policy – a discipline at once both less tractable and more impersonal.

The key is the wider range of options that comes to more privileged elements of the private sector with the globalisation of financial activity. For societal actors in a position to take advantage of the opportunities afforded by market integration, capital mobility means more degrees of freedom – more room for manoeuvre in response to the actual or potential decisions of government. Higher taxes or regulation may be evaded by moving investment funds offshore: tighter monetary policies may be circumvented by accessing foreign sources of finance. And this broader latitude, in turn, means a significant increase of leverage in relation to political authority. Recalling the language of Albert Hirsehman (1970), influence in the policy process may be thought to depend on the relative availability of the options of Exit, Voice, and Loyalty. The greater the ability of market actors to evade the preferences of public officials (Exit), the less will government be able to count on or command submissive Loyalty. 'Investors vote with their feet', as sociologist Saskia Sassen (1996: 39) puts it. As a result, more Voice is gained to promote private priorities and objectives.

In effect, therefore, financial globalisation gives selected societal actors a measure of *de facto* veto power over state behaviour, elusive but effective. It is elusive because it is exercised indirectly, through market processes rather than formal lobbying. Policy autonomy is threatened, but not from intent that is purposive or hostile. The leverage is effective because it involves a menace, the risk of exit, that may never be implemented but is forever present. The pressure on government officials is without end. The imperative for governments is to avoid provoking exercise of the Exit option. This means, above all, maintaining insofar as possible the confidence and good will of the private sector. The full implications of this new veto power have been aptly summarised, albeit with approval, by a former finance minister of France:

> The world economy is increasingly dominated by financial markets, and we have to get used to accepting their verdicts, whether favorable to us or not. I think I understand their mind-set. They've become watchdogs who will promptly punish any country that lets inflation or public debt get out of control. But they reward good economic policies. A champion of free markets like me thinks that they provide good discipline.[5]

The Capital Mobility Hypothesis thus does correctly identify the nature of the challenge to government. Its logic is impeccable. Public policy, more and more, is indeed pressured to conform to what markets appear to desire, whether or not this coincides with the preferences of elected officials. Less and less can governments ignore the signals of the financial marketplace. Yet in pursuing that logic the proposition manages simultaneously both to *understate* and *overstate* the constraints presently imposed on state behaviour.

Constraints are understated because a focus on capital mobility, emphasising financial-market integration, highlights only one function of money; its use for store-of-value purposes. In fact, that is only part of the story. Cross-border competition is really far more extensive, involving all the standard functions of currency for both international and foreign–domestic use – not just money's role as a private investment medium – and penetrating to the very core of what is meant by national political sovereignty. Much more is involved here than just financial markets alone. It is, indeed, a matter of the basic effectiveness and legitimacy of government itself.

At the same time, constraints are overstated because a focus on capital mobility, stressing the preferences of currency users, highlights only one side of the market: the demand side. That too ignores an important part of the story – namely *supply*, which even in a deterritorialised world remains largely the privilege of the state. We must not forget that governments are still the principal source of the currencies that now compete so vigorously across political frontiers. The Darwinian struggle may be intense, but it is a struggle that remains, for now at least, limited almost exclusively to national moneys. Thus, though challenged, governments still retain a considerable influence of their own in relation to the private sector. The era of territorial money may be over, but that does not mean that states have become an anachronism in the governance of currency relations.

Competition on the supply side

Government dominance of the supply side is not absolute, of course. Even that remaining privilege could be croded in time by competition from non-state sources. A variety of private moneys already exist, both domestically and internationally, to rival the official issue of central banks. Until now, however, none has had an impact on the Darwinian struggle that might be described as anything more than marginal – though that too could change significantly in the future.

At the domestic level, private moneys circulate in some countries in fairly sizeable numbers. In the United States alone there are as many as 85 local currencies in 26 states, the best known being the system of 'Ithaca Hours' based in Ithaca, New York (Frick 1996). In 1993, *The Economist* (1993) reported the existence of some 45 local currencies in Britain – many with exotic, not to say eccentric, names like beaks, bobbins, cockles, and kreds – and perhaps 300 world-wide. Such currencies, however, really are little different from institutionalised systems of multilateral barter and remain self-consciously local, circulating on a very restricted scale.[6] None trades across national frontiers.

At the international level, private substitutes for national moneys have long existed in the form of what economists call 'artificial currency units' (ACUs) – non-state alternatives designed to perform one or more of the conventional roles of money. Traditionally, though, most ACUs have functioned mainly as a unit of account or store of value, rather than as a medium of exchange, thus posing little direct threat to government dominance of supply. Currently the only non-state form of money used to any substantial degree internationally is a pool of privately issued assets denominated in ECUs, the European Union's old European Currency Unit that came into existence with the European Monetary System in 1979.[7] But despite having attained limited success in global bond markets, the ECU has never been widely accepted for private transactional purposes.

In fact, the only real threat of competition on the supply side would appear to lie still in the future – in the developing realm of cyberspace, the 'virtual' geography of the internet and World Wide Web. Clearly, present-day physical money is bound to become decreasingly important over time once digital entries in a computer can substitute effectively for everyday cash and checking accounts. Around the world, as communications and information technologies continue to develop, entrepreneurs are racing to develop effective electronic means of payment: electronic cash or e-cash, as it is sometimes called. If and when they succeed, governments will face a competitive challenge like none they have experienced in living memory – full-bodied ACUs beyond their individual or even collective control. Then dominance of supply, not just demand, truly would be lost.[8]

That future, however, could be rather distant, if it arrives at all, given the difficulties of introducing any credible new form of money into the market. The key issue, as it is for all moneys, is trust; how to command confidence in the general acceptability of any species of e-cash. Initially at least, value is likely to be assured only by promising full and unrestricted convertibility into more conventional legal tender. Later on, as *The Economist* has written, 'it is possible to imagine the development of e-cash reaching [a] final evolutionary stage ... in which convertibility into legal tender ceases to be a condition for electronic money; and electronic money will thereby become indistinguishable from – because it will be the same as – other, more traditional sorts of money' (*The Economist* 1994: 23). But that day, surely, is still a long way off. Until then, officially sponsored moneys alone will continue to dominate the supply side for both international and foreign domestic purposes. Governments, therefore, will continue to play a role that is anything but insignificant.

The state as oligopolist

What, then, is the true nature of the relationship between states and societal actors in the governance of currency relations? In essence, the interaction has been transformed from monopoly to oligopoly. The monetary role of government has not so much been diminished as redefined. The status of states, once totally dominant in their own territories, has now become something like that of competing firms in an oligopolistic industry.

The point is simple. Markets have two sides: supply and demand. Hence not one but two sets of actors are involved – not just the users of money but also its principal producers, who happen still to be governments. With deterritorialisation states have lost the sole authority they once enjoyed over demand: their local monopolies. Since many transactors now have an alternative, the happy option of Exit, government can no longer easily enforce Loyalty, an exclusive role for their own currency within established political frontiers. But states do still dominate the supply side of the industry, largely retaining control over the issue of money. Thus they are still in a position, like oligopolistic firms, to exercise influence over demand insofar as they can successfully compete, inside or across borders, for the allegiance of market agents. Relevance, accordingly, is retained to the extent that user preferences can be swayed. Like oligopolists, governments find themselves driven to join the competitive fray; to do what they can, consciously or unconsciously, to preserve or promote market share for their product by shaping or managing demand. In this sense, producers of currency are essentially no different from producers of cars, chemicals, or computers.

Commercial rivalry between states is nothing new, of course. Governments have always competed with one another for markets and resources as part of the great game of world politics. Nor is the idea that states now vie to attract diverse market agents any longer particularly novel. More than a decade ago, Susan

Strange had already noted how the spreading globalisation of world markets was pushing governments into a new kind of geopolitical rivalry, 'competing for world market shares as the surest means to greater wealth' (Strange 1987: 564).[9] More recently, Philip Cerny crystallised the idea in his notion of the 'competition state' – governments 'driven by the imperatives of global competition to expand transnationalization' (Cerny 1994: 225). The competition state, however, participates in markets only indirectly, mainly as a catalyst to alter incentives confronting agents on both the demand and supply sides. What is unique about cross-border currency competition is that the state participates directly, as the dominant actor on the supply side. It is the government's own creation, its money, that must be marketed and promoted.

Furthermore, all states (excluding those few scattered enclaves, like Monaco or San Marino, that have formally adopted another nation's money in lieu of one of their own) must be considered part of the oligopolistic struggle, no matter how competitive or uncompetitive their respective currencies may be. Rivalry is not limited merely to the small handful of moneys at the very top of the global hierarchy, as is sometimes suggested.[10] That would be so only if cross-border competition were restricted to international use alone; a few key currencies vying for shares of global investment portfolios or for use in trade invoicing. But deterritorialisation extends to foreign–domestic use as well – CS as well as CI – hence involving all national currencies, to some degree, in direct competition with one another, the weak as well as the strong. Money's oligopoly is truly global.[11]

Role of the market

In this altered environment, we are entitled to ask: Who now governs currency relations? Governments have clearly lost much of their privileged status in relation to societal actors. Yet private agents too remain subject to enormous influence through state efforts to manage the demand side of the market. How, therefore, is monetary authority actually exercised? Who makes the rules, how are they enforced, and where are outcomes determined?

Authority or anarchy?

For some observers, the answer to these crucial questions is simple: When power shifts to markets, *no one* governs.[12] Authority is replaced by anarchy. In fact, nothing could be more mistaken.

Representative is the view of Susan Strange, as expressed in a recent commentary aptly entitled *The Retreat of the State* (1996). Like many other scholars. Strange focuses on the challenge posed by economic globalisation to the traditional Westphalian model of state sovereignty. Her starting point is conventional, as she readily concedes: 'There is no great originality in the underlying assumption of this book, which is that the territorial boundaries of states no longer coincide with the extent or the limits of political authority over economy and society' (Strange 1996: ix). Nor is there anything particularly unusual in her observations about the increased 'hollowness of state authority' caused by the growing influence of 'impersonal forces of world markets' (Strange 1996: 4, 6). In her words:

> The authority of the governments of all states, large and small, strong and weak, has been weakened as a result of technological and financial change and of the accelerated integration of national economies into one single global market economy. (Strange 1996: 13–14)

More dramatic, however, is the conclusion that she draws from her analysis, which is that the system of governance itself is weakened in the process. The erosion of state authority, she argues, has left no one in charge. Again in her words:

> Some of the fundamental responsibilities of the state in a market economy – responsibilities first recognised, described and discussed at considerable length by Adam Smith over 200 years ago – are not now being adequately discharged by anyone. At the heart of the international political economy, there is *a vacuum....* What some have lost, others have not gained. The diffusion of authority away from national governments has left *a yawning hole of non-authority*, ungovernance it might be called. (Strange 1996: 14, italics added)

In a formal sense, of course, Strange is absolutely right. Aspects of governance that we all take for granted at the national level – what Adam Smith called the 'magistracy' of the state, including protection of property rights, standardisation of weights and measures, and provision of a general framework of law, order, and justice – are obviously diluted or absent at the global level, where no legal government exists. To that extent, ungovernance is not an unfair characterisation. True, a wide range of substitutes for a single supranational authority, systematically institutionalised in multilateral organisations or in regularised procedures for inter-governmental cooperation, have been established over time to take on at least some of the responsibilities traditionally assumed by states. But without the powers that go with the notion of absolute sovereignty, such proxies are bound to remain pale imitations at best; less effective in providing outcomes that may be regarded as efficient, stable, or equitable. There can be little doubt that in today's increasingly globalised marketplace, many functions of governance are indeed no longer being discharged in a way that might be described as adequate.

But does this mean that no one remains in charge – that we are left with nothing but a vacuum? In fact such a bold claim, though widely shared, is based on a serious misconception of the meaning of authority in social relations. In politics and law, authority is commonly understood to embody a capacity to enforce compliance.[13] Like its synonym, the concept of governance, it represents an ability to exert influence over the behaviour and decisions of actors. Authority is inseparable from power, which in its many guises is the *sine qua non* for effective control of outcomes. But it is indeed separable from the state, which is by no means the only agent capable of making and enforcing rules. Authority may be exercised under the banner of sovereignty – the Westphalian model – but it can also originate in a wide variety of other social institutions, some of which may be far less visible to the naked eye than the formal offices and explicit rules of governments or multilateral agencies. In other words, governance can also take more informal or implicit forms.

As a mode of organising political space, authority falls somewhere between the contrasting modalities of coercion and persuasion. In the words of philosopher Hannah Arendt: 'If authority is to be defined at all, it must be in contradistinction to both coercion by force and persuasion by argument' (Arendt 1968: 93). Hints of each approach may be implicit in the notion of authority, but by presumption only. Persuasion, for example, works its will through systematic argument and appeal – what is generally termed a 'capacity for reasoned elaboration'. Coercion, at the opposite extreme, rests on the naked use of force – a capacity for repressive violence. Both alternatives may lurk in the background of governance, as possibilities to be brought forward should deviant behaviour occur. In certain circumstances, compliance may in fact be promoted by a belief that a capacity for either persuasion or coercion exists. But neither argument nor violence is a necessary condition for the effective exercise of authority.

The core issue is: Where does authority originate and how is it conveyed? For most scholars the usual starting point for analysis is Max Weber's familiar typology, which lists no fewer than three distinct foundations for authority: law, tradition, and charisma. In Weber's own words:

There are three pure types of legitimate authority. The validity of their claims to legitimacy may be based on:

1   Rational grounds – resting on a belief in the 'legality' of patterns of normative rules and the right of those elevated to authority under such rules to issue commands (legal authority);
2   Traditional grounds – resting on an established belief in the sancitity of immemorial traditions and the legitimacy of the status of those exercising authority under them (traditional authority); or finally
3   Charismatic grounds – resting on devotion to the specific and exceptional sanctity, heroism or exemplary character of an individual person, and of the normative patterns or order revealed or ordained by him (charismatic authority). (Weber 1947: 328)

From this perspective, it is easy to see that much more may be involved here than governance by government alone. For Weber, of course, authority was directly associated with the state. His concern was with the sources of legitimacy for the traditional Westphalian model of governance. In fact, however, only one of his three categories, the *de jure* 'rational-legal' mode of authority, is truly exclusive to the notion of formal government. Authority may indeed derive from juridical supremacy as embodied in the familiar institutions of the sovereign state.

But if Weber's two remaining categories are to be believed, that is clearly not authority's only possible provenance. Neither tradition nor charisma may be regarded as a monopoly of the state.

In fact, authority may be manifested through any number of *de facto* channels of control. Tradition and charisma are two of them; others include opinion, ideology, or even mere intellectual convention. It is by no means true, therefore, that we are left with a 'yawning hole of non-authority' just because power in the world economy has shifted away from national governments. Market forces may be 'impersonal', but that does not make them any less capable of governance.

The key point is simple. Authority, ultimately, is socially constructed – a product of intersubjective understandings built up from our own ideas and experiences. John Ruggie captures the point in his notion of 'social epistemes', which he defines as 'the mental equipment that people draw upon in imagining and symbolizing forms of political community' (Ruggie 1993: 157). As political philosopher R.B. Friedman writes, following Weber's logic, the effectiveness of authority is derived from 'some mutually recognized normative relationship' (Friedman 1990: 71). Its legitimacy is based on historically and culturally conditioned expectations about what constitutes appropriate conduct. A practical distinction between societal orders based on formal design and organisation (e.g., the state) and more spontaneous orders that emerge naturally from the mutual accommodations of many diverse and autonomous actors has long been a staple feature of Western social philosophy, going back to Bernard Mandeville's justly famous 'Fable of the Bees', first published in 1714. The unplanned spontaneous model may be regarded as no less legitimate – no less authoritative – than the deliberately devised variety.

Governance, therefore, does not necessarily demand the tangible institutions of government. It may not even call for the presence of explicit actors, whether state-sponsored or private, to take responsibility for rule-making and enforcement. To suffice, all that is really needed is a valid social consensus on relevant rights and values. As summarised by James Rosenau:

> Governance refers to activities backed by shared goals that may or may not derive from legal and formally prescribed responsibilities and that do not necessarily rely on police powers to overcome defiance and attain compliance. Governance, in other words, is a more encompassing phenomenon than government. It embraces governmental institutions, but it also subsumes informal, non-governmental mechanisms. ... Governance is thus a system of rule that is as dependent on inter-subjective meanings as on formally sanctioned constitutions and charters. (Rosenau 1992: 4)

Authority may be formally articulated in explicit rules outlining specific prescriptions or proscriptions for action. But it may also express itself more informally as implicit norms defining standards of behaviour in terms of understood rights and obligations. Rules are normally enforced by 'rightful' rulers, which since the Peace of Westphalia have been most closely identified with the territorial state. Norms, by contrast, tend to exercise their influence more through the power of social institutions, including such familiar arrangements as the family, religion, and, of course, the market. Both explicit rules and implicit norms are part of what we mean by governance. We do not face a vacuum whenever influence is redistributed from the former to the latter.

Admittedly, governance may not be as tidy when it is effectuated through social institutions rather than national governments. The greater ambiguity of norms, as compared with rules, leaves actors more room for strategic manoeuvre; lack of overt compliance mechanisms (police, judiciary, etc.) heightens the temptation to renege on commitments when convenient. Outcomes, therefore, may be neither as stable nor as equitable as we might prefer. As indicated, Susan Strange is undoubtedly right when she suggests that many functions of governance are no longer being discharged as adequately as they could be. The certitude of formal government is replaced by the less predictable force of social convention. But that is not the same as 'ungovernance'. We must not confuse the *form* of authority with its *consequences*.

Hence it is not at all accurate to conclude, as Strange's argument suggests, that no one now governs money's new deterritorialised landscape. The monopoly power of states has been replaced not by anarchy but by the 'invisible hand' of competition. The authority that once derived solely from legal-tender laws and other political interventions has come to be embodied more in the norms and expectations that rule the Darwinian struggle among currencies. The power of governance, in short, now resides in that social institution we call the market.

Supply or demand?

But that still leaves us with our underlying question: Who in the market governs? The market is not a unitary actor, after all; we must avoid the social-science sin of reification. At least two sets of actors are involved here – the producers of money on the supply side, the users of money on the demand side. Who really is in charge?

In fact, both sides govern – producers of money as well as users. As in any market setting it is supply and demand together, interacting synergistically, that determine the organisation of currency space. The basic point was made many years ago by the renowned English economist Alfred Marshall, commenting on whether it is demand ('utility') or supply ('cost of production') that governs market outcomes ('value'): 'We might as reasonably dispute whether it is the upper or the under blade of a pair of scissors that cuts a piece of paper, as whether value is governed by utility or cost of production' (Marshall 1948: 348).

Likewise, in our own time, we might as reasonably dispute whether it is the state or society that shapes the new geography of money. In reality, as with Marshall's scissors, it is both, each playing a critical reciprocal role in an ongoing dialectical process. What links the two sides in their synergy are the transactional networks that define the functional domains of individual currencies. And what lies at the heart of these social spaces is, once again, the issue of trust: the collective faith of a group of like-minded transactors in a money's general usefulness and future acceptability. Governance is provided by whatever may influence market confidence in individual currencies.

In short, if money is accurately comprehended as a social institution derived from self-reinforcing patterns of historical practice, it becomes clear that neither formal organisation nor explicit rules are required for the effective exercise of monetary authority. The system of governance is the collectivity of actors, public as well as private, that comprise both sides of the market. Through their ongoing interaction, it is these agents together who jointly, if uneasily, make the rules and shape the contours of today's monetary geography.

A crisis of legitimacy

In the end, then, we find that the traditional Westphalian model has become little more than a convenient fiction – a 'territorial trap' for the unwary, to borrow from the language of geographer John Agnew (1994). In fact, today's monetary geography is governed by a hybrid patchwork of authority that is both diffuse and contingent. Where the sovereign state once ruled, market forces now prevail.

Does it matter? Given money's central role in modern economics, the answer is most certainly yes. Money affects us all, every day of our lives; its impacts are manifold and direct. The real issue is the *legitimacy* of decision-making in this new deterritorialised system of governance – a decidedly normative question. Should we be content with this dramatically new geography of money?

Many, particularly partisans of a more libertarian political persuasion, might well respond in the affirmative, since liberty would appear to be promoted. Ever distrustful of excessive governmental authority, libertarians celebrate all limitations on political behaviour imposed by the decentralised decision-making of the marketplace. For them, the market serves two valuable functions, dispersing power in society and also providing a potent counterweight to the awesome power of the state. Hence many would undoubtedly applaud such a passing of privilege from the public to the private sector – from despised politicians to competitive market forces. The monopoly appropriated by governments during the era of territorial money was frequently mismanaged or abused, as we well know, often resulting in corrosive inflation or macroeconomic instability. Are we not all better off if states must now act as oligopolists, competing keenly with one another for the allegiance of market actors? In lieu of compulsory Loyalty, we now have the option of voluntary Exit. Hence instead of the arbitrary actions of public officials, we may now enjoy the fruits of market rationality.

Moreover, libertarians continue, markets are inherently democratic because they reflect the attitudes and decisions of millions of individual transactors, functioning in effect as a sort of perpetual opinion poll – a kind of 'automatic, nonpolitical system for grading [policy] performance', as one economist has approvingly put it (Meigs 1993: 717). Why should we not be content with a governance structure that yields more power to the people?

The libertarian response, however, is seriously deficient in two respects, neglecting issues of both equity and accountability. It is true, for example, that cross-border competition gives many societal actors more voice in relation to governmental authority; the right to 'vote with their feet' if they disapprove of official policy. But votes are distributed not by person, the traditional 'One Person, One Vote', but by wealth. The constitutional notion of equality before the law is thus effectively violated, if not fatally compromised. In the words of economist Arthur Okun, writing of the 'big tradeoff' between the principles of democracy and capitalism, 'money transgresses equal political rights' (Okun 1975: 29). Those with the most money have the most votes. Such a skewed franchise seems greatly inconsistent with contemporary views of political legitimacy.

Worse, there is less accountability in a system of governance that gives as much voice to a privileged class of market agents as it does to elected officials. As an approach to political rule, such a transformation may be regarded as regressive or even pernicious, insofar as it subverts the will of the general electorate. Politicians may be ineffectual or unsavoury, but in many countries – certainly in representative democracies – they are supposed to govern with the consent of the governed. In other words they can, at least to some degree, be held accountable for their actions. Market actors, by contrast, are neither elected nor politically accountable, and may not even be citizens. If the will of the majority, however poorly refracted through the lens of representative government, can be thwarted by the economic power of an anonymous minority, democracy itself is threatened. This too would seem at odds with contemporary views of legitimacy.

That economic globalisation may threaten a crisis of legitimacy in political rule – what one source calls a 'legitimacy deficit' (Underhill 1996: 6) – has only recently begun to attract the attention of students of world politics.[14] The growing concern is well captured by the title of a recent book by Louis Pauly: *Who Elected the Bankers?* (1997). As Saskia Sassen puts the point:

> Central banks and governments appear now to be increasingly concerned about pleasing the financial markets rather than setting goals for social and economic well-being. ... Do we want the global capital market to exercise this discipline over our governments? And to do so at all costs – jobs, wages, safety, health – and without a public debate? While it is true that these markets are the result of multiple decisions by multiple investors and thus have a certain democratic aura, all the 'voters' have to own capital. ... This leaves the vast majority of a country's citizens without any say. (Sassen 1996: 50–1)

No one who believes in either equity or accountability in politics should be content with such a structure of authority. Currency deterritorialisation *does* matter.

Conclusion

The issue, therefore, is not that states have lost all role in the management of currency relations. They are still part of money's implicit system of governance. But in the new deterritorialised geography that has supplanted the old Westphalian model, governments must consciously adapt to a dramatic transformation of their status, from monopolists to oligopolists, if they are adequately to represent the interests of all their citizens in monetary affairs. Whether governments are up to coping with this new challenge to their traditional sovereignty is not at all clear.

Notes

1 Useful sources on currency internationalisation include Krugman (1992), Black (1993). General introductions to currency substitution include Giovannini and Turtelboom (1994), Mizen and Pentecost (1996).
2 Representative samples can be found in Thygesen *et al.* (1995), Eichengreen and Frankel (1996), Tavlas (1997), Cohen (1998).
3 For two recent surveys, see Cohen (1996), Andrews and Willett (1997).
4 In fact, much of Andrews' analysis is appropriately directed to qualifications and limits of the proposition. In his words: 'Caution is warranted when generalizing about the effects of heightened capital mobility on individual states' monetary autonomy' (1994: 193). Andrews does not concur unreservedly with the Capital Mobility Hypothesis, as I regrettably implied in my 1996 survey (Cohen 1996: 281).
5 Alain Madelin, a political conservative, quoted in the *International Herald Tribune*, 16 October, 1995, two months after he resigned from the government of Prime Minister Alain Juppé.
6 For some discussion, see Morehouse (1989), Solomon (1996).
7 Other examples include the IMF's Special Drawing Right (SDR) and an early predecessor of the ECU labelled the European Unit of Account (EUA). For more discussion, see Aschheim and Park (1976).
8 For some discussion, see Dorn (1997), Kobrin (1997).
9 Strange contrasts this with the older, more traditional rivalry between states for such things as territory and the wealth-creating resources that might be located within territory.
10 See e.g., De Boissieu (1988). De Boissieu, a French economist, writes of an 'oligopolistic monetary equilibrium' consisting of the dollar, DM (or EU common currency), and the yen. Such a perspective is common among mainstream international economists.
11 For further discussion of state responses to money's new oligopoly, see Cohen (1998).
12 Hirst and Thompson (1995) label such observers 'extreme globalisation theorists'. See this source for further references.
13 The literature on authority is voluminous, involving specialists from several disciplines. Intense debate is attracted by the relationship of the concept of authority to notions of duty or obligation, on the one hand, and to issues of liberty, rights, and the autonomy of the individual on the other. For a useful survey, see Miller (1987).
14 See e.g., Hirst and Thompson (1995), Pauly (1995), Sassen (1996).

Bibliography

Agnew, J.A. (1994) 'The territorial trap: the geographical assumptions of international relations theory', *Review of International Political Economy* 1, 1: 53–80.
Andrews, D.M. (1994) 'Capital mobility and state autonomy: toward a structural theory of international monetary relations', *International Studies Quarterly* 38, 2: 193–218.
Andrews, D.M. and Willett, T. (1997) 'Financial interdependence and the state: international monetary relations at century's end', *International Organisation* 51, 3: 479–511.
Arendt, H. (1968) 'What is authority?', in H. Arendt, *Between Past and Future*, New York: Viking Press.

Aschheim, J. and Park, Y.S. (1976) *Artificial Currency Units: The Formation of Functional Currency Areas*, Essays in International Finance No. 114, Princeton: International Finance Section.

Bank for International Settlements (1999) *Central Bank Survey of Foreign Exchange and Derivatives Market Activity*, Basle: Bank for International Settlements.

Black, S.W. (1993) 'The international use of currencies', in D.K. Das (ed.) *International Finance*, London: Routledge.

Cerny, P.G. (1994) 'The infrastructure of the infrastructure? Toward "embedded financial orthodoxy" in the international political economy', in R.P. Palan and B. Gills (eds) *Transcending the State–Global Divide: A Neostructuralist Agenda in International Relations*, Boulder: Lynne Rienner.

Cohen, B.J. (1996) 'Phoenix risen: the resurrection of global finance', *World Politics* 48, 2: 268–96.

Cohen, B.J. (1998) *The Geography of Money*, Ithaca, NY: Cornell University Press.

De Boissicu, C. (1988) 'Concurrence entre monnaies et polycentrisme monétaire', in D.E. Fair and C. De Boissieu (eds) *International Monetary and Financial Integration – The European Dimension*, Boston: Kluwer Academic Publishers.

Deutsche Bundesbank (1995) 'The circulation of Deutsche Mark abroad', *Monthly Report*, 47, 7: 65–71.

Dorn, J.A. (ed.) (1997) *The Future of Money in the Information Age*, Washington: Cato Institute.

Eichengreen, B. and Frankel, J.A. (1996) 'The SDR, reserve currencies, and the future of the international monetary system', in Michael Mussa, James M. Boughton, and Peter Isard (eds) *The Future of the SDR in the Light of Changes in the International Financial System*, Washington: International Monetary Fund.

Frick, R.L. (1996) 'Alternative monetary systems: the Ithaca HOUR; *Durell Journal of Money and Banking*, 8, 2: 29–35.

Friedman, R.B. (1990) 'On the concept of authority in political philosophy', in J. Raz (ed.) *Authority*, Oxford: Basil Blackwell.

Giovannini, A. and Turtleboom, B. (1994) 'Currency substitution', in F. Van Der Ploeg (ed.) *The Handbook of International Macroeconomics*, Oxford: Basil Blackwell.

Hale, D.D. (1995) 'Is it a yen or a dollar crisis in the currency market?'. *Washington Quarterly*, 18, 4: 145–71.

Hansson, A.H. (1993) 'The trouble with the ruble: monetary reform in the former Soviet Union', in A. Aslund and R. Layard (eds) *Changing the Economic System in Russia*, London: Pinter.

Hirschman, A.O. (1970) *Exit, Voice and Loyalty: Responses to Decline in Firms, Organizations, and States*, Cambridge: Harvard University Press.

Hirst, P. and Thompson. G. (1995) 'Globalisation and the future of the nation state', *Economy and Society*, 21, 3: 108–42.

Kobrin, S.J. (1997) 'Electronic cash and the end of national markets', *Foreign Policy*. 107: 65–77.

Krueger, R. and Ha, J. (1996) 'Measurement of cocirculation of currencies,' in P.D. Mizen and F.J. Pentecost (eds) *The Macroeconomics of International Currencies: Theory, Policy and Evidence*, Brookfield, VT: Edward Elgar.

Krugman, P.R. (1992) 'The international role of the dollar', in P.R. Krugman. *Currencies and Crises*. Cambridge and London: MIT Press.

Marshall, A. [1920] (1948) *Principles of Economics*, eighth edition, New York: Macmillan.

Meigs, A.J. (1993) 'Eurodollars: a transition currency', *Cato Journal* 12, 3: 711–27.

Miller, D. (ed.) (1987) 'Authority', *The Blackwell Encyclopedia of Political Thought*, Oxford: Basil Blackwell.

Mizen, P.D. and Pentecost, E.J. (eds) (1996) *The Macroeconomics of International Currencies: Theory, Policy and Evidence*, Brookfield, VT: Edward Elgar.

Morehouse, W. (ed.) (1989) *Building Sustainable Communities: Tools and Concepts for Self-Reliant Economic Change*, New York: Bootstrap Press.

Okun, A.M. (1975) *Equality and Efficiency: The Big Tradeoff*, Washington: Brookings Institution.

Pauly, L.W. (1995) 'Capital mobility, state autonomy and political legitimacy', *Journal of International Affairs*, 48, 2: 369–88.

Pauly, L.W. (1997) *Who Elected the Bankers? Surveillance and Control in the World Economy*, Ithaca, NY: Cornell University Press.

Porter, R.D. and Judson, R.A. (1996) 'The location of U.S. currency: how much is abroad?', *Federal Reserve Bulletin*, 82, 10: 883–903.

Rosenau, J.N. (1992) 'Governance, order, and change in world politics', in J.N. Rosenau and E.-O. Czempiel (eds) *Governance Without Government: Order and Change in World Politics*, New York: Cambridge University Press.

Ruggie, J.G. (1993) 'Territoriality and beyond: problematizing modernity in international relations', *International Organisation*, 47, 1: 139–74.

Sassen, S. (1996) *Losing Control?: Sovereignty in an Age of Globalisation*, New York: Columbia University Press.

Solomon, L.D. (1996) *Rethinking Our Centralized Monetary System: The Case for a System of Local Currencies*, Westport, CN: Praeger.

Strange, S. (1987) 'The persistent myth of lost hegemony', *International Organisation*, 41, 4: 551–74.

Strange, S. (1996) *The Retreat of the State: The Diffusion of Power in the World Economy*, Cambridge: Cambridge University Press.

Tavlas, G.S. (1997) 'The international use of the US dollar: an optimum currency area perspective', *The World Economy*, 20, 6: 709–47.

The Economist (1993) 'Slip me a beak', (24 April), 60.

The Economist (1994) 'Electronic money: so much for the cashless society', (26 November), 21–3.

Thygesen, N. *et al.* (1995) *International Currency Competition and the Future Role of the Single European Currency*, Final Report of a Working Group on European Monetary Union – International Monetary System, London: Kluwer Law International.

Underhill, G.R.D. (1996) 'Financial market integration, global capital mobility, and the ERM Crisis 1992–1995', paper prepared for the 1996 annual meeting of the International Studies Association (manuscript).

Weber, M. [1925] (1947) *The Theory of Social and Economic Organisation*, Glencoe, IL: Free Press.

11 Monetary governance in a world of regional currencies[1]

Source: From Miles Kahler and David A. Lake (eds), *Governance in a Global Economy*, 2003.

One of the most remarkable developments in the world economy at the dawn of the new millennium is the rapid acceleration of cross-border competition among currencies – what I have elsewhere called the *deterritorialization* of money (Cohen 1998). Circulation of national currencies no longer coincides with the territorial frontiers of nation-states. A few popular monies, most notably the U.S. dollar and the euro (succeeding Germany's deutsche mark, the DM), have come to be widely used outside their country of origin, competing directly with local rivals for both transactions and investment purposes. The origins of this development, which economists call "currency substitution," can be found in the broader process of globalization, which, for the purposes of this chapter and following conventional practice, may be understood to refer to economic integration at the global level. The result is a fundamental transformation in the way money is governed. Where once existed *monopoly*, each state claiming absolute control over the issue and circulation of money within its own territory, we now find something more like *oligopoly*, a finite number of autonomous suppliers, national governments, all vying ceaselessly to shape and manage demand for their respective currencies. Monetary governance, at its most basic, has become a political contest for market loyalty, posing difficult choices for policymakers.

Among the alternative policy choices available to governments today, an option that is attracting increasing attention is replacement of national currencies with a *regional* money of some kind. Currency regionalization occurs when two or more states formally share a single money or equivalent. Broadly speaking, two main variants are possible. First, countries can agree to merge their separate currencies into a new joint money, as members of Europe's Economic and Monetary Union (EMU) have done with the euro. This is *currency unification*, a strategy of alliance. Alternatively, any single country can unilaterally or by agreement replace its own currency with an already existing money of another, an approach typically described as full or formal *dollarization*.[2] This variant, a more subordinate strategy of followership, has long been official policy in a miscellany of tiny enclaves or microstates around the world, from Monaco to the Marshall Islands, as well as in Panama and, for many years, Liberia, and was more recently adopted by Ecuador and El Salvador, each of which now uses America's greenback in place of its own former currency.

The emergence of regional currencies can be regarded as a logical corollary of the intense competitive contest among monies – a Darwinian struggle where, ultimately, only the fittest may survive. Among informed observers today it is rapidly becoming conventional wisdom that the number of currencies in the world will soon decline.[3] The only question is: What will the resulting population of monies look like? Scholars are just beginning to explore this critical issue.[4]

Not all local currencies will disappear, of course. Even in today's globalizing world, many states remain determined to preserve some semblance of their traditional monetary sovereignty. But the range of countries likely to choose the regional option, in one form or another, is certainly great enough to raise significant questions for the future of monetary governance. Currency regionalization, in contrast to a strictly national money, implies an upward shift in the delegation of formal authority. Monetary sovereignty is either *pooled* in a partnership of some sort, shifting authority to a joint institution like the European Central Bank (ECB), or else *surrendered* wholly or in part to a dominant foreign power such as the United States.[5] Many governments thus are faced with a tricky tripartite choice: traditional sovereignty, monetary alliance, or formal subordination. How will they decide?

The aim of this chapter is to provide the first building blocks for a positive theory of currency regionalization. In the spirit of actor-oriented framework, the analytical focus here is the state – specifically, central decision makers responsible for currency policy. The working assumption is that economic globalization is driving policymakers to reconsider their historical preference for strictly national money. The question is: What delegation of authority is most likely to emerge in individual countries? What conditions are most likely to influence the choice among available options?

The chapter is organized as follows. I begin in the first section with a brief look back at the dramatic transformation of global monetary relations that has occurred in recent decades – a period during which many governments, finding it increasingly difficult to sustain the market position of uncompetitive national currencies, have begun to reflect instead on the possibility of a regional currency of some kind.[6] The second section then highlights the considerable leeway available in designing alternative forms of either currency unification or dollarization, while the third section identifies key factors that can be expected to dominate the calculations of rational policymakers in thinking about the choices before them. Taking all factors into account, it is clear that for many states traditional sovereignty will remain the preferred option. But taking account of possible variations in the degree of regionalization, it is also clear that for many other countries some form of monetary alliance or subordination could turn out to be rather more appealing.

Can individual state preferences be predicted? The fourth section surveys the empirical record, looking at countries that have rejected regionalization, as well as those that have embraced it. Comparative analysis suggests that outcomes will depend most on country size, economic linkages, political linkages, and domestic politics. The relevance of these variables is then illustrated with some brief case studies in the fifth section. The sixth section concludes the chapter with a few generalizations about the future of monetary governance in a world of regional currencies.

The new geography of money

That the global monetary environment has been greatly transformed in recent decades is undeniable. A half-century ago, after the ravages of the Great Depression and World War II, national monetary systems – with the notable exception of the United States – were generally insular and strictly controlled. Starting in the 1950s, however, barriers separating local currencies gradually began to dissolve, first in the industrial world and then increasingly in many emerging-market economies, as well. Partly this was the result of an increased volume of trade, which facilitated monetary flows between states. But even more it was the product of intense market competition, which, in combination with technological and institutional innovation, offered an increasingly freer choice among currencies. Currency substitution widened the range of opportunities for a growing number of actors at all levels of society.

Deterritorialization and governance

Most scholarly attention has been paid to the remarkable growth in recent decades of capital mobility, reflected in a scale of international financial flows unequaled since the glory days of the nineteenth-century gold standard. The high level of capital mobility today is commonly cited as one of the most visible artifacts of contemporary globalization. But these flows are just part of the story of money's growing deterritorialization. A focus on capital mobility, emphasizing integration of financial markets, highlights only one of the standard functions of money: its use as a store of value. In fact, the interpenetration of monetary systems today has come to be far more extensive, involving *all* of the functions of currency – not just money's role as a private investment medium but also its use as a medium of exchange and unit of account for transactions of every kind, domestic as well as international. Crossborder currency competition means much more than capital mobility alone.

Deterritorialization is by no means universal, of course – at least, not yet. But it is remarkably widespread. Krueger and Ha (1996) estimate that foreign currency notes in the mid-1990s accounted for twenty percent or more of the local money stock in as many as three dozen nations inhabited by at least one-third of the world's population. In all, as much as one-quarter to one-third of the world's paper money supply is now located outside its country of issue. Most currency substitution is concentrated in Latin America, the Middle East, and republics of the former Soviet Union, where the dollar is favored; or in East-Central Europe and the Balkans, where the DM traditionally predominated. By a different measure, focusing on foreign currency deposits rather than paper money, the International Monetary Fund identifies some eighteen nations where, by the mid-1990s, another state's money accounted for at least thirty percent of broad money supply.[7] The most extreme cases, with ratios above 50 percent, included Azerbaijan, Bolivia, Croatia, Nicaragua, Peru, and Uruguay. Another thirty-nine economies had ratios approaching 30 percent, indicating "moderate" penetration.

The implications of deterritorialization for monetary governance are only beginning to be understood. For specialists in open-economy macroeconomics, who typically focus narrowly on capital mobility, the significance of recent developments lies mainly in implications for the choice of exchange-rate regime. Traditionally, the exchange-rate issue was cast in simple binary terms: fixed versus flexible rates. A country could adopt some form of peg for its currency or it could float. Pegs might be anchored on a single currency or a basket of currencies; they might be formally irrevocable (as in a currency board) or based on a more contingent rule; they might crawl or even take the form of a target zone. Floating rates, conversely, might be managed or just left to the interplay of market supply and demand. More recently, the issue has been recast – from fixed versus flexible rates to a choice between, on the one hand, contingent rules of any kind and, on the other, the so-called corner solutions of either free floating or some form of monetary union. Today, according to an increaingly fashionable argument known as the bipolar view or two-corner solution, no intermediate regime can be regarded as tenable (Fischer 2001). Owing to the development of huge masses of mobile wealth capable of switching between currencies at a moment's notice, governments can no longer hope to defend policy rules designed to hit explicit exchange-rate targets. The middle ground of contingent rules has in effect been "hollowed out," as Barry Eichengreen (1994) memorably put it.

But that too is just part of the story. In reality, more is involved here than simply a choice of exchange-rate regime. At its most fundamental, what is involved is nothing less than a challenge to the long-standing convention of national monetary sovereignty. Once we look beyond capital mobility alone to the broader phenomenon of currency competition, we see that in many areas of the world the traditional dividing lines between separate national monies are becoming less and less distinct. No longer are most economic actors restricted to a single currency – their own home money – as they go about their business. Crossborder circulation of currencies, which had long been common prior the emergence of the modern state system, has dramatically reemerged, resulting in a new geography of money. The functional domains of many monies no longer correspond precisely with the formal jurisdiction of their issuing authority.

Currency deterritorialization poses a critical challenge because governments have long relied upon the advantages derived from formal monetary monopoly to promote their conception of state interest. In fact, five main benefits are derived from a strictly territorial currency: first, a potential reduction of domestic transactions costs to promote economic growth; second, a potent political symbol to promote a sense of national identity; third, a powerful source of revenue (seigniorage) to underwrite public expenditures; fourth, a possible instrument to manage the macroeconomic performance of the economy; and finally, a practical means to insulate the nation from foreign influence or constraint. But all of these gains are eroded or lost when a government is no longer able to exert the same degree of control over the use of its money, by either its own citizens or others. Instead, in a growing number of countries, policymakers are driven to compete, inside and across borders, for the allegiance of market agents – in effect, to sustain or cultivate market share for their own brand of currency. The monopoly of monetary sovereignty yields to something more like oligopoly, and monetary governance is reduced to little more than a choice among marketing strategies designed to shape and manage demand.

Broadly speaking, for affected states, four strategies are possible, depending on two key considerations – first, whether policy is defensive or aggressive, aiming either to preserve or promote market share; and second, whether policy is unilateral or collective. These four strategies are:

1 *Market leadership*: an aggressive unilateralist policy intended to maximize use of the national money, analogous to predatory price leadership in an oligopoly.
2 *Market preservation*: a status-quo policy intended to defend, rather than augment, a previously acquired market position for the home currency.
3 *Market alliance*: a collusive policy of sharing monetary sovereignty in a monetary union of some kind, analogous to a tacit or explicit cartel.
4 *Market followership*: an acquiescent policy of subordinating monetary sovereignty to a stronger foreign currency via a currency board or full dollarization, analogous to passive price followership in an oligopoly.

Of these four, a strategy of market leadership is of course generally available only to governments with the most widely circulated currencies, such as the dollar, euro, or yen. For the vast majority of states with less competitive monies, decision making is limited to the remaining three – a tricky, tripartite choice.

The basic question

The basic question is plain. What constraints on national policy are states willing to accept? Should policymakers seek to sustain their traditional monetary sovereignty (market preservation)? Or, alternatively, should they countenance delegating some or all of that authority upward, either to the joint institutions of a monetary union (market alliance) or to a dominant foreign power (market followership)? A former president of the Argentine central bank put the point bluntly (Pou 2000, 244): "Should a [country] produce its own money, or should it buy it from a more efficient producer?" Buying money from a more efficient producer necessarily implies a degree of regionalization in monetary affairs.

Many states, for the present at least, appear resolved to continue producing their own money. They would prefer to keep the national currency alive, no matter how uncompetitive it may be. Monetary sovereignty can be defended by tactics of either persuasion or coercion. Persuasion entails trying to sustain demand for a currency by buttressing its reputation, above all by a public commitment to credible policies of "sound" monetary management. The idea is to preserve market confidence in the value and usability of the nation's brand of money – the "confidence game," as Paul Krugman has ironically dubbed it (Krugman 1998). Coercion means applying the formal regulatory powers of the state to avert any significant shift by users to a more popular foreign money. Possible measures range from standard legal-tender laws, which specify what money creditors must accept in payment of a debt, to limitations on foreign currency deposits in local banks and even to the extremes of capital controls or exchange restrictions. Both floating and contingent exchange-rate rules are consistent with a strategy of market preservation.

A desire to continue producing a national money is understandable, given the historical advantages of a formal monetary monopoly. But at what cost? As currency competition accelerates, tactics of persuasion or coercion become increasingly expensive. Growth and employment may have to be sacrificed, more and more, in order to keep playing the confidence game; widening distortions in the allocation of resources may be introduced by controls or restrictions. The costs of defending monetary sovereignty are real, a direct result of the transformation of the global currency environment. And as they continue to mount, the alternative of buying from a more efficient producer becomes increasingly appealing – or, at least, less unappealing. Not surprisingly, therefore, in a growing number of countries more attention is being paid today to the corner solution of monetary union, in the form of either formal dollarization or currency unification.

In Latin America, for example, the idea of dollarization has become a topic of intense public debate since Argentina's former President, Carlos Menem, spoke out in its favor in early 1999. Likewise, in East-Central Europe and the Mediterranean, "euroization" increasingly is touted as a natural path for countries with close ties to the European Union (EU) or hopes of one day joining the EU. Should more governments decide to go the route of dollarization, emulating the recent examples of Ecuador and El Salvador, it is not too difficult to imagine the gradual emergence of two giant monetary blocs, one centered on the United States and one on EMU's "Euroland." (Eventually a third bloc could also coalesce around the Japanese yen, though not any time soon.) As one observer has predicted, "By 2030 the world will have two major currency zones–one European, the other American. The euro will be used from Brest to Bucharest, and the dollar from Alaska to Argentina–perhaps even in Asia. These regional currencies will form the bedrock of the next century's financial stability."[8]

Much will depend, of course, on the policies adopted by the market leaders, which could significantly alter the relative costs and benefits of followership as contrasted with strategies of either market preservation or alliance. Unfortunately, these policies cannot be easily predicted. On the one hand, monetary leadership can yield substantial benefits, both economic and political. Economic gains include additional opportunities for seigniorage as well as an enhanced degree of macroeconomic flexibility. Politically, an international currency may yield dividends in terms of both power and prestige. The prospect of such benefits could lead the United States and Europe (and/or Japan) to offer explicit incentives to the potential dollarizer, especially if, as I have suggested elsewhere (Cohen 2000b), active competition for market share breaks out among the market leaders. But, on the other hand, there are also considerable risks in monetary leadership, including, in particular, policy constraints that could be imposed by pressures to accommodate the needs of followers. Such risks might prompt Washington and others to seek to discourage rather than encourage formal adoption of their currencies.

Absent material incentives to dollarize, some governments might instead prefer to look to the idea of currency unification, a less subordinate form of monetary union on the model of EMU. One long-standing currency union, the CFA Franc Zone, already exists in Africa; another, the Eastern Caribbean Currency Union (ECCU), functions smoothly in the Caribbean; and since the Maastricht treaty in 1991, which set the timetable for EMU, prospects for more such alliances have been discussed in almost every region of the world.[9] EMU is clearly viewed as a test case for a strategy of pooling, rather than surrendering, monetary sovereignty. If Europe's experiment comes to be seen as a success, it could have a powerful demonstration effect, encouraging similar initiatives elsewhere. Alongside two (or three) major currency zones, a variety of new joint currencies in addition to the euro could also eventually come into existence.

Scenarios of currency regionalization, therefore, seem not only plausible, but even likely – indeed, arguably for many states the most reasonable outcome to be expected from today's accelerating deterritorialization of money. At present there are more than 170 central banks in the world, as compared with fewer than twenty a century ago; and more than one hundred currencies that formally float more or less freely. Can anyone really believe that such a polyglot universe represents a stable equilibrium? "Convergence on regional monies is a no-brainer," writes Rudi Dornbusch (2001, 242). The logic of competition suggests that many governments could eventually yield to the market power of more efficient producers, replacing national monies with regional currencies of some kind. Regionalization of the world's monies has happened before, in medieval Europe and again during the nineteenth century, as Eichengreen and Sussman (2000) remind us. Obviously, it can happen again. For Ricardo Hausmann, formerly chief economist of the Inter-American Development Bank, the process has an almost historical inevitability about it: "National currencies are a phenomenon of the twentieth century; supranational currencies are the solution of the future" (Hausmann 1999b, 96). That formulation may be a bit too deterministic. Nonetheless, there is little doubt that alongside national monies a new geography of regional currencies is beginning to emerge as a byproduct of globalization.

Degrees of regionalization

The question is: What might that new geography look like? For individual countries a wide range of scenarios is possible, depending on the *degree* of regionalization involved. Whichever strategy a government is considering, whether alliance or followership, considerable leeway exists for variations of design along two key dimensions. These dimensions are institutional provisions for (1) the issuing of currency and (2) the management of decisions. Examples of currency regionalization have differed dramatically along each dimension, providing policymakers a rich menu. A guide to this diversity is provided in appendix 6A, which contains a complete listing of all cross-border currency arrangements presently in existence among sovereign states.

Currency issue

The highest degree of currency regionalization is of course when a single money is used by all participating countries. That is the way dollarization works in many of the small enclaves and microstates that have eschewed any currency of their own, such as Micronesia and Liechtenstein (table 11*a*.1).[10] That is also the way it works in a case of currency unification such as the ECCU, which shares the Eastern Caribbean dollar, and of course Europe's EMU. But a single money is by no means universal in regional currency arrangements. Relationships, in practice, may involve not one money but two or more bound together more or less tightly – an exchange-rate union.

Though the idea might seem counterintuitive, parallel circulation of two or more monies is in fact fully consistent with formal dollarization. Two currencies, for instance, has long been the case in Panama, where token amounts of locally issued coins (Panamanian balboas) circulate freely alongside the greenback at a fixed rate of exchange. Ecuador and El Salvador, too, are expected to maintain limited circulation of their own currencies even with formal dollarization, as do Kiribati and Tuvalu in the Pacific (table 11*a*.2). Local coins also used to be issued by several independent enclaves in Europe, such as San Marino and Andorra, prior to the introduction of the euro. In all of these cases, which may be labeled *near-dollarized* countries, the foreign currency dominates domestic money supply but falls short of absolute monopoly – a somewhat lower degree of dollarization.

Even lower on the scale is a *currency board*, such as has long existed in Brunei, Djibouti, and Hong Kong. With a currency board, the home money continues to account for a large, if not dominant, part of domestic money supply. In principle, though, issue of the local money is firmly tied to the availability of a designated foreign currency – usually referred to as the anchor currency. The exchange rate between the two monies is rigidly fixed, ostensibly irrevocably (an exchange-rate union); both currencies circulate as legal tender in the dependent country; and any increase in the issue of local money must be fully backed by an equivalent increase of reserve holdings of the anchor currency. During the 1990s new currency boards were established in a number of economies, including most notably Argentina, Bulgaria, Estonia, and Lithuania (table 11*a*.3). All of these arrangements still continue in operation except for Argentina's, which collapsed in early 2002.[11]

The lowest degree of dollarization is a *bimonetary* relationship, where legal-tender status is extended to one or more foreign monies, but without the formal ties characteristic of a currency board. Local money supply is not dependent on the availability of an anchor currency, and the exchange rate is not irrevocably fixed. Bimonetary relationships exist in a diverse range of states, from Bhutan to the Bahamas (table 11*a*.4).

Parallel circulation of two or more currencies is also consistent with a strategy of monetary alliance, as several present and past examples demonstrate (table 11*a*.5). Closest in spirit to a single money is today's CFA Franc Zone, born out of France's former colonial empire in Africa, which combines two separate regional currencies for West Africa and Central Africa, each cleverly named to preserve the CFA franc appellation, plus one national currency, the Comorian franc (CF) for the Comoros. Together the two regional groups comprise the *Communauté Financière Africaine* (African Financial Community). Technically each of the two regional currencies is legal tender only within its own region and managed by its own regional central bank. But the arrangement is very strict in the sense that it makes no allowance for any change of the exchange rate between the two CFA francs, and circulation between the two regions is not at all uncommon.

Essentially similar were two notable exchange-rate unions established in late nineteenth-century Europe – the Latin Monetary Union (LMU), which grouped together Belgium, France, Italy, Switzerland, and Greece; and the Scandinavian Monetary Union (SMU), comprising Denmark, Norway, and Sweden. The LMU was created in 1865, the SMU eight years later. The purpose of both was to standardize existing gold and silver coinages on the basis of a common monetary unit – in the LMU, the franc, and in the SMU, the krone (crown). Within each group, national currencies and central banks continued to exist. The separate currencies circulated freely at par, and no changes of official rates were even contemplated until the breakdown of the gold standard during World War I, which ultimately led to formal dissolution of both unions in the 1920s.

A less symmetrical, albeit comparably strict, model was provided by the Belgium-Luxembourg Economic Union (BLEU), which lasted nearly eight decades from 1922 until absorbed into EMU in 1999. Separate national monies were issued by each government, as in the LMU and SMU; but only one, the Belgian franc, enjoyed full status as legal tender in both states. The Luxembourg franc was limited in supply by a currency board–type arrangement and was legal tender only within Luxembourg itself. The arrangement was quite binding. Only once, in 1935, was there ever a change in the exchange rate between the two francs (subsequently reversed during World War II).

At the opposite extreme is the so-called Common Monetary Area (CMA) combining the Republic of South Africa – a sovereign state for decades – with two former British colonies, Lesotho and Swaziland, and South Africa's own former dependency, Namibia (formerly the United Nations trust territory of South West Africa). The origins of the CMA go back to the 1920s when South Africa's currency, now known as the rand, became the sole legal tender in several of Britain's nearby possessions, including Basutoland (later Lesotho) and Swaziland, as well as in South West Africa, previously a German colony. But following decolonization, an arrangement that began as an early example of dollarization based on the rand has gradually been transformed into a much looser scheme representing a much lower degree of regionalization, as each of South Africa's partners has introduced a distinct currency of its own. Today the CMA encompasses no fewer than four national currencies, only one of which, the rand, is legal tender outside its country of issue. The rand circulates legally in Lesotho and Namibia – both of which can now be described as bimonetary countries – but no longer in Swaziland. The rand serves as anchor for South Africa's three neighbors, but each government formally retains the right to change its own exchange rate at will.

Decision-making

Provisions for the delegation of decision-making authority may be equally varied, whether we are speaking of dollarization or currency unification. The logic of a regional currency, by analogy with national money, would seem to call for a single central agency with strong supranational powers – the highest possible degree of regionalization – and indeed that is the case in several instances. Microstates like Micronesia or Liechtenstein, totally without any money of their own, naturally cede all powers to the central bank of the country whose currency they use. The relationship is strictly *hierarchical*, with no assurance at all that the dependent state's specific views will be taken into account when monetary decisions are made. Likewise, both the ECCU and EMU have created joint institutions (respectively, the Eastern Caribbean Central Bank and the ECB) with exclusive authority to act on behalf of the group. Monetary sovereignty is fully pooled on a principle of *parity*, officially a relationship of equals.[12] But these are by no means the only possibilities. Other examples exist to demonstrate how formal powers may be more decentralized, reducing the degree of regionalization involved.

Most unusual is the CFA Franc Zone, with its two subregional central banks – a case of shared or dual supranationality. More common is the persistence of national monetary authorities with more or less symmetrical rights and responsibilities. The greater the degree of symmetry, the weaker is the element of supranationality.

Closest in spirit to a single central authority is the sort of highly asymmetric relationship characteristic of near-dollarized countries like Panama or Ecuador. A national monetary agency exists but without significant powers. Somewhat less demanding is a currency-board relationship, as in Hong Kong today or Luxembourg under BLEU, where local authorities may retain a significant degree of discretion depending on how the rules are written. A currency-board relationship is inherently asymmetrical, plainly favoring the central bank of the dominant partner, but need not be entirely one-sided. And yet less demanding are bimonetary relationships of the sort that exist in countries like the Bahamas and Bhutan. Least demanding is a wholly decentralized model of the sort practiced in the nineteenth century's LMU and SMU, where monetary management remained the exclusive responsibility of the members' separate central banks. Though in each case there was one central bank that could be said to enjoy disproportionate influence (the Banque de France in the LMU, the Swedish Rijksbank in the SMU), powers within each bloc were in principle symmetrical. The element of supranationality was minimal. The same principle of decentralization, implying a minimal degree of regionalization, is also characteristic of the CMA today.

Costs and benefits

With such a rich menu to choose from, how will governments decide among the three broad options of market preservation, alliance, or followership? At issue are potential benefits and costs, both economic and political. Rational policy-makers must take five key factors into account, all of which can be expected to vary systematically with the form and degree of currency regionalization under consideration.

Economic factors

On the economic side, three factors stand out. These are implications for (1) transactions costs; (2) macroeconomic stabilization; and (3) the distribution of seigniorage.[13] The first of these three factors argues clearly for currency regionalization in some form. The remaining two can be expected to reinforce a preference for market preservation.

Transactions costs

As compared with a world of separate territorial monies, currency regionalization has one unambiguous benefit. That is a reduction of transactions costs – the expenses associated with search, bargaining, uncertainty, and enforcement of contracts. When diverse local monies are replaced by a single regional currency, whether via monetary union or dollarization, there is no longer a need to incur the expenses of currency conversion or hedging in transactions between participating economies. Trade, as a result, could be increased substantially – by as much as a factor of three, according to empirical estimates by Andrew Rose – generating considerable efficiency gains.[14] This is the standard economic argument for monetary integration.

Indeed, nothing demonstrates the power of economies of scale more than money, whose usefulness is a direct function of the size of its functional domain. The larger a currency's transactional network, the greater will be the economies of scale to be derived from its use – what economists call money's "network externalities." Ceteris paribus, this factor implies a preference for the biggest currency regions possible. At the extreme, network externalities would be maximized if there were but a single currency in circulation everywhere – one global money.

Related to this factor are three other efficiency gains that also enhance the appeal of currency regionalization. First is a reduction of administrative costs, since individual governments will no longer be obliged to incur the expense of maintaining an infrastructure dedicated to production and management of a sep-arate national money. That saving would of course be of most interest to poorer or more diminutive sovereignties because of the diseconomies of small scale involved in monetary governance. Second, as a supposedly irreversible institu-tional change, currency regionalization could also establish a firm basis for a sounder financial sector – a benefit that would be of particular value to states that previously have not enjoyed much of a reputation for price stability or fiscal responsibility. Finally, with regionalization there could be a substantial reduction of interest rates for local borrowers in countries that have not yet succeeded in establishing a solid credit rating in international financial markets. All of these gains represent additional transactions-costs savings and, as such, carry the same implied preference for the biggest currency regions possible.

Because of the power of economies of scale, savings will be substantial for even a low degree of regionalization. Marginal benefits will diminish with successively higher degrees of regionalization.

Macroeconomic stabilization

Counterbalancing regionalization's efficiency gains, however, which are all of a microeconomic nature, is a potentially serious cost at the macroeconomic level: the loss of an autonomous monetary policy to manage the aggregate performance of the economy. This is the standard economic argument *against* monetary integration. Individually, governments give up control of both the money supply and exchange rate as policy instruments to cope with domestic or external disturbances. The more shocks there are likely to be and the more they can be expected to be asymmetric between economies, the greater will be the disadvantage of a single regional money. Ceteris paribus, this factor thus implies a preference for *avoiding* currency regionalization to the extent possible – just the reverse of the transactions-cost factor. As Krugman has written, the challenge "is a matter of trading off macroeconomic flexibility against microeconomic efficiency" (Krugman 1993, 4).[15]

On balance, the loss will be least onerous for countries that have already experienced substantial erosion of monetary autonomy owing to the growing deterritorialization of money. The greater the degree of informal currency substitution that has already occurred – reflecting a local currency's lack of competitiveness – the greater is the degree of constraint imposed even now on a government's ability to manage macroeconomic conditions; this is precisely the circumstance that is leading increasing numbers of countries to look for a more efficient producer of money. Indeed, the loss of autonomy might even be welcomed in some countries where past abuses of a monetary monopoly have led to persistent price instability or even hyperinflation. Currency regionalization in some form, by tying the hands of policymakers, may be seen as the only way to restore a reasonable degree of monetary stability. Conversely, the loss of policy flexibility will be felt most acutely in more insulated states that still enjoy a measure of monetary autonomy.

Comparing degrees of regionalization, it is evident that relatively little autonomy is sacrificed in bimonetary relationships or relatively symmetrical alliances like the CMA. Both money supply and the exchange rate can still be changed should circumstances warrant. The impact on policy flexibility, at the margin, will rise significantly with successively higher degrees of regionalization.

The distribution of seigniorage

A final economic issue involves seigniorage – the spending power that accrues from the state's ability to create money. Technically identified as the excess of the nominal value of a currency over its cost of production, seigniorage in the modern era derives from the difference between the interest-free liabilities of the central bank – cash in circulation – and the interest earned on the central bank's counterpart assets. It is, in effect, a pure profit attributable to the central bank's traditional position as a monopolist. In absolute terms seigniorage may not be very large, amounting to just a small fraction of a percent of GDP. But as the equivalent of a supplemental source of finance for government expenditure, it is apt to be considered of substantial value – a privilege not to be abandoned lightly.

Ceteris paribus, this factor, too, implies a preference for avoiding currency regionalization to the extent possible. With any form of regional currency, a certain amount of seigniorage profit will by definition be diverted elsewhere, going to either a joint institution or a dominant foreign power. Here also relatively little is sacrificed when the degree of regionalization is low. A bimonetary relationship or even a currency board keeps a national currency in circulation, permitting retention of some measure of seigniorage revenue; the same is true of a decentralized monetary union, as well. But here again the impact, at the margin, will rise significantly with successively higher degrees of regionalization, unless provisions can be agreed upon to compensate governments for interest earnings forgone. One precedent for such compensation is provided by the CMA, where the South African government makes annual payments to Lesotho and Namibia according to an agreed-upon formula for seigniorage-sharing, in order to encourage continued use of the rand. Another is provided by EMU, where net profits of the ECB are distributed proportionately to each of the member central banks.

Political factors

On the political side, two factors stand out. These involve issues of (1) social symbolism and (2) diplomatic influence. Both also can be expected to reinforce a preference for market preservation. In fact, each goes to the heart of the fundamental purpose of the state in world politics: to permit a community to live in peace and to preserve its own social and cultural heritage.

Social symbolism

Money has long played a powerful role in politics as a symbol to help promote a sense of national identity. As Eric Helleiner (1998) has noted, a territorial currency, enjoying sole place as legal tender within the political frontiers of the state, serves to enhance popular patriotism in two ways. First, because it is issued by the government or its central bank, the currency acts as a daily reminder to citizens of their connection to the state and oneness with it. Second, by virtue of its universal use on a daily basis, the currency underscores the fact that everyone is part of the same social entity – a role not unlike that of a single national language, which many governments also actively promote for nationalistic reasons. Both aspects help explain why so many governments are still determined to stick to monetary strategies of market preservation, keeping their currencies on life support no matter how uncompetitive they may have become. Such behavior is not at all irrational insofar as value continues to be attached to allegiance to a distinct political community.

Once in place, a territorial currency can also take on a psychological life of its own in defiance of all economic or political logic. Indeed, it is difficult to over-estimate the emotional attachment that most communities come to feel for their monies – even monies that have clearly failed the test of market competition.

The symbolic role of money would obviously be compromised by regionaliza-tion in any form, whether via dollarization or currency unification. Ceteris paribus, therefore, this factor, too, would appear to imply a preference for avoiding cur-rency regionalization to the extent possible. Here also, however, relatively little is sacrificed when the degree of regionalization is low. Even with a currency board or decentralized monetary union a national currency is preserved, thus continuing to provide a basic symbol to help sustain a society's sense of community. It is only at the highest degrees of regionalization – full or near-dollarization or something like EMU or ECCU – that the full impact of this factor will be felt.

Diplomatic influence

Money has also long played a role as an instrument of diplomatic influence. Indeed, as Jonathan Kirshner has written, "Monetary power is a remarkably efficient component of state power … the most potent instrument of economic coercion available to states in a position to exercise it" (Kirshner 1995, 29, 31). Money, after all, is, at its most basic, simply command over real resources. If a nation can be threatened with a denial of access to the means to acquire vital goods and services, it is clearly vulnerable in geopolitical terms.

This factor, too, implies a preference for avoiding currency regionalization to the extent possible. Monetary sovereignty enables policymakers to avoid depen-dence on some other source for their purchasing power. In effect, government is insulated from outside influence or constraint in formulating and implementing policy. Conversely, that measure of insulation will be compromised by any form of dollarization or currency unification. Again, the sacrifice is relatively modest when the degree of regionalization is low, since exit costs will be correspondingly limited. So long as national currency remains in circulation, with some degree of decentralization of decision making, room exists for a restoration of monetary sovereignty to escape painful diplomatic coercion. But here again the impact, at the margin, will rise significantly with successively higher degrees of regionalization.

Maximum acceptable regionalization

Taking all five factors into account, two implications become clear. First, it is evident why so many states appear resolved to continue producing their own money. A regional currency's saving of transactions costs, on its own, would seem unlikely to outweigh the considerable negatives implied: the losses of macroeconomic flexibility, seigniorage, a social symbol, and political insulation. In effect market preservation – defense of national monetary sovereignty – is a government's default strategy.

Second, it is evident why there is such wide variation in the design of regional currencies. Lower degrees of regionalization help to alleviate of some of the perceived disadvantages of an upward shift of authority. The considerable leeway for variations of design offers more opportunity to accommodate the interests of individual participants.

Is there, then, some degree of regionalization that will encourage more governments to depart from their default strategy? At the risk of oversimplifying a highly difficult decision, the key elements for rational policymakers can be reduced to a two-dimensional diagram comparing the cost of market preservation with the costs of either an alliance strategy or a followership strategy, as in figure 11.1.

Along the horizontal axis of the figure are alternative degrees of regionalization, ranging from the lowest forms at the left (e.g., a bimonetary system, or something like the CMA) to the highest at the right (e.g., pure dollarization, or something like the EMU). In principle one should distinguish not one but two metrics for regionalization, corresponding to the two separate dimensions involved – institutional provisions for currency issue and decision making. But in practice such an approach would only complicate the analysis with little promise of

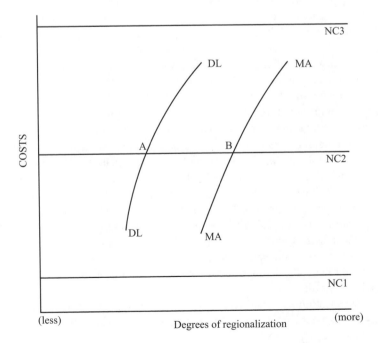

Figure 11.1 Choice diagram

additional insight. For the heuristic purposes of this essay, it is sufficient to collapse the two dimensions into a single scale that may be read from left to right as a rough measure of the share of formal authority delegated upward from the individual state.

On the vertical axis are total costs as perceived by a nation's policymakers. Begin with the cost of maintaining a strictly national currency (*NC*). *NC* may be represented by a horizontal line, since the estimated cost of a national currency is invariant to the degree of regionalization. The height of the line, low or high, will vary considerably from country to country reflecting differences in the cost of a default strategy of market preservation. Overall, for most states, it is clear that the height of *NC* is dramatically rising owing to the growing deterritorialization of money. Indeed, it is this upward movement that is the driving force connecting globalization and currency regionalization. As currency competition grows, the net benefits of monetary sovereignty are correspondingly reduced. Where a half-century ago most governments might have faced a line as low as *NC1*, today they may be confronted with lines as high as *NC2* or even *NC3*.

Curves *DL* and *MA* represent the net costs of, respectively, dollarization and monetary alliance. Each is a composite of the five factors just outlined – microeconomic efficiency gains, which decline at the margin with successively higher degrees of regionalization; and the losses of macroeconomic flexibility, seigniorage, social symbolism, and political insulation, all of which are a rising function of the degree of regionalization. Though it is manifestly difficult, a priori, to assign specific weights to each of these five factors, the overall direction of the relationship is clear. The greater the share of formal authority that is delegated upward, the higher is the estimated net cost as compared with a national currency. For any single country, the maximum acceptable degree of currency unification is represented by point A, where the cost of preserving a national currency equals the cost of the least demanding form of a followership strategy. By similar reasoning, the maximum acceptable degree of monetary alliance is point *B*.

The positions of *DL* and *MA* relative to *NC* will vary considerably from country to country, yielding diverse outcomes. For some, the cost of maintaining a national currency may already have become so elevated that it is now somewhere in the neighborhood of *NC3*, where there is no point of intersection with either *DL* or *MA*. Even the strictest form of monetary alliance or dollarization would thus be an acceptable option. By contrast, for others the position of *NC* might still be closer to *NC1*, below both *DL* and *MA*, making neither regionalization strategy acceptable in even its most diluted form. For some, *DL* might lie below *MA*, making some form of dollarization acceptable (*A*); for others, *MA* might lie below *DL*, resulting in just one point of intersection (*B*) where monetary alliance is the preferred option; and for yet others, *DL* and *MA* could lie close together, making the choice between dollarization and monetary alliance especially difficult.

The key question is: What determines the relative position of the three curves for any given country? Therein lies the core of a positive theory of currency regionalization.

Determining state preferences

At issue are state preferences. The more we know about what it is that influences policymakers' estimates of prospective benefits and costs, the easier it will be to predict preferences and therefore the delegation of authority that is ultimately likely to emerge in individual countries. Although policymakers can be expected to vary the weights they attach to particular gains or losses, depending on each state's individual circumstances, study of the empirical record does reveal some reasonably consistent patterns of behavior. Three conditions seem especially influential in determining strategic choices: (1) country size; (2) economic linkages; and (3) political linkages. In addition, domestic politics must also be assumed to play a key role.

The empirical record

There are limitations to the empirical record, of course. We do have an abundant population of states committed to one form of currency regionalization or another, as the appendix shows: some eighteen fully dollarized or near-dollarized economies, seven currency boards, ten bimonetary systems, and thirty-seven countries in a total of four different monetary unions, adding up to nearly a third of all sovereign entities in the world. This would certainly seem a large enough sample to look for meaningful patterns of behavior. But it is also evident that relatively few of these arrangements arc the product of calculated decisions by fully independent governments. The majority, in fact, grew out of relationships that originated in colonial times or in United Nations trusteeships. These include most of the fully dollarized and near-dollarized economies listed in tables 11a.1 and 11a.2 as well as three of the four monetary unions listed in table 11a.5 (all but EMU). In all such cases it was currency regionalization that was the default position, not some form of exclusive national currency.

Moreover, the empirical record is at best only an *indirect* indicator of preferences, since government choices are rarely fully unconstrained. In most cases it must be assumed that observed relationships are the outcome of strategic interactions and bargaining rather than unilateral decision making.

Nonetheless much can be learned, despite such limitations. Path dependency may be pervasive, but governments were not, after all, *compelled* to preserve inherited arrangements. A decision *not* to abandon a regional currency can tell us as much about preferences as a decision to adopt one. Moreover to this sample we may add other governments that, once given the opportunity, *did* in fact abandon a regional currency. These cases, too, tell us something about government attitudes. One instructive set of precedents is offered by the host of Third World countries that, once decolonization began after World War II, rapidly chose to abandon colonial-era currency boards for independent national monies. These also include the interesting case of the East African shilling, a joint currency shared by Kenya, Tanzania, and Uganda, which notably failed to outlive decolonization. Other precedents are provided by the successor states of recently failed federations – the former Soviet Union, Czechoslovakia, and Yugoslavia – nearly all of which chose to establish monies of their own in one form or another as soon as they gained their independence.

Likewise, choices may not be unconstrained, but outcomes may still be interpreted as evidence of revealed preference. The difficulty of inferring preferences from outcomes is a familiar one in social-science methodology but is generally not considered an insuperable barrier to analysis, so long as observations are handled with caution.

So what does the record tell us?

Country size

One thing the record tells us is that country size clearly matters, at least for the world's smallest states. Of all the economies that were fully or near-dollarized until recently, the largest was Panama, with a population of less than three million. Most are truly tiny enclaves or microstates. Small size also dominates among nations that have adopted currency boards or bimonetary systems and is an accurate description of the members of both the ECCU and CFA Franc Zone. One safe bet, ceteris paribus, is that the smaller an economy's size – whether measured by population, territory, or GDP – the greater is the probability that it will be prepared to surrender the privilege of producing a money of its own.

The logic is simple. Smaller states are least able to sustain a competitive national currency. The *NC* curve is already greatly elevated. Conversely, these are the economies that stand to gain most from a reduction of transactions costs. Whether in the form of dollarization or currency unification, some degree of regionalization offers both enhanced network externalities and lower administrative costs. Moreover, since in most cases these countries are also inherently vulnerable in political terms, less importance is likely to be attached to the risks that go with dependence on some other source for their purchasing power. Indeed, advantage may be seen in the protection that could be offered by association with either a powerful patron or a local partnership. Hence either *DL* or *MA*, or both, may fall below *NC*, encouraging governments to abandon strategies of market preservation.

How small must a state be? Until recently, regionalization seemed the preference of only the poorest and most diminutive specks of sovereignty around the globe. The threshold was very high. But as globalization has gradually elevated the NC curve, even bigger nations, as we know, have begun to join in, such as Ecuador and El Salvador. The threshold is clearly shifting downward, increasing the number of potential candidates.

Size, however, by no means explains all. Obviously there are many small states that have elected *not* to go the route of regionalization – at least, not yet. These include many former colonies and trust territories, as well as most of the successor states of recently failed federations, which even today remain intent on preserving, to the extent possible, the privileges of a national monetary monopoly. Small size per se is by no means a sufficient condition to predict the choice of strategy. Conversely, there are also some larger nations that have indeed chosen to delegate monetary authority elsewhere, most notably Bulgaria, Estonia, and Lithuania, with their currency boards, and the members of EMU. Small size is not a necessary condition, either.

Economic linkages

Another condition that appears to matter, not surprisingly, is the intensity of economic linkages between nations. Many of the countries that make use of a popular foreign currency have long been closely tied to a market leader economically. This is especially true of the numerous dollarized or bimonetary systems in the Caribbean and Central America, as well as the several dollarized enclaves of Europe and the Pacific. Likewise, we know that nearly a half-century of deepening integration preceded the start of EMU. Another safe bet, ceteris paribus, is that closer economic bonds will also increase the probability that a government will be prepared to surrender the privilege of producing its own money.

Here again, the logic is simple. Economies that are already closely linked would, because of the efficiency gains involved, appear to be natural candidates for a regional money of some kind. Linkages might operate through trade, as is evident in the European Union, or through financial relationships developed from formal or informal currency use. The higher the level of interaction, the more we would expect to see both greater savings of transactions costs and closer convergence of economic activity. If relations are mostly concentrated on a market leader, lowering the *DL* curve, some form of dollarization might prevail. This especially would be the case in countries where currency substitution has now become widespread, as in Latin America or East-Central Europe. Conversely, if links are closer within a group of neighboring states – say, as a result of a common integration project like the EU – MA would be lowered, making currency unification more likely.

It is clear, however, that this condition, too, on its own is neither necessary nor sufficient for predictive purposes. Both Mexico and Canada are more closely tied to the United States than most other Hemispheric economies, yet to date each remains firmly committed to defending its traditional monetary sovereignty. Conversely, both the ECCU and CFA Franc Zone continue to thrive despite an absence of much reciprocal trade, while successor states of recently failed federations have mostly preferred to produce their own national monies in spite of the previously close integration of their economies. Economic linkages alone are rarely decisive. The reason is that they bear on only two of the five factors of interest to rational policymakers: the trade-off between microeconomic efficiency and macroeconomic flexibility. Governments are undoubtedly sensitive to such considerations, but not exclusively.

Political linkages

A third condition that appears to matter is the intensity of political linkages between nations, whether formal or informal. Ties may take the form of a patron-client relationship, often descended from a previous colonial or trusteeship association; or they may be embodied in a network of cooperative diplomatic arrangements, possibly institutionalized in a formal alliance. Whatever the form, the influence of such ties is unmistakable – in currency groupings that have failed, as well as those that have survived.

On the negative side, I have already mentioned the several monetary unions that broke up in recent decades: in East Africa following decolonization, as well as in the former Soviet bloc following the end of the Cold War. We also know that many former dependencies of the old imperial powers, once granted independence, quickly rejected dollarization or colonial-era currency boards in favor of a money of their own. Plainly, in all of these cases, governments were motivated by a desire to assert their newfound rights and prerogatives as sovereign states; in other words, to *reduce* political linkages. Conversely, in the monetary unions that survived decolonization (ECCU and CFA Franc Zone), as well as in EMU and CMA, inter-state ties have always been stronger; and the same is true of most of today's dollarized entities, as well, which have long been accustomed to a hierarchical relationship with the source of their money. These are cases where governments are *least* interested in a reduction of political linkages.

Thus a third safe bet, ceteris paribus, is that closer political bonds, too, will increase the probability that a government will be prepared to surrender the privilege of a national money. The logic is that political linkages reduce two of the key costs associated with regionalization – the loss of a social symbol and the increase of vulnerability to outside influence. For states with already close ties to one of the market leaders, this means a lower DL curve, making some form of followership relatively more attractive. Candidates might include many of the countries of Latin America, ever in the shadow of the United States; or numerous economies of the former Soviet bloc, Mediterranean basin, or sub-Sahara Africa, with their close links to Europe. Likewise, for states already engaged in a common integration project, such as Mercosur in South America or the Association of Southeast Asian Nations (ASEAN), political linkages lower the MA curve, making a strategy of monetary alliance seem an increasingly natural choice.

Here again, however, as with size or economic linkages, the condition is rarely decisive, since it, too, bears directly on only a subset of the factors of interest to policymakers. Djibouti, for example, has a currency board that has always been based on the dollar despite the absence of any direct relationship with the United States. Israel, conversely, has expressly rejected dollarization in spite of its close ties to Washington (Cohen 1998, 38). Political linkages, too, on their own, are neither necessary nor sufficient for predictive purposes.

Domestic politics

Finally, what of domestic politics? The material interests of specific constituencies are systematically influenced by what a government decides to do with its money. State strategies thus are bound to be sensitive to the interplay among domestic political forces, as well as the institutional structures through which interest-group preferences are mediated.

Unfortunately, no studies yet exist that directly probe the role of domestic interest groups in currency regionalization. Strong hints, however, are provided by a related literature focusing on the wave of financial liberalization that swept emerging-market economies in the 1980s and 1990s.[16] Though details differ from country to country, it is clear that critical constituencies benefited measurably from the integration of local financial markets into the growing structure of global finance, including in particular big tradable-goods producers, banks and other financial-services firms, and large private asset-holders – those that Jeffry Frieden (1991a, b) refers to as "integrationist" interests. Exporters and importers, as well as domestic banks, gained improved access to loanable funds and lower borrowing costs; the owners and managers of financial wealth were freed to seek out more profitable investments or to develop new strategies for portfolio diversification. Most of these integrationist interests, research reveals, were active in lobbying policymakers to reduce or eliminate past restraints on capital mobility. Extrapolation from this literature suggests that many of these same powerful constituencies are likely to favor currency regionalization, as well, since a regional money offers the same advantage of financial openness. These are the actors who will benefit most from the anticipated reduction of transactions costs; for them, the *DL* and *MA* curves appear lower than they do to others. And they are not the type of actors who are apt to be shy about promoting their own interests.

Much rests, therefore, on the degree of political influence exercised by such groups as compared with other domestic constituencies, such as producers of nontradables and workers, who might oppose abandoning a national currency – "anti-integrationist" forces who feel they would benefit more from preservation of some measure of monetary autonomy. Integrationists' degree of influence, in turn, will be a function of domestic institutions and political structures. The issue is the extent to which government decision making is insulated from the pressures of such groups. How much attention is paid to their specific preferences and demands? This is less a matter of formal regime type than of practical access to the corridors of power. The greater the relative influence of integrationist interests, the more probable it is that policymakers will be prepared to delegate monetary authority elsewhere. This seems another safe bet, again ceteris paribus.

Illustrations

Generalization is of course difficult when no single variable can be considered either necessary or sufficient to forecast behavior. A parsimonious predictive model is simply not possible. Nonetheless, much insight can be gained by looking at all relevant conditions together in the context of specific cases. Two brief comparisons serve to illustrate the value of such an analytical approach.

Argentina versus Ecuador

Consider first Argentina and Ecuador, a pair of states that, as indicated, have chosen strategies of market followership – but to significantly different degrees and with very different outcomes. Argentina moved first, in 1991, when it adopted a currency board tied firmly to the dollar. Subsequently, following former President Menem's expression of interest, the idea of full dollarization was considered but ultimately rejected by the government of Menem's successor, Fernando de la Rúa, even before the currency board's eventual collapse. Ecuador, by contrast, decided in 2000 to adopt the dollar formally, leaving only token amounts of its own previous currency in circulation. What explains the difference in the degree of regionalization attempted by the two countries?

In two key respects, the pair are quite similar. Each state has strong economic linkages with the United States, particularly through currency substitution. At the end of 1999, the dollar accounted for some 56 percent of total bank deposits in both Argentina and Ecuador.[17] And each is close to the United States politically, long accustomed to Washington's leadership role in the Western Hemisphere. In terms of figure 6.1, both conditions suggest a lowered DL, helping to explain why each country might have been predisposed to dollarization in some form.

But in two other respects, the pair are quite dissimilar. One obvious difference is size. Whereas Argentina, Latin America's third largest economy, is a middle-income emerging market with a fair amount of industry, Ecuador is much smaller in territory and population and far less developed economically. The other difference has to do with domestic politics, which since the late 1980s have been rather more open and pluralistic in Argentina than in Ecuador. In Ecuador, particularly in the crisis circumstances prevailing in early 2000 when the dollarization decision was taken, few opportunities existed for opposition to mobilize against the new currency strategy. Integrationist forces were able to dominate decision making. In Argentina, by contrast, anti-integrationist forces are much better organized and represented politically, creating a more level playing field. The first contrast suggests a more elevated NC curve for Ecuador, raising the maximum acceptable degree of regionalization as compared with Argentina. The second suggests a higher DL curve for Argentina, lowering the maximum acceptable degree of regionalization as compared with Ecuador.

Hence we should not be surprised by the differing outcomes in the two cases, following President Menem's remarks in 1999. At the very time that Ecuador embraced full dollarization, unilaterally delegating all of its monetary authority to Washington, Argentina was holding out for a better deal, preferably in the form of a bilateral treaty of monetary association with Washington. If the nation was to surrender what remained of its historical monetary sovereignty, proud Argentinians wanted to be seen as partners with the United States, not a mere dependency. When Washington politely declined, Buenos Aires decided to remain instead with its less demanding currency board, until even that degree of commitment proved impossible to sustain.

Eastern Caribbean versus East Africa

A second instructive comparison is between the Eastern Caribbean and East Africa, two regions that have had strikingly different experiences with strategies of market alliance. Each region inherited a common currency from its former colonial master, Great Britain, upon receiving independence in the 1960s – respectively, the West Indian dollar (now the Eastern Caribbean dollar) and the East African shilling. But whereas the Eastern Caribbean Currency Union, as indicated, has functioned smoothly for decades, its East African equivalent, the East African Community (EAC), fell apart almost as soon as the British left the scene. First the East African shilling was replaced by separate national currencies in a looser exchange-rate union; and then in the mid-1970s even the exchange-rate union was abandoned as all three constituent members extended exchange restrictions to each other's money. The contrast between outcomes in the two regions could not be greater. Again, we may ask what explains the difference.

In fact, similarities between the two cases are considerable. The economies in both regions are among the smallest and poorest in the world. For all of them, the cost of preserving a strictly national currency is undoubtedly high (a greatly elevated *NC*). There is also relatively little difference between the regions in the intensity of economic linkages within each group or, so far as one can judge, in the political influence of integrationist interests. On all of these counts we would not expect much variance in the degree of regionalization elected by the two groups.

But the two cases do differ significantly along the political dimension, where postcolonial ties proved to be far more durable in the Eastern Caribbean than in East Africa. In the EAC, as I have noted elsewhere (Cohen 2000a), decolonization left little feeling of solidarity among the three constituent members, despite their legacy of common services and institutions. Much more influential was a pervasive sensitivity to any threat of encroachment on newly won sovereignty, which raised the perceived cost of currency unification (elevating *MA*). Once independent, each was more concerned with building national identity than with preserving regional unity. In the Eastern Caribbean, by contrast, identities have always been defined more in regional than national terms, institutionalized in a dense web of related political and economic agreements. From the start, the *MA* curve was seen as much lower, removing any incentive to alter strategy.

Conclusions and implications

What, then, can we say about the future of monetary governance in a world of regional currencies? The working assumption, to repeat, is that economic globalization is driving states to reconsider their historical attachment to strictly national money. The question, once again, is: What delegation of authority, then, is most likely to emerge?

While firm predictions are difficult, four broad generalizations seem reasonable. First, while the deterritorialization of currency is clearly imposing growing constraints on traditional forms of monetary governance, it by no means dictates the choices that governments will eventually make. Many countries will consider some form of either dollarization or currency unification – but by no means all.

Second, we should expect to see relatively few *pure* cases of dollarization or currency unification. Few countries are apt to go the way of the Marshall Islands or Monaco, which willingly forgo any claim to a national money of their own. Likewise, even in the small handful of common integration projects now under way in the developing world – most notably, Mercosur and ASEAN – partnerships remain far from the degree of closeness that would be required to establish something as far-reaching as EMU or the ECCU. Regionalization may for many be a logical corollary of currency competition, but it does not follow that sovereign states will spontaneously delegate *all* of their monetary authority upward, either to a market leader or to a joint central bank. Most governments are likely to prefer somewhat more mixed models, involving a more limited element of regionalization.

Third, what those mixed models might in practice look like will vary considerably, depending very much on *bargaining context*. Practical experience demonstrates that many different degrees of regionalization are possible to accommodate the economic and political interests of participating states. No uniform outcome should be expected for either dollarization or currency unification.

Finally, bargaining context in turn will depend greatly on the key conditions of country size, economic linkages, political linkages, and domestic politics. Higher degrees of regionalization are more likely where states are small, economic and political linkages are strong, and domestic politics is heavily influenced by tradable-goods producers and financial interests. Conversely, lower degrees of regionalization may be expected insofar as countries are larger, economic and political linkages with others are weaker, and the domestic political setting is more pluralistic. In the largest states, with the weakest economic and political linkages and the most pluralistic politics, defense of national monetary sovereignty will remain the default strategy.

In short, there seems little doubt that a new geography of regional currencies is emerging as a byproduct of globalization. But as it evolves, the world's monetary map will in all probability come to look more like a messy, highly variegated mosaic than any simple structure of giant blocs and joint currencies. The essential elements of a positive theory of currency regionalization can be identified. What cannot be foretold is how these elements will work out in specific bargaining contexts. Standard microeconomic theory teaches that when monopoly yields to oligopoly, outcomes become indeterminate and multiple equilibria are possible. So, too, it would appear, is this true in matters of money.

Appendix

Table 11a.1 Fully Dollarized Countries[1]

Country	Currency used	Since
Andorra	euro	2002
Cyprus (Northern)[2]	Turkish lira	1974
East Timor	U.S. dollar	2000
Kosovo[3]	euro	2002
Liechtenstein	Swiss franc	1921
Marshall Islands	U.S. dollar	1944
Micronesia	U.S. dollar	1944
Monaco	euro	2002
Montenegro[3]	euro	1999
Nauru	Australian dollar	1914
Palau	U.S. dollar	1944
San Marino	euro	2002
Vatican City	euro	2002
TOTAL = 13		

Sources: International Monetary Fund, Europa World Year Book, various government sources.

[1] Independent states that extend exclusive legal-tender rights to a single foreign currency.
[2] De facto independent; under the protection of Turkey.
[3] Semi-independent; formally still part of Yugoslavia.

Table 11a.2 Near-Dollarized Countries[1]

Country	Currency used	Since	Local currency
Ecuador	U.S. dollar	2000	sucre
El Salvador	U.S. dollar	2001	colon
Kiribati	Australian dollar	1943	own coins
Panama	U.S. dollar	1904	balboa
Tuvalu	Australian dollar	1892	Tuvaluan dollar
TOTAL = 5			

[1] Independent states that rely primarily on one or more foreign currencies, but also issue a token local currency.

Table 11a.3 Currency Boards[1]

Country	Anchor currency	Since	Local currency
Bosnia and Herzegovina	euro (formerly deutsche mark)	1998	Bosnian marka
Brunei Darussalam	Singapore dollar	1967	Brunei dollar
Bulgaria	euro (formerly deutsche mark)	1997	lev

(Continued)

Table 11a.3 Continued

Country	Anchor currency	Since	Local currency
Djibouti	U.S. dollar	1949	Djibouti franc
Estonia	euro (formerly deutsche mark)	1992	kroon
Hong Kong[2]	U.S. dollar	1983	Hong Kong dollar
Lithuania	euro (formerly U.S. dollar)	1994	litas
TOTAL = 7			

[1] Countries with a formally irrevocable exchange-rate link to a foreign currency, both of which circulate domestically as legal tender and are fully interchangeable.
[2] Special Administrative Region of China.

Table 11a.4 Bimonetary Countries[1]

Country	Currencies used	Since
Bahamas	Bahamanian dollar, U.S. dollar	1966
Belarus	Belarusian rubel, Russian ruble	1991
Bhutan	Bhutan ngultrum, Indian rupee	1974
Cambodia	Cambodian riel, U.S. dollar	1980
Guatemala	Guatemala quetzal, use of other currencies permitted	2001
Haiti	Haitian gourde, U.S. dollar	n.a.
Lao P.D.R.	Lao kip, Thai baht, U.S. dollar	n.a.
Liberia[2]	Liberian dollar, U.S. dollar	1982
Palestinian territories[3]	Israeli shekel, Jordanian dinar	1967
Tajikistan	Tajik ruble, use of other currencies permitted	1994
TOTAL = 10		

[1] Countries with one or more foreign currencies in circulation that are recognized legally but are subsidiary to the local currency as legal tender.
[2] Near-dollarized, with only token amounts of Liberian dollars in circulation, from 1944 until 1982.
[3] Occupied by Israel since 1967. The Israeli shekel is the exclusive legal tender in the Gaza Strip; both the shekel and Jordanian dinar are recognized in the West Bank.

Table 11a.5 Monetary Unions

Union	Member countries	Institutional arrangements	Since
Eastern Caribbean	Antigua and Barbuda, Dominica, Grenada, St. Kitts-Nevis, St. Lucia, St. Vincent and the Grenadines	Single currency (Eastern Caribbean dollar), currency union, single central bank	1965

(*Continued*)

Table 11a.5 Continued

Union	Member countries	Institutional arrangements	Since
Economic and Monetary Union (European Union)	Austria, Belgium, Finland, France, Germany, Greece, Ireland, Italy, Luxembourg, Netherlands, Portugal, Spain	Single currency (euro), single central bank	1999
CFA Franc Zone	Benin, Burkina Faso, Cameroon, Central African Republic, Chad, Comoros, Congo-Brazzaville, Côte d'Ivoire, Equatorial Guinea, Gabon, Guinea-Bissau, Mali, Niger, Senegal, Togo	Two regional currencies (both named CFA franc) and one national currency (Comorian franc); two regional central banks and one national central bank (Comoros)	1962–64
Common Monetary Area	Lesotho, Namibia, South Africa, Swaziland	Three currencies pegged to South African rand, four central banks (South African rand is legal tender in Lesotho and Namibia)	1986
TOTAL = 37			

Notes

1 This essay has benefited from comments by other contributors to this collective project and especially by the editors, Miles Kahler and David Lake. Special thanks, as well, to Jeffrey Chwieroth, Eric Helleiner, Barbara Koremenos, and Richard Steinberg for valuable insights and suggestions. The research assistance of Tom Knecht is gratefully acknowledged.
2 The adjectives "full" or "formal" are frequently added to distinguish this policy choice from the market-driven process of currency substitution, which in the past was also often popularly labeled dollarization (now unofficial or informal dollarization). Dollarization, of course, does not necessarily require the dollar. Some other currency, such as the euro or yen, may also be chosen to replace a country's currency.
3 See, for example, Alesina and Barro (2001); Dornbusch (2001); Fischer (2001); and Rogoff (2001).
4 See, for example, Alesina and Barro (2002).
5 The distinction between pooling and surrender of sovereignty, which is generic to the question of how to organize political authority, is of course a familiar one in political

science and is used in a variety of contexts – in analyzing differences between confederal states and empires, for instance.

6 The discussion in the beginning of the first section – on deterritorialization and governance – is necessarily condensed and is based on arguments presented at greater length in Cohen (1998).

7 Baliño, Bennett, and Borensztein (1999). Broad money supply (*M*2) is defined to include all coins and notes in circulation, demand deposits (checking accounts), and all other "reservable" deposits (time-deposits).

8 Beddoes (1999, 8). See also Eichengreen (1994); Hausmann (1999a,b) and Mundell (2000).

9 These include prospects in Asia (Eichengreen and Bayoumi 1999), Africa (Honohan and Lane 2001), Latin America (Levy Yeyati and Sturzenegger 2000), Australia-New Zealand (Grimes and Holmes 2000), and even between the United States and Canada (Buiter 1999).

10 I include here only politically sovereign entities, excluding all monetary arrangements with scattered dependent territories left over from the era of colonialism. In most cases, dependent territories make exclusive use of the currency of the "mother" country. These include the external dependencies of Australia, Denmark, France, New Zealand, Norway, the United Kingdom, and the United States. Exceptions include, inter alia, Bermuda, the British Virgin Islands, and the Turks and Caicos Islands, all of which use the U.S. dollar though they are territories of the United Kingdom.

11 For a discussion of factors leading up to the collapse of Argentina's currency board, see Pastor and Wise (2001).

12 Von Furstenberg (2000) characterizes these as, respectively, "uncooperative unilateral monetary unions" and a "multilateral sharing model of monetary union."

13 Not surprisingly, these three factors dominate discussions by economists. See, for example, Alesina and Barro (2002).

14 Rose (2000). Though frequently challenged, Rose's results have been consistently confirmed by other studies, as Rose (2002) demonstrates in a comprehensive analysis.

15 Readers will recognize a more-than-passing familiarity of this trade-off to the central tension identified by Charles Tiebout and others interested in the optimal level of governance in world affairs – a tension between scale economies and externalities, on the one hand, which argue for larger units and greater centralization of authority; and on the other hand, heterogeneity of preferences, which argues for the reverse. Scale economies and externalities are at the heart of the efficiency gains offered by currency regionalization, while macroeconomic flexibility is valued precisely because of the persistence of national differences. But that is not the only trade-off implicated in currency regionalization, as the discussion will make clear, and may not even be the most salient. Functionalist Tiebout-type models are too narrow to capture all of the elements of the policy choices involved.

16 Notable examples include Auerbach (2001); Haggard, Lee, and Maxfield (1993); Loriaux et al. (1997); Maxfield (1990); Pauly (1988).

17 Confidential source. In addition, substantial amounts of U.S. bank notes can be assumed to be in circulation in both countries.

References

Alesina, Alberto, and Robert J. Barro. 2001. "Dollarization." *American Economic Review* 91, 2 (May): 381–85.

——. 2002. "Currency Unions." *Quarterly Journal of Economics* 117, 2 (May): 409–36.

Auerbach, Nancy Neiman. 2001. *States, Banks, and Markets: Mexico's Path to Financial Liberalization in Comparative Perspective.* Boulder, Colo.: Westview Press.

Baliño, Tomás, J.T., Adam Bennett, and Eduardo Borensztein. 1999. *Monetary Policy in Dollarized Economies.* Washington, D.C.: International Monetary Fund.

Beddoes, Zanny Minton. 1999. "From EMU to AMU? The Case for Regional Currencies." *Foreign Affairs* 78, 4 (July/August): 8–13.

Buiter, Willem H. 1999. "The EMU and the NAMU: What is the Case for North American Monetary Union?" *Canadian Public Policy/Analyse de Politiques* 25, 3 (September): 285–305.

Cohen, Benjamin J. 1998. *The Geography of Money.* Ithaca, N.Y.: Cornell University Press.

——. 2000a. "Beyond EMU: The Problem of Sustainability." In *The Political Economy of European Monetary Integration,* 2d ed., edited by Barry Eichengreen and Jeffry A. Frieden. Boulder, Colo: Westview Press.

——. 2000b. "Life at the Top: International Currencies in the Twenty-First Century." In *International Economics* 221. Princeton, N.J.: International Economics Section.

Dornbusch, Rudi. 2001. "Fewer Monies, Better Monies." *American Economic Review* 91, 2 (May): 238–42.

Eichengreen, Barry. 1994. *International Monetary Arrangements for the Twenty-First Century.* Washington, D.C.: Brookings Institution.

Eichengreen, Barry and Tamim Bayoumi. 1999. "Is Asia an Optimum Currency Area? Can It Become One? Regional, Global, and Historical Perspectives on Asian Monetary Relations." In *Exchange Rate Policies in Emerging Asian Countries,* edited by Stefan Collignon, Jean Pisani-Ferry, and Yung Chul Park. London: Routledge.

Eichengreen, Barry and Nathan Sussman. 2000. "The International Monetary System in the (Very) Long Run." In *World Economic Outlook Supporting Studies.* Washington, D.C.: International Monetary Fund.

Fischer, Stanley. 2001. "Exchange Rate Regimes: Is the Bipolar View Correct?" *Journal of Economic Perspectives* 15, 2 (spring): 3–24.

Frieden, Jeffry. 1991a. "Invested Interests: The Politics of National Economic Policies in a World of Global Finance." *International Organization* 45, 4 (autumn): 425–51.

——. 1991b. *Debt, Development, and Democracy.* Princeton, N.J.:Princeton University Press.

Grimes, Arthur, and Frank Holmes. 2000. *An ANZAC Dollar? Currency Union and Business Development.* Wellington: Victoria University of Wellington, Institute of Policy Studies.

Haggard, Stephan, Chung H. Lee, and Sylvia Maxfield, eds. 1993. *The Politics of Finance in Developing Countries.* Ithaca, N.Y.: Cornell University Press.

Hausmann, Ricardo. 1999a. "Should There Be Five Currencies or One Hundred and Five?" *Foreign Policy* 116 (fall): 65–79.

——. 1999b. "Why the Interest in Reform?" In *Rethinking the International Monetary System,* edited by Jane Sneddon Little and Giovanni P. Olivei, 94–96. Boston: Federal Reserve Bank of Boston.

Helleiner, Eric. 1998. "National Currencies and National Identities." *American Behavioral Scientist* 41, 10 (August): 1409–436.

Honohan, Patrick, and Philip Lane. 2001. "Will the Euro Trigger More Monetary Unions in Africa?" In *EMU and Its Impact on Europe and the Developing Countries,* edited by Charles Wyplosz. Oxford: Oxford University Press.

Kirshner, Jonathan. 1995. *Currency and Coercion: The Political Economy of International Monetary Power.* Princeton. N.J.: Princeton University Press.

Krueger, Russell, and Jiming Ha. 1996. "Measurement of Cocirculation of Currencies." In *The Macroeconomics of International Currencies: Theory, Policy, and Evidence,* edited by Paul D. Mizen and Eric J. Pentecost. Brookfield, VT.: Edward Elgar.

Krugman, Paul R. 1993. "What Do We Need to Know about the International Monetary System?" In *International Finance* 190. Princeton, NJ: Princeton University, International Finance Section.

Krugman, Paul R. 1998. "The Confidence Game." *The New Republic,* 5 October, 23–25.

Levy Yeyati, Eduardo, and Federico Sturzenegger. 2000. "Is EMU a Blueprint for Mercosur?" *Latin American Journal of Economics* 110 (April): 63–99.

Loriaux, Michael, Meredith Woo-Cumings, Kent E. Calder, Sylvia Maxfield, and Sofía A. Pérez. 1997. *Capital Ungoverned: Liberalizing Finance in Interventionist States.* Ithaca, N.Y.: Cornell University Press.

Maxfield, Sylvia. 1990. *Governing Capital: International Finance and Mexican Politics.* Ithaca, N.Y.: Cornell University Press.

Mundell, Robert. 2000. "A Reconsideration of the Twentieth Century." *American Economic Review* 90, 3 (June): 327–40.

Pastor, Manuel, and Carol Wise. 2001. "From Poster Child to Basket Case." *Foreign Affairs* 80, 6 (July/August): 60–72.

Pauly, Louis W. 1988. *Opening Financial Markets: Banking Politics on the Pacific Rim.* Ithaca, NY: Cornell University Press.

Pou, Pedro. 2000. "Is Globalization Really to Blame?" In *Rethinking the International Monetary System,* edited by Jane Sneddon Little and Giovanni P. Oliveri, 243–50. Boston: Federal Reserve Bank of Boston.

Rogoff, Kenneth. 2001. "Why Not a Global Currency?" *American Economic Review* 91, 2 (May): 243–47.

Rose, Andrew K. 2000. "One Money, One Market: The Effect of Common Currencies on Trade." *Economic Policy* 30 (April): 7–45.

Von Furstenberg, George. 2000. "A Case Against U.S. Dollarization." *Challenge* 43, 4 (July/August): 108–20.

12 The geopolitics of currencies and the future of the international system

Source: Working paper prepared for the Real Instituto Elcano, Madrid, November 2003.

Geopolitics, the dictionary tells us, is about international great-power rivalries – the struggle for dominance among territorially defined states. Conflict is at the heart of geopolitics. Geopolitical relations are dynamic, strategic, and hierarchical. In geopolitics, the meek definitely do not inherit the earth.

Today, much the same can be said about currencies, which in recent years have become increasingly competitive on a global scale. Monetary relations, too, have become conflictual and hierarchical; and the meek are similarly disadvantaged. At issue is a breakdown of the neat territorial monopolies that national governments have historically claimed in the management of money, a market-driven process that elsewhere I have described as the deterritorialization of money (Cohen 1998, 2003a). In lieu of monopoly, what we have now is more like oligopoly – a finite number of autonomous suppliers, national governments, all vying ceaselessly to shape and manage demand for their respective currencies. Since most states are no longer able to exercise supreme control over the circulation and use of money within their own frontiers, they must instead do what they can to preserve or promote market share. As a result, the population of the monetary universe is becoming ever more stratified, assuming the appearance of a vast Currency Pyramid – narrow at the top, where the strongest monies dominate; and increasingly broad below, reflecting varying degrees of competitive inferiority.

What are the geopolitical implications of this new geography of money? At present, one currency stands head and shoulders above the rest – the US dollar, familiarly known as the greenback. The dollar is the only truly global currency, used for all the familiar purposes of money – medium of exchange, unit of account, store of value – in virtually every corner of the world. From its dominant market share, the United States gains significant economic and political advantages. The question is: can the dominance of the dollar be challenged? The answer comes in two parts: first, if we look at the logic of market competition; and, secondly, if we factor in government preferences as well.

Looking at the logic of market competition alone, the answer is clear. The dollar will continue to prevail. Presently, only two other currencies are used at all widely outside their countries of issue. These are the euro, the new joint money of the European Union (EU), and the Japanese yen. Together, these are the Big Three of currency geopolitics. But neither the euro nor the yen, I submit, poses a serious competitive threat to the greenback in today's global marketplace.

Once we factor in government preferences, however, the outlook becomes cloudier. That the Europeans and Japanese will do all they can to sustain the market appeal of their currencies may be taken for granted. But whether they will go further, to seek formation of organized monetary blocs with foreign governments, is less certain. Japan may well to seek to challenge the dollar's present dominance in East Asia; likewise, Europe could be tempted to make a battleground of the Middle East. Neither, however, is likely to carry currency confrontation with the United States to the point where it might jeopardize more vital political and security interests. Mutual restraint among the Big Three would appear to be the safest bet.

The dollar

I begin with the dollar. Broadly speaking, currencies may be employed outside their country of origin for either of two purposes: for transactions either between nations or within foreign states. The former is conventionally referred to as international currency use or currency internationalization; the latter goes under the label currency substitution and can be referred to as foreign-domestic use. For both purposes America's greenback today is indisputably the market leader, the Top Currency perched at the peak of the Currency Pyramid. Its only possible rivals are the euro and, more distantly, the yen. Because of the dollar's market leadership, it may be argued, the United States is privileged both economically and politically.

The dollar's market leadership

The clearest signal of the dollar's leadership in international currency use is sent by the global foreign-exchange market where, according to the Bank for International Settlements (2002), the dollar is the most favoured vehicle for currency trading worldwide, appearing on one side or the other of some 90% of all transactions in 2001 (the latest year for which such data are available). The euro, in distant second place, appeared in just 38% of transactions – higher than the share of its popular predecessor, the deutsche mark (DM), which had appeared in 30% of transactions in 1998, but lower than that of all the euro's constituent currencies taken together that same year (53%). The yen was even further behind with only 23%.[1]

The greenback is also the most favoured vehicle for the invoicing of international trade, where it has been estimated to account for nearly half of all world exports (Hartmann 1998), more than double America's share of global trade. The DM's share of invoicing in its last years, prior to its replacement by the euro, was 15%, roughly equivalent to Germany's proportion of world exports. Preliminary evidence from the European Central Bank, the ECB (2002: 39–42), suggests that the euro's share may have increased modestly since its introduction as a 'virtual' currency in 1999, albeit mainly for Europe's own trade with the outside world rather than in exchanges between third countries. The yen's share of global invoicing was just 5%, significantly less than Japan's proportion of world exports.

A parallel story is evident too in international markets for financial claims, including bank deposits and loans as well as bonds and stocks. Using data from a variety of sources, Thygesen et al. (1995) calculated what they call 'global financial wealth', the world's total portfolio of private international investments, estimated at more than US$4.5 trillion in 1993. Again the dollar dominated, accounting for close to two-fifths of international bonds and nearly three-fifths of foreign-currency deposits. The DM accounted for 10% of bonds and 14% of deposits; the yen for 14% of bonds and 4% of deposits. More recently, the euro has cut into the greenback's share of the bond market, accounting now for close to 30% of all issues as against 44% for the dollar and just 13% for the yen (ECB 2002: 17–19). But in international banking the dollar still dominates, with a share of 55% of deposits compared with 24% for the euro and 7% for the yen (ECB 2002: 16).

The clearest signal of the greenback's leadership in foreign-domestic use is sent by the swift increase in the currency's physical circulation outside the borders of the United States, mostly in the form of US$100 bills. Authoritative studies by the Federal Reserve (Porter and Judson 1996) and the US Treasury (2000) put the value of all Federal Reserve notes in circulation abroad at between 50% and 70% of the total outstanding stock – equivalent at the turn of the century to roughly US$275 billion to US$375 billion in all.[2] Estimates also suggest that as much as three-quarters of the annual increase of US notes now goes directly abroad, up from less than one-half in the 1980s and under one-third in the 1970s. By the end of the 1990s, as much as 90% of all US$100 notes issued by the Federal Reserve were going directly abroad to satisfy foreign demand (Lambert and Stanton 2001). Appetite for the greenback appears to be not only strong but growing.

By contrast, estimates by Germany's central bank, the Bundesbank (1995), put foreign circulation of the DM in its last years, mainly in East-Central Europe and the Balkans, at no more than 30% to 40% of total stock, equivalent at year-end 1994 to some DM65–90 billion (US$45–65 billion).[3] It remains unclear to what extent euro notes may surpass the level of popularity previously enjoyed by the DM (ECB 2002: 48–52). On the other side of the world, Bank of Japan officials have been privately reported to believe that of the total supply of yen bank notes, amounting to some US$370 billion in 1993, no more than 10% was located in neighbouring countries (Hale 1995).[4]

Advantages for the United States

Not surprisingly, all this international and foreign-domestic use of the dollar appears to translate into considerable advantages for the United States, both economic and political. Though minimized by some (eg, Wyplosz 1999: 97–100), the benefits of market leadership in currency affairs can in fact be quite substantial. Four distinct gains may be cited.

Most familiar is the potential for seigniorage. Expanded cross-border circulation of a country's money generates the equivalent of a subsidized or interest-free loan from abroad – an implicit transfer that represents a real-resource gain for the economy as a whole. Consider just the circulation of Federal Reserve notes, which are a form of non-interest bearing liability. Updating earlier estimates by Jeffrey A. Frankel (1995) and Alan S. Blinder (1996), current interest savings from foreign circulation of the greenback may be conservatively calculated at some US$16–22 billion a year. To this may be added a saving of interest payments on US government securities, which are uniquely attractive to foreign holders because of their greater liquidity. Richard Portes and Hélène Rey (1998: 309) call this an 'often neglected source of seigniorage to the issuer of the international currency'. In their words (1998: 309): 'This international currency effect reduces the real yields that the United States government has to pay' –a 'liquidity discount' that they suggest could amount to at least US$5–10 billion a year. Put these numbers together and, paraphrasing former Republican Senator Everett Dirksen's celebrated remark about the Federal budget, we are beginning to talk about real money.

A second gain is the increased flexibility of macroeconomic policy that is afforded by the privilege of being able to rely on one's own money to help finance foreign deficits. Expanded cross-border circulation reduces the real cost of adjustment to unanticipated payments shocks by internalizing through credit what otherwise would be external transactions requiring scarce foreign exchange. In effect, it reduces the need to worry about the balance of payments in formulating and implementing domestic policy. Who can remember the last time Washington decision makers actively incorporated concern for our large current deficits or our exchange rate in debating the course of monetary and fiscal policy?

Third, more psychological in nature, is the gain of status and prestige that goes with market dominance. Money, as I have written elsewhere (Cohen 1998), has long played a key symbolic role for governments, useful – like flags, anthems and postage stamps – as a means to cultivate a unique sense of national identity. But that critical role is eroded to the extent that a local currency is displaced by a more popular foreign money, especially a money like the greenback that is so widely used on a daily basis. Foreign publics are constantly reminded of America's elevated rank in the community of nations. 'Great powers have great currencies', Nobel laureate Robert Mundell once wrote (1993: 10). In effect, the dollar has become a potent symbol of American primacy – an example of what political scientist Joseph S. Nye (1990) has called 'soft power', the ability to exercise influence by shaping beliefs and perceptions. Though obviously difficult to quantify, the role of reputation in geopolitics should not be underestimated.

Finally, there is the gain of 'hard' geopolitical power that derives from the monetary dependence of others. On the one hand, an issuing country is better insulated from outside influence in the domestic arena. On the other hand, it is also better positioned to pursue foreign objectives without constraint, or even to exercise a degree of coercion internationally. As political scientist Jonathan Kirshner reminds us (1995: 29, 31): 'Monetary power is a remarkably efficient component of state power...the most potent instrument of economic coercion available to states in a position to exercise it'. Money, after all, is simply command over real resources. If another country can be denied access to the means needed to purchase vital goods and services, it is clearly vulnerable in political terms. Kirshner lists four ways in which currency dependence can be exploited: (a) enforcement – manipulation of standing rules or threats of sanctions; (b) expulsion – suspension or termination of privileges; (c) extraction – use of the relationship to extract real resources; and (d) entrapment – transformation of a dependent state's interests. The dollar's widespread use puts all of these possibilities in the hands of Washington policymakers.

Admittedly there are limits to these benefits, which are likely to be greatest in the early stages of cross-border use when confidence in a money is highest. Later, as external liabilities accumulate increasing supply relative to demand, gains may be eroded, particularly if an attractive alternative comes on the market. Foreign holders may legitimately worry about the risk of future depreciation or even restrictions on the usability of their holdings. Thus the currency leader's autonomy may eventually be constrained, to a degree, by a need to discourage sudden or substantial conversions through the exchange market. Both seigniorage income, on a net basis, and macroeconomic flexibility will be reduced if a sustained increase of interest rates is required to sustain market share. Likewise, overt exploitation of political power will be inhibited if foreigners can switch allegiance easily to another currency. But even admitting such limits, there seems little doubt that on balance these are advantages of considerable significance, as numerous sources acknowledge (eg, Portes and Rey 1998: 308–310).

The logic of market competition

Can the dominance of the dollar be challenged? As indicated, the greenback's only possible rivals at the moment are the euro and the yen. But the logic of market competition, I contend, suggests that neither will able to match, let alone surpass, the dollar's popularity in the foreseeable future. Left to their own devices to choose among the Big Three, market actors will continue to give a distinct preference to the dollar.

Barriers to displacement

Displacement of a market leader is not easy, for two reasons: first, because the qualities required for competitive success tend to be highly demanding; and, secondly, because of inertia, which is a characteristic inherent in all monetary behaviour.

Fundamentally, currency choice in the global marketplace is shaped by three essential attributes. First, at least during the initial stages of a money's cross-border use, is widespread confidence in its future value backed by political stability in the country of origin. Second are the qualities of 'exchange convenience' and 'capital certainty' – a high degree of transactional liquidity and reasonable predictability of asset value. The key to both qualities is a set of well developed financial markets, sufficiently open to ensure full access by non-residents. Markets must not be encumbered by high transactions costs or formal or informal barriers to entry. They must also be broad, with a large assortment of instruments available for temporary or longer-term forms of investment, and resilient, with fully operating secondary markets for most if not all financial claims. And third, a money must promise a broad transactional network, since nothing enhances a currency's acceptability more than the prospect of acceptability by others. Historically, this factor has usually meant an economy that is large in absolute size and well integrated into world markets. The greater the volume of transactions conducted in or with a country, the greater are the potential network externalities to be derived from use of its money. Not many currencies can meet all these demanding conditions. Today there are only the Big Three.

Moreover, even with the requisite attributes, displacement is difficult because of inertia in currency choice. The principle source of inertia is the pre-existence of already well established transactional networks, which generate a well documented stickiness in user preferences – what specialists call hysteresis or ratchet effects. In effect, prior use confers a certain natural advantage of incumbency. Switching from one money to another is costly, involving an expensive process of financial adaptation. Considerable effort must be invested in creating and learning to use new instruments and institutions, with much riding on what other market agents may be expected to do at the same time. Hence as attractive as a given money may seem, adoption will not prove cost-effective unless others appear likely to make extensive use of it too. In the words of economists Kevin Dowd and David Greenaway (1993: 1180): 'Changing currencies is costly – we must learn to reckon in the new currency, we must change the units in which we quote prices, we might have to change our records, and so on.... [This] explains why agents are often reluctant to switch currencies, even when the currency they are using appears to be manifestly inferior to some other'.

Inertia is also promoted by the exceptionally high level of uncertainty that is inherent in any choice between alternative monies. Uncertainty encourages a tendency toward what psychologists call 'mimesis': the rational impulse of risk-averse actors, in conditions of contingency, to minimize anxiety by imitative behaviour based on past experience. Once a currency gains a degree of acceptance, its use is apt to be perpetuated – even after the appearance of powerful new competitors – simply by regular repetition of previous practice. In effect, a conservative bias is inherent in the dynamics of the marketplace. As one source has argued (Orléan 1989: 81–83), 'imitation leads to the emergence of a convention [wherein] emphasis is placed on a certain "conformism" or even hermeticism in financial circles'.

The salience of inertia in this context is well illustrated by the dollar's own experience when it first began to rival the pound sterling, the dominant currency of the nineteenth century. Even after America's emergence as the world's richest economy, it took literally decades for the greenback to ascend to top rank among currencies. As Paul Krugman has commented (1992: 173): 'The impressive fact here is surely the inertia; sterling remained the first-ranked currency for half a century after Britain had ceased to be the first-ranked economic power'. Similar inertias have been evident for millennia in the prolonged use of such international moneys as the Byzantine solidus (otherwise known as the bezant) or the Spanish silver peso (later known as the Mexican silver dollar) long after the decline of the imperial powers that first coined them (Cohen 1998: ch. 2). In fact, such inertias are very much the rule, not the exception, in global monetary relations.

Exceptional or not, even the most stubborn inertias can in time be overcome, as these historical examples also illustrate. But to defeat the conservative bias in market behaviour, a new contender must do more than merely match the attributes of the market leader. It must be able to offer substantial advantages over the exist-ing incumbent. The dollar was able to do that in relation to sterling once New York overtook London as the world's pre-eminent source of investment capital. The problem for the euro and yen is that for the foreseeable future, neither can realistically hope to offer comparable advantages in relation to the greenback.

The yen

Consider first the yen. Little probability can be attached to a successful challenge by the vaunted Japanese currency, despite Japan's evident strengths as the world's top creditor nation and its enviable long-term record of success in controlling inflation and promoting exports. Cross-border use of the yen did accelerate significantly in the 1970s and 1980s, during the heady years of Japanese economic expansion. Internationalization was strongest in bank lending and secu-rities markets, where because of an appreciating exchange rate yen-denominated claims were especially attractive to investors. But the yen never came close to overtaking the popularity of the dollar, or even the DM, and was little used for either trade invoicing or currency substitution Worse, its upward trajectory was abruptly halted in the 1990s, following the bursting of Japan's 'bubble economy', and there seems little prospect of resumption in the near term so long as Japanese domestic stagnation persists.

In fact, use of the yen abroad in recent years has, in relative terms, actually decreased rather than increased. In exchange markets, the 23% yen share of global turnover reported in 2001 represented a considerable decline from a high of 27% in 1989; similarly, in central-bank reserves, the yen's share of the total has shrunk from some 7% at the end of the 1980s to under 5% a decade later. Overall, the yen's position near the peak of the Currency Pyramid has slipped substantially below both the other market leaders, as informed observers now readily acknowl-edge. In the words of one knowledgeable group of experts (Bergsten et al. 2001: 234), 'the yen is now a distant third among global currencies, far behind the new euro as well as the dollar'.[5]

Largely, the yen's decline of popularity abroad mirrors Japan's economic troubles at home, which include not only a fragile banking system but also a level of public debt, relative to GDP, that is now the highest of any industrial nation. Perhaps the greatest burden for the yen is Japan's financial system, which despite recent improvements has long lagged behind American and even many European markets in terms of openness or efficiency. Starting in the mid-1970s, a process of liberalization began, prompted partly by a slowing of domestic economic growth and partly by external pressure from the United States. Most dramatic was a multi-year liberalization programme announced in 1996, dubbed the Big Bang in imitation of the swift deregulation of Britain's financial markets a decade earlier. But the reform process is still far from complete and could take many years to come even close to approximating market standards in the United States or Europe, where transaction costs are considerably lower.

Without further progress in financial-market liberalization, the yen will remain at a distinct competitive disadvantage. International traders and investors will have little incentive to bear the costs and risks of switching from either the dollar or the euro to the yen. Indeed, if left to market forces alone, the trend is more likely to continue moving the other way, towards gradual erosion of the yen's standing as an international currency in a manner reminiscent of sterling's long decline in an earlier era.

The euro

In principle, prospects for the euro should be much brighter. Europe's new currency started life in January 1999 with many of the attributes necessary for competitive success already well in evidence. Together, the twelve present members of the EU's Economic and Monetary Union (EMU) – familiarly known as 'Euroland'– constitute an economy nearly as large as that of the United States, with extensive trade relations not only in the European region but around the world. The potential for network externalities is considerable. Likewise, Euroland started with both unquestioned political stability and an enviably low rate of inflation, backed by a joint monetary authority, the European Central Bank, that is fully committed to preserving confidence in the euro's future value. Much room exists, therefore, for a quick ascendancy towards the peak of the Currency Pyramid, as many have predicted. Typical is the attitude of Robert Mundell, who expresses no doubt that the euro 'will challenge the status of the dollar and alter the power configuration of the system' (2000: 57). In the oft-quoted words of Jacques Delors, former head of the European Commission, 'le petit euro deviendra grand'.

In practice, however, the outlook for the euro is anything but rosy. Indeed, with each passing year it becomes increasingly clear that serious obstacles lie in the path of the euro's ascent. Within the European region, of course, the euro will dominate easily; and its influence may even be extended as well to some neighbouring areas, such as the Mediterranean littoral or sub-Saharan Africa – what the ECB (2001) has called the 'Euro-time zone'. In these areas the euro is the natural currency of choice. As Wyplosz remarks: 'This is the euro's turf' (1999: 89). But that appears to be as far as the new money's domain will expand as a result of market forces alone. Virtually all the growth of cross-border use of the euro since its introduction has occurred within the Euro-time zone (ECB 2002: 54). Elsewhere, left to the logic of market competition, the currency seems fated to remain a distant second to the greenback. In a recent analysis (Cohen 2003b), I spell out three critical reasons for this negative assessment.

Transactions costs

First is the cost of doing business in euros, which directly affects the currency's attractiveness as a vehicle for foreign-exchange transactions or international trade. Euro transactions costs, as measured by bid-ask spreads, are historically higher than those on the more widely traded dollar. Whether they can be lowered to more competitive levels will depend directly on what happens to the structural efficiency of Europe's financial markets. On the face of it, prospects for euro transactions costs look good. In purely quantitative terms, introduction of the euro promises to create the largest single-currency capital market in the world; and that expansion, in turn, should trigger major qualitative improvements in depth and liquidity as previously segmented national markets are gradually knitted together into an integrated whole. As a practical matter, however, progress to date has been disappointing, owing to stubborn resistance to many market-opening measures; and as a result it is not at all clear that the euro's promise in this respect can ever be converted fully into performance. As a recent EU report on Europe's financial markets – the so-called Lamfalussy Report – firmly insisted (European Union 2001: 8): 'The European Union has no divine right to the benefits of an integrated financial market. It has to capture those benefits' – and so far, at least, the EU has not done a very good job at doing so.

In certain key respects the dollar's advantages will persist no matter what the EU does. Most important is the lack of a universal financial instrument in Europe to rival the US Treasury bill for liquidity and convenience – a deficiency that will be difficult, if not impossible, to rectify so long as the Europeans, with their separate national governments, lack a counterpart to the Federal Government in Washington. Full consolidation of Euroland's markets for public debt is stymied by the persistence of differential credit and liquidity risk premiums among participating countries as well as by variations in legal traditions, procedures, issuance calendars and primary dealer systems. Market segmentation has also been prolonged by intense competition among governments to establish their own issues as EMU benchmarks.

On balance, therefore, it seems unlikely that anticipated efficiency gains, though substantial, will soon suffice on their own to displace the greenback from top rank. To date, there is little evidence of reduced transactions costs for Europe's new money. Indeed, for some types of transactions, bid-ask spreads have actually increased relative to the corresponding spreads for the DM, Europe's most widely traded currency prior to EMU (Hau et al. 2002a, 2002b). In reality, no one expects that euro transactions costs will ever decline to a level substantially below those presently quoted for the dollar.

Anti-growth bias

A second critical factor is a serious anti-growth bias that appears to be built into the institutional structure of EMU. By impacting negatively on yields on euro-denominated assets, this structural bias directly affects the new currency's attractiveness as an investment medium. When EMU first came into existence, eliminating exchange risk within the European region, a massive shift was predicted in the allocation of global savings as compared with holdings of European assets in the past. In fact, however, international portfolio managers have been slow to move into the euro (Detken and Hartmann 2002), evidently because of doubts about prospects for longer-term growth. In turn, the main cause for such doubts seems to lie in the core institutional provisions of EMU governing monetary and fiscal policy, the key determinants of macroeconomic performance. In neither policy domain is priority attached to promoting real production. Rather, in each, the main emphasis is on other considerations that can be expected to limit opportunities for future expansion – imparting a distinct anti-growth bias to the economy of Euroland as a whole.

On the monetary policy side, the European Central Bank, unlike many other monetary authorities, was created with just a single policy mandate – to maintain price stability. Moreover, the ECB is endowed with absolute independence, insulating it from political influence of any kind. Legally, the ECB is free to focus exclusively on fighting inflation, even if over time this might be at the cost of stunting real growth. In practice, naturally, the ECB is not wholly insensitive to growth concerns. Nonetheless, the overall orientation of ECB priorities is clear. Since EMU's start, monetary conditions in Euroland have been among the tightest in the industrial world. The bias of policy has plainly been towards restraint, not expansion.

Likewise, on the side of fiscal policy, Euroland governments have formally tied their own hands with their controversial Stability and Growth Pact (SGP), which mandates a medium-term objective of fiscal balance in all participating economies as well as a strict cap on annual budget deficits. These fiscal restraints make it exceedingly difficult for elected officials to use budgetary policy for contracyclical purposes, to offset the anti-growth bias of monetary policy. Here too, we know, practice has at times diverged from principle; and many specialists in Europe have called for revision or repeal of the Pact's principle provisions. Until now, however, such appeals have made little headway. So long as the SGP remains officially binding on all Euroland governments, an anti-growth bias will be perpetuated in fiscal policy too.

Governance

Finally, there is the governance structure of EMU, which for the euro's prospects as an international currency may be the biggest obstacle of all. The basic question is: who is in charge? The answer, regrettably, has never been clear. From the start, much confusion has reigned concerning the delegation of authority among governments and EU institutions. The Maastricht Treaty, which brought EMU into existence, embodies a variety of artful compromises and deliberate obfuscations in provisions for the political management of the euro, resulting in a high level of ambiguity. Prospective users of the new currency, therefore, may be excused for hesitating to commit themselves to what seemingly amounts to a pig in a poke – even if in fact transactions costs could be lowered to competitive levels and rewards to European capital could be significantly improved.

Three key provisions are at issue. First is the governance of EMU's core institution, the European Central Bank itself. Immediate operational control of monetary policy lies in the hands of the ECB's Executive Board, made up of the President, Vice-President and four other members. Ultimate authority, however, is formally lodged in the Governing Council, which in addition to the six-member Executive Board includes heads of central banks of the participating states – a number seemingly greater than consistent with efficient collective decision making. Sooner or later, therefore, as so often happens in large multinational institutions, real power will have to devolve to a smaller 'inner' group formally or informally charged with resolving differences on critical issues. But who will be allowed to join this exclusive club? Would it be the members of the Executive Board, who might be expected to take a broad approach to Euroland's needs and interests? Or would it be a select coterie of central-bank governors, whose views could turn out to be more parochial? For the moment, no one knows.

Second is the critical matter of exchange-rate policy. Under the Maastricht Treaty, the ECB is assigned day-to-day responsibility for the euro's external value. Authority over the more general orientation of policy, however, is uneasily shared with both the Council of Ministers, representing national governments, and the European Commission in Brussels. Plainly, power over exchange rates was meant to be shared in some form of consensual process. But, equally, these provisions could turn out to be a sure recipe for political deadlock and drift. Again, no one knows.

Finally, there is the issue of external representation. Who is to speak for Euroland on broader macroeconomic issues such as policy coordination, crisis management or reform of the international financial architecture? Here there is no answer at all, leaving a vacuum at the heart of EMU. No single body is designated to represent EMU at the International Monetary Fund or in other global forums. Instead, the Maastricht Treaty simply lays down a procedure for resolving the issue at a later date, presumably on a case-by-case basis. This is a cop-out that, at a minimum, compounds confusion about who is in charge. At worst, the vacuum condemns Euroland to lasting second-class status, since it limits the group's ability to project power in international negotiations. As one source warns (McNamara and Meunier 2002: 850): 'As long as no "single voice" has the political authority to speak on behalf of the euro area, as the US Secretary of the Treasury does for the American currency, the pre-eminence of the US in international monetary matters, as in other realms, is likely to remain unchallenged'.

Government preferences

But is Europe really likely to accept such an unfavourable geopolitical outcome? Is Japan? Whatever the logic of market competition, the Europeans and Japanese can hardly be expected to leave market actors entirely to their own devices – particularly if that means passively submitting to the continued dominance of the dollar. Currency rivalries, in practice, reflect the influence of government preferences as well as market forces. However, once we introduce government preferences, the outlook for the geopolitics of currencies becomes considerably more cloudy.

A critical distinction

One thing is certain. A strategy to maintain or enhance market position will be the preferred choice of both Europe and Japan. Rational policymakers are unlikely to turn their back on the considerable benefits that may be derived from broader circulation of their currency. But following a suggestion I have made elsewhere (Cohen 2003a), a critical distinction must be drawn between two different kinds of geopolitical monetary conflict: informal and formal.

Given the stakes involved, there seems little doubt that both Europe and Japan will all do what they can to sustain the underlying competitiveness of their currencies, with the objective of defending or promoting widespread use by market actors. Rivalry for market share – what I call informal conflict – is natural in an oligopoly. It is less evident, however, whether either will be motivated to go a step further, to seek to influence the behaviour of state actors – that is, to sponsor formation of an organized currency bloc, what I call formal conflict. Will Europe or Japan seek to offer direct inducements to foreign governments to encourage greater reliance on their money? About this prospect there is more uncertainty, not least because the balance of benefits and costs implied by that extra step is not at all clear.

What is clear is that whatever either one does is sure to be closely watched by Washington. Any move to promote organized currency blocs would transform the low politics of market competition, by definition, into the high politics of diplomatic confrontation. The risk is that policy manoeuvring could lead to increased geopolitical tensions, particularly if monetary initiatives were perceived to be encroaching on established regional relationships. Precisely for that reason, however, it is more likely that both Japan and Europe, ultimately, will act with restraint to avoid direct confrontations with the United States that could jeopardize more vital political and security interests. The safest bet is that currency rivalries among the Big Three will be restricted mainly to the realm of market transactions. The one exception could be in the Middle East, where rivalry for the monetary favour of OPEC governments could conceivably generate a serious battle between Europe and Washington.

Informal conflict

In the oligopolistic setting created by deterritorialization, both Europe and Japan have obvious incentives to promote the competitiveness of their respective currencies – to 'sell' their brand of money to as many potential users as possible. On the European side, the successful launch of EMU has created a golden opportunity to move up significantly in the Currency Pyramid. Conversely, on the Japanese side, recent setbacks have increased pressure to take defensive measures to prevent any further slide down in global ranking. The obvious target for both is the dollar, the incumbent Top Currency. Rivalry at the market level, therefore, is apt to be intense.

Japan, for example, has given every indication that it intends to stay in the race, competing actively to preserve as much as possible of the yen's shrinking international role. Indeed, reversal of the currency's slide in standing was made an official policy objective in 1998 and was given further impetus the next year by a widely publicized report of a Ministry of Finance advisory group, the Council on Foreign Exchange and Other Transactions (1999). Declared the Council (1999: 1–2): 'Internationalization has not necessarily kept pace with what is warranted by the scale of the Japanese economy...Recent economic and financial environments affecting Japan point to the need for the greater internationalization of the yen...The question of what Japan must do to heighten the international role of the yen has re-emerged as a vital issue'.

Most emphasis in Japan has been placed on continued implementation of the Big Bang reform process, which it is hoped will eventually succeed in lowering yen transactions costs to levels more like those for the dollar or euro. Along the same lines, the government has also floated a plan to drop two zeros from the yen, currently valued at over one hundred yen for either the dollar or the euro. Establishing a rough parity with the US and European monies, Japanese authorities think, might also facilitate wider use of their currency. Simplifying the yen's denomination, said one official when the plan first came to light, 'would be good for internationalizing and regaining trust in the yen'.[6] Commented a foreign banker in Tokyo: 'If there's a liquid market in dollars and a liquid market in euros, there's a risk of Japan becoming a sort of second-string market...They don't want the yen to become the Swiss franc of Asia'.[7] It is evident that Tokyo will not allow further erosion of its currency's market standing without a fight.

On the European side, official aspirations remain more modest. According to authoritative statements by the European Central Bank, the development of the euro as an international currency – to the extent it happens – will mainly be a market-driven process, simply one of many possible by-products of EMU. Europe, says the ECB (2002: 11), 'does not pursue the internationalisation of the euro as an independent policy goal...It neither fosters nor hinders this process'. These carefully considered words, however, may be dismissed as little more than diplomatic rhetoric, revealing nothing. Behind the scenes it is known that there is considerable disagreement within European elites, with the eventual direction of policy still unsettled. Many in Europe are indeed inclined to leave the future of the euro purely to the logic of market competition. But many others, resentful of the dollar's strong incumbency advantages, favour a more proactive stance to reinforce EMU's potential. Few Europeans are unaware of the advantages that the United States derives from the greenback's perch atop the Currency Pyramid – what Charles De Gaulle famously denounced as America's 'exorbitant privilege'. The euro has long been viewed in some circles, particularly in France, as the EU's best chance to challenge US pre-eminence in monetary affairs. Charles Wyplosz (1999: 76) calls this 'the hidden agenda of Europe's long-planned adoption of a single currency'.

Much more revealing, therefore, is not what the ECB says but what it does. Especially suggestive is the bank's controversial decision to issue euro notes in denominations as high as 100, 200, and 500 euros – sums far greater than most Eurolanders are likely to find useful for everyday transactions. Why issue such large notes? Informed sources suggest that the plan may have been decided in order to reassure the German public, fearful of losing their beloved deutsche mark, that notes comparable to existing high-denomination DM bills would be readily available. But that is hardly the whole story. As knowledgeable experts such as Wyplosz (1999) and Kenneth Rogoff (1998) have observed, it is also likely that the decision had something to do with the familiar phenomenon of currency substitution: the already widespread circulation of large-denomination dollar notes, especially US$100 bills, in various parts of the world. In Rogoff's words (1998: 264): 'Given the apparently overwhelming preference of foreign and underground users for large-denomination bills, the [ECB's] decision to issue large notes constitutes an aggressive step toward grabbing a large share of developing country demand for safe foreign currencies'. Europeans who favour more widespread use of the euro have openly applauded the plan. Writes one (Hüfner 2000: 25): 'The United States is able to obtain goods and services by simply giving foreigners pieces of green paper that cost pennies to print.... There is no reason why the United States should monopolize these benefits'.

What more could Europe do, apart from issuing high-denomination notes? The answer lies in the three reasons for the euro's sluggish ascent to date. More could be done to lower transactions costs for non-residents in European financial markets. International investments in euro bonds and stocks might be encouraged with selected tax incentives, including abolition of any withholding or reporting requirements. Similarly, broader cross-border use of the euro as a vehicle currency could be underwritten with targeted subsidies for European banks, lowering the cost of commercial credit for third-country trade. More could also be done to reverse the anti-growth bias built into Euroland's institutional structure and to clarify the governance structure of EMU. As indicated, much room exists for policy actions to make the euro more appealing to market actors.

How will Washington react to such competition? Officially, the United States remains unconcerned. Policy statements regarding prospective challenges from the yen or euro have been studiously neutral, avoiding provocation. But such words too may be dismissed as diplomatic rhetoric, concealing as much as they reveal. As Richard Portes (1999: 34) observes: 'It is difficult to believe that the American authorities are indifferent'. In fact, in Washington too there is considerable disagreement behind the scenes about what should be the eventual direction of policy. But much sentiment exists to respond in kind to any direct threat to the dollar. Introduction of the ECB's large-denomination bills, for example, quickly generated counterproposals to issue a rival US$500 Federal Reserve note, designed to preserve America's seigniorage earnings abroad. Japan's efforts to revive the yen are no less likely to arouse opposition and even irritation in Washington. As even a yen enthusiast like David Hale acknowledges (1995: 162), there is 'a risk that [Japanese initiatives] will be interpreted as a threat by some

Americans [and] could intensify the economic conflicts that are already straining US-Japan relations'. The probability is that aggressive policy measures from either Japan or Europe will ultimately provoke countermeasures from Washington, with all of the Big Three doing what they can to maximize market use.

Formal conflict

This does not mean, however, that either Japan or Europe must necessarily go the next step, to seek to influence state behaviour. Compared with the benefits of market leadership, the additional gains from sponsoring a formal currency bloc could be considerable. But so too could be the costs, political as well as economic, discouraging new initiatives. Prediction, therefore, is chancy. The safest bet is that both Japan and Europe, ultimately, will act with restraint to avoid direct geopolitical confrontation with the United States. A key exception, however, could be in the Middle East, where serious friction between Europe and Washington is a distinct possibility.

Japan

From the Japanese side, a formal challenge of some kind must be anticipated. The reason is simple. If Tokyo does nothing, the yen's slide in standing could become irreversible, even in East Asia, a region that the Japanese prefer to think of as their own backyard. It is difficult to imagine that Tokyo will accept such a loss of status without a struggle. But it is also difficult to imagine that any Japanese challenge would be carried to the point of open confrontation with the United States, which has its own established relationships in East Asia. There are good reasons to believe that tensions between the two governments on currency matters, though almost certainly unavoidable, will not be unmanageable.

Japanese officials have made no secret of the fact that their aspirations now extend well beyond mere market competitiveness. The best defence for a beleaguered yen, they seem to have decided, is a strong offence. Beyond 'selling' its brand of money to market users, the Japanese seem intent on 'selling' it to neighbouring governments, too – in short, to do what they can to build a formal East Asian currency bloc – even though this would unavoidably come at the expense of America's dollar. Tokyo hopes to persuade neighbours to anchor their exchange rates to the yen and to make the yen their principal reserve currency, displacing the greenback. Efforts along these lines have persisted despite the risk of provoking Washington.

Symptomatic was Japan's response to the great Asian financial crisis that began in mid-1997. Tokyo seized the occasion to propose a new US$100 billion regional financial facility, quickly dubbed the Asian Monetary Fund (AMF). Ostensibly, the aim of the AMF was to help protect local currencies against speculative attack. In practice, an 'Asia-for-Asians' fund excluding the United States would have gone far to institutionalize Japanese dominance in regional currency affairs, undermining American interests. Though the Japanese denied any ulterior motives, the prospect frankly dismayed US officials, and the proposal was quickly suppressed.

Nonetheless, despite economic troubles at home and the steady repatriation of private investments from abroad, Tokyo has persisted in seeking new ways to promote its regional currency role. In October 1998, the then Finance Minister Kiichi Miyazawa offered some US$30 billion in fresh financial aid for Asia in a plan soon labelled the New Miyazawa Initiative; and more recently, in May 2000, agreement was reached on a planned new network of swap arrangements with Asian nations, named the Chiang Mai Initiative after the town in Thailand where negotiations took place. Because both initiatives were confined to the so-called 'ASEAN+3' (the ten nations of the Association of South-east Asian Nations plus China, Japan, and Korea), with no explicit part for the United States, many see them as a further affirmation of Tokyo's continued interest in the creation of an exclusive yen bloc – subtle attempts to achieve the aims of the AMF by incremental means while avoiding the politically more provocative step of establishing a formal institution. As such initiatives multiply, tensions with Washington seem set to continue, perhaps even to grow.

Tension, however, is not the same as conflict. Tokyo may aspire to assume more of the role of a great monetary power, but almost certainly not at the expense of the broader political and security relationship that it has long enjoyed with the United States. 'The bilateral relationship with the United States', writes one expert (Green 2001: 3–4), 'is the indispensable core of Japan's position in the world...On issues of fundamental interest to the United States, Japan remains deferential and cautious'. In fact, a delicate balancing act is involved, as students of Japanese foreign policy have long understood (Vogel 2002). The delicacy of the balance is well illustrated by the Chiang Mai Initiative, which is directly premised on involvement of the International Monetary Fund – and thus indirectly assumes a part for the United States, the IMF's most influential member – as a condition for assistance.

Nor can Japan ignore the threat of an emergent China looming on the horizon, which increases even more the value of preserving a special relationship with Washington. China has already gained a good deal of diplomatic clout throughout East Asia as a result of its rapid economic expansion in recent years and shows every sign of intending to challenge Japanese aspirations for regional leadership. Resistance to the Chinese juggernaut would be especially difficult without backing from the Americans.

Tokyo, in short, has no interest in alienating its most powerful ally. Nor is Washington eager to jeopardize a decades-old relationship that is still valued highly for the stability it helps bring to a troubled part of the world. Both sides can be expected to continue to manoeuvre for advantage in Asian finance. But neither is likely to let their monetary rivalry get out of control.

Europe

A formal challenge from Europe is also possible – but, outside the Middle East, improbable. The Europeans, as indicated, will no doubt make every effort to promote use of their new money at the market level wherever they can. It is also evident that they will not discourage greater reliance on the euro by nearby governments, particularly in East-Central Europe and the Balkans. But none of this will trigger geopolitical conflict with Washington unless the EU's aspirations begin to spread beyond its immediate neighbourhood to regions more traditionally aligned with the United States. Arguably, only in the Middle East is there a significant risk of direct confrontation.

That is not to say that there are no Europeans with more global ambitions for the euro. Quite the contrary. Portes and Rey (1998), for example, plainly favour what they call the 'big euro' scenario, where the euro would join the dollar at the peak of the Currency Pyramid. The dollar, they declare (1998: 308), 'will have to share the number-one position'. But this is a minority view. Most informed opinion in Europe accepts that there are limits to what might be regarded as the natural home for a formal euro zone.

An EMU bloc would naturally include most if not all of the countries of Europe itself, including first and foremost the ten applicant states due to join the EU in 2004. Beyond EMU's present dozen members, six regional jurisdictions have already adopted the euro as their exclusive legal tender, including the tiny enclaves of Andorra, Monaco, San Marino and the Vatican, as well as Montenegro and Kosovo, two special cases in the Balkans. In addition, several regional economies are pegged to the euro via currency boards, including Bosnia and Herzegovina, Bulgaria, Estonia and Lithuania; and most other nearby currencies are more loosely linked. Some maintain basket pegs that give greatest weight to the euro; others have adopted systems of managed floating with the euro unofficially used as an anchor. Momentum toward full 'euroization' will only grow as EU enlargement proceeds. As Pier Carlo Padoan suggests (2000: 101): 'The case is easily stated. What matters is not "if" but "when"'. Every regional government aspiring to join the EU club expects to adopt the euro, too.

Indeed, for the EU, the problem is not whether to speed up the euro's spread to the rest of Europe but rather to slow it down. Though all new entrants must commit to adopting the euro as a condition of EU membership, full participation in EMU will not occur automatically. Formally, after joining the EU, governments will first be obliged to meet a number of demanding conditions – the same 'convergence criteria' that were demanded of present participants before they could become full partners in EMU. Aspirants must also participate successfully for a minimum of two years in the pegging arrangement to the euro known as the Exchange Rate Mechanism. Several of the candidate countries, however, have spoken openly of the possibility of adopting the euro unilaterally, without waiting first to meet the Maastricht conditions. Why postpone the advantages of access to one of world's leading currencies?

EU authorities, however, have been doing all they can to forestall a rush to the euro, mainly on the grounds that participation without adequate preparation could prove unmanageable, straitjacketing governments at just the time when flexibility will be most needed. Strains could arise because of changing economic structures and shifts in monetary demand, as well as sizable and possibly volatile capital flows and differential growth trends in productivity. A gradual approach has been forcefully advocated by both the Council of Ministers and European Parliament. In November 2001, EU heads of government formally insisted that candidate countries should follow the prescribed path. In public, the European Central Bank is more equivocal, suggesting that candidates could adopt the euro if they wish so long as they understand that the ECB would not be obliged to take them into account when making policy. In private, monetary officials are more adamant, worrying about the impact that unilateral 'euroizations' might have on their control of the supply of euros in circulation. The last thing they want at this stage is to be burdened with responsibility for underwriting still underdeveloped and fragile banking systems.

Whatever the rate of momentum, though, Washington is unlikely to take offence. The United States has never questioned the EU's privileged interests in what is universally acknowledged to be its own backyard. Indeed, for geopolitical reasons Washington might even be inclined to prod the Europeans along. More positive support for inclusion of candidate countries promises to bring greater stability to a potentially volatile region. As Randall Henning has observed (2000: 18): 'The consolidation of the monetary union contributes to economic and political stability in Central and Eastern Europe...If the monetary union were to fail, Central and Eastern Europe would probably be considerably less stable...As a consequence, US manpower and resource commitments would have to be correspondingly greater. This geopolitical consideration is profoundly important for US foreign policy'.

Nor is Washington likely to take offence if the growing EMU bloc were extended to encompass as well countries of the Mediterranean littoral and sub-Saharan Africa that have close economic and political linkages with the EU. These too are regarded as Euro-time zone states. Some of their currencies are already pegged to the euro, including most prominently the CFA Franc in central and west Africa, for which Europe's new money has seamlessly taken over the anchor role previously played by the French franc; and for most the euro is already an important reserve currency. Here too Washington might even prod the Europeans along in the interest of regional stabilization.

The critical question is: might Europe aspire to go further? There is no evidence that the EU would seriously consider challenging the dollar in Latin America or Asia, where it is Washington's interests that are clearly seen as privileged. These areas, Europeans acknowledge, are America's turf. But what about the Middle East, with its concentration of wealthy oil exporters? If the geopolitics of currencies is to lead to direct confrontation anywhere, it will be here.

The Middle East

Three factors explain why the Middle East could become a currency battleground. First is the sheer scale of monetary riches in the area controlled directly or indirectly by national governments. Exports of oil generate massive revenues for state authorities in Saudi Arabia, Kuwait and other countries scattered around the Persian Gulf; and much of this wealth, in turn, is either stored away in central bank reserves or invested abroad in publicly held portfolios. What these governments decide to do with their money can have a major impact on the relative fortunes of international currencies.

Second is the instability of great-power alignments in the area. Within the Euro-time zone, the United States may happily defer to Europe; conversely, across Latin America and Asia, Europe may still accept Washington's strategic dominance. But in geopolitical terms the Middle East is a contested region, as the still unfinished business of Iraq clearly testifies. For the moment, most governments in the region find it prudent to accept US leadership and even US troops. But with their ample economic and cultural ties to the area, Europe's governments remain committed to playing an important regional role. Resentment of Washington's displacement of Europe's historical pre-eminence in the area is rife among Europeans.

And third is the seeming contradiction between the region's commercial ties with the outside world and its financial relations. Foreign trade is dominated by Europe, which is by far the biggest market for the Middle East's oil exports as well as the largest source of its imports. Yet financial relations are dominated by the United States and the almighty greenback. America's dollar is not only the standard for invoicing and payments in world energy markets. It also accounts for the vast majority of central bank reserves and government-held investments in the region and is the anchor, de jure or de facto, for most local currencies. In the eyes of many the disjunction seems anomalous, even irrational. Repeatedly, the question is asked: would it not make more sense to do business with the area's biggest trading partner, Europe, in Europe's own currency rather than the greenback? And if so, would it not then make sense to switch to the euro as a reserve currency and monetary anchor as well?

Together, these three factors add up to an obvious recipe for geopolitical conflict, should Europe choose to turn up the heat. Certainly, the possibility of a switch to the euro is tempting from a European perspective. Almost immediately, given the large sums involved, the EU's new currency would be vaulted to the 'big euro' scenario favoured by Portes and Rey (1998) and others, while restoring a measure of Europe's historically privileged position in the Middle East. Arguably, the prospect might be tempting from the perspective of local governments too, for sound financial reasons as well as to curb America's presently overweening influence. It is well known that from time to time oil exporting states have actively explored alternatives to the dollar, only to be discouraged by the lack of a suitable substitute. Now, with the arrival of the euro, they see the possibility of a truly competitive rival for their affections. In the artfully composed words of a high official of the Organization of Petroleum Exporting Countries (OPEC): 'It is worthwhile to note that in the long run the euro is not at such a disadvantage versus the dollar... I believe that OPEC will not discount entirely the possibility of adopting euro pricing and payments in the future'.[8]

Indeed, some straws are already in the wind. As early as October 2000, in a deliberate snub to the United States, Iraq's now deposed dictator Saddam Hussein began demanding payment in euros for his country's oil exports. He also converted his US$10 billion United Nations reserve fund into euros, making a considerable profit once Europe's currency began to appreciate two years later. And, more recently, Iran is known to have considered a similar strategy. Should Europe seek directly to 'sell' its brand of money to regional governments, it might find itself pushing against an open door.

Any effort along these lines, however, would surely provoke determined opposition from the United States, which clearly prefers to keep the region's door as firmly shut to the euro as possible. For Washington today, there is no higher politics than the Great Game being played out in the Middle East. With so much at stake, the level of tolerance for a formal currency challenge from Europe would be correspondingly low, making geopolitical conflict a virtual certainty. For some observers, the conflict has already begun with America's attack on Iraq, which is said to have been motivated above all by the euro's threat to the dollar. In the words of one widely circulated commentary (Clark 2003: 1): 'It is an oil currency war. The Real Reason for [the war] is this administration's goal of preventing further OPEC momentum towards the euro as an oil transaction currency standard'. Such a theory, wholly unsubstantiated by plausible evidence, obviously smacks of conspiratorial thinking.[9] But one does not have to be a sensationalist to recognize the seeds of truth it contains. A battle of currencies in the Middle East could become serious.

Would Europe risk it? In the end, however strongly tempted, Europeans are more likely to keep their aspirations in check, in order to avert direct confrontation with Washington. Like the Japanese, most Europeans have no wish to jeopardize the broader political and security relationship that they have long enjoyed with the United States. Hence like the Japanese, they too can be expected to act with restraint beyond their currency's natural home. In the Middle East, as in East Asia, manoeuvring for advantage will persist, but monetary rivalry, most likely, will not be allowed to get out control.

Conclusion

Overall, therefore, the outlook for the geopolitics of currencies appears relatively benign. In the global marketplace, competition between the dollar and its two main rivals, the euro and yen, will continue to be intense, and governments will do all they can to sustain the competitive appeal of their currencies. But at the level of inter-state relations, the low politics of market competition is unlikely to be transformed into the high politics of diplomatic confrontation, largely because neither Japan nor Europe will be eager to seriously provoke the United States. Miscalculations are always possible, of course, despite the best of intentions. Japan could overstep its efforts to sustain the role of the yen in Asia; Europe, likewise, might well go too far in promoting use of the euro in the Middle East. The safest bet, however, is for mutual restraint by all of the Big Three at the top of the Currency Pyramid, keeping great-power rivalries in check.

Notes

1 Because each foreign-exchange transaction involves two currencies, the total of shares adds up to 200% rather than 100%.
2 Porter and Judson 1996; US Treasury 2000; Judson and Porter 2001. But see also Feige 1996 and 1997, who suggests a lower figure of about 40%.
3 The estimate, based on Seitz 1995, may be conservative. According to Doyle 2000, a more accurate figure for the mid-1990s could have been as high as 69%. See also Feige and Dean 2002. On the other hand, there is evidence to suggest that after 1999, when Europe's monetary union first got under way, foreign holdings of German currency declined some-what owing to uncertainties about the conversion of DM notes into euro notes that was scheduled for January 2002. See Sinn and Westermann 2001a, 2001b; Stix 2001.
4 Hale 1995. Rogoff 1998, inferring from indirect evidence, suggests a higher figure of 25%. Publicly, the Bank of Japan is unwilling to offer any kind of official estimate. See, eg, Bank of Japan 1994.
5 The yen's retreat since the start of the 1990s is well documented by Katada 2002.
6 As quoted in *The Economist*, 30 October 1999, p. 85.
7 As quoted in the *New York Times*, 19 November 1999, C4.
8 Yarjani 2002. Yarjani is head of OPEC's Petroleum Market Analysis Department.
9 For a direct critique of the oil-currency war theory, see Caffentzis 2003.

References

Bank for International Settlements (2002): *Triennial Central Bank Survey: Foreign Exchange and Derivatives Market Activity in 2001* (Basle, Switzerland).
Bank of Japan (1994): 'The Circulation of Bank of Japan Notes', *Quarterly Bulletin*, November, p. 90–118.
Bergsten, C. Fred, Takatoshi Ito, and Marcus Noland (2001): *No More Bashing: Building a New Japan-United States Economic Relationship* (Washington, DC: Institute for International Economics).
Blinder, Alan S. (1996): 'The Role of the Dollar as an International Currency', *Eastern Economic Journal* 22:2 (Spring), p. 127–136.
Bundesbank (1995): 'The Circulation of Deutsche Mark Abroad', *Monthly Report* 47: 7 (July), p. 65–71.
Caffentzis, George (2003): 'A Note on the "Euro" Explanation of the War' (Infoshop News), available at http://www.infoshop.org.
Clark, William (2003): 'The Real Reasons for the Upcoming War With Iraq: A Macroeconomic and Geostrategic Analysis of the Unspoken Truth' (Independent Media Center), available at http://www.indymedia.org.
Cohen, Benjamin J. (1998): *The Geography of Money* (Ithaca, NY: Cornell University Press).
—— (2003a): *The Future of Money* (Princeton, NJ: Princeton University Press).
—— (2003b): 'Global Currency Rivalry: Can the Euro Ever Challenge the Dollar?', *Journal of Common Market Studies* 42:4 (September), p. 575–595.
Council on Foreign Exchange and Other Transactions (1999): 'Internationalization of the Yen for the 21st Century' (Tokyo, 20 April), available at: www.mof.go.jp/english/if/e1b064a.htm.
Detken, Carsten and Philipp Hartmann (2002): 'Features of the Euro's Role in International Financial Markets', *Economic Policy* 35 (October), p. 553–569.
Dowd, Kevin and David Greenaway (1993): 'Currency Competition, Network Externalities and Switching Costs: Towards an Alternative View of Optimum Currency Areas', *Economic Journal* 103 (September), p. 1180–1189.

Doyle, Brian M. (2000): ' "Here, Dollars, Dollars…" Estimating Currency Demand and Worldwide Currency Substitution', International Finance Discussion Paper 657 (Washington, DC: Federal Reserve Board of Governors).

European Central Bank (2001): *Review of the International Role of the Euro* (Frankfurt, Germany).

—— (2002): *Review of the International Role of the Euro* (Frankfurt, Germany).

European Union (2001): *Final Report of the Committee of Wise Men on the Regulation of European Securities Markets* (Brussels).

Feige, Edgar L. (1996): 'Overseas Holdings of U.S. Currency and the Underground Economy', in Susan Pozo, ed., *Exploring the Underground Economy* (Kalamazoo, MI: W.E. Upjohn Institute for Employment Research), p. 5–62.

—— (1997): 'Revised Estimates of the Underground Economy: Implications of US Currency Held Abroad', in Owen Lippert and Michael Walker, eds., *The Underground Economy: Global Evidence of its Size and Impact* (Vancouver, BC: Simon Fraser Institute), p. 151–208.

Feige, Edgar and James W. Dean (2002): 'Dollarization and Euroization in Transition Countries: Currency Substitution, Asset Substitution, Network Externalities and Irreversibility', paper prepared for a Conference on The Euro and Dollarization, Fordham University, New York, 5–6 April.

Frankel, Jeffrey A. (1995): 'Still the Lingua Franca: The Exaggerated Death of the Dollar', *Foreign Affairs* 74: 4 (July), p. 9–16.

Green, Michael Jonathan (2001): *Japan's Reluctant Realism: Foreign Policy Challenges in an Era of Uncertain Power* (New York: Palgrave).

Hale, David D. (1995): 'Is it a Yen or a Dollar Crisis in the Currency Market?', *Washington Quarterly* 18: 4 (Autumn), p. 145–171.

Hartmann, Philipp (1998): *Currency Competition and Foreign Exchange Markets: The Dollar, the Yen and the Euro* (Cambridge, UK: Cambridge University Press).

Hau, Harald, William Killeen, and Michael Moore (2002a): 'The Euro as an International Currency: Explaining Puzzling First Evidence from the Foreign Exchange Markets', *Journal of International Money and Finance* 21:3 (June), p. 351–383.

—— (2002b): 'How Has the Euro Changed the Foreign Exchange Market?', *Economic Policy* 34 (April), p. 149–191.

Henning, C. Randall (2000): 'US-EU Relations after the Inception of the Monetary Union: Cooperation or Rivalry?', in C. Randall Henning and Pier Carlo Padoan, *Transatlantic Perspectives on the Euro* (Washington, DC: Brookings Institution), ch. 1.

Hüfner, Martin (2000): 'Give the Euro Greater Currency', *The International Economy* (November/December), p. 24–25, 50.

Judson, Ruth A. and Richard D. Porter (2001): 'Overseas Dollar Holdings: What Do We Know?', *Wirtschaftspolitische Blätter* 4 (April), p. 431–440.

Katada, Saori N. (2002): 'Japan and Asian Monetary Regionalisation: Cultivating A New Regional Leadership after the Asian Financial Crisis', *Geopolitics* 7:1 (Summer), p. 85–112.

Kirshner, Jonathan (1995): *Currency and Coercion: The Political Economy of International Monetary Power* (Princeton, NJ: Princeton University Press).

Krugman, Paul R. (1992): 'The International Role of the Dollar', in Paul R. Krugman, *Currencies and Crises* (Cambridge, MA: MIT Press), ch. 10.

Lambert, Michael J. and Kristin D. Stanton (2001): 'Opportunities and Challenges of the US Dollar as an Increasingly Global Currency: A Federal Reserve Perspective', *Federal Reserve Bulletin* 87:9 (September), p. 567–575.

McNamara, Kathleen R. and Sophie Meunier (2002): 'Between National Sovereignty and International Power: What External Voice for the Euro?', *International Affairs* 78:4 (October), p. 849–868.

Mundell, Robert A. (1993): 'EMU and the International Monetary System: A Transatlantic Perspective', Working Paper 13 (Vienna: Austrian National Bank).

—— (2000): 'The Euro and the Stability of the International Monetary System', in Robert A. Mundell and Armand Cleese, eds., *The Euro as a Stabilizer in the International Economic System* (Boston, MA: Kluwer Academic), ch. 5.

Nye, Joseph S. Jr. (1990): 'Soft Power', *Foreign Policy* 80 (Fall), p. 153–171.

Orléan, Andre (1989): 'Mimetic Contagion and Speculative Bubbles', *Theory and Decision* 27:1–2, p. 63–92.

Padoan, Pier Carlo (2000): 'The Role of the Euro in the International System: A European View', in C. Randall Henning and Pier Carlo Padoan, *Transatlantic Perspectives on the Euro* (Washington, DC: Brookings Institution), ch. 2.

Porter, Richard D. and Judson, Ruth A. (1996): 'The Location of U.S. Currency: How Much Is Abroad?', *Federal Reserve Bulletin* 82: 10 (October), p. 883–903.

Portes, Richard and Hélène Rey (1998): 'The Emergence of the Euro as an International Currency', in David Begg, Jürgen von Hagen, Charles Wyplosz, and Klaus F. Zimmermann, eds., *EMU: Prospects and Challenges for the Euro* (Oxford, UK: Blackwell), p. 307–343.

Rogoff, Kenneth (1998): 'Blessing or Curse? Foreign and Underground Demand for Euro Notes', in David Begg, Jürgen von Hagen, Charles Wyplosz, and Klaus F. Zimmerman, eds., *EMU: Prospects and Challenges for the Euro* (Oxford, UK: Blackwell), p. 261–303.

Seitz, Franz (1995): 'The Circulation of Deutsche Mark Abroad', Discussion Paper 1/95 (Frankfurt: Deutsche Bundesbank).

Sinn, Hans-Werner and Frank Westermann (2001a): 'The Deutschmark in Eastern Europe, Black Money and the Euro: On the Size of the Effect', *CESifo Forum* 3, p. 35–40.

—— (2001b): 'Why Has the Euro Been Falling? An Investigation into the Determinants of the Exchange Rate', Working Paper 8352 (Cambridge, MA: National Bureau of Economic Research).

Stix, Helmut (2001): 'Survey Results about Foreign Currency Holdings in Five Central and Eastern European Countries', *CESifo Forum* 3, p. 41–48.

Thygesen, Niels et al. (1995): *International Currency Competition and the Future Role of the Single European Currency*, Final Report of a Working Group on European Monetary Union-International Monetary System (London: Kluwer Law International).

United States Treasury (2000): *The Use and Counterfeiting of United States Currency Abroad* (Washington, DC).

Vogel, Steven K., ed. (2002): *US-Japan Relations in a Changing World* (Washington, DC: Brookings Institution).

Wyplosz, Charles (1999): 'An International Role for the Euro?', in Jean Dermine and Pierre Hillion, eds., *European Capital Markets with a Single Currency* (Oxford, UK: Oxford University Press), ch. 3.

Yarjani, Javad (2002): 'The Choice of Currency for the Denomination of the Oil Bill', speech prepared for a meeting of European Union financial officials (April 14), available at http://www.opec.org/NewsInfo/Speeches.

13 Dollarization

Pros and cons

Source: Paper prepared for the workshop "*Dollars, Democracy and Trade: External Influences on Economic Integration in the Americas*", Los Angeles, CA, May 18, 2000.

In the wake of the recurrent financial crises of the last decade – Mexico in 1994–95, East Asia in 1997–98, Brazil in 1999 – it is not surprising that governments today would look for new ways to cope with the old risks of currency fragility and volatility. The ever-elusive goal is to construct a sustainable regime of exchange-rate stability. The challenge, as always, is to make a commitment to stable exchange rates credible. In 1991 Argentina thought it found the solution in a currency board, an ostensibly permanent peg to the U.S. dollar. But as subsequent developments have demonstrated, not even the guarantees of a Convertibility Law may suffice to convince investors that an exchange-rate peg is truly irrevocable. So now attention has focused on an even more radical solution: dollarization. The idea of dollarization has become a topic of intense public debate throughout Latin America since Argentina's former President, Carlos Menem, spoke out in its favor a year ago.

Dollarization is not new, of course. On an informal basis, America's greenback has long circulated alongside national monies throughout much of the Hemisphere as well as elsewhere. This is the familiar phenomenon of currency substitution. In similar fashion, Germany's Deutsche mark (DM) is used widely in the Balkans and East-Central Europe. What is new among our southern neighbors today is a growing interest in *formal* dollarization: legal adoption of the dollar as a full *replacement* for local money. Until now, formal dollarization (or its equivalent using some other major currency) was seen as an option limited only to tiny enclaves or micro-states like San Moreno or the Marshall Islands. In all, only some dozen sovereign entities – including only one country (Panama) with a population exceeding 100,000 – currently use the currency of a larger neighbor or patron in lieu of a money of their own. Today, however, even nations as big as Argentina or Mexico are debating the merits of the approach; and one country, Ecuador, has actually gone from talk to action, enacting legislation intended to implement formal dollarization before the end of the year.

The purpose of this chapter is to assess the case for dollarization in Latin America today. The general advantages of dollarization are clear. They are the standard economic benefits of financial and monetary integration: reduced transactions costs, reflecting an enhanced usefulness of money for all its basic functions (medium of exchange, unit of account, store of value). With replacement of the local money there is no longer a need to incur the expenses of currency conversion or hedging in trade and investment transactions between the partner economies. Efficiency gains could be considerable and will be shared commensurately by both sides, the United States as well as the country that dollarizes.

In addition to these general benefits, however, there will also be more specific effects – some positive, some negative – for each side. Implications for the partners are as much political as economic. The first section of this paper will examine the pros and cons of dollarization from the point of view of the dollarizing country. The second section will take up the perspective of the United States. For both sides a complex calculus of potential gains and losses is required, leaving much room for disagreement over the underlying issues. The third section of the paper will address the policy questions involved: What, if anything, should the United States do about dollarization, and what policy alternatives might there be? A final section asks what might be learned in this context from Europe's experience with its own form of monetary integration.

Implications for the dollarizing country

Advantages of dollarization

From the point of view of the dollarizing country, replacement of the local currency offers three major benefits (apart from the general advantage of reduced transactions costs). First, **administrative expenses** are reduced. No longer must the government incur the cost of maintaining an infrastructure dedicated solely to production and management of a separate national money. Admittedly, such savings are apt to be most attractive to poorer or more diminutive sovereignties because of the diseconomies of small scale involved. But even for bigger and wealthier countries the potential reduction of expenses would not be inconsiderable.

Second, dollarization can also establish a firm basis for a sounder **financial sector**. Dollarization means more than merely the adoption of a foreign currency. It also means financial integration with the United States, which will force domestic financial institutions to improve their efficiency and the quality of their services. Even more, as a supposedly irreversible institutional change, it signals a permanent commitment to low inflation, fiscal responsibility, and transparency. That would be of particular value to countries that previously have not enjoyed much of a reputation for price or fiscal stability.

Also importantly, with dollarization there could be a substantial reduction of **interest rates** for local borrowers. Dollarization establishes a stable relationship with a currency whose reputation is already well established and secure. Instead of investing heavily in efforts to build market confidence in its own monetary policy, a government can achieve instant credibility by "hiring" the respected Federal Reserve instead. Fed policy become the country's policy. With luck, the reduction of interest rates will result in substantially higher levels of domestic investment and future economic growth.

Presently, Latin American countries must pay a considerable premium when borrowing in world capital markets, reflecting two perceived risks for lenders. One is devaluation risk (or currency risk): a fear of depreciation of the local money's exchange rate. The other is default risk (or sovereign risk): a fear of disruption or suspension of a country's payments on foreign debt. Dollarization can do nothing directly to reduce default risk (the "country" premium), which is a reflection of the political reality of national sovereignty. An independent government can always, *in extremis*, suspend or abrogate its external obligations if faced with, say, a fiscal emergency or political turmoil. But dollarization can reasonably be expected to eliminate devaluation risk (the "currency" premium) since the reform, at least in principle, is supposed to be irrevocable. And it might even indirectly reduce default risk, insofar as some part of default risk reflects the possibility of future currency crises. Barring reintroduction of the local money, exchange-rate disturbances should become a thing of the past, making it easier for governments to meet foreign commitments.

Disadvantages of dollarization

Counterbalancing these benefits, however, are several potentially substantial costs. Economists, not surprisingly, tend to focus on disadvantages that are essentially economic in nature. These include forfeiture of national monetary autonomy and prospective losses of both seigniorage and an effective lender of last resort for domestic banks. In reality, however, none of these costs are apt to be as serious as frequently alleged. The more critical disadvantages of dollarization are *political*, not economic, involving losses of a powerful symbol of national identity, an emergency source of state revenue, and an important measure of diplomatic insulation. Though frequently discounted by economists, who are inclined to view political behavior as mostly interest-driven or even "irrational," these are in fact the costs that are likely to matter most in practice.

Economic costs

It is easy to exaggerate the purely economic costs of dollarization. It is certainly true, for example, that in formal terms **monetary autonomy** is forfeited, since the dollarizing country can no longer exercise unilateral control over its own money supply or exchange rate. The relationship is inherently hierarchical. All authority is ceded to the Federal Reserve, with little promise that the dollarizing country's specific circumstances would be taken into account when monetary decisions are made. In practical terms, however, it is likely that much of the country's monetary autonomy has already been greatly eroded. Otherwise, the country would not even be considering dollarization in the first place. In Argentina, the big step was taken when its currency board was established. The Argentines have already lived without an independent monetary policy for most of a decade. And in many other Latin American countries monetary autonomy has long since been compromised by the steady growth of informal dollarization. The greater the degree of currency substitution that has already occurred, reflecting market pressures and preferences, the greater is the degree of constraint imposed even now on a government's ability to manage macroeconomic conditions – and hence the smaller will be the actual loss of monetary autonomy if the local money is eliminated formally in the future.

Likewise, it is true that with dollarization a government forfeits a potentially powerful tool for underwriting public expenditures – the capacity to create money, otherwise known as **seigniorage**. Technically defined as the excess of the nominal value of a currency over its cost of production, seigniorage can be understood as an alternative source of revenue for the state beyond what can be raised via taxation or by borrowing from financial markets at home or abroad. What cannot be paid for with tax receipts or borrowed funds can be paid for, in effect, by using the printing press. Dollarization automatically terminates that revenue unless explicitly offset by some kind of agreed formula for seigniorage-sharing with the United States. But once again, in practical terms, the loss will be smaller, the greater is the degree of prior informal dollarization. For many of the countries of Latin America, where the greenback even now accounts for a large part of local money supply, the privilege of seigniorage has already been greatly diminished.

Finally, it is true that a dollarizing country forfeits a formal **lender of last resort**, since in adopting a foreign currency it also gives up a central bank capable of discounting freely in times of financial crisis. Domestic banks may thus be more exposed to potential liquidity risks. In practical terms, however, this alleged cost can be rather easily offset on a unilateral basis. Dollarization reduces the overall need for international reserves, since a share of external transactions that previously required foreign exchange can now be treated as the equivalent of domestic transactions. A portion of the central bank's dollar assets could therefore be dedicated instead to a public stabilization fund to help out domestic financial institutions under stress. Alternatively a contingency fund could be built up over time from tax revenues, or flexible credit lines with foreign banks or monetary authorities could be negotiated, using future tax revenues or seigniorage-sharing as collateral. A model for a foreign credit line already exists in Argentina where, in support of its currency board, the government has established a Contingent Repurchase Facility allowing it to sell dollar-denominated bonds to selected international banks when needed in exchange for cash dollars.

Political costs

It is more difficult to exaggerate the political costs of dollarization, which are highly visible and could be quite dramatic.

At the **symbolic level**, preservation of a national currency is particularly useful to governments wary of internal division or dissent. Centralization of state authority is facilitated insofar as citizens all feel themselves bound together as members of a single social unit – all part of the same political and historical community. Cultural anthropologists teach us that states are made not just through force but through loyalty, a voluntary commitment to a joint identity. The critical distinction between "us" (the nation) and "them" (everyone else) can be heightened by all manner of tangible symbols: flags, anthems, postage stamps, public architecture, even national sports teams. And among the most potent of these symbols is money, which serves to enhance a unique sense of national identity in two ways. First, because it is issued by the government or its central bank, a currency acts as a daily reminder to citizens of their connection to the state and oneness with it. Second, by virtue of its universal use on a daily basis, the currency underscores the fact that everyone is part of the same social entity – a role not unlike that of a single national language, which many governments also actively promote for nationalistic reasons. Both effects are lost when the money of a foreign state is adopted. Insofar as value continues to be attached to loyalty to a distinct political community, it can no longer be promoted through the tangible symbol of a separate national currency.

Similarly, at the level of state policy, preservation of a national currency is useful to governments as a kind of **insurance policy against risk**. This takes us back to seigniorage, which is more than just a marginal source of revenue for the state. More importantly, it can serve as an *emergency* source of revenue – a way of finding needed purchasing power quickly when confronted with unexpected contingencies, up to and including war. As John Maynard Keynes once wrote, "A government can live by this means when it can live by no other." Resources can be mobilized immediately without being forced to wait for tax returns to be filed or loans to be negotiated. That privilege too is lost when the money of another state is adopted.

Finally, at the level of **foreign policy and diplomacy**, preservation of a national currency is useful to governments wary of external dependence or threat. National monetary autonomy enables policymakers to avoid dependence on some other source for this most critical of all economic resources. In effect, a clear economic boundary is drawn between the state and the rest of the world, promoting political authority. This insulation also is lost when a foreign money is adopted. Indeed, with dollarization the United States gains a potentially powerful instrument of influence over the dependent dollarized economy. Hierarchy unavoidably implies vulnerability.

For a case in point consider Panama, which since its independence in 1903 has used the greenback as legal tender for most domestic monetary purposes. Although a national currency, the balboa, notionally exists, only a negligible amount of balboa coins actually circulates in practice. The bulk of local money supply, including all paper notes and most bank deposits, is accounted for by the dollar. In economic terms, most observers have rightly had only praise for Panama's currency dependence. Reliance on the dollar has created an environment of stability that has both suppressed inflation – a bane of most of Panama's hemispheric neighbors – and helped establish the country as an important offshore financial center. In political terms, however, Panama has been extremely vulnerable in its relations with Washington, which of course could sour at any time. In the late 1980s, Panamanians learned just how exposed to external coercion they really were.

The critical moment came in 1988, following accusations of corruption and drug smuggling against General Manuel Noriega, the country's de facto leader. In March 1988, Panamanian assets in U.S. banks were frozen, and all payments and dollar transfers to Panama were prohibited as part of the Reagan administration's determined campaign to force Noriega from power. The impact was swift. Most local banks were forced to close, and the economy was squeezed by a severe liquidity shortage. The effect on the economy was devastating despite rushed efforts by the Panamanian authorities to create a substitute currency, mainly by issuing checks in standardized denominations that they hoped recipients would then treat as cash. The country was effectively demonetized. Over the course of the year, domestic output fell by a fifth.

As it happens, the sanctions turned out to be insufficient to dislodge Noriega on their own. Ultimately, in 1989, Washington felt it necessary to mount a military invasion that led to a temporary occupation of the country until a new, friendlier government could be installed. But there can be no doubt that the liquidity squeeze was painful and contributed greatly to Noriega's downfall. Dollarization clearly makes a country more vulnerable to threats of manipulation or coercion.

Conclusion

So what can we conclude? For Latin Americans the purely economic costs of dollarization, while hardly trivial, nonetheless appear limited in scope and essentially manageable. Overall, on economic grounds alone, dollarization should be attractive to many countries. But governments cannot ignore the fact that there are also potential political costs, which could be substantial and may in fact be far more threatening to a nation's internal cohesion and external independence. The political implications of dollarization go to the heart of the fundamental purpose of the state: to permit a community to live in peace and preserve its own social and cultural heritage. Such matters cannot be lightly dismissed as mere "politics as usual." Latin American governments have real reason to hesitate over such a momentous decision.

Implications for the United States

For the United States too, as for the dollarizing country, there are potential costs as well as benefits associated with dollarization. And for the United States too, the more critical implications are likely to be political rather than economic in nature.

Advantages of dollarization

On the economic side, in addition to the general advantage of reduced transactions costs, the United States would enjoy one major benefit: an increase of **seigniorage**, mirroring the dollarizing country's revenue loss. Dollarization means that a government must give up interest-bearing dollar reserves in order to acquire the greenbacks needed to replace local cash in circulation. The interest payments thus foregone represent a net saving for the United States which, while not large, could cumulate significantly over time. In the case of Argentina, for example, it is estimated that the amount of seigniorage that would be transferred to Washington as a result of formal dollarization might amount to something like $750 million a year. That number helps explain why Argentina has so far hesitated to abandon its own currency irrevocably without first obtaining some agreed formula for seigniorage-sharing with the U.S. Treasury.

On the political side, the United States would enjoy three main benefits, all also mirroring corresponding disadvantages for the dollarizing country. At the symbolic level, for example, the dollarizing country's loss of a vital token of national identity is matched by America's gain in **international status and prestige**. Our money's global circulation is a constant reminder to others of our elevated rank in the community of nations. Certainly foreign publics cannot help but be impressed when the dollar formally takes over the domestic monetary system. "Great powers have great currencies," Robert Mundell once wrote. In effect, the greenback becomes a tangible symbol of American primacy, if not hegemony, on the world stage. Likewise, at the level of state policy, the dollarizing country's loss of seigniorage as an emergency source of revenue is matched by a corresponding increase of **fiscal opportunities** for the United States. Now foreigners as well as Americans can be counted upon to accept new dollars issued to underwrite public expenditures in the event of a sudden crisis or threat to national security. In effect, Washington's tax base is broadened. And finally, at the level of foreign policy and diplomacy, the dollarizing country's increased vulnerability is of course matched by America's enhanced **political authority**. Washington's capacity to exercise influence or coercion is broadened too.

Disadvantages of dollarization

Despite all these benefits, however, the United States too has reasons to hesitate. Dollarization also poses potentially serious risks for U.S. policy in the future.

Economists, again, tend to focus on the economic side, stressing in particular possible disadvantages for the conduct of U.S. **monetary policy**. Dollarization, it is alleged, could impose an awkward constraint on Federal Reserve decisionmakers, since a larger share of greenbacks would now be placed in circulation abroad. Money demand in the dollarizing country could be subject to sudden or frequent shifts, generating net international flows that might increase the short-term volatility of U.S. monetary aggregates. Such liquidity shocks could make it tougher for the Fed to maintain a steady course over time. But this risk is also easy to exaggerate. In fact, a large share of the outstanding stock of U.S. banknotes – conservatively estimated at some 55–70 percent of the total – is already in circulation outside the country, with little or no evident impact on policy. The Fed recognizes the phenomenon of informal dollarization and, as part of its daily open-market operations targeting the federal-funds rate, already factors overseas circulation into its behavior. In any event the additional sums involved, even if several governments were to choose formally to dollarize, are unlikely to be great enough to make much practical difference in an economy as large as that of the United States.

More critical, once again, are possible political risks that could ensue from dollarization. By voluntarily adopting the greenback as its own currency, a country makes itself a monetary dependency of the United States. Like it or not, therefore, Washington might find itself under **pressure to accommodate** the country's specific needs or fragilities should conditions warrant. The Fed might be pressured to take explicit account of the priorities of the dollarized economy in setting its policy goals – especially in the event of asymmetric payments shocks – or to extend its lender-of-last-resort facilities formally to local financial institutions. In time, the country might even begin to lobby for indirect or even direct representation on the Federal Reserve Board or Federal Open-Market Committee. Likewise, the Treasury might be importuned to come to the country's rescue in the event of financial crisis or instability. Even in the absence of any formal inter-state agreement, dollarization could create an implicit expectation of future monetary bailouts – a kind of contingent claim on U.S. Government resources. Such an expectation is the flip side of America's enhanced political authority. With primacy comes not only greater influence but also, potentially, greater responsibility.

Conclusion

For the United States too, therefore, political considerations – positive as well as negative – appear to far outweigh purely economic implications. On strictly economic grounds dollarization appears not unattractive, as it should for many Latin American governments. But on the political side the calculus is more uncertain, reflecting risks as well as possible gains that are by definition unknowable *ex ante*. The U.S. Government also, no less than Latin Americans, has reason to hesitate over such a decision.

U.S. policy options

What, then, should the United States do? In practical terms, three broad policy strategies suggest themselves: (1) active discouragement of dollarization; (2) passive neutrality; or (3) active encouragement. Each option carries with it its own calculus of potential benefits and risks.

Active discouragement

One strategy would be to actively discourage dollarization by all means possible. Governments considering such a course would be told in no uncertain terms that no help will be forthcoming from Washington – no seigniorage-sharing, no access to the Fed's discount window, no special accommodation of their monetary needs. Dollarize if you will, they would be advised, but you do so only at your own peril.

The main reason for such an uncooperative strategy would be to avoid even a hint of responsibility for backstopping the financial affairs of Latin American economies. Americans have long enjoyed a high degree of insularity in the making of monetary policy and would be unlikely to welcome any obligation, however limited, to compromise domestic priorities for the sake of undisciplined, perhaps even ungrateful, foreigners. Granted, this course would also mean foregoing the acknowledged benefits of dollarization, political as well as economic. But for many U.S. citizens, all that would be a small price to pay to maintain our traditional monetary autonomy.

Much depends, of course, on the historical counterfactual: What will happen in Latin America if the choice of dollarization is foreclosed? Several scenarios are possible. Easiest to imagine is a future in which governments seek to maintain and manage their own independent monies, just as they have done in the past. In that case, however, the risks of currency fragility and volatility would remain as salient as ever. Would the United States really be better off if our southern neighbors continue to suffer periodic bouts of monetary and financial crisis? An alternative possibility is that some Hemispheric governments might consider promoting monetary unification on their own, on the model of Europe's Economic and Monetary Union (EMU). In the southern cone of South America, for example, there has already been discussion of a proposed common currency for Mercosur, which some have suggested might be called the gaucho. In such a case, the United States would avoid any responsibility but would also undoubtedly suffer a decline of status and influence, as well as opportunities for seigniorage, as the new currency matures. Finally, a third possibility is that some Latin American countries might decide to throw in their lot with Europe, adopting the euro ("euroization") in lieu of the dollar as a replacement for their own national monies. In that case, America's status and influence would be even more directly challenged by a strengthened European Union.

Passive neutrality

A second possible strategy would be passive neutrality – a policy of "benign neglect," to borrow a phrase from another era. Governments considering dollarization would be given moral support, and perhaps some technical assistance, but otherwise would be left more or less on their own. No formal bilateral agreement would be offered, along the lines sought by Argentina over the past year, outlining mutual rights and obligations. Adoption of the greenback would have to be entirely unilateral, as is presently happening in Ecuador.

In fact, benign neglect is the best description of U.S. policy today. The main reason for the policy is the same as before: to try to avoid even a hint of responsibility for backstopping Latin American economies. But at the same time, by not discouraging dollarization undertaken on a unilateral basis, the United States can still hope to harvest the potential gains to be derived, including especially seigniorage and enhanced political authority. The main risk of such a course involves an empirical question: How many countries will actually be willing to transform themselves into a monetary dependency, with all the disadvantages implied, without some sort of formal quid pro quo from Washington? The Argentine government has already made plain that it is unlikely to commit itself in the absence of a bilateral treaty. Ecuador proceeded on its own only because of a massive financial collapse that seemed to leave policymakers in Quito no plausible alternative. The reality would appear to be that so long as Washington's current policy persists, the number of countries that finally do choose dollarization will remain comparatively small.

Active encouragement

That leaves one other possibility: active encouragement of dollarization initiatives. Governments would be offered specified incentives and perhaps even the public affirmation of a formal treaty. The element of dependency would be de-emphasized. Instead, dollarizing countries would be welcomed as sovereign partners in a great new monetary enterprise.

The most obvious incentive to offer would, of course, be seigniorage-sharing. From the dollarizing country's point of view, the government's revenue loss is by far the most visible cost involved. It also seems the least equitable since it reverts directly to the U.S. Treasury as a pure windfall gain. Why, Latin Americans are entitled to ask, should the wealthy United States profit at the expense of poorer neighbors? Should they not be entitled to reclaim at least a part of their foregone earnings as compensation for their surrender of mone-tary autonomy? Seigniorage-sharing can be most easily accomplished simply by giving the dollarizing country the cash greenbacks needed to replace local currency. The greenbacks may be a pure gift or may be offered in exchange for a dollar-denominated, non-interest-bearing government bond (in effect, a currency swap). Either way, the advantage is that the country can retain its existing dollar reserves and thus continue to receive interest in the future. Alternatively, if reserves are used to retire the local currency, the U.S. could make regular transfers to the country calculated to replace some or all of the interest earnings foregone. Precedent for this approach already exists in southern Africa, where South Africa makes annual transfers to two of its neighbors, Lesotho and Namibia, to compensate for their continued use of the South African rand as domestic legal tender.

In fact, legislation to offer a form of seigniorage-sharing has already been proposed by Senator Connie Mack of Florida, chairman of the Joint Economic Committee of the Congress. Entitled the International Monetary Stability Act, the bill would allow rebates to dollarizing countries of up to 85 percent of all lost seigniorage. (The remaining 15 percent would finance rebates to countries that are already dollarized, such as Panama, and to help pay related costs of the

Federal Reserve and Treasury.) Seigniorage would be paid in the form of interest on a consol (a perpetual debt instrument) that would be issued to each country as soon as the U.S. Treasury certifies that its money supply is officially dollarized. The measure's purpose, as Senator Mack emphasized, was quite self-consciously to promote adoption of the greenback. "It is time," he declared, "for the U.S. to show leadership and encourage dollarization." Though greeted cautiously by the Fed and Treasury officials, Mack's initiative appears to have drawn some degree of support from legislators on both sides of Capitol Hill.

Is the Mack bill the best way to encourage dollarization? From a strictly U.S. perspective, critics worry about other obligations that may be implicit in the legislation. Explicitly, the act formally provides "that the United States is not obligated to act as a lender of last resort to officially dollarized countries, consider their economic or financial conditions in setting monetary policy, or supervise their financial institutions." Yet not even such blunt wording may be enough to convince skeptics. Once having encouraged countries to adopt the greenback, can Washington really be expected to turn its back if any of them get into serious trouble? Conversely, from the point of view of potential dollarizers, there is much justifiable concern about the uncompromising unilateralism that is built into the bill. Certification of eligibility for seigniorage rebates would be at the sole discretion of the U.S. Treasury and could be withdrawn at any time. Might this privilege become yet one more handy instrument for the exercise of U.S. influence in Latin America?

For Latin Americans, accordingly, dollarization would be more palatable if accomplished through a bilateral or multilateral treaty, as sought by Argentina, rather than exclusively at the pleasure of the United States. Admittedly, any sort of written agreement would only serve to heighten skeptics' concerns about future contingent claims on the U.S. Government. But expectations of an implied commitment, it is evident, are likely to be generated no matter how strong the disclaimers emanating from Washington. If so, denials of responsibility would literally not be worth the paper they were written on. More preferable, it could be argued, would be an agreed contract spelling out mutual rights and obligations in clear and explicit detail. A manageable balance between the sensitivities of the two sides may not be easy to find. But there seems no satisfactory alternative if a strategy of encouraging dollarization is to be made to work effectively.

Conclusion: lessons from the European experience

What lessons for dollarization can be learned from Europe's experience with monetary integration? On the face of it, the parallels are weak. EMU, with its newly created currency – the euro – and its jointly managed European Central Bank (ECB), is formally a partnership of equals. Everyone has a seat at the table where policy is made. Dollarization, by contrast, is by definition a relationship of unequals: a hierarchical structure with just one country, the United States, firmly in charge. There is one common money, but it is America's currency. There is one central bank, but it is the Federal Reserve, accountable to Americans alone.

Much more germane might seem the CFA Franc Zone in Africa, which has long functioned as a monetary dependency of France. Though officially maintaining their own separate currency (actually a collection of regional currencies all labeled CFA francs), the fourteen members of the Zone – all but two former French colonies – voluntarily subordinate their monetary policies to the Treasury in Paris. The CFA franc has been firmly anchored on the French franc (a role now seamlessly taken over by the euro) and the bulk of the Zone's foreign reserves have been deposited in Paris. In return, the French government enhances the credibility of the CFA franc by guaranteeing its convertibility, with monetary discipline implemented through rules that determine access to Treasury credit. In reality, however, it is difficult to imagine that Latin Americans would view the Zone as an attractive model for their own relations with the United States. Their preference is certain to be for something far less obviously "neo-colonial."

Most relevant is Europe's experience with EMU's predecessor, the European Monetary System, which was de facto (though not formally) a hierarchical relationship centered on Germany. Begun in 1979, the EMS quickly evolved into a pegged-rate arrangement dominated by the policies of the Deutsche Bundesbank. For Germany's partners in the so-called Exchange Rate Mechanism (ERM), the advantage was the monetary stability imported via the DM, not unlike the main economic advantage claimed for dollarization. Policy credibility was instantly attained by "hiring" the highly respected Bundesbank. But there was also a clear disadvantage, which became most evident after German unification in 1990. Unification, a manifestly costly undertaking, brought in its wake extremely high interest rates, to which Germany's partners, being subordinate, felt constrained to adapt until ultimately forced to abandon their pegs under the pressure of speculative currency flows in 1992–93. The lesson, Europeans felt, was that they could not always rely on the good behavior of one dominant country. Hegemony could be abused, unconsciously if not deliberately. Hence the widespread acceptance of the initiative to replace the EMS with EMU, which involves a much more collective decisionmaking process. For Latin Americans, this is undoubtedly the key lesson to be learned from the European experience.

In short, dollarization has its attractions, but not if it means unqualified subordination to the dominant partner. Some countries, like Ecuador, may feel they have no choice. But most, like Argentina, will prefer to look for greater assurances that their monetary subordination, once entered into, will not be exploited by Washington, the long-dreaded colossus of the north. In effect, America's hands must be tied – albeit not so much that the whole project becomes politically infeasible for the United States. Ultimately, therefore, the debate boils down to one basic question: Can the sovereign rights of both sides be adequately protected? Should dollarization prove more than just a passing fancy, diplomats will surely have their hands full.

Bibliography

Baliño, Tomás J.L., Adam Bennett, and Eduardo Borensztein (1999), *Monetary Policy in Dollarized Economies* (Washington: International Monetary Fund).

Barro, Robert J. (1999), "Let the Dollar Reign from Seattle to Santiago," *Wall Street Journal* (March 18), A18.

Berg, Andrew and Eduardo Borensztein (2000), "The Dollarization Debate," *Finance and Development* (March), 38–41.

Berg, Andrew and Eduardo Borensztein (2000), "The Pros and Cons of Full Dollarization," Working Paper WP/00/50 (Washington, DC: International Monetary Fund).

Bogetić, Željko (1999), "Official or 'Full' Dollarization: Current Experiences and Issues" (International Monetary Fund, unpublished).

Bogetić, Željko (2000), "Full Dollarization: Fad or Future," *Challenge* 43:2 (March/April), 17–48.

Calvo, Guillermo A. (1999), "On Dollarization" (University of Maryland, unpublished).

Cohen, Benjamin J. (2000), "Dollarisation: la dimension politique," *L'Economie Politique* 5 (January), 88–112.

Cohen, Benjamin J. (2000), "Political Dimensions of Dollarization," remarks prepared for a Conference on Dollarization, Dallas, TX, March 6–7 (available online at: http://www.dallasfed.org/htm/dallas/pdfs/cohen.pdf).

Fraga, Arminio, Pablo Guidotti, and Sebastian Edwards (1999), "From Floating Exchange Rates to Full Dollarization: What Works for Latin America?," a symposium, *Global Emerging Markets* (Deutsche Bank) 2:2 (April), 29–41.

Hausmann, Ricardo (1999), "Should There Be Five Currencies or One Hundred and Five?," *Foreign Policy* (Fall), 65–79.

Hausmann, Ricardo and Andrew Powell (1999), "Dollarization: Issues of Implementation," paper prepared for a Conference on Alternative Exchange Rate Regimes for the Region, Panama City, July 23–24.

International Monetary Fund (1999), "Dollarization: Fad or Future for Latin America," an IMF Economic Forum, June 24 (online at http://www.imf.org/external/np/tr/1999/TR990624.HTM)

Joint Economic Committee of the Congress (1999), "Encouraging Official Dollarization in Emerging Markets," staff report (April).

Joint Economic Committee of the Congress (2000a), "Basics of Dollarization," staff report (January, updated from July 1999).

Joint Economic Committee of the Congress (2000b), "Dollarization: A Guide to the International Monetary Stability Act," staff report (February).

Katzman, Julie T. (2000), "Dollarization," in Patrick J. DeSouza (ed.), *Economic Strategy and National Security: A Next Generation Approach* (Boulder, CO: Westview Press), ch. 12.

Moreno-Villalaz, Juan Luis (1999), "Lessons from the Monetary Experience of Panama: A Dollar Economy with Financial Integration," *Cato Journal* 18: 3 (Winter), 421–439.

Pou, Pedro (1999), "Is Globalization Really to Blame?," in Jane Sneddon Little and Giovanni P. Olivei (eds.), *Rethinking the International Monetary System* (Boston, MA: Federal Reserve Bank of Boston), 243–250.

Sachs, Jeffrey and Felipe Larrain (1999), "Why Dollarization is More Straightjacket than Salvation," *Foreign Policy* (Fall), 80–92).

Samuelson, Robert J. (1999), "Dollarization – A Black Hole," *Washington Post* (May 12), A27.

U.S. Senate (1999a), "Official Dollarization in Emerging-Market Countries," Hearings before the Subcommittee on Economic Policy and the Subcommittee on International Trade and Finance, Committee on Banking, Housing, and Urban Affairs (April).

U.S. Senate (1999b), "Issues Regarding Dollarization," Staff Report of the Subcommittee on Economic Policy, Committee on Banking, Housing, and Urban Affairs (July).

Velde, François R. and Marcelo Veracierto (2000), "Dollarization in Argentina," *Economic Perspectives* (Federal Reserve Bank of Chicago) 24:1, 24–35.

14 Are monetary unions inevitable?*

Source: *International Studies Perspectives* 8, 3, August 2003.

One of the most remarkable developments in the world economy in recent years has been the rapid growth of cross-border competition among currencies – a demand-driven process of currency substitution that I have elsewhere called the *deterritorialization* of money (Cohen, 1998). No longer, in many countries, are market actors restricted to using the national money alone, despite governmental efforts to preserve the exclusivity of their currencies. Now popular foreign monies are also widely employed, competing directly with the state's own monetary issue for the favor of transactors and investors. In effect, currencies are increasingly caught up in an intense Darwinian struggle for survival, posing difficult choices for policymakers.

What will be the outcome of this struggle? In the opinion of many informed observers, the answer is obvious. The number of currencies must necessarily shrink, as the least competitive monies fall by the wayside. At present there are more than 150 state-sanctioned currencies around the globe, from market leaders like the U.S. dollar and Europe's euro to dozens of weaker rivals in many of the world's poorer economies – what one economist scornfully dismisses as mere "junk currencies" (Harris, 2001:35). Can anyone believe that such a crowded population, including large numbers of small currencies with very limited circulation, represents a stable equilibrium? As another economist, George von Furstenberg (2000b:112) remarks, "small really is not beautiful in matters of money." For many the only solution is monetary union, a strategy of currency alliance on the model of Europe's Economic and Monetary Union (EMU), replacing diverse "junk currencies" with more appealing joint brands of money. Typical is the prediction of Michel Camdessus (2000:35), former managing director of the IMF, who suggests that "[i]n the long run, we are moving toward a world of fewer currencies." Von Furstenberg (2000a:199–200) is even more forthright. Monetary unions, he asserts, are "inevitable ... the wave of the future." As he summarizes (2000b: 109): "[Governments] will reclaim co-ownership and comanagement of their monetary asset in multilateral monetary union with likeminded countries."

* *Author's note*: This article has benefited from helpful comments and suggestions by David Andrews, Eric Helleiner, Peter Kenen, Louis Pauly, and three anonymous reviewers. The research assistance of Tom Knecht is also gratefully acknowledged.

But are monetary unions truly inevitable? In fact, predictions such as these are misleading and almost certainly wrong. The aim of this chapter is to explain why they are wrong. Previously (Cohen, 2001) I have used comparative historical analysis to identify the key conditions that appear to determine the *sustainability* of monetary unions over time: that is, the factors that influence whether joint currencies, once established, are fated to live or die. In this article I use the same conditions to assess prospects for the *creation* of monetary unions. A survey of possible candidates around the world, from Canada to Argentina and from East Asia to West Africa, suggests that prospects for full new monetary unions are dim at best, though conceivably some governments could be attracted to less demanding forms of currency alliance depending on bargaining context.

The key issue is *commitment*. A currency merger implies an upward shift in the delegation of formal authority. Involved is what Karen Litfin (1997) calls a "sovereignty bargain" – a voluntary agreement to accept certain limitations on national authority in exchange for anticipated benefits. Monetary sovereignty is pooled in a partnership of some sort. The main advantage is that participating governments might find it easier to promote the market share of a single joint currency as compared with the thankless task of trying to defend separate national brands. But therein also lies the main disadvantage, since pooling necessarily implies some measure of *collective* action in the issue and management of money. An alliance requires *allies* – other states with similar preferences and a disposition to act cooperatively. In practice, willing partners among sovereign states are just not all that plentiful.

Monetary union

Monetary union, in the strictest sense of the term, means complete abandonment of a separate national currency. Only a newly created joint money is recognized as legal tender for a designated group of countries, and all decision making is lodged in a single central agency with strong supranational powers. As compared with the status quo of separate national currencies, a full monetary union offers distinct advantages. But there are also potential disadvantages that create serious obstacles to a successful sovereignty bargain. The conditions needed to facilitate the requisite degree of commitment are demanding and exist only rarely in practice.

Effects

Analytically, the effects of a monetary union are easy to identify. Most obvious are potential costs, which are not inconsiderable. Each state individually loses all the benefits that are traditionally associated with a national monetary monopoly: first, a powerful instrument to manage the macroeconomic performance of the economy; second, a possible source of revenue (seigniorage) to underwrite public expenditures; third, a potent political symbol to promote a sense of national identity; and finally, a practical means to insulate the nation from foreign influence or constraint.[1] For sovereign governments, these are not easy sacrifices to contemplate.

All is not lost, however. On the positive side, partners can anticipate a reduction of transactions costs – an efficiency saving on all exchanges and investments within the group. Moreover, what is sacrificed at the national level is recouped at the group level. Authority is not surrendered but pooled – delegated to the joint institutions of the currency partnership, to be shared and in some manner collectively managed by all the countries involved. Each partner's loss, therefore, is simultaneously also each other's gain. The individual state may no longer have much latitude to act unilaterally, but every government retains a voice in decision making for the group as a whole. They are all, in this sense, gainers.

Net effects for participants, therefore, could turn out to be distinctly favorable. Like a cartel, a monetary union aims to improve the market position of its members – to create a single joint currency that, as compared with weakly competitive national monies, will have more appeal to market actors. The greater the appeal of the new currency, the more the benefits of monopoly, eroded at the national level, will be replicated at the group level; the more governments will be able to resurrect the privileges once enjoyed before the advent of deterritorialization, albeit now collectively rather than separately. By joining together, policy-makers will be more strongly positioned to resist market pressures. They will thus be better able to guide macroeconomic performance, generate seigniorage revenue, promote a sense of community, and avoid external dependence. On all these scores the group could gain substantially as compared with what each government might achieve on its own. Joint gains could exceed the sum of individual losses by a sizable margin.

Obstacles

Why, then, do we not see more monetary unions sprouting up around the globe? Despite potential advantages, the number of monetary unions remains tantalizingly small. In addition to two arrangements left over from the era of colonialism – the CFA Franc Zone in Africa and the Eastern Caribbean Currency Union (ECCU) – only one new union, EMU, has come on the scene in recent years. Clearly, obstacles lie in the path of an alliance strategy – most notably, in the very fact that the strategy must be *shared*. Monetary union is by definition mutual, an exercise in collective action. An alliance requires allies, and it must be negotiated. Willing partners in a sovereignty bargain like monetary union are difficult to find and may be even more difficult to negotiate with.

Can the obstacles be overcome? Regrettably the contemporary empirical record, with only one new monetary union – Europe's EMU – to date, offers few direct clues. Indirectly, though, much can be learned from my previous analysis of the conditions that have determined the sustainability of monetary unions in the past (Cohen, 2001). The historical sample of currency unions, including all those that have eventually failed as well as those that survived, is quite a bit larger – certainly large enough to make clear just why an alliance strategy can be so challenging. The same factors that *sustain* monetary unions can be assumed to be instrumental in promoting their *creation* as well.

Economic linkages, my previous analysis suggests, are clearly insufficient on their own to sustain the necessary commitment. In assessing prospects for monetary unions, economists typically rely on the familiar theory of optimum currency areas (OCAs), which compares the benefit of reduced transactions costs with the potential cost of doing without either an autonomous monetary policy or a flexible exchange rate. A diverse range of variables is identified that arguably will affect the magnitude of losses at the macroeconomic level, by influencing either the severity of payments disturbances or the ease of needed adjustments. Included among these so-called country characteristics are wage and price flexibility, labor and capital mobility, geographic trade patterns, size and openness of economies, and the nature, source, and timing of potential economic shocks. States are expected to be more amenable to an alliance strategy to the extent that prices and wages are flexible, factors of production are mobile, trade interdependence is high, economies are open, and shocks tend to be synchronized rather than asymmetric.

As often noted, however, the explanatory power of OCA theory appears limited at best. For every one of the characteristics stressed in this approach, there are contradictory historical examples – cases that conform to expectations suggested by the theory and others that do not (Cohen, 2001). Moreover, for any one country it is rare that all the factors cited point in the same direction, adding to the difficulties of forecasting; nor are all the variables necessarily mutually independent or easy to measure or compare for relative importance. In practice, none appears sufficient to explain observed outcomes. This is not to suggest that economic factors are therefore unimportant. Clearly they do matter insofar as they tend, through their impact on adjustment costs and speculative incentives, to ease or exacerbate the challenge of an alliance strategy. But it is equally clear, as one astute observer concludes (Goodhart, 1995:452), that OCA theory on its own "has relatively little predictive value."

Nor is much help offered by the details of institutional design – that is, the legal provisions agreed to govern the issuing of currency and the management of decisions. Such organizational formalities have differed sharply in various cases. In principle, such differences might be thought to matter insofar as they affect the net costs of commitment by individual states. Recent theoretical literature on transactions costs emphasizes the key role that institutional design can play in promoting credible commitments, by structuring arrangements to match anticipated incentive problems (Martin and Simmons, 1999). The higher the exit costs involved, the greater the disincentive for any government to defect. In looking at historical experience, therefore, we might reasonably expect to see a direct correlation between the degree of centralization of a monetary union and its practical sustainability over time. In practice, however, no such relationship can be found. Again, contradictory examples abound (Cohen, 2001).

Most decisive, it appears, are *political* linkages, which may take either of two forms. One, suggested by traditional realist approaches to international relations theory, is the presence or absence of a powerful state committed to using its influence to keep a monetary union functioning effectively on terms agreeable to all. The other, suggested by more institutional approaches to world politics, is the presence or absence of a broad constellation of related ties and commitments sufficient to make the sacrifice of monetary sovereignty, whatever the costs, basically acceptable to each partner. Judging from the historical record, I conclude that one or the other of these two types of linkage is necessary to sustain the requisite degree of commitment among independent states. Where both types have been present, they have been a sufficient condition for success. Where neither was present, unions have tended to erode or fail.[2]

The first type of linkage calls for a locally dominant country – a leader or "hegemon" – and is a direct reflection of the distribution of interstate power. Scholars have long recognized the critical role that the leadership of a powerful state can play in maintaining the stability of a monetary regime. At issue, as David Lake (1993) has emphasized, is the provision of a type of public good – an essential "infrastructure" that will support both short-term stabilization and longer-term growth. The leader must be not only able but also willing to use its power, via sidepayments or sanctions, to lower the costs or raise the benefits of commitment for its partners.

The second type of linkage calls for a well-developed set of institutional connections and reflects, more amorphously, the degree to which a genuine sense of solidarity – of *community* – exists among the countries involved.[3] Scholars have also long recognized the demanding psychological dimension of bargains to pool sovereignty. Participating states, at a quite fundamental level, must come to accept that individual interests can best be realized through joint commitments – through what Keohane and Hoffmann (1991:13) call a "network" form of organization "in which individual units are defined not by themselves but in relation to other units." Without such a sense of solidarity, governments will be more preoccupied with the costs of commitment than with the benefits.

The underlying logic of these linkages is clear. Sovereign governments need strong incentives to stick to bargains that might, at some point, turn out to be inconvenient. In practice, such incentives may derive either from the encouragement or discipline supplied by a single powerful state or from the opportunities and constraints posed by a network of institutional linkages. Economic ties may be weak or strong; likewise, organizational details may differ. But such factors appear to be of secondary importance at best. What matters most is a convergence of state preferences, supported either by a committed local hegemon or by a common project of integration. Von Furstenberg's reference (2000b) to "like-minded countries" is apt.

In turn, this logic suggests why a full monetary union may be so challenging to implement in the first place. In how many places can a suitably committed hegemon or necessary sense of community be said to exist? Where in the quarrelsome family of nations can the requisite like-mindedness be found? The obstacles to finding willing partners are formidable and, in most instances, likely to turn out to be insurmountable.

Europe

As a case in point consider Europe, home to the one new monetary union to be successfully negotiated in recent decades. For EMU, willing partners were in fact found – twelve in all by the time euro notes and coins made their appearance in 2002 – with even more countries throughout East Central Europe and the Balkans clamoring to join at the earliest possible date. At first glance, the successful launch of the euro would seem to suggest that the obstacles to a full currency merger are not so formidable after all. But upon reflection it is clear that just the opposite conclusion is warranted, given the considerable time and effort Europeans had to put into getting the enterprise to this point. In many ways a unique undertaking, EMU is best understood not as evidence for enthusiasts but as the exception that proves the rule.

That EMU is exceptional is unquestioned. Never before, in modern history, has a group of fully independent states voluntarily agreed to replace existing national currencies with one newly created type of money. Even while retaining political sovereignty, member governments have formally delegated all monetary sovereignty to a common authority, the European Central Bank (ECB). These are not former overseas dependencies like the members of ECCU or the CFA Franc Zone, inheriting arrangements that had originated in colonial times. Rather, these are established states of long standing and include some of the biggest national economics in the world engaged in a gigantic experiment of unprecedented proportions. Not without reason, EMU is being closely watched around the globe as a test case for an alliance strategy.

But what does EMU prove? Obviously, the Europeans have demonstrated that the obstacles involved are not insurmountable. Participating governments did indeed find it possible to make a firm commitment. Under the 1992 Maastricht Treaty, which set the timetable for EMU, four so-called convergence criteria were specified, including tough restrictions on inflation, interest rates, fiscal deficits, and public debt. By the time the euro came into existence in 1999, most members of the European Union (EU) were judged to have met the Maastricht conditions or at least to have made substantial progress toward achieving them. The one exception, Greece, was permitted to enter the monetary union two years later.

But it is also obvious that the path to EMU was not easy, requiring more than four decades of determined effort despite unusually favorable circumstances. The European Union was in fact a near ideal setting for implementation of an alliance strategy. On the one hand, members were already intimately connected to one another through a dense network of institutional linkages that have only continued to spread and deepen over time. Growing like-mindedness was implicit in their common integration project. At the same time there was also a powerful local hegemon, Germany, whose policy commitment to monetary integration was never in doubt. For historical reasons, the Federal Republic has long found it useful to confirm its European credentials in this way even at the cost of sacrificing its own monetary independence. Yet resistance to creation of a joint currency was fierce. Two generations had to pass before EMU could be realized. If it took so long to get a monetary union started in Europe, why should we expect it to be any easier elsewhere?

Reasons for the long resistance to monetary union in Europe are not difficult to find. The problem has never been the prospective loss of the seigniorage privilege, to which little attention is paid. Unlike in many developing nations, governments in Europe have long ceased to rely regularly on money creation to finance public deficits, and most have developed ample alternatives to augment spending when needed. But many Europeans do worry about removing yet another layer of insulation against outside influence, to be wielded in this instance by a supranational ECB. Many worry as well about the diminished capacity of national governments to manage their own economy in the event of unanticipated shocks. With activist fiscal policy severely constrained by the Maastricht Treaty's restrictions on budget deficits, what would compensate for the loss of the money supply and exchange rate as instruments of macroeconomic policy? And in at least some member countries, there was also a deep reluctance to sacrifice what many regarded as a vital symbol of national identity. This is more than just a matter of what one noted economist has dismissed as mere "misplaced pride" (Alesina, 2001:223). Politicians concerned about remaining in office could hardly afford to ignore such strongly held sentiments.

What EMU proves, therefore, is that even in the most favorable circumstances, monetary union is difficult if not impossible to achieve. An alliance strategy is bound to encounter stiff resistance, for reasons both rational and emotional. In Europe, opposition has stemmed from worries about outside control, macroeconomic stabilization, and political symbolism. Elsewhere, potential seigniorage losses could also be a legitimate issue of concern. The obstacles to monetary union are surely not insurmountable, given appropriate leadership and political linkages. But even in those exceptional circumstances where willing partners might be found, the process is unlikely to be consummated swiftly or easily.

Unwilling hegemons

In this light, the outlook for many new monetary unions around the globe seems dim at best. The idea of currency alliance has been touted in almost every region of the world. In some cases, the aim of proponents has been to marry a smaller state in bilateral union with a larger neighbor. Examples include Canada, New Zealand, and Belarus. In each of these countries there has been lively discussion of the possibility of a currency merger with a larger power next door – respectively, the United States, Australia, and Russia. In other cases, the aim has been to build on regional integration projects comparable, in some degree, to the successful model of the European Union – including, most notably, groupings in Southeast Asia, South America, the Caribbean, West Africa, and the Persian Gulf. Talk, however, is cheap. The real question is whether the necessary political linkages exist or can be promoted. In practice, the obstacles remain overwhelming. Smaller countries considering a bilateral union have not found a suitably committed hegemon; likewise, in existing regional projects, the necessary sense of community has been most notable for its absence. A survey of all these cases confirms the difficulty of cultivating the requisite like-mindedness among potential partners.

Canada–United States

We begin our survey with the three bilateral cases. Consider, first, Canada, where the possibility of a monetary union with the United States has been actively debated in recent years.[4] The two neighbors are already closely linked economically through the North American Free Trade Agreement (NAFTA), which came into operation in 1993, as well as through a variety of other political and military arrangements and through closely related cultures and social histories. Though by no means a single community, the two certainly do not lack for a significant sense of solidarity. If in similar circumstances Europeans could agree to complement their free-trade zone with a common currency, many Canadians ask, why cannot North Americans do the same? A name has even been invented for a future joint money – the *amero* (Grubel, 1999), in flattering emulation of the euro. Unfortunately for its advocates, however, the idea of the amero has elicited no interest whatsoever south of the longest unguarded border in the world.

Most prominent among Canadian champions of a North American Monetary Union (NAMU) are economists like Thomas Courchene (1999) and Herbert Grubel (1999), who naturally tend to focus on the standard economic benefits and costs of currency regionalization. Efficiency gains, in particular, are stressed. Canada, it is argued, is becoming an increasingly open economy, in terms of both trade and investment. With up to 85 percent of Canadian exports now going to the United States, accounting for upwards of 40 percent of GDP, transactions costs would be significantly reduced by a merger of currencies. The result could be a substantial growth of trade and income. At the same time, potential costs are discounted. Little, allegedly, would be sacrificed in terms of macroeconomic stabilization, since Canadian inflation and employment rates are already so sensitive to developments below the border. Owing to the overwhelming dominance of America's economy, which is twenty times larger than Canada's, business cycles in the two countries have long been highly synchronized. Nor would the government be forced to forego any of the seigniorage that it currently earns from printing money, estimated at about C\$2 billion a year (Grubel, 1999:16), since NAMU would presumably include provisions for seigniorage-sharing. On balance, Canada would come out a winner.

Not everyone agrees, of course. The NAMU also has its opponents, who raise two principal types of objection. The first, essentially economic in nature, concerns exchange rates.[5] Canada's dollar – familiarly known as the "loonie" after the loon, a native bird, depicted on dollar coins – is presently allowed to float freely vis-à-vis all other currencies, including its U.S. counterpart. The advantage, in principle, is that a floating rate can function as a shock absorber to help cushion producers of primary goods from external disturbances. Commodity prices, as we know, tend to be relatively volatile, and among advanced economies Canada remains disproportionately dependent on its farming and extractive sectors, which still account for as much as a third of all exports. Independent analysis confirms that exchange-rate flexibility plays a useful role in buffering the Canadian economy against asymmetric shocks (Arora and Jeanne, 2001). By contrast, the currency cushion would be lost in the event of a monetary union with the United States. For all the synchronization of business cycles, the structures of the two economies remain strikingly divergent, with their terms of trade tending to move in opposite directions in response to fluctuations of commodity prices. The pair can hardly be described as an optimum currency area.

There are some grains of truth here, reply NAMU proponents. The exchange rate cushion does help buffer the domestic economy – but at what price? In fact, they contend, the costs of preserving a separate Canadian dollar with a floating rate are considerable. In the short term, Canada's flexible rate tends to be volatile and subject to a good deal of "noise," sending confusing signals to the domestic economy. Over the longer term, floating is said to contribute to poor economic performance by reducing labor-market flexibility and delaying adjustment to a secular decline in global natural resource prices. Overall, NAMU proponents conclude, Canadians have suffered a marked loss of real income relative to their American neighbors, reflected in the sustained drop in the value of the loonie from near parity with the greenback as recently as the mid-1970s to not much more than sixty U.S. cents at the end of 2001 – the currency's lowest level in over a century. The NAMU, by contrast, would supposedly send clearer price signals and encourage a quicker shift of resources from commodity production to more profitable sectors such as technology and services, accelerating growth of productivity and living standards.

The second type of objection encompasses familiar concerns about sovereignty and symbolism. Are Canadians really prepared to give up their embattled loonie and all it represents about the distinctiveness of Canada's culture and society? As Eric Helleiner (2003) writes, "the political battle over NAMU is inevitably a debate over Canada's national identity." More tangibly, are Canadians really willing to become junior partners of the Americans, as they inevitably would in any joint institution created to manage the amero? With less than one-tenth of America's population, Canada could hardly expect to receive equal representation in decision making. More likely, the country would simply become "a thirteenth district of a widened Federal Reserve System," as one critic suggests (Laidler, 1999:327).

Again some grains of truth are there, reply NAMU proponents, but are they overwhelming? Critics are cautioned against exaggeration. Many of the same arguments were made against NAFTA before its ratification and ultimately proved far from the mark. In fact, giving up a national currency by no means implies surrender of cultural autonomy or political independence. In all respects other than money, the nation would remain as sovereign as ever. As Grubel (1999:19–20), a former member of Parliament, concludes:

> The basic fact is that the introduction of the amero does nothing to the existing national border and the ability of Canadian governments to pursue policies that get them re-elected. Nationalists do not have a good case to oppose the amero except on the grounds that it results in the loss of national monetary sovereignty. But [even] this loss is incurred in the expectation of large economic gains.

Though neither side in the debate lands a knockout blow, it is clear that the case for the amero cannot be dismissed out of hand. In fact, NAMU has roused widespread interest among Canadians and has even been the subject of parliamentary hearings in the nation's capital, Ottawa. Popular support is substantial, including key elements of the business community. At the end of 2001, according to a major opinion survey (Centre for Research and Information on Canada, 2002), some 55 percent of Canadians favored a monetary union of some kind with the United States. Typical are the remarks of one prominent business economist, once an opponent of a currency merger who has now come around to champion it. "Let's face it," she says, "our currency does not float, it sinks.... Let's [negotiate a currency union] and get it over with.... I do believe it's inevitable."[6]

Inevitable or not, though, Canada faces a serious problem. Even if approval among Canadians were to become universal, a towering impediment remains – namely, a total lack of interest on the part of the United States. As the much larger of the two countries, the United States clearly is in a position to play the role of supportive hegemon. But as even the most enthusiastic of NAMU proponents acknowledge, currency union holds little appeal below the border and has attracted even less attention. Americans show no enthusiasm whatsoever for the idea of sharing their traditional monetary sovereignty. The point is well put by Canadian economist John McCallum (2000:2), who observes, "the European Union model, in which independent states share decision-making and sovereignty, is alien to American thinking and American history.... [The United States] is obviously light years away from according [Canada] any formal role in the setting of US policy, let alone contemplating a move to a supranational, euro-style currency." Grubel regretfully concurs. "The biggest obstacle," he concedes (1999:39), "will be indifference in the United States."

In short, Canada lacks a willing partner; and without a willing partner, no collective action will be possible.

New Zealand–Australia

A similar problem looms in the South Pacific, where the possibility of a monetary union between Australia and New Zealand is also actively debated. Like the United States and Canada, the two antipodean neighbors are already closely linked through a free-trade accord, the Closer Economic Relations (CER) Agreement dating from 1983, as well as through other political and military arrangements and closely related cultures and social histories. And as in North America, interest has been piqued by the precedent of the euro. Here too a name has even been invented for the future money to replace the present Australian and New Zealand dollars. It would be called the ANZAC dollar – "Zac," for short. The problem is that here too the debate so far has been largely confined to the smaller of the two neighbors, New Zealand.

Interest at the eastern end of the Tasman Sea is evident. Acutely aware of their country's tiny size and geographic isolation, many New Zealanders feel that close integration with Australia, a market seven times larger, is imperative to ensure their future economic security. The CER is viewed as just the beginning, with monetary union a natural corollary – simply, as one source puts it (Grimes, 2000:14), "the next logical step in the CER process." Discussion received a particularly strong impetus from the appearance in 2000 of a public manifesto for monetary union authored by two locally prominent economists, Arthur Grimes and Frank Holmes (2000).

Direct savings on transactions costs, advocates admit, would not be especially large, since only about a fifth of New Zealand's trade is with Australia, accounting for less than 5 percent of gross domestic product (GDP). At most, according to a study at the country's central bank (Hargreaves and McDermott, 1999:23), savings might amount to a minuscule 0.13 percent of GDP. But New Zealanders could gain substantially from lower and more stable interest rates, which by promoting economic growth might, in turn, generate further expansion of trade and investment.

Furthermore, advocates argue, New Zealand would have relatively little to lose in terms of macroeconomic stabilization, since the two economies are essentially alike both structurally and cyclically. Because each exports mainly primary commodities, terms-of-trade movements in the two countries are highly correlated, and business cycles tend to be synchronized. Consequently, New Zealand should have less need of a flexible exchange rate to buffer itself against adverse developments originating from its larger partner. Indeed, empirical evidence is cited to suggest that a joint money with Australia might actually provide a more effective shock absorber than the New Zealand dollar can do on its own (Grimes, 2000:12). Likewise, as in Canada, there would presumably be little, if any, revenue loss for the government, since an arrangement for revenue sharing could be anticipated.

In fact, the evidence on the cushioning role of New Zealand's floating exchange rate is mixed, as numerous studies demonstrate (Scrimgeour, 2002). While the correlation of shocks is high, it is far from perfect, owing to the differing composition of commodity exports from the two countries. Whereas Australia relies more on minerals, New Zealand ships more dairy and forestry products. Simulation exercises suggest that if New Zealand were to lose its ability to set monetary policy independently, the variability of both inflation and output could increase, rather than decrease, over the course of a typical business cycle (Drew et al., 2001).

Nonetheless, support for an ANZAC dollar is widespread among New Zealanders. In a survey of some four hundred local business firms, Grimes and Holmes (2000) found nearly 60 percent – three of five – in favor of a monetary union with Australia, with only 14 percent against. Opinion polls show a majority of the general public also backing an alliance strategy.[7] Even the prime minister, Helen Clark, has reversed her long-standing opposition. "If the largest countries in Europe see benefit in a currency merger," she said in late 2000, "what is so sacrosanct about the currency of a country with 3.8 million people? It might be one of those things that becomes inevitable as we have closer economic integration with Australia."[8]

But would Australians agree? The problem for New Zealand, as it is for Canada, is that the potential partner is just not interested. Like the United States,

Australia clearly is in a position to play the role of supportive hegemon. But the issue is hardly debated at all by Australians, largely because direct benefits of a merger with their smaller neighbor would appear to be negligible at best. Australia's currency already enjoys a modest leadership role in the South Pacific and might even acquire additional followers. If New Zealand is so eager for a monetary alliance, Australians suggest, it should simply adopt Australia's dollar as its own, just as have some other nearby island states (de Brouwer, 2000). When asked by a reporter what he thought of Helen Clark's remarks, Australia's finance minister flatly declared:

> We're not interested in any new currency, any third currency. We are happy with our monetary arrangements and we intend to keep them.... It's open to other countries to say we would like to adopt your currency.... We are not proposing to change the Australian dollar nor are we proposing to go into some new currency.[9]

Unless New Zealanders can find some way to change Australian minds, the whole notion of an ANZAC dollar must be regarded as a nonstarter.

Belarus–Russia

A third example is provided by Belarus, formerly a republic of the Soviet Union, which in Czarist times was known as White Russia or Little Russia. With only eleven million people, an economy overwhelmingly dependent on Russian oil, and an uncertain sense of its own nationhood, Belarus has attached little importance to preservation of any significant degree of monetary sovereignty for itself. On the contrary, its own currency, the Belarusian rubel – derisively known as the "bunny" (zaichyk) after the rabbit that appears on the face of bank notes – was adopted only reluctantly, when the old Soviet ruble zone broke up in 1992–93. Repeatedly, agreements have been signed with Russia calling for renewed monetary union between the two countries, most recently in 1999. Negotiations have been driven by the country's autocratic ruler, Aleksandr Lukashenko, whose fondest dream has been to engineer a political reunification with Russia. Moscow, however, is at best a grudging partner, wary of taking responsibility for Belarus's feeble economy. The Russians have been prepared to sign one document after another to appease a strategically placed segment of their "near abroad." But they have clearly been averse to going any further, toward any kind of practical implementation. Each accord, Russia's foreign minister has said pointedly, is "a declaration, not a treaty."[10] Belarus may be eager for monetary union, but like Canada and New Zealand it lacks a willing partner.

Insufficient solidarity

Elsewhere, as indicated, monetary unions have been proposed that would build on regional integration projects already in existence. But nowhere does the local sense of solidarity seem sufficient to sustain the requisite degree of commitment.

East Asia

One region where monetary union has come up for a good deal of discussion is East Asia. Particularly since the financial crisis that hit the area in 1997–98, the idea has been widely mooted as a safeguard against future disruptions. The crisis seemed to suggest that the cost of defending diverse national currencies was, for most regional governments, becoming too high to bear. Perhaps a single regional currency could serve their interests better.

Typical were the remarks of the head of Hong Kong's monetary authority in early 1999, calling for an Asian monetary union to make the region less vulnerable to speculative attacks. "The time may come," he averred, "when we may want to consider the possibility of our own Asian currency."[11] The goal of a joint money has been promoted by Mahathir Mohamad of Malaysia[12] and has been formally endorsed as a "distinct possibility" by the heads of government of the Association of Southeast Asian Nations (ASEAN).[13] Numerous private specialists have also spoken in favor, including most notably Nobel laureate Robert Mundell.[14] Most experts emphasize the potential saving of transactions costs involved as well as the prospect for greater insulation against future crises. A common currency would reduce the risk of incompatible exchange-rate movements or other negative regional spillovers of the sort observed after the Thai baht's crash in 1997. One economist with expertise in the region flatly predicts an Asian Monetary Union (AMU) by 2010 (Walter, 1998).

But there are problems – not least, the challenge of identifying just which countries might become involved. The ASEAN would seem to be the most natural focus. Its ten members are in the process of building a free-trade area, first agreed to in 1992. An AMU, like an ANZAC dollar or NAMU, would seem a logical next step. But not even ASEAN's most ardent admirers think it likely that a monetary merger can be negotiated any time soon. When asked about prospects for a common currency, ASEAN's secretary general looks around the room for the youngest person present and responds, "Perhaps in her lifetime."[15] Noting how long it took Europe to conceive the euro, the Philippines finance minister has grimly commented, "perhaps it will also take us that time."[16]

The reasons for such doubts are evident. In the first place the ASEAN partners are an obviously diverse lot in terms of economic structure and development, ranging from modern high-tech Singapore and emerging manufacturing centers like Malaysia and Thailand, to rural and still primarily agrarian economies such as Cambodia, Laos, and Myanmar. Trade relations tend to be highly diversified geographically, with relatively little intragroup trade, and there is no evidence of significant convergence in terms of either economic shocks or macroeconomic performance. Econometric studies confirm that the group remains far from anything that might be described as an optimum currency area (Eichengreen and Bayoumi, 1999), meaning that the economic costs of a merger could be painfully high.

Even more critically, ASEAN is still at an early stage of evolution as a political community. For all their protestations of amity, member governments remain noticeably distrustful of one another and place a high premium on preservation of as much national sovereignty as possible. In fact, the group is rife with historical antagonisms, ethnic and cultural conflicts, and border disputes. Unlike Europeans, East Asians are as yet unwilling to pay even lip service to the notion of "an ever closer union" among their peoples. Most, having only recently emerged from colonial status, are more intent on individual state-building than on promoting regional solidarity. Few demonstrate much inclination to define themselves in relation to one another rather than in their own terms.

Efforts to promote regional solidarity have not been absent, of course. On the contrary, ASEAN governments have invested considerable effort in building a variety of linkages across their borders, including not only their free-trade accord but also agreements to integrate key infrastructure elements like railways, high-ways, and electrical grids. In monetary matters, central banks have cultivated closer ties through annual meetings of governors and enhanced cooperation on training and technical matters, and member-states have several times pledged to institute a system of mutual surveillance of economic policies. For the most part, however, ASEAN governments continue to rely primarily on informal arrangements and market processes rather than formal institutions to pursue their objectives. The ASEAN, they insist, is a voluntary association of independent states, not an EU in the making. Representative are the admonitory words of the managing director of Singapore's monetary authority: "Eventually some form of cooperation will emerge as market forces bring about economic integration. I would caution against forcing the process."[17]

Mercosur

The story is much the same in Mercosur, the four-member Common Market of the South located in the southern cone of South America, where there has also been discussion of a possible monetary union. These countries too have had their share of currency crises, including Brazil's devaluation in 1999 and the collapse of Argentina's currency board in late 2001. However, these too are a diverse lot in terms of economic structure and development and are still at an early stage of evolution as a political community. Willing partners for a monetary merger are in scarce supply in Mercosur as well.

Recent discussion was kicked off by Carlos Menem when he was still president of Argentina, who began calling for a common currency for Mercosur as early as 1997. Part of Menem's motivation was to find a way to prevent Argentina's peso – tied as it was by its now-defunct currency board to the strong U.S. dollar – from appreciating relative to the Brazilian real. Argentina needed to maintain price competitiveness in relation to its biggest trading partner. Partly also he was driven by a genuine commitment to Mercosur as an integration project. Although his proposal initially received a frosty reception from the government of Brazilian President Fernando Cardoso, a common currency has now officially become part of Mercosur's agenda. Brazil's early response was motivated mainly by a visceral distaste for any sharing of monetary sovereignty. But by the end of 1999,

President Cardoso had publicly warmed to the idea, saying that "[i]t takes some time to realize just how ... important it is."[18] Cardoso's newfound enthusiasm was echoed in turn by his successor, Luiz Inácio Lula da Silva, following presidential elections in late 2002.[19] At the end of 2000, a timetable was agreed for a "mini-Maastricht" – a set of macroeconomic convergence targets similar to those specified by the EU's Maastricht Treaty – aiming to establish the preconditions for an eventual monetary union. The long-term goal of a joint currency is now regularly endorsed at Mercosur meetings.

In practice, however, no one expects to see a monetary merger any time soon. The idea has its fans. But as one informed observer suggests (Wheatley, 2001:25): "The idea of creating a common currency à la the euro remains a distant dream." One reason is that like ASEAN, Mercosur is still far from anything that might be described as an optimum currency area, as numerous studies attest (Levy-Yeyati and Sturzenegger, 2000). Hence, as in ASEAN, the economic costs of a merger could be painfully high. Price trends and cyclical developments in the participating economies remain highly divergent. Mercosur is still not even a true common market, despite the pledges that were made to remove all mutual trade barriers when the group was started back in 1988. In fact there was some regression after the start of 1999, when Brazil's devaluation led to new import restraints in Argentina and tit-for-tat retaliation by the Brazilians. Intra-Mercosur trade dropped from a high of 25 percent of member exports in 1998 to under 18 percent three years later. Some hope for greater macroeconomic convergence was raised after Argentina abandoned its currency board in late 2001, but little progress seemed likely in the short term.

Even more critically, the four participants are also still far apart politically, all protestations to the contrary notwithstanding. This is especially true of the group's two dominant members, Argentina and Brazil, traditional rivals for South American leadership. Despite their historic reconciliation in the late 1980s, which made Mercosur possible, the Argentines and Brazilians remain wary of one other and fundamentally resistant to any initiative that might make one subject to the dominance of the other. On both sides, political elites have shown great reluctance to cede any significant amount of policy autonomy to joint institutions (Kaltenthaler and Mora, 2002). Real progress toward a Mercosur common currency will be impossible without a much higher level of mutual trust between these two uneasy neighbors.

The Caribbean

Monetary union has also come up for discussion in the Caribbean, building on the already established Eastern Caribbean Currency Union. The six sovereign members of the ECCU, embedded in a network of related agreements including the Eastern Caribbean Common Market and the Organization of Eastern Caribbean States, are in turn partnered with eight neighboring states in a broader regional grouping known as the Caribbean Community and Common Market (CARICOM).[20] In 1992, the governors of CARICOM central banks put forward a detailed proposal to launch a Caribbean Monetary Union (CMU) to include all members of CARICOM by the year 2000. The plan was quickly accepted in principle by CARICOM heads of government and officially remains a key objective of the organization.

In practice, however, CMU remains a distant dream. The 2000 deadline has long since passed, and few in the region expect to see the birth of a new joint money any time soon. Typical are the words of the prime minister of Barbados, speaking in 1999: "The ideal is to achieve the common currency.... We know it can work. But it took the Europeans forty years to do it.... This will take some time."[21] Little has been done to formally implement the 1992 plan, which many informed observers regard as unrealistic for such a diverse set of economies (Anthony and Hughes Hallett, 2000). Though all are relatively small and open, they differ greatly in level of development and export structure. Some, like the ECCU states as well as Bahamas and Barbados, rely mainly on tourism and services, while others depend more on mining (Guyana, Suriname), oil and petrochemicals (Trinidad and Tobago), or light manufacturing (Haiti, Jamaica). The CMU has been justified, first and foremost, as a way of imposing discipline on the more inflationary members of CARICOM. (The worst offenders have been Jamaica and Suriname.) But despite the existence of multiple economic and political linkages, the notion has been resisted by some non-ECCU countries fearful of any compromise of their traditional monetary sovereignty. Most of the non-ECCU countries prefer to continue producing and managing their own separate currencies, however uncompetitive they may be.

West Africa

A detailed plan to launch a new monetary union has also been agreed to by six countries of West Africa – Gambia, Ghana, Guinea, Liberia, Nigeria, and Sierra Leone. All are members of the Economic Community of West African States (ECOWAS) together with the eight members of the West African Economic and Monetary Union (WAEMU), which in turn is part of the CFA Franc Zone. In April 2000, the leaders of the six non-CFA members of ECOWAS declared their intention to complete a "second" monetary union among themselves by January 2003, as a first step toward a wider merger to include all ECOWAS states by 2004. Initially, the six agreed to create a Convergence Council to help coordinate monetary policies, as well as a West African Monetary Institute to begin setting up a central bank. Eventually, the new monetary authority would be consolidated with the already existing central bank of WAEMU, the Banque Central des Etats de l'Afrique de l'Ouest (BCEAO).

The West African plan is ambitious and, if ultimately it were to combine with all of the CFA Franc Zone, could encompass nearly half the states of sub-Saharan Africa. Proponents stress the usual efficiency gains of a common currency and discount any costs that might be involved. In the words of a member of the ECOWAS Secretariat,[22] "Given the propensity over the years for monetary mismanagement in West Africa, the costs associated with the loss of national monetary instruments would not really amount to much." Much emphasis is also placed on the psychological importance of monetary union as a high-profile symbol of regional integration. Officials acknowledge that their inspiration comes directly from the euro and its role in the promotion of European unity (Irving, 2001).

Others, however, question whether the project is realistic. At a technical level, the challenges are considerable. On the model of the EU's Maastricht Treaty, the plan calls for each country to meet a number of macroeconomic convergence criteria no later than 2003, requiring inter alia steep reductions in inflation rates and budget deficits. Given past policy performance in the region, many wonder whether all this could really be accomplished in two years – or even in ten or twenty. As one analysis dryly comments (Masson and Pattillo, 2001:7), "it is not clear how the list of planned policy measures can be reconciled with the timetable." Likewise, does it really make sense to create an entirely new monetary authority for the six, only to merge it with the BCEAO a year later? Once established, would the new central bank truly be prepared to give up its institutional independence? The practical obstacles to implementation seem imposing.

Even more formidable are challenges at the political level. Apart from their common membership in ECOWAS, the six states have few direct linkages. Even a minimal sense of community is missing. Mutual trade is small, at a little over ten percent of the average of exports and imports, while historical antagonisms in some instances remain deep and persistent. Moreover, most of these countries have only recently emerged from extended civil strife, making implementation of such demanding new commitments highly problematic.

The project's best hope is that Nigeria, by far the biggest state in the region, might play the role of supportive hegemon. The political will appears to be there. Indeed, it was as a direct result of Nigeria's leadership, together with Ghana, that the six countries were able to reach agreement in the first place. But even if the Nigerians are willing to lead, will others be prepared to follow? It could be difficult enough to persuade other former British colonies in the region, each determined to assert its own distinct nationality, to cede pride of place to Nigeria. It would undoubtedly be even more distasteful to the francophone states of the CFA Franc Zone, with their quite different cultural and political orientations.

In fact, prospects for full implementation of the West African plan are limited at best. Nor, despite much talk, does there seem any likelihood of new currency mergers elsewhere on the African continent, according to recent studies (Honohan and Lane, 2001). In Africa, as in the Caribbean, there is still much resistance to any significant compromise of monetary sovereignty.

The Persian Gulf

Finally, there is the strategic Persian Gulf, where since 1981 the six Arab monarchies of Bahrain, Kuwait, Oman, Qatar, Saudi Arabia, and the United Arab Emirates have been grouped together in a loose association known as the Gulf Cooperation Council (GCC). The GCC was initially established as a security alliance, to help safeguard members against possible fallout from the 1979 revolution in Iran and the Iran-Iraq War that began in 1980. To say that the Gulf region was – and, for that matter, still is – unstable would be an understatement. Six countries that otherwise had never felt much solidarity with one another were drawn together in hopes of better protecting themselves against threats of external aggression or internal unrest.

Interpreting security broadly, the GCC soon added an economic dimension with a Unified Economic Agreement in 1982, inter alia calling on the six partners to "seek to coordinate their financial, monetary and banking policies and enhance cooperation between monetary agencies and central banks, including an endeavor to establish a common currency."[23] In matters of trade the economic agreement has been relatively successful, leading to the elimination of all customs duties among the members and a broad harmonization of external tariff rates. But in matters of money little has been done, in practical terms, to translate rhetoric into accomplishment, despite repeated reaffirmations of monetary union as a goal. The closest members have come to serious action was in 1987, when they agreed in principle to coordinate their exchange rates. But the effort was soon abandoned when governments could not concur on a common anchor. Little evidence exists of any degree of macroeconomic convergence.

More recently, at a summit meeting in January 2002, GCC leaders renewed their call for a common currency as part of a broad plan for deepening their economic integration. But the deadline for the projected monetary merger was set for 2010, far enough in the future so that, conveniently, no immediate action would be required. Few observers expect to see significant progress any time soon.

Conclusion

The conclusion, then, is plain. Predictions of many full new monetary unions around the globe, on the model of Europe's EMU, appear premature at best. The difficulty of defending uncompetitive national currencies is certainly growing. But for most governments, the disadvantages of monetary union continue to look more formidable still. Few states share enough group loyalty to make the requisite sacrifice of monetary sovereignty seem acceptable: and even for those that might be prepared to make the commitment, willing partners are hard to find.

Of course, full monetary union is not the only option. Less demanding forms of alliance strategy are also possible, requiring something short of a complete pooling of monetary sovereignty. Indeed, much room exists for variation in the degree of formal authority to be delegated to joint institutions to accommodate the interests of individual countries. Monetary powers need not be as centralized as they are in the ECCU and EMU. The merit of a more decentralized alliance is that it offers a possible compromise between the pressure of defending uncompetitive national currencies and the lack of willing partners for a full monetary union. Policies can be decided jointly, including especially goals for monetary growth and interest rates, but implemented individually in accordance with local circumstances. Likewise, the degree of fixity of exchange rates can be made a matter of negotiation. The idea is to enhance the market appeal of participating currencies while retaining at least some of the historical advantages of monetary sovereignty. Might some governments elect this more limited option?

In the case of possible bilateral mergers, the answer is almost certainly negative. Smaller countries like Canada, New Zealand, and Belarus, seeking an alliance with a much larger neighbor, might see virtue in the option. They would gain a voice in joint decision making yet not lose their own national currency. But they would face the same problem as with a full monetary union – namely, lack of a willing partner. For the United States, Australia, or Russia, there would be little direct benefit in sharing even a limited amount of their monetary authority with a smaller neighbor. Their interests would be better served if the smaller neighbor simply adopted the larger neighbor's currency as their own, as Australians suggest to New Zealand.

Elsewhere, where monetary union is discussed in the context of a broader integration project, the probability of some lesser form of monetary alliance is greater. In some instances, a foundation is already laid – in Mercosur, for instance, with its intended "mini-Maastricht," or in West Africa with its Convergence Council and Monetary Institute. In others, the task will be to build on related institutional links and commitments. Chances that governments will elect to go this route are lowest in places like the Caribbean or Africa, where ties to the United States or Europe are also strong. In these regions, many countries might be attracted more to some form of currency board or hard peg anchored on either the dollar (in the Caribbean) or the euro (in Africa). Chances would be higher in regions where there is no obvious alternative to such an approach, as in ASEAN, Mercosur, or the Gulf. In these groups, there will be more incentive for a mutual commitment of some sort. At a minimum, a limited partnership might enhance the market appeal of their individual currencies. At a maximum, it could eventually generate the kind of like-mindedness that is needed to realize the still distant goal of a common currency.

In short, *pace* Michel Camdessus, George von Furstenberg, and others, the number of currencies around the world is not about to shrink dramatically. The world's monetary map may include a growing number of limited alliances but few, if any, new joint currencies like the euro. Monetary unions are not inevitable. Quite the contrary, in fact. The purported wave of the future, most likely, will turn out to be little more than a ripple.

Notes

1 For more discussion see Cohen (1998).
2 This interpretation of the historical record, first articulated in 1994 in an earlier edition of Cohen, 2001, has been explicitly endorsed by most subsequent discussions. See, for example, Goodhart, 1998; Bordo and Jonung, 1999. Objections to my analysis have been raised by only one source. Andrews and Willett, 1997, who contend that a combination of economic and organizational factors perform as well as the political considerations I identify as decisive – despite the fact that, as Andrews and Willett themselves admit, half the cases examined fail to confirm their alternative view.

3 This type of linkage is stressed as well by Scott Cooper (1999), in a systematic political analysis of regional monetary cooperation. Cooperation is facilitated, he argues, by a high level of intraregional trust, which may be understood as synonymous with what I call a sense of solidarity or community.

4 Though of recent origin, the current debate in Canada actually has roots going back to the first days of Canada's national currency in the nineteenth century, as Eric Helleiner (2003) has ably demonstrated.

5 See, for example, Laidler, 1999; McCallum, 1999.

6 Sherry Cooper, as quoted in the *Globe and Mail*, 9 November 2001:B1.

7 As reported in the *Dominion* (Wellington), 20 September 2000: 12.

8 As quoted in the *International Herald Tribune*, 19 September 2000:17.

9 Press conference, 13 September 2000 (available at http://www.treasurer.gov.au).

10 Igor Ivanov, as quoted in the *New York Times*, 26 December 1998: Al.

11 Joseph Yam, as quoted in the *Financial Times*, 6 January 1999.

12 See, for example, *The Economist*, 19 December 1999:47.

13 Final communiqué of the meeting of ASEAN heads of government in Manila, Philippines, 28 November 1999.

14 As reported in *IMF Survey*, 8 October 2001:318–319.

15 Rodolfo Severino, as quoted in *The Economist*, 12 February 2000.

16 Edgardo Espiritu, as quoted in *The Economist*, 12 February 2000.

17 Tharman Shanmugaratnam, as quoted in the *Financial Times*, 5 June 2001.

18 As quoted in the *Financial Times*, 10 November 1999:19.

19 See, e.g., the *New York Times*, 3 December 2002:A6.

20 The six sovereign members of the ECCU are Antigua and Barbuda, Dominica, Grenada, St. Kitts and Nevis, St. Lucia, and St. Vincent and the Grenadines (along with two British dependencies, Anguilla and Montserrat). The eight neighboring states that are their partners in CARICOM are Bahamas, Barbados, Belize, Guyana, Haiti, Jamaica, Suriname, and Trinidad and Tobago.

21 Owen Arthur, as quoted in *Journal of Commerce*, 7 December 1999:17.

22 R. D. Asante, head of the Money and Payments Division of the ECOWAS Secretariat, in Irving, 2001:26.

23 GCC Unified Economic Agreement, 8 June 1982, Article 22.

References

Alesina, A. (2001) Interview. *IMF Survey*, July 2.

Andrews, D. M., and T. D. Willett (1997) "Financial Interdependence and the State: International Monetary Relations at Century's End." *International Organization* 51(3):479–511.

Anthony, M. L., and A. Hughes Hallett (2000) "Is the Case for Economic and Monetary Union in the Caribbean Realistic?" *The World Economy* 23(1):119–144.

Arora, V., and O. Jeanne (2001) *Economic Integration and the Exchange Rate Regime: Some Lessons from Canada*. Policy discussion paper PDP/01/1. Washington, DC: International Monetary Fund.

Bordo, M. D., and L. Jonung (1999) *The Future of EMU: What Does the History of Monetary Unions Tell Us?* Working paper 7365. Cambridge, MA: National Bureau of Economic Research.

Camdessus, M. (2000) Council on Foreign Relations Address. *IMF Survey*, February 7.

Centre for Research and Information on Canada (2002) *Portraits of Canada 2001*. Montreal, Quebec: CRIC.

Cohen, B. J. (1998) *The Geography of Money*. Ithaca, NY: Cornell University Press.

Cohen, B. J. (2001) "Beyond EMU: The Problem of Sustainability." In *Political Economy of European Monetary Unification*, 2nd ed., edited by B. Eichengreen and J. A. Frieden, pp. 179–204. Boulder, CO: Westview Press.

Cooper, S. B. (1999) *Regional Monetary Cooperation Beyond Western Europe*. Ph.D. dissertation, Duke University.

Courchene, T. J. (1999) "Towards a North American Common Currency: An Optimal Currency Area Analysis." In *Room to Manoeuvre? Globalization and Policy Convergence*, edited by T. J. Courchene, pp. 271–334. Kingston, ON: Queens University.

de Brouwer, G. (2000) "ANZAC Dollar." *Agenda* 7(3):273–276.

Drew, A., V. Hall, J. McDermott, and R. St. Clair (2001) *Would Adopting the Australian Dollar Provide Superior Monetary Policy in New Zealand?* Discussion paper DP2001/03. Wellington, NZ: Reserve Bank of New Zealand.

Eichengreen, B., and T. Bayoumi (1999) "Is Asia an Optimum Currency Area? Can It Become One? Regional, Global, and Historical Perspectives on Asian Monetary Relations." In *Exchange Rate Policies in Emerging Asian Countries*, edited by S. Collignon, J. Pisani-Ferry, and Y. Chul Park, pp. 347–366. London: Routledge.

Goodhart, C. A. E. (1995) "The Political Economy of Monetary Union." In *Understanding Interdependence: The Macroeconomics of the Open Economy*, edited by P. B. Kenen, pp. 448–505. Princeton, NJ: Princeton University Press.

Goodhart, C. A. E. (1998) "The Two Concepts of Money: Implications for the Analysis of Optimal Currency Areas." *European Journal of Political Economy* 14:407–432.

Grimes, A. (2000) "An Anzac Dollar: Does It Make Sense?" *Policy* 16(3):10–14.

Grimes, A., and F. Holmes (2000) *An ANZAC Dollar? Currency Union and Business Development*. Wellington, NZ: Victoria University, Institute of Policy Studies.

Grubel, H. G. (1999) *The Case for the Amero: The Economics and Politics of a North American Monetary Union*. Vancouver, BC: Simon Fraser Institute.

Hargreaves, D., and J. McDermott (1999) "Issues Relating to Optimal Currency Areas: Theory and Implications for New Zealand." *Reserve Bank of New Zealand. Bulletin* 62(3):16–29.

Harris, R. G. (2001) "Mundell and Friedman: Four Key Disagreements." *Policy Options/ Options Politiques* (May):34–36.

Helleiner, E. (2003) "Toward a North American Common Currency?" In *Changing Canada: Political Economy as Transformation*, edited by W. Clement and L. Vosko. Montreal: McGill-Queen's University Press, forthcoming.

Honohan, P., and P. Lane (2001) "Will the Euro Trigger More Monetary Unions in Africa?" In *The Impact of EMU on Europe and the Developing Countries*, edited by C. Wyplosz, pp. 315–338. Oxford: Oxford University Press.

Irving, J. (2001) "The Pros and Cons of Expanded Monetary Union in West Africa." *Finance and Development* (March):24–28.

Kaltenthaler, K., and F. O. Mora (2002) "Explaining Latin American Economic Integration: The Case of Mercosur." *Review of International Political Economy* 9(1):72–97.

Keohane, R. O., and S. Hoffmann (1991) "Institutional Change in Europe in the 1980s." In *The New European Community: Decisionmaking and Institutional Change*, edited by R. O. Keohane and S. Hoffmann, ch. 1. Boulder, CO: Westview Press.

Laidler, D. (1999) "Canada's Exchange Rate Options." *Canadian Public Policy/Analyse de Politiques* 25(3):324–332.

Lake, D. A. (1993) "Leadership, Hegemony, and the International Economy: Naked Emperor or Tattered Monarch with Potential?" *International Studies Quarterly* 37(4):459–489.

Levy-Yeyati, E., and F. Sturzenegger (2000) "Is EMU a Blueprint for Mercosur?" *Latin American Journal of Economics* 110:63–99.

Litfin, K. (1997) "Sovereignty in World Ecopolitics." *Mershon International Studies Review* 41(2):167–204.

Martin, L. L., and B. Simmons (1999) "Theories and Empirical Studies of International Institutions." In *Exploration and Contestation in the Study of World Politics*, edited by P. J. Katzenstein, R. O. Keohane, and S. D. Krasner, pp. 89–117. Cambridge, MA: MIT Press.

Masson, P. R., and C. Pattillo (2001) *Monetary Union in West Africa: An Agency of Restraint for Fiscal Policies?* Working paper WP/01/34. Washington, DC: International Monetary Fund.

McCallum, J. (2000) "Engaging the Debate: Costs and Benefits of a North American Common Currency." *Current Analysis*, Royal Bank of Canada (April).

Scrimgeour, D. (2002) "Exchange Rate Volatility and Currency Union: New Zealand Evidence." Unpublished paper. Wellington, NZ: Reserve Bank of New Zealand.

von Furstenberg, G. M. (2000a) "Can Small Countries Keep Their Own Money and Floating Exchange Rates." In *Shaping a New International Financial System*, edited by K. Kaiser, J. J. Kirton, and J. P. Daniels, pp. 187–202. Aldershot, UK: Ashgate.

von Furstenberg, G. M. (2000b) "A Case Against U.S. Dollarization." *Challenge* 43(4):108–120.

Walter, N. (1998) "An Asian Prediction." *The International Economy* 12(3):49.

Wheatley, J. (2001) "The Mercosur Marriage Is in Trouble." *Business Week*, January 29, p. 25.

Bibliography

The complete works of Benjamin J. Cohen

Books (authored)

Cohen, Benjamin J. (1969) *Balance-of-Payments Policy*, London and Baltimore: Penguin Books.
[Spanish-language edition: Madrid, Alianza Editorial, 1975]
—— (1971) *The Future of Sterling as an International Currency*, London: Macmillan.
[American edition: New York, St. Martin's Press, 1972]
—— (1973) *The Question of Imperialism: the political economy of dominance and dependence*, New York: Basic Books.
[British edition: Macmillan Ltd., 1974]
[Portuguese-language edition: Rio de Janeiro, Zahar Editores, 1976]
[Spanish-language edition: Mexico City, Editores Associados, 1977]
[Special edition in simplified English: United States International Communications Agency, Current Thought Series, 1979; subsequently published in Thai, Korean, and Arabic translations]
—— (1977) *Organizing the World's Money: the political economy of international monetary relations*, New York: Basic Books.
[British edition: Macmillan Ltd., 1978]
[Spanish-language edition: Mexico City, Fondo de Cultura Economica, 1981]
—— (1981) *Banks and the Balance of Payments: private lending in the international adjustment process*, in collaboration with Fabio Basagni, Montclaire, New Jersey: Allenheld Osmun for the Atlantic Institute for International Affairs.
[British edition: Croom Helm, 1981]
[Italian-language edition: Bologna, Il Mulino, 1982]
—— (1986) *In Whose Interest? International Banking and American Foreign Policy*, New Haven, CT and London, England: Yale University Press for the Council on Foreign Relations.
[Spanish-language edition: Mexico City, Editorial Limusa, 1990]
—— (1991) *Crossing Frontiers: explorations in international political economy*, Boulder, CO: Westview Press.
—— (1998) *The Geography of Money*, Ithaca and London: Cornell University Press.
[Korean-language edition: Seoul, ShiYu Shi Publishing, 1999]
[Japanese-language edition: Tokyo, Springer Verlag Tokyo, 2000]
[Chinese-language edition: Southwest Financial University Press, 2004]
—— (2004) *The Future of Money*, Princeton, NJ: Princeton University Press.
—— (2006) *The Future of the Dollar*, Hyderabad, India: ICFAI University Press.

Books (edited or co-edited)

Cohen, Benjamin J. (1968) *American Foreign Economic Policy: essays and comments*, New York: Harper and Row. [editor and contributor]

—— (1993) *The International Political Economy of Monetary Relations*, London: Edward Elgar Publishing. [editor and contributor]

—— (1997) *International Trade and Finance: new frontiers for research, essays in honor of Peter B. Kenen*, New York: Cambridge University Press. [editor and contributor]

—— (1999) *Issues and Agents in International Political Economy: an International Organization reader*, edited with Charles Lipson, MIT Press.

—— (1999) *Theory and Structure in International Political Economy: an International Organization reader*, edited with Charles Lipson, MIT Press.

—— (2004) *International Monetary Relations in the New Global Economy*, two volumes, London: Edward Elgar Publishing. [editor and contributor]

—— (2005) *International Political Economy*, London: Ashgate. [editor]

Monographs

Cohen, Benjamin J. (1966) *Adjustment Costs and the Distribution of New Reserves*, Princeton Studies in International Finance, No. 18, Princeton: International Finance Section.

—— (1969) *The Reform of Sterling*, Princeton Essays in International Finance, No. 77, Princeton: International Finance Section.

—— (1974) *Commercial Policy*, General Learning Press Module in Economics, Morristown, New Jersey: General Learning Press.

—— (1981) *The European Monetary System: an outsider's view*, Princeton Essays in International Finance, No. 142, Princeton: International Finance Section.

—— (1989) *Developing-Country Debt: a middle way*, Princeton Essays in International Finance, No. 173, Princeton: International Finance Section.

—— (1997) *The Financial Support Fund of the OECD: a failed initiative*, Princeton Essays in International Finance, No. 204, Princeton: International Finance Section.

—— (2000) *Life at the Top: international currencies in the twenty-first century*, Princeton Essays in International Economics, No. 221, Princeton: International Economics Section.

Contributions to conference proceedings and edited volumes

Cohen, Benjamin J. (1968–1975) "Foreign Economic Aid," "Foreign Exchange," and "International Trade," annual contributions to *Funk and Wagnalls New Encyclopedia*, New York: Funk and Wagnalls, Inc.

—— (1972) "Foreign Trade," "Free Trade and Protection," "Tariffs," and "Tariffs, United States," in *Funk and Wagnalls New Encyclopedia*, New York: Funk and Wagnalls, Inc.

—— (1972) "Stabilization Policies in a Dependent Economy: comment," in Emil Claassen and Pascal Salin (eds) *Stabilization Policies in Interdependent Economies*, Amsterdam: North-Holland Publishing Co.

—— (1972) "The United Kingdom as an Exporter of Capital," in Fritz Machlup, Walter S. Salant, and Lorie Tarshis (eds) *International Mobility and Movement of Capital*, New York: National Bureau of Economic Research.

—— (1973) "On United States 'Imperialism'," in James H. Weaver (ed.) *Modern Political Economy: radical and orthodox views on crucial issues*, Boston: Allyn and Bacon.

Cohen, Benjamin J. (1974) "The Historical Setting: comments," in Lawrence B. Krause and Walter S. Salant (eds) *European Monetary Unification and Its Meaning for the United States*, Washington: Brookings Institution.

—— (1974) "The Revolution in Atlantic Economic Relations: a bargain comes unstuck," in W.F. Hanrieder (ed.) *The United States and Western Europe: Political, Economic and Strategic Perspectives*, Cambridge, MA: Winthrop Publishers.

—— (1975) "International Reserves and Liquidity," in Peter B. Kenen (ed.) *International Trade and Finance: frontiers for research*, New York and Cambridge: Cambridge University Press.

—— (1976) "Major Issues of World Monetary Reform," in *Critical Choices for Americans*, Vol. 5, *Trade, Inflation and Ethics*, Lexington, MA: D.C. Heath.

—— (1976) "Mixing Oil and Money," in J.C. Hurewitz (ed.) *Oil, the Arab-Israel Dispute, and the Industrial World: horizons of crisis*, Boulder, CO: Westview Press.

—— (1976) "Problems of Organizing the International Monetary Order," in Fabio Basagni (ed.) *International Monetary Relations After Jamaica*, Atlantic Papers, 4/1986, Paris: Atlantic Institute for International Affairs.

—— (1977) "Great Britain," in Wilfrid F. Kohl (ed.) *Economic Foreign Policies of Industrial States*, Lexington, MA: D.C. Heath.

—— (1979) "The European Monetary System in the Broader Setting of the Community's Economic and Political Development: comments," in Philip H. Trezise (ed.) *The European Monetary System: its promise and prospects*, Washington: Brookings Institution.

—— (1980) "United States Monetary Policy and Economic Nationalism," in Otto Hieronymi (ed.) *The New Economic Nationalism*, London: Macmillan.

—— (1980) Contributor to dialogue recorded in Randall Hinshaw (ed.) *Domestic Goals and Financial Interdependence: the Frankfurt dialogue*, New York and Basle: Marcel Dekker.

—— (1980) Contributor to roundtable discussion recorded in Wilfrid L. Kohl and Giorgio Basevi (eds) *West Germany: a European and global power*, Lexington, MA: D.C. Heath.

—— (1980) "The EMS, the Dollar and the Future of the International Monetary System – An American View," in Giorgio Basevi and Wilfrid L. Kohl (eds) *The Political Economy of the European Monetary System: a conference report*, Occasional Paper No. 31, Bologna, Italy: Johns Hopkins University Research Institute.

—— (1981) "Balancing the System in the 1980s: private banks and the IMF," in Gary Clyde Hufbauer (ed.) *The International Framework for Money and Banking in the 1980s*, Washington: International Law Institute.

—— (1982) "Three Challenges for Better International Monetary Management," in Gregory Flynn (ed.) *Economic Interests in the 1980s: convergence or divergence?* Atlantic Papers, No. 44–45, Paris: Atlantic Institute for International Affairs. [This paper was published under the same title in *Fletcher Forum*, 6:6 (Summer 1982), and under the title "L'avenir du système monétaire international" in *Politique Étrangère*, No. 1 (March 1980).]

—— (1983) "Balance-of-Payments Financing: evolution of a regime," in Stephen D. Krasner (ed.) *International Regimes*, Ithaca, NY: Cornell University Press. [This volume was first published as a special issue of *International Organization*, 36:2 (Spring 1982).]

—— (1983) "An Explosion in the Kitchen? Economic Relations with Other Advanced Industrial States," in Kenneth Oye, Robert Lieber, and Donald Rothchild (eds) *Eagle Defiant: United States foreign policy in the 1980s*, Boston: Little, Brown.

—— (1984) "High Finance, High Politics," in Richard E. Feinberg and Valeriana Kallab (eds) *Uncertain Future: commercial banks and Third World debt*, New Brunswick, NJ: Transactions Books for the Overseas Development Council.

—— (1986) "Politics, Trade and Money: comment," in Loukas Tsoukalis (ed.) *Europe, America and the World Economy*, Oxford: Basil Blackwell.

—— (1986) "International Debt and Linkage Strategies: some foreign-policy implications for the United States," in Miles Kahler (ed.) *The Politics of International Debt*, Ithaca, NY: Cornell University Press. [This chapter was first published in *International Organization*, 39:4 (Autumn 1985).]

—— (1987) "An Explosion in the Kitchen? Economic Relations with Other Advanced Industrial States," in Kenneth Oye, Robert Lieber, and Donald Rothchild (eds) *Eagle Resurgent? The Reagan Era in American Foreign Policy*, Boston: Little, Brown. [This chapter updates an earlier version published under the same title in *Eagle Defiant* (1983).]

—— (1987) "Implications of the European Monetary System for Developing Nations," in Sidney Dell (ed.) *The International Monetary System and its Reform*, Papers prepared for the Group of Twenty-Four, Part I, Amsterdam: North-Holland.

—— (1988) "Global Debt: why is cooperation so difficult?" in Paolo Guerrieri and Pier-Carlo Padoan (eds) *The Political Economy of International Cooperation*, London: Croom Helm.

—— (1989) "European Financial Integration and National Banking Interests," in Pier-Carlo Padoan and Paolo Guerrieri (eds) *The Political Economy of European Integration*, London: Harvester Wheatsheaf.

—— (1989) "LDC Debt: toward a genuinely cooperative solution," in Omar Hamouda, Robin Rowley, and Bernard Wolf (eds) *The Future of the International Monetary System: change, coordination or instability?* London: Edward Elgar.

—— (1989) "LDC Debt: is activism required?" in Graham Bird (ed.) *Third World Debt: the search for a solution*, London: Edward Elgar.

—— (1989) "The Brady Plan: good news and bad," in Mojmir Mrak (ed.) *External Debt Problem: current issues and perspectives*, Ljubljana, Yugoslavia: Centre for International Cooperation and Development.

—— (1990) "North American Policy Toward the International Credit Organizations," in Roberto Bouzas and Roberto Russell (eds) *Estados Unidos and la Transition Argentina*, Buenos Aires: Legasa.

—— (1990) "Debt and the International Financial System from the Perspective of the United States," in Eduardo Ferrero Costa (ed.) *La Reinsercion del Peru en el Sistema Financiero Internacional*, Lima: CEPEI.

—— (1992) "Towards a Mosaic Economy: relations with other advanced industrial nations," in Kenneth A. Oye, Robert J. Lieber, and Donald Rothchild (eds) *Eagle in a New World: American grand strategy in the post-Cold War era*, New York: Harper-Collins.

—— (1992) "U.S. Debt Policy in Latin America: the melody lingers on," in Robert Bottome *et al.*, *In the Shadow of the Debt: emerging issues in Latin America*, New York: Twentieth Century Fund.

—— (1992) "Currency Areas" and "Sterling Area," in Peter Newman, Murray Milgate, and John Eatwell (eds) *The New Palgrave Dictionary of Money and Finance*, London: Macmillan; and New York: Stockton.

—— (1993) "The Triad and the Unholy Trinity: lessons for the Pacific Region," in Richard A. Higgott, Richard Leaver, and John Ravenhill (eds) *Pacific Economic Relations in the 1990s: cooperation or conflict?* Sydney: Allen and Unwin and Boulder, CO: Lynne Rienner.

Cohen, Benjamin J. (1993) "Critical Questions on the Future Role of the ECU," in Leonce Bekemans and Loukas Tsoukalis (eds) *Europe and Global Economic Interdependence*, Brussels: European Interuniversity Press.

—— (1994) "Beyond EMU: the problem of sustainability," in Barry Eichengreen and Jeffry A. Frieden (eds) *The Political Economy of European Monetary Unification*, Boulder: Westview Press. [This essay was first published as part of a special issue of *Economics and Politics*, 5:2 (July 1993).]

—— (1996) "'Return to Normalcy'? Global Economic Policy at the End of the Century," in Robert J. Lieber (ed.) *Eagle Adrift: American foreign policy at the end of the century*, New York: Longman.

—— (1996) "Gulliver o Lilliputiense? Los Estados Unidos en la Economia Mundial de Hoy" ("Gulliver or Lilliputian? The United States in the World Economy Today"), in Roberto Bouzas and Roberto Russell (eds) *Globalizacion y Regionalismo en las Relaciones Internacionales de Estados Unidos*, Buenos Aires: Grupo Editor Latinamericano.

—— (1996) "La Dinámica de las Relaciones Económicas: viviendo con el elefante" ("The Dynamics of Economic Relations: living with the elephant"), in Felipe A.M. de la Balze and Eduardo A. Roca (eds) *Argentina y EE UU: Fundamentos de una Nueva Allianza*, Buenos Aires: Asociación de Bancos de la República Argentina.

—— (1997) "Dollar Diplomacy," "International Debt," and "Third World Debt," in Bruce W. Jentleson and Thomas G. Paterson (eds) *Encyclopedia of U.S. Foreign Relations*, New York: Oxford University Press.

—— (1997) "The Political Economy of Currency Regions," in Edward D. Mansfield and Helen V. Milner (eds) *The Political Economy of Regionalism*, New York: Columbia University Press.

—— (1997) "Optimum Currency Area Theory: bringing the market back in," in Benjamin J. Cohen (ed.) *International Trade and Finance: New Frontiers for Research*, New York: Cambridge University Press.

—— (1998) "When Giants Clash: the OECD financial support fund and the IMF," in Vinod D. Aggarwal (ed.) *Institutional Designs for a Complex World*, Ithaca: Cornell University Press.

—— (1999) "The New Geography of Money," in Emily Gilbert and Eric Helleiner (eds) *Nation-States and Money: the past, present and future of national currencies*, New York and London: Routledge.

—— (2000) "Marketing Money: currency policy in a globalized world," in Aseem Prakash and Jeffrey A. Hart (eds) *Coping with Globalization*, New York and London: Routledge.

—— (2000) "Money in a Globalized World," in Ngaire Woods (ed.) *The Political Economy of Globalization*, London: Macmillan.

—— (2000) "Taming the Phoenix? Monetary Governance After the Crisis," in Greg Noble and John Ravenhill (eds) *The Asian Financial Crisis and the Architecture of Global Finance*, Cambridge University Press.

—— (2000) "Money and Power in World Politics," in Thomas C. Lawton, James N. Rosenau, and Amy C. Verdun (eds) *Strange Power: shaping the parameters of international relations and international political economy*, Ashgate.

—— (2000) "La Política de las Uniones Monetarias: reflexiones para el mercosur," in Jorge Carrera and Federico Sturzenegger (eds) *Coordinación de Políticas Macroeconómicas en el Mercosur*, Buenos Aires: Fondo de Cultura Económica.

—— (2001) "Beyond EMU: the problem of sustainability," in Barry Eichengreen and Jeffry Frieden (eds) *The Political Economy of European Monetary Unification*, second edition, Westview.

—— (2001) "Containing Backlash: foreign economic policy in an age of globalization," in Robert J. Lieber (ed.) *Eagle Rules? Foreign Policy and American Primacy in the 21st Century*, Prentice Hall.

—— (2001) "EMU and the Developing Countries," in Charles Wyplosz (ed.) *The Impact of EMU on Europe and the Developing Countries*, Oxford University Press.

—— (2002) "International Finance," in Walter Carlsnaes, Thomas Risse, and Beth A. Simmons (eds) *Handbook of International Relations*, Sage.

—— (2002) "Bretton Woods system," in R.J. Barry Jones (ed.) *Routledge Encyclopedia of International Political Economy*, Routledge.

—— (2002) "Capital Controls: why do governments hesitate?" in Leslie Elliott Armijo (ed.) *Debating the Global Financial Architecture*, SUNY Press.

—— (2002) "Monetary Instability: are national currencies becoming obsolete?" in Stephen McBride *et al.* (eds) *Global Instability: uncertainty and new visions in political economy*, Kluwer Academic Publishers.

—— (2002) "Is a Dollarized Hemisphere in the U.S. Interest?" in Carl A. Cira and Elisa N. Gallo (eds) *Dollarization and Latin America: quick cure or bad medicine?* Summit of the Americas Center.

—— (2003) "Monetary Unions," *Online Encyclopedia of Economic History*, Available HTTP: <http://www.eh.net/encyclopedia>.

—— (2003) "Capital Controls: the neglected option," in Geoffrey R.D. Underhill and Xiaoke Zhang (eds) *International Financial Governance Under Stress: global structures versus national imperatives*, Cambridge University Press.

—— (2003) "Monetary Governance in a Globalized World," in C. Roe Goddard, Patrick Cronin, and Kishore C. Dash (eds) *International Political Economy*, 2nd edition, Lynne Rienner.

—— (2003) "Monetary Union: the political dimension," in Dominick Salvatore, James W. Dean, and Thomas D. Willett (eds) *The Dollarization Debate*, Oxford University Press.

—— (2003) "Monetary Governance in a World of Regional Currencies," in Miles Kahler and David A. Lake (eds) *Governance in a Global Economy*, Princeton University Press.

—— (2004) "America's Interest in Dollarization," in Volbert Alexander, Jacques Mélitz, and George M. von Furstenberg (eds) *Monetary Unions and Hard Pegs: effects on trade, financial development, and stability*, Oxford University Press.

—— (2005) "Living with the Euro: comment," in Loukas Tsoukalis (ed.) *Governance and Legitimacy in EMU*, Florence, Italy: European University Institute.

—— (2006) "Monetary Governance and Capital Mobility in Historical Perspective," in Rainer Grote and Thilo Marauhn (eds) *The Regulation of International Financial Markets: perspectives for reform*, Cambridge University Press.

—— (2006) "The Euro and Transatlantic Relations," in Thomas L. Ilgen (ed.) *Hard Power, Soft Power and the Future of Transatlantic Relations*, Ashgate.

—— (2006) "The Macrofoundations of Monetary Power," in David M. Andrews (ed.) *International Monetary Power*, Cornell University Press.

—— (2006) "Are National Currencies Becoming Obsolete?" in Giuseppe Felloni (ed.) *La Casa di San Giorgio: il potere del credito*, Genoa: Brigati.

—— (2006) "North American Monetary Union: A United States Perspective," in Amy Verdun (ed.) *Britain and Canada and their Large Neighboring Monetary Unions*, Nova Science Publishers.

—— (2007) "Enlargement and the International Role of the Euro," in Joaquin Roy and Pedro Gomis–Porqueras (eds) *The Euro and the Dollar in a Globalized Economy*, Ashgate.

Articles

Cohen, Benjamin J. (1963) "The Euro-Dollar, the Common Market, and Currency Unification," *Journal of Finance* Vol. 18 December.

—— (1964) "Balance of Payments Adjustment in a Disequilibrium System," *Kyklos* Vol. 17 March. [Co-authored with Staffan B. Linder]

—— (1964) "A Note on the Definition of International Liquidity," *Economia Internazionale* Vol. 17 August.

—— (1964) "Exchange Rates During the Process of Customs Union," *Oxford Economic Papers* Vol. 16 November.

—— (1965) "Capital Controls and the U.S. Balance of Payments: comment," *American Economic Review* Vol. 55 March.

—— (1967) "Can We Alter Tastes to Suit our Balance of Payments Problem?" *Challenge*, March/April.

—— (1967) "Voluntary Foreign Investment Curbs: a plan that really works," *Challenge*, March/April.

—— (1967) "Reparations in the Postwar Period: a survey," *Banca Nazionale del Lavoro Quarterly Review* No. 82 September.

—— (1969) "The Benefits and Costs of Sterling," *Euromoney*, September.

—— (1970) "Sterling and the City," *The Banker*, February.

—— (1970) "Measuring the Benefits and Costs of Sterling," *Euromoney*, April.

—— (1971) "U.S. Foreign Economic Policy in the 1970s," *ORBIS* Vol. 15 Spring.

—— (1971) "The Seigniorage Gain of an International Currency: an empirical test," *Quarterly Journal of Economics* Vol. 85 August.

—— (1971) "What to Do About Sterling," *Euromoney*, July.

—— (1971) "Sterling After the Vote," *International Currency Review*, November/December.

—— (1973) "The Future Role of Sterling," *National Westminster Bank Quarterly Review*, May.

—— (1976) "The Political Economy of Monetary Reform Today," *Journal of International Affairs* 30:1 Spring/Summer.

—— (1978) "Managing Floating Exchange Rates," *Intereconomics*, January/February [printed in German as *"Zur Steuerung floatender Wechselkurse," Wirtschafts Dienst*, July 1977].

—— (1978) "The U.S. Trade Deficit: a cause for alarm?" *Fletcher Forum* 2:2 May.

—— (1978) "Financial Aspects of the North-South Dialogue," *Marzhaye Now* [*New Frontiers*, a Farsi-language magazine once published in Iran] 22:6.

—— (1978) "Cutting Japan's Trade Surplus," *Challenge*, July/August.

—— (1979) "Europe's Money, America's Problem," *Foreign Policy* No. 35 Summer.

—— (1980) *"Le SME, le dollar, et l'avenir du système monétaire international"* ["EMS, the Dollar, and the Future of the International Monetary System"], *Politique Étrangère* No. 1 March.

—— (1980) "Inflation, the Terms of Trade and Flexible Exchange Rates: comment," *Kredit und Kapital*, Heft 6.

—— (1980) "Monetary Relations Between the U.S. and Japan," *Trends* [a Japanese-language magazine published in Japan] No. 10.

—— (1982) "Balance-of-Payments Financing: Evolution of a Regime," *International Organization* 36:2 Spring.

—— (1983) "Trade and Unemployment: Global Bread and Butter Issues," *Worldview* 26:1 January.

—— (1983) "Banking Gone Bad," *Worldview* 26:10 October.

—— (1985) "International Debt and Linkage Strategies: some foreign-policy implications for the United States," *International Organization* 39:4 Autumn.

—— (1988) "Bankruptcy Treatment for LDC Debt," *The International Economy* 2:6 November/December.

—— (1989) "Third World Debt: is there an unexploited opportunity for joint gain?" *Business in the Contemporary World* 1:2 Winter.

—— (1989) "A Global Chapter 11," *Foreign Policy* No. 75 Summer.

—— (1989) "Debtors in Wonderland," *Challenge*, November/December.

—— (1989) "The United States and the International Economic Scene," *Revista Espanola de Estudios Norteamericanos* No. 2 Autumn.

—— (1990) "The Political Economy of International Trade," *International Organization* 44:2 Spring.

—— (1991) "What Ever Happened to the LDC Debt Crisis?" *Challenge* May/June.

—— (1991) "Toward a Mosaic Economy: economic relations in the post-Cold War era," *The Fletcher Forum of World Affairs* 15:2 Summer.

—— (1993) "Beyond EMU: the problem of sustainability," *Economics and Politics* 5:2 July.

—— (1996) "Phoenix Risen: the resurrection of global finance," *World Politics* 48:2 January.

—— (1996) "EMU and the Dollar: who threatens whom?" *Swiss Political Science Review* 2:3 Fall.

—— (1997) *"L'Euro contre le Dollar: un défi pour qui?"* ["The Euro Against the Dollar: a challenge for whom?"], *Politique Étrangère* No. 4.

—— (1998) "Money in a Globalized World: from monopoly to oligopoly," *Oxford Development Studies* 26:1 February.

—— (2000) *"Dollarisation: la dimension politique"* ["Dollarization: the political dimension"], *L'Economie Politique* No. 5 January.

—— (2000) "Life at the Top: international currencies in the 21st century," *Latin American Journal of Economics* 110 April.

—— (2000) "Capital Controls: why do governments hesitate?" *Kokusai Kin-yuh/ International Finance Journal*, 15 September and 1 October (Japanese translation in two parts).

—— (2001) *"Contrôle des Capitaux: pourquoi les gouvernements hestitent-ils?"* ["Capital Controls: why do governments hesitate?"], *Revue Économique* 52:2 March.

—— (2001) *"Politica de los Estados Unidos sobre la dolarización: un análisis politico"* ["United States Policy on Dollarization: a political analysis"], *Cuestiones Económicas* 17:1 1st quarter.

—— (2001) "Electronic Money: new day or false dawn?" *Review of International Political Economy* 8:2 Summer.

—— (2002) *"Monnaie électronique: un jour nouveau ou une aube trompeuse?"* ["Electronic Money: new day or false dawn?"], *L'économie politique* No. 14 2e trimestre.

—— (2002) "U.S. Policy on Dollarization: a political analysis," *Geopolitics* 7:1 Summer.

—— (2003) "Are Monetary Unions Inevitable?" *International Studies Perspectives* 8:3 August.

—— (2003) "Global Currency Rivalry: can the euro ever challenge the dollar?" *Journal of Common Market Studies* 41:4 September.

—— (2003) "Pourquoi l'euro n'est pas près de remplacer le dollar," *L'Economie politique* No. 20 October.

—— (2005) "Dollarization, Rest In Peace," *International Journal of Political Economy* 33:1 Spring.

Cohen, Benjamin J. (2006) "North American Monetary Union: a United States perspective," *Current Economics and Politics of Europe* 17:1 January.

—— (2006) "The Euro and Transatlantic Relations" (Russian translation), *Ural Survey of International Studies.*

—— (2007) "The Transatlantic Divide: why are American and British ipe so different?", *Review of International Political Economy* 14:2 May.

Shorter commentaries

Cohen, Benjamin J. (1971) "Calling in Postwar Debts Won't Help," *Boston Globe*, 4 October.

—— (1983) "The Williamsburg Summit: a failure of political will," *Nihon Keizai Shimbun* [Japan Economic Journal], 20 June.

—— (1983–1985) "Current Account," *Worldview* [a bi-monthly column published June 1983–June 1985].

—— (1985) "The Politics of Latin Debt," *The New York Times*, 8 August [reprinted as "No Choice But to Shift the Burden," *International Herald Tribune*, 9 August l985].

—— (1986) "Let Them Eat Fantasy," *San Jose Mercury News*, 6 February.

—— (1987) "Third World Debt (Cont'd.)," *The New York Times*, 5 March [reprinted as "So Much for All That Progress on Debt," *International Herald Tribune*, 6 March l987].

—— (1987) "An International Chapter 11," *The New York Times*, 11 August, 1987 [reprinted in *International Herald Tribune*, 12 August 1987].

—— (1991) "GATT Setback Won't Lead to Trade Wars," *Christian Science Monitor*, 10 January.

—— (1991) "Adapting to a Mosaic-Like World Economy," *Trends* [a monthly publication of the Institute of Southeast Asian Studies, Singapore, distributed with *The Sunday Times*], 26 May.

—— (1993) "Globalnomics: Clinton missed an opportunity in Tokyo," *Santa Barbara News-Press*, 16 July.

—— (1993) "Tax Breaks Are Not the Best Lures," *Santa Barbara News-Press*, 31 October.

—— (1994) "Gold: barbarous relic?" *Global Competitor* 1:3 Summer.

—— (1998) *"Qui gagnera le match euro-dollar?"* ["Who Will Win the Euro-Dollar Contest?"], *Capital* No. 76 January.

—— (1998) "The Approaching Monetary Earthquake," *Santa Barbara News-Press*, 17 May.

—— (1999) *"Surprise Argentine"* ["Argentine Surprise"], *Alternatives Economiques*, May.

—— (1999) "World Economy in the Next Century and Beyond," *Santa Barbara News-Press*, 20 June.

—— (2000) *"Ce Que Mundell a Dit"* ["What Mundell Said"], *Alternatives Economiques*, January.

—— (2000) *"La monnaie et le pouvoir des Etats"* ["Money and the Power of States"], *Alternatives Economiques* No. 45.

—— (2000) *"L'euro a la carrure pour defier le roi dollar"* ["The Euro at the Crossroads to Defy the King Dollar"], *Le Soir*, Brussels, 8 May.

—— (2000) *"Es Irreversible la Globalización?"* ["Is Globalization Irreversible?"], *La Razon*, Buenos Aires, 31 August.

—— (2002) *"Euro identité"* ["Euro Identity"], *Alternatives Economiques* No. 199.

—— (2002) *"Bush est-il protectionniste?"* ["Is Bush a Protectionist?"], *Alternatives Economiques* No. 204.

—— (2002) *"Gestion des crises financières: enfin!"* ["Management of Financial Crises: at last!"], *Alternatives Economiques*, No. 209.

—— (2004) *"Éstan obsoletas las monedas nacionales?"* ["Are National Currencies Becoming Obsolete"], *Cinco Dias*, 7 June.

—— (2006) "Do Not Rush to Write Off National Currencies", *Financial Times*, 19 April.

Published working papers

Cohen, Benjamin J. (1994) *The Geography of Money: Currency Relations Among Sovereign States*, OFCE Working Paper No. 94–07, Paris: Observatoire Français des Conjonctures Économiques.

—— (1996) *When Giants Clash: The OECD Financial Support Fund and the IMF*, Working Paper 2.34, Berkeley: Center for German and European Studies.

—— *Technology, Globalization, and the Future of Money*, Working Paper T99–1, Atlanta: European Union Center of the University System of Georgia. Online. Available HTTP: <http://www.inta.gatech.edu/eucenter/wpapers99/pdf/cohen.pdf>.

—— *The Geography of Money*, Research Brief No. 1, Claremont, CA: European Union Center of California.

—— *Political Dimensions of Dollarization*, Dallas: Federal Reserve Bank of Dallas. Online. Available HTTP: <http://www.dallasfed.org/htm/dallas/pdfs/cohen/pdf>.

—— *EMU and the Developing Countries*, WIDER Working Paper 177, Helsinki: World Institute for Economic Development Research. Online. Available HTTP: <http://www.wider.unu.edu/publications/publications.htm>.

—— *Dollarization: Pros and Cons* (Center for Applied Policy Research, Munich. Online. Available HTTP: <http://www.cap.uni-muenchen.de/transatlantic/papers/americas.html>.

—— *The Geopolitics of Currencies and the Future of the International System*, Real Instituto Elcano, Madrid, Spain. Online. Available HTTP: <http://realinstitutoelcano.org/documentos/69.asp>.

—— *The Macrofoundation of Monetary Power*, EUI Working Papers, RSCAS No. 2005/08, Robert Schuman Centre for Advanced Studies, European University Institute, Florence, Italy.

—— "Super Debt: Managing America's Foreign Debt," in *U.S. Foreign Policy in Bush's Second Administration*, Davis Institute, Hebrew University, Jerusalem [in Hebrew translation].

Index